AD BOY

Vintage Advertising with Character

Warren Dotz • Masud Husain

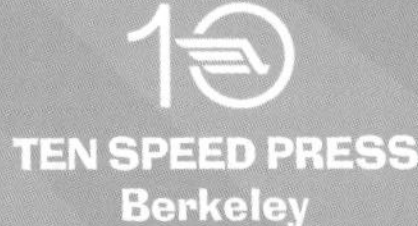

TEN SPEED PRESS
Berkeley

Tiger • c. 1962
Tiger bread
Pin-back button

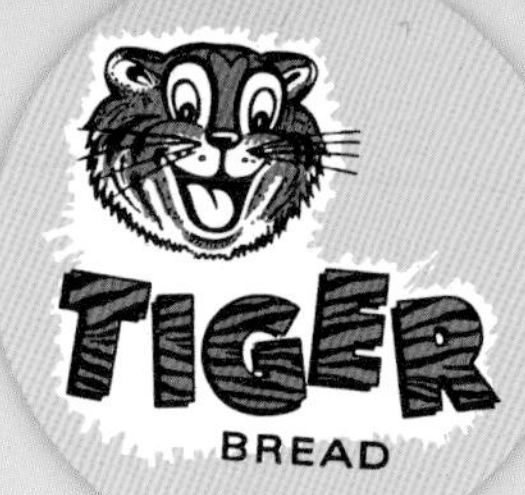

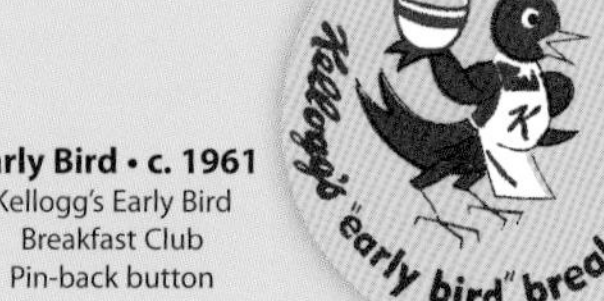

Early Bird • c. 1961
Kellogg's Early Bird
Breakfast Club
Pin-back button

TABLE OF CONTENTS

Buzzy Bee • c. 1960
Unknown
Pin-back button

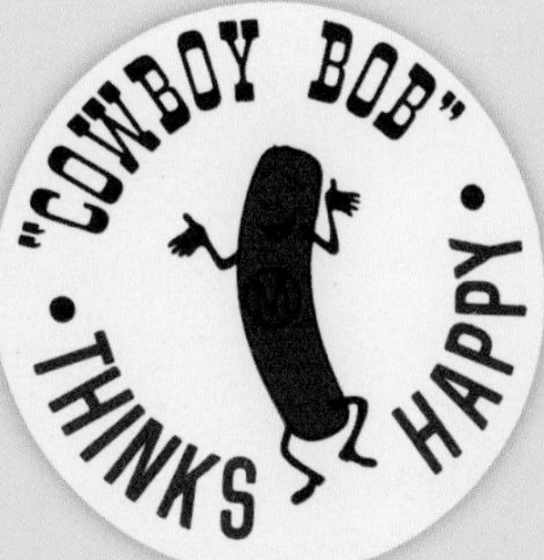

Cowboy Bob • 1971
Marhoefer hot dogs
Pin-back button

INTRODUCTION

There is a classic axiom among ad men: "Don't sell the steak, sell the sizzle." In other words—don't sell the product, sell the feeling—it isn't about what's for sale, it's about the emotional response of the customer who's being courted.

Perhaps that's why, in an increasingly unpredictable world, the friendly faces and forms of the critters and characters in the print ads and TV commercials we grew up with seem so reassuring. But why do they reach us in ways other images don't? Familiarity? Certainly. They've been coming into our homes (and our heads) through magazines and television since the 1950s. But nostalgia isn't the only reason we think fondly of these imaginative creations. Commercial images and slogans, some of which even attained the status of pop-culture icons, were often cleverly amusing, but they weren't made to entertain, although that was often a by-product. Company mascots were advertising ambassadors created not only to entice people to acquire a product or use a service, but also to brand or differentiate their products from the competition—even if there was little distinction.

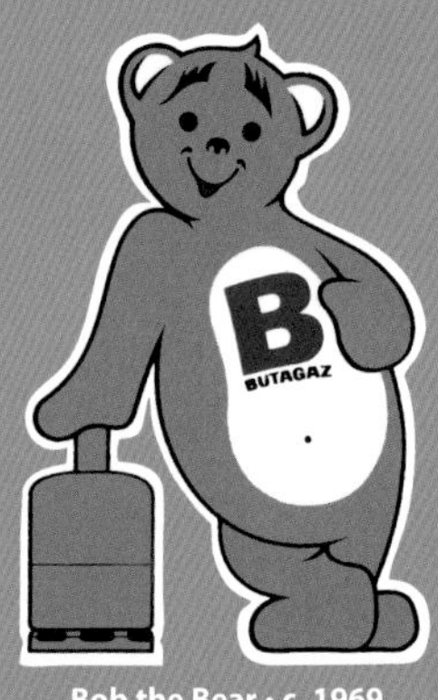

Bob the Bear • c. 1969
Butagaz gasoline
Promotional sticker

Product characters were designed to comfort consumers, to reassure them that they were making the smartest, safest, best-quality choices and thus were wise, secure, good people. Whatever form it took—human, animal, vegetable, or inanimate object each was given a personality that an eager audience would find easy to relate to and even easier to identify with the product or service it represented. After all, what homemaker wouldn't want the muscle power of a very buff and immaculately groomed Mr. Clean? Surely Mr. Peanut's dapper top hat, monocle, and spats would elevate the once lowly goober to the status of swanky snack, wouldn't he? (Mr. P's spit-and-polish appearance has remained undimmed for decades, by the way.) What about the stylish, European sophistication of Paul Rand's Dubonnet ads? They were meant to remind middle-class Americans of their upwardly mobile aspirations. And there's the Land-O-Lakes Indian maiden who hasn't aged a day and is as freshly youthful, and therefore as promising of freshness, as ever.

It's important to recall that prior to the 1950s manufacturers did not market to children. After all, kids didn't have money to spend, so why spend money on them? But as baby boomers populated the burgeoning suburbs and television reached out for the hearts and minds of America's offspring, a vast, heretofore untapped audience for new merchandise was discovered. Advertisers took note and kids were targeted to sway their parents' spending.

Thus, kid-friendly critters proliferated faster than you could say Froot Loops! Smokey the Bear (who was based on a very real, wild orphaned cub), was transformed into a creature as cute and cuddly as any toy teddy; the Kool-Aid Pitcher was portrayed with a permanent smile on what should have been a fleetingly frosty face; and tykes all over the country identified with the fractious foibles of the Trix Rabbit and his endless quest for sweet cereal treats. These characters became not only familiar—they were trusted. They were, in a sense, the visual equivalent of comfort food and helped shepherd a young generation through uncertain times.

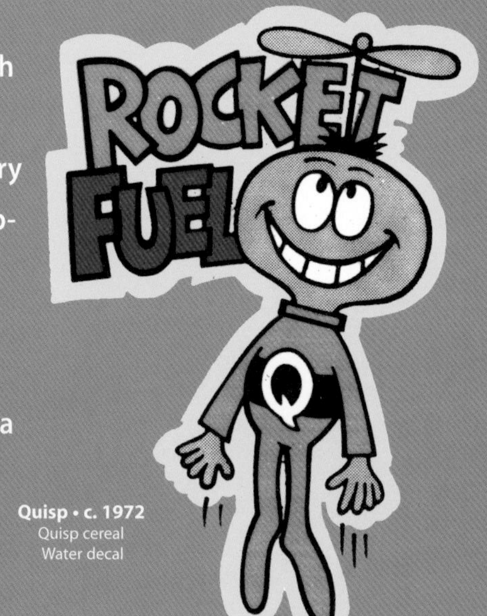

Quisp • c. 1972
Quisp cereal
Water decal

INTRODUCTION

Not every mascot achieved the status of icon. Some of these long forgotten faces once fronted for now defunct companies. And in some cases, the business is still in business, but its mascot or pitchman has long since retired. Strangely (or perhaps not so strangely) some of the characters are not only recognizable, they would look perfectly at home in today's marketing campaigns. Why couldn't Tuffy Tooth make a comeback for Colgate and fight dental battles right alongside the other toothpaste brands? And who would say no to Miss Fluffy if she returned to preside over the next batch of rice you make for dinner?

So, look a little closer when you pick up a box, bottle, or can and watch a little more attentively when the hapless AFLAC Duck flaps across the screen or the GEICO Geko chats in his charming cockney accent. They're part of a modern legacy of an old tradition and one we celebrate in the pages that follow.

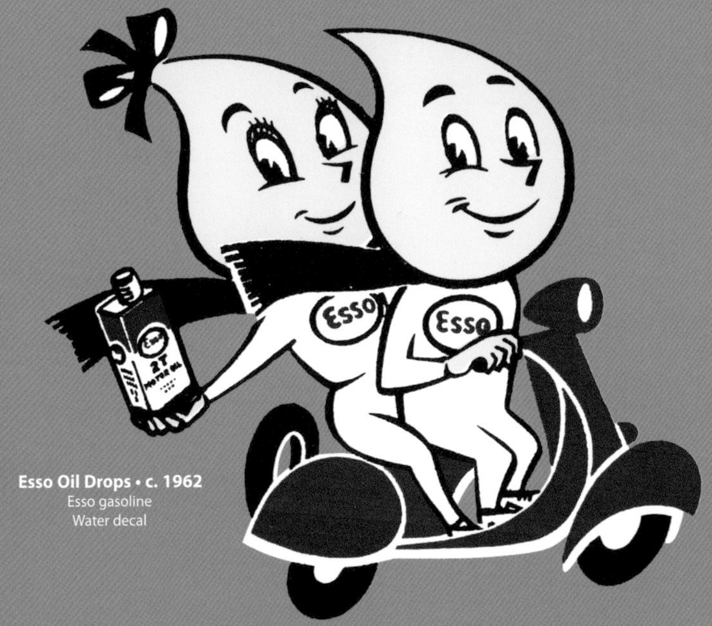

Esso Oil Drops • c. 1962
Esso gasoline
Water decal

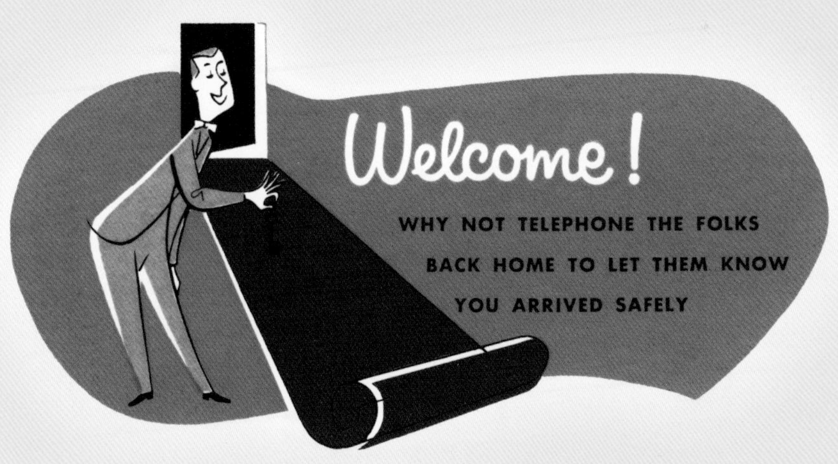
Welcome!
WHY NOT TELEPHONE THE FOLKS
BACK HOME TO LET THEM KNOW
YOU ARRIVED SAFELY

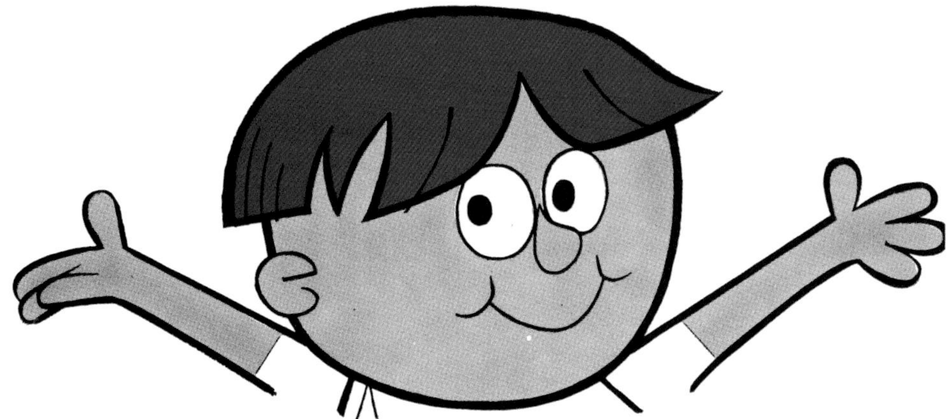

MICKEY is the new salesman

Mickey's a television star!

He's selling Cook Book Cake Treats to children on the top-rated kid shows in your city!

The fact is—you get full-time support from TV the most effective (and expensive) medium known . . . at no cost to you!

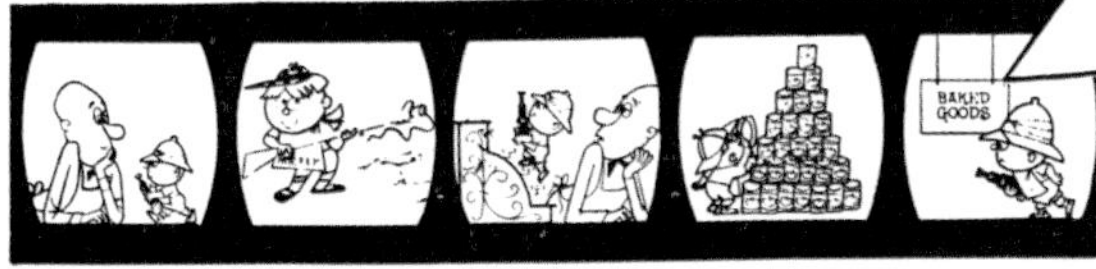

Mickey's on the labels!

Mickey is on the labels . . . for quicker brand identification . . . more product interest . . . increased impulse buying attraction!

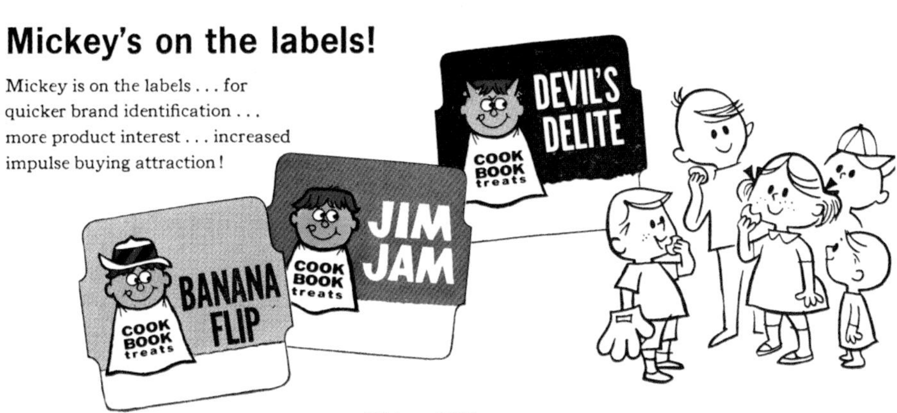

Mickey • 1959
Cook Book cake treats
Trade journal ad

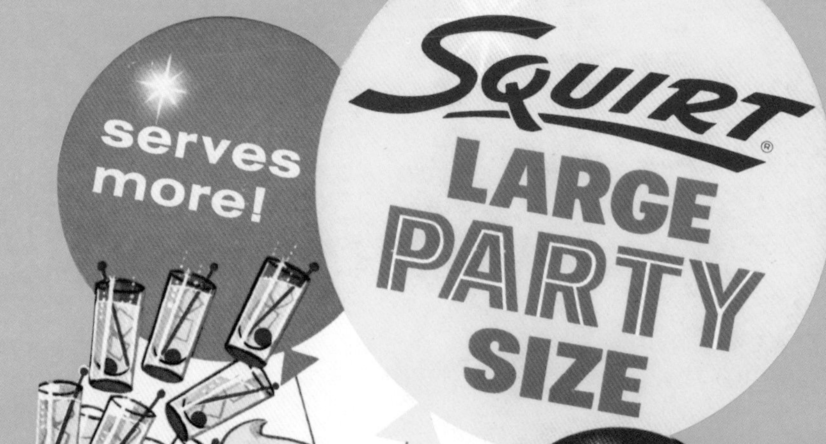

Squirt • 1960
Squirt soda
Bottle topper

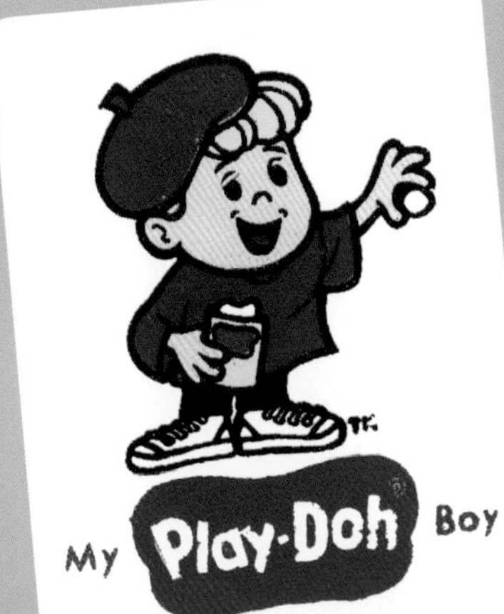

Play•Doh Pete • c. 1968
Play•Doh modeling compound
Night light facing

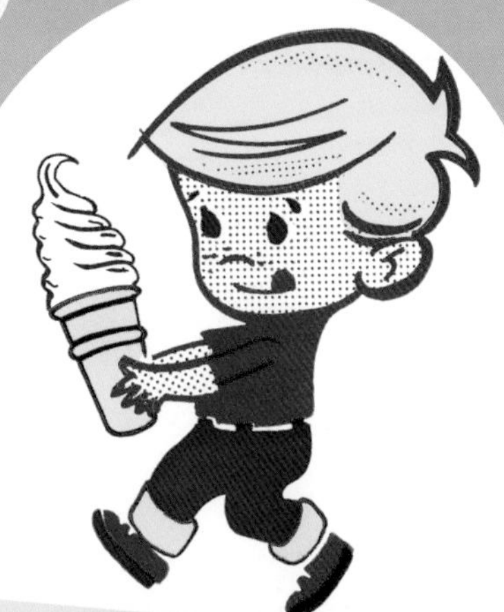

Frosty Boy • 1976
Frosty Boy ice cream
Promotional sticker

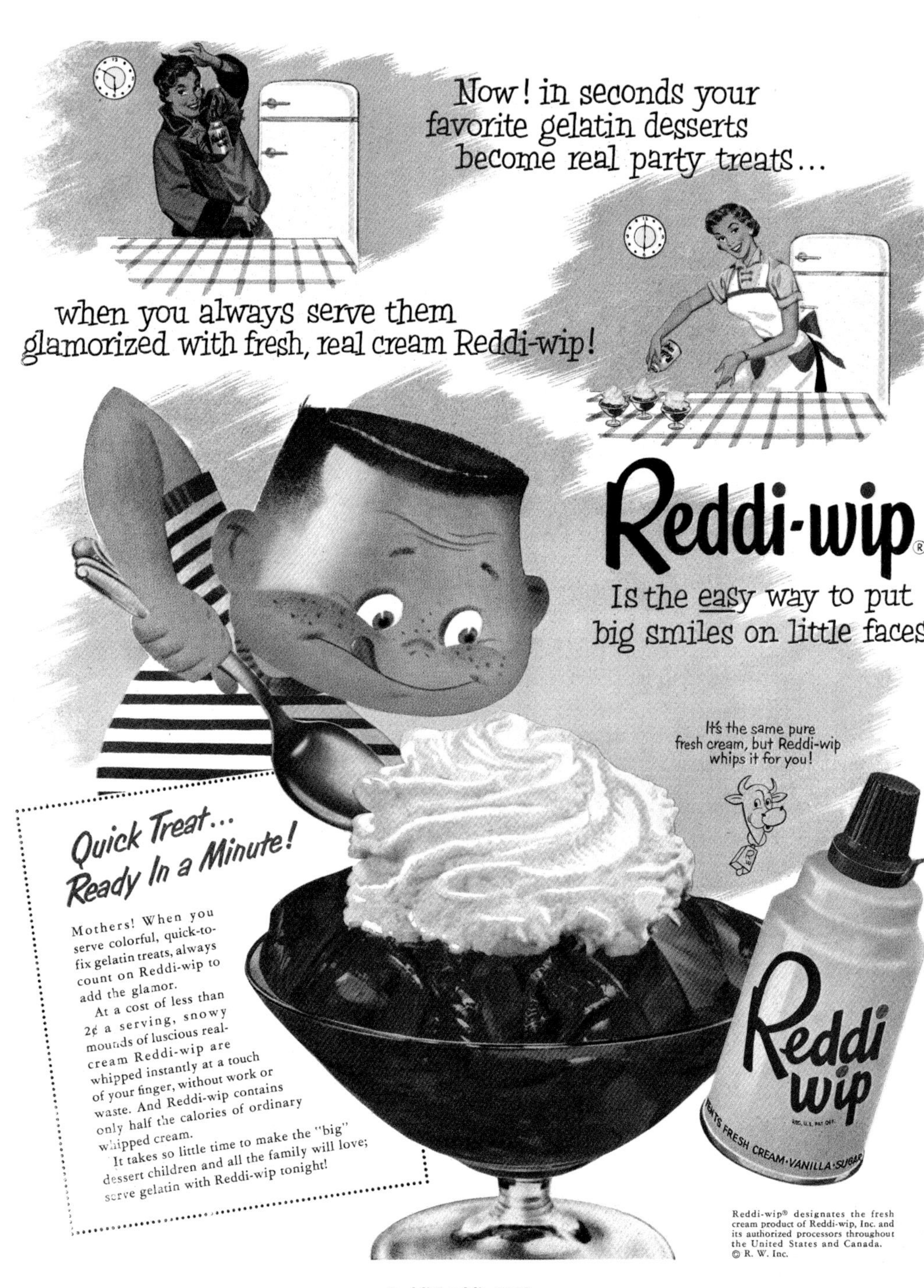

Reddi Freddi • 1953
Reddi-wip whipped cream
Magazine ad

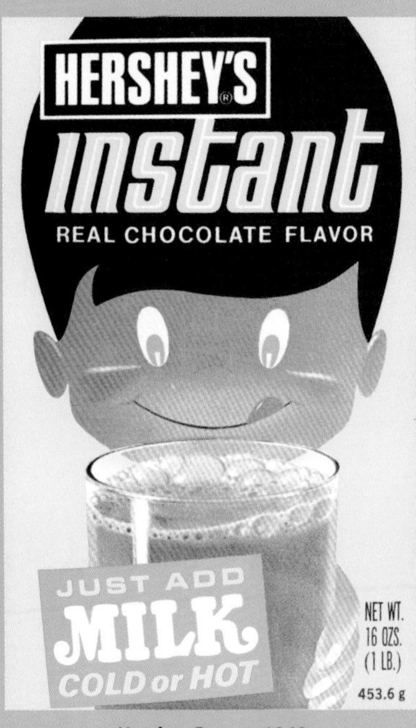

Hershey Boy • c. 1969
Hershey's chocolate milk mix
Container front

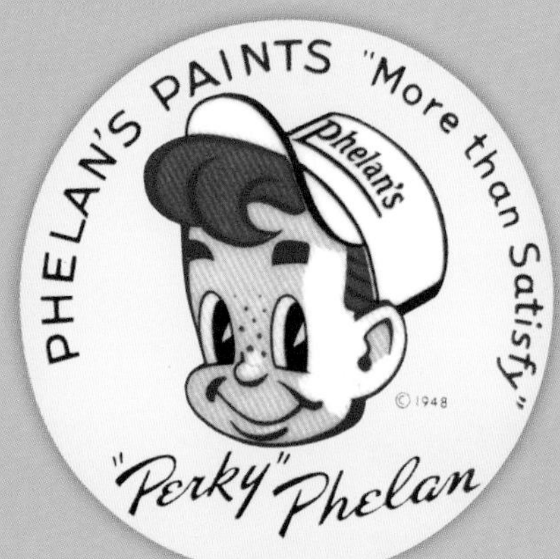

Perky Phelan • 1948
Phelan's paints
Pin-back button

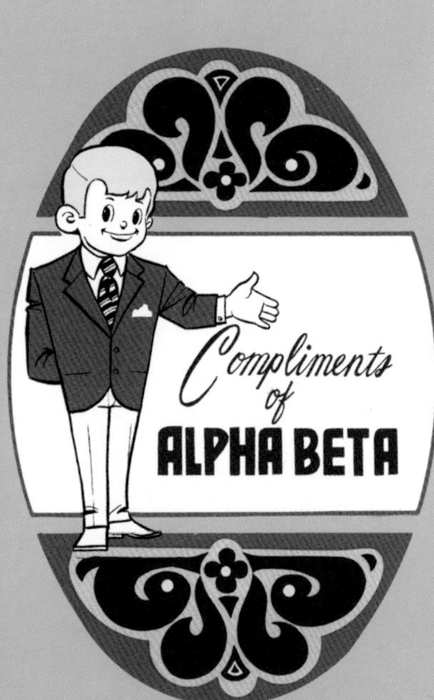

Alphy • c. 1970
Alpha Beta supermarkets
Sewing kit cover

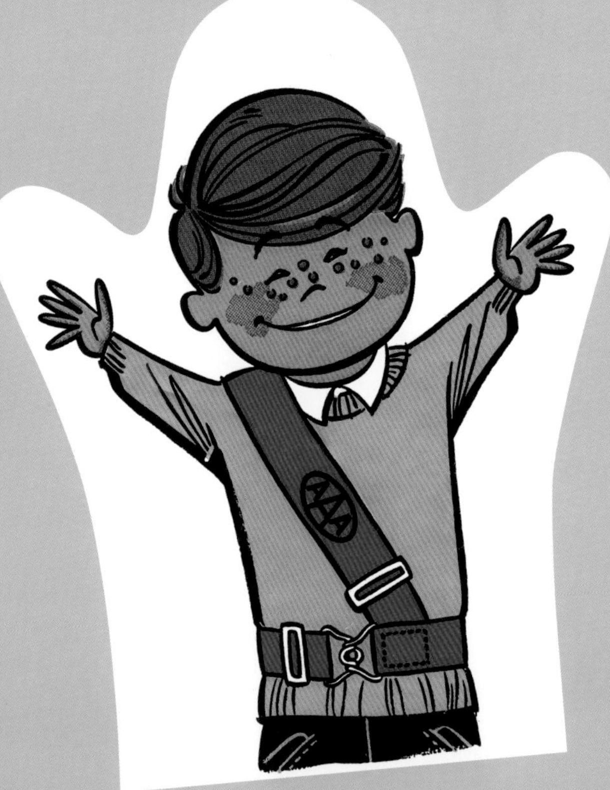

AAA Boy • c. 1972
Bring 'Em Back Alive campaign
Hand puppet

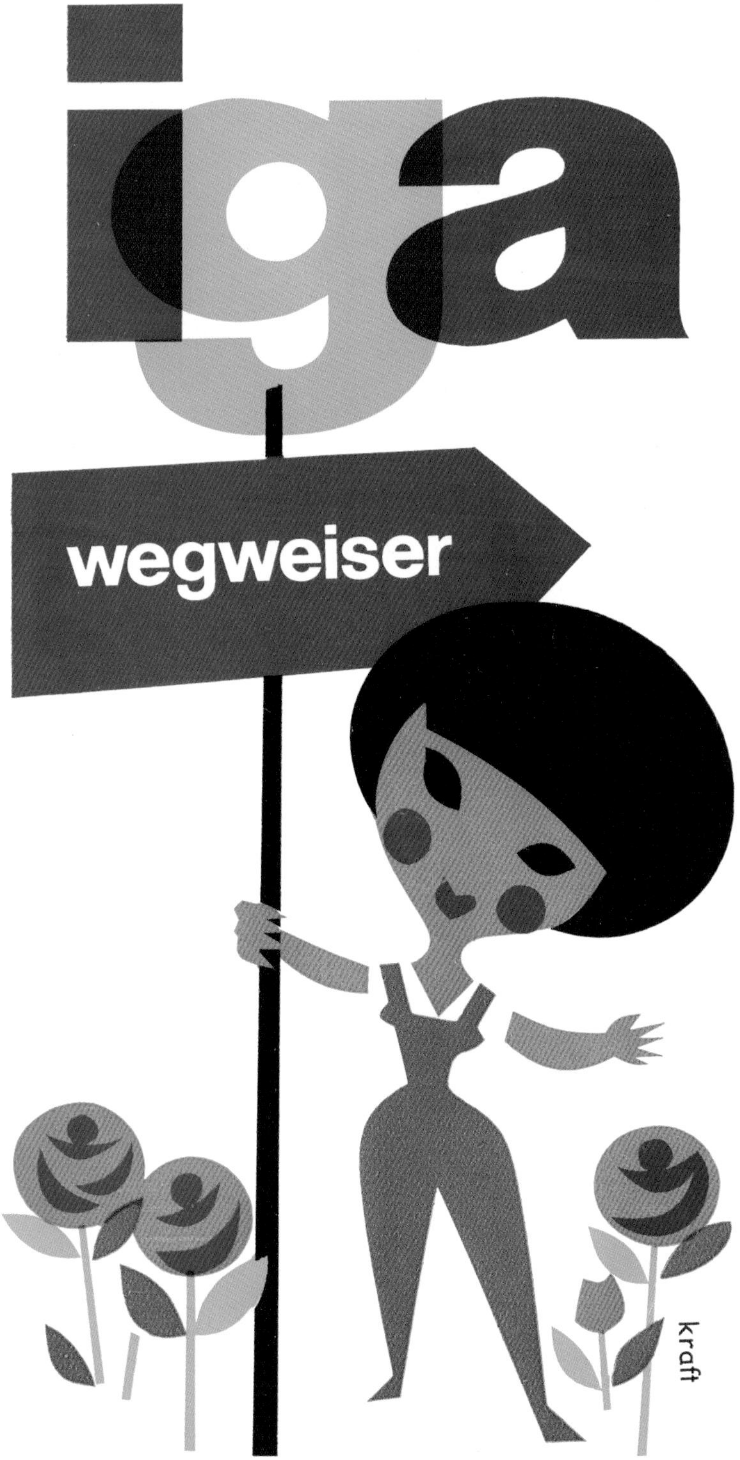

iga

wegweiser

kraft

Florinchen • 1966
IGA horticulture exhibition
Program cover

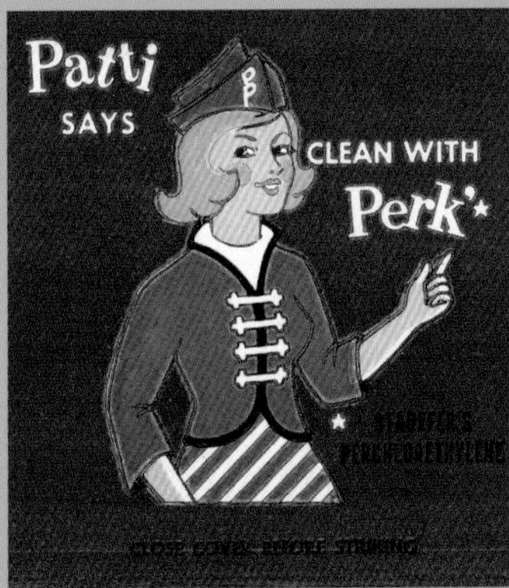

Patti Perk • c. 1957
Perk dry cleaning solvent
Matchbook cover

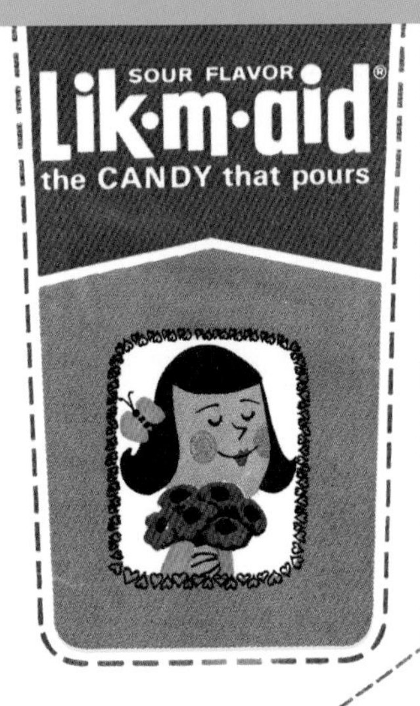

Lik•m•aid Girl • c. 1970
Lik•m•aid candy
Pack front

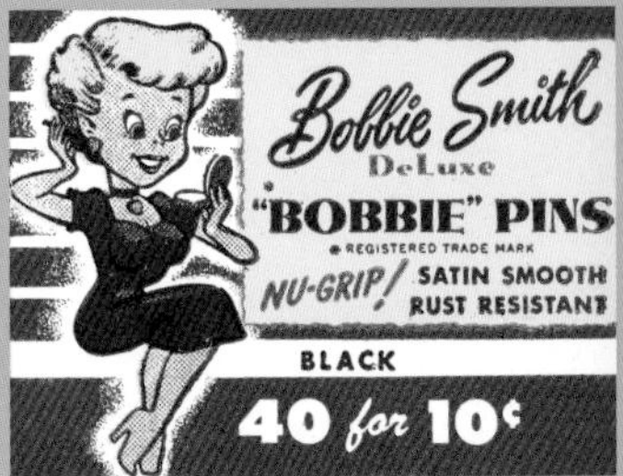

Bobbie Smith • c. 1947
Bobby Smith bobby pins
Box front

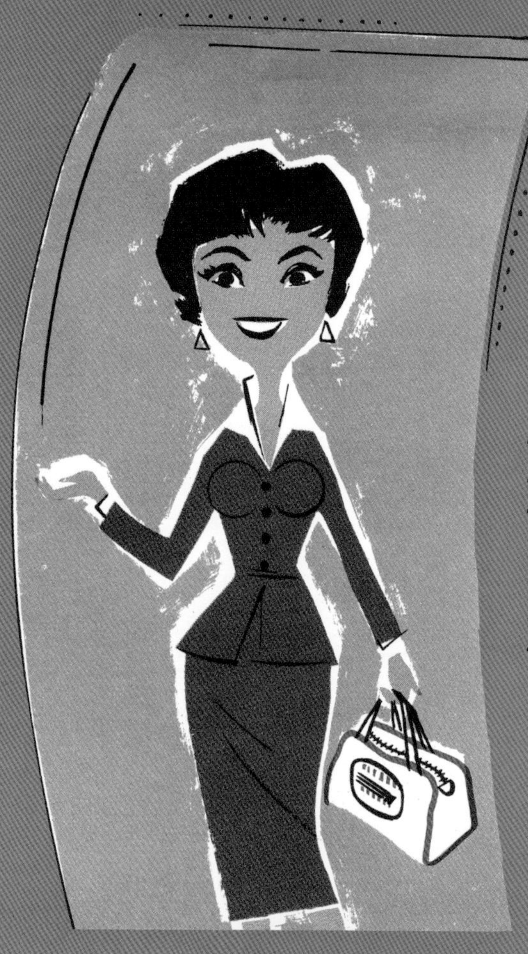

BETTY
WEST
INVITES
YOU...

Betty West • 1960
Western airlines
Promotional brochure detail

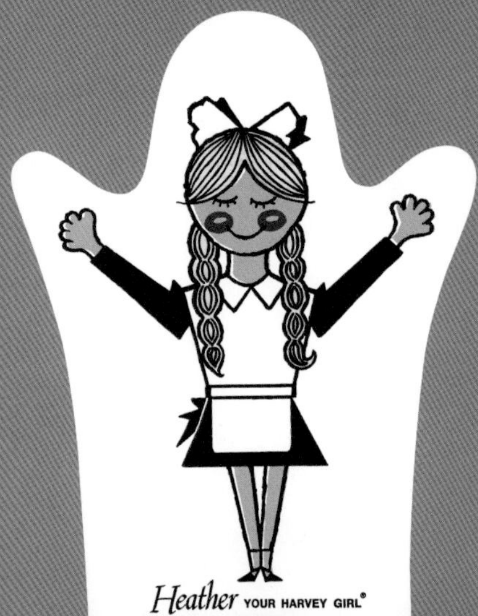

Heather • c. 1969
Harvey House restaurants
Hand puppet

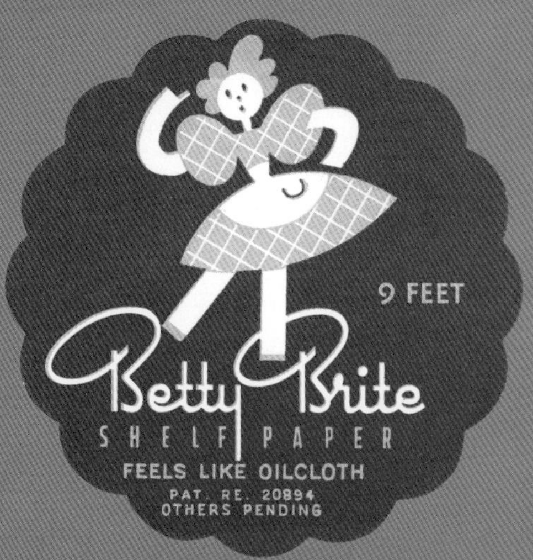

Betty Brite • c. 1946
Betty Brite shelf paper
Paper label

C and H Kids • 1963
C and H cane sugar
Store poster

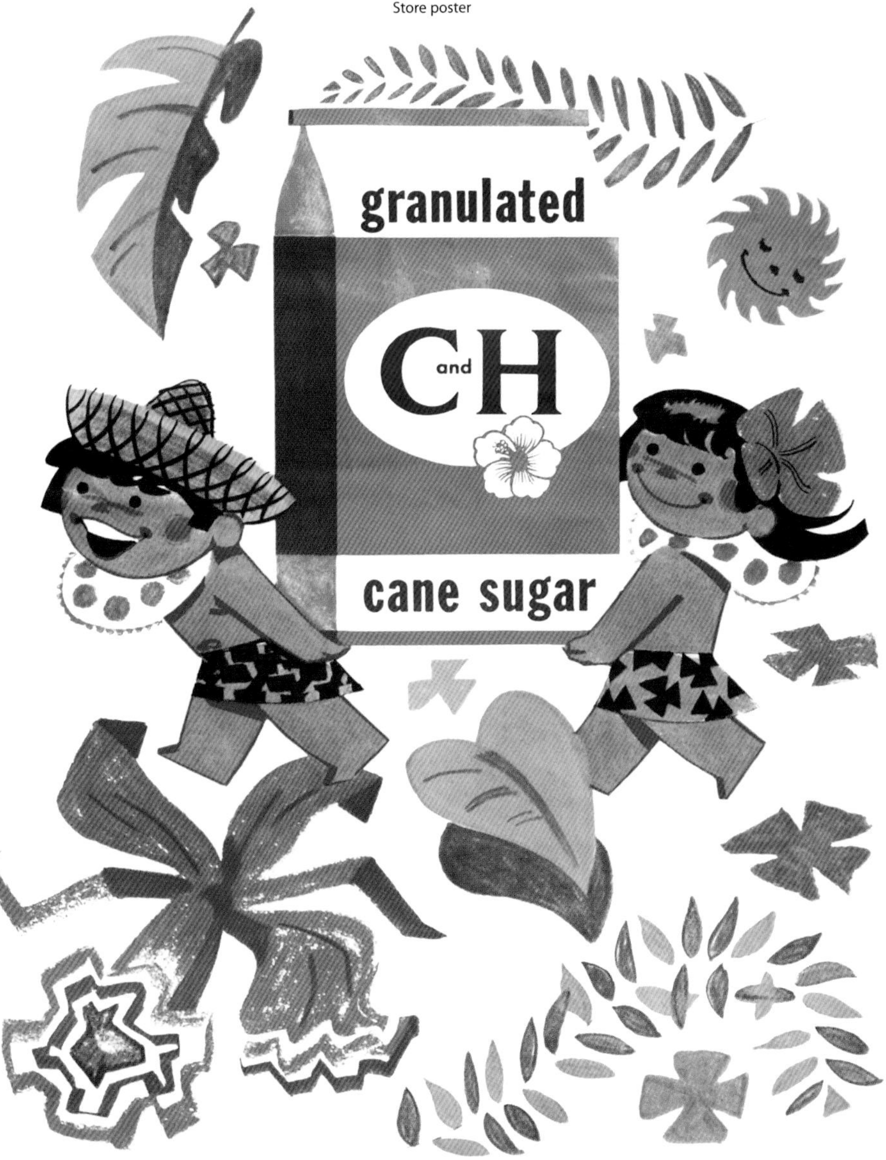

Aloha! FROM C AND H

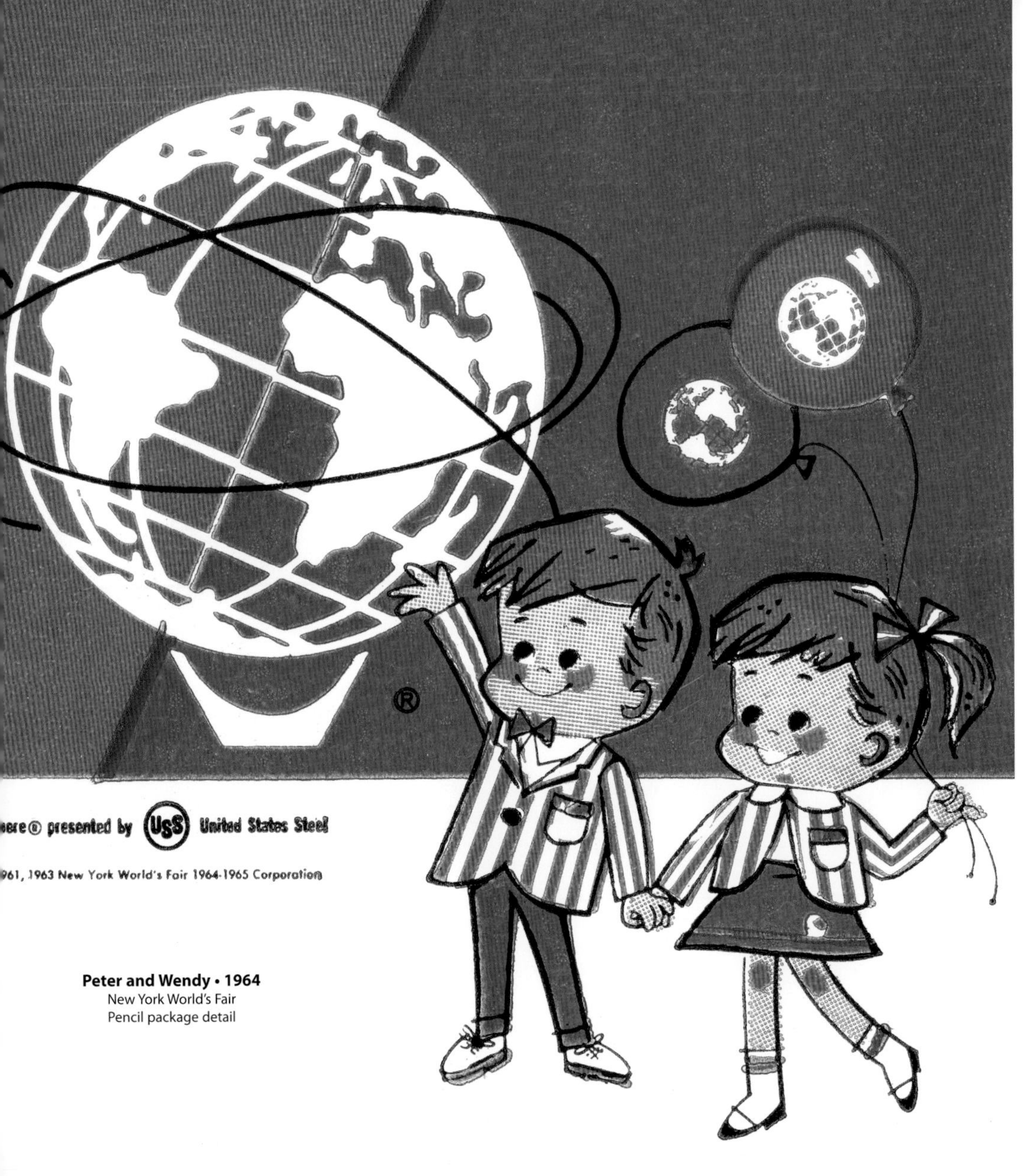

Peter and Wendy • 1964
New York World's Fair
Pencil package detail

Prior to the advent of television, children had not been identified as a consumer group. But as children's programming began to outpace adult shows in terms of viewership, advertisers began to realize that kids could be addressed directly in a TV commercial. And who better to sell to kids than a kid like Mickey as the 1959 trade journal ad on page 10 acknowledges?

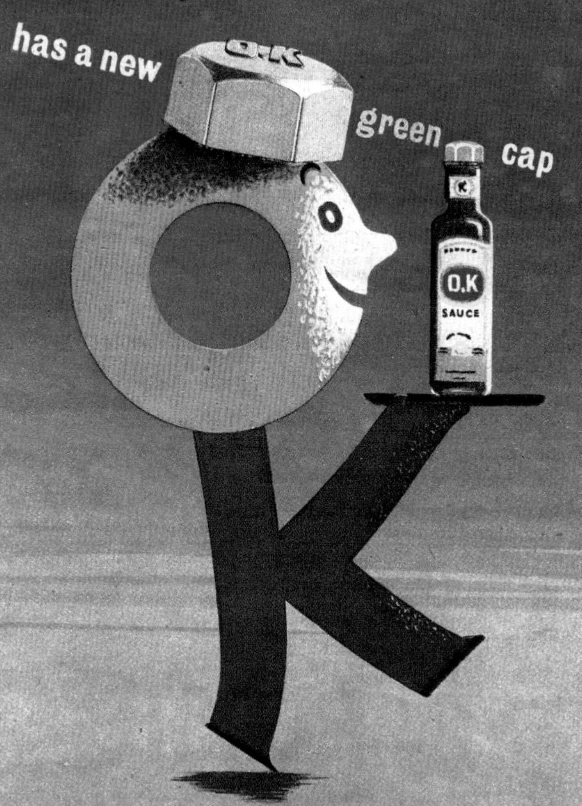

O.K Man • 1954
O.K sauce
Magazine ad

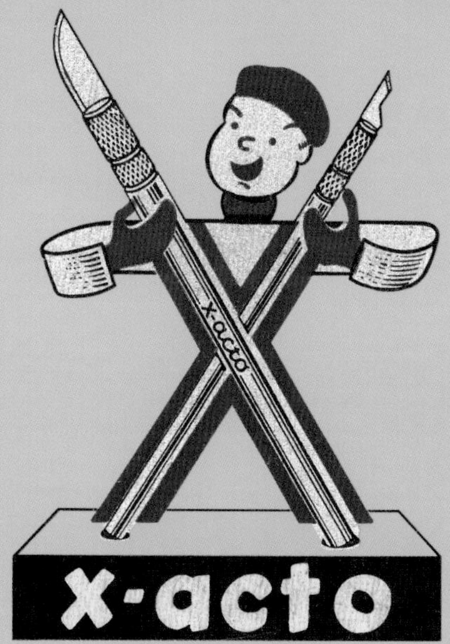

X-acto Boy • c. 1958
X-acto blades and knives
Water decal

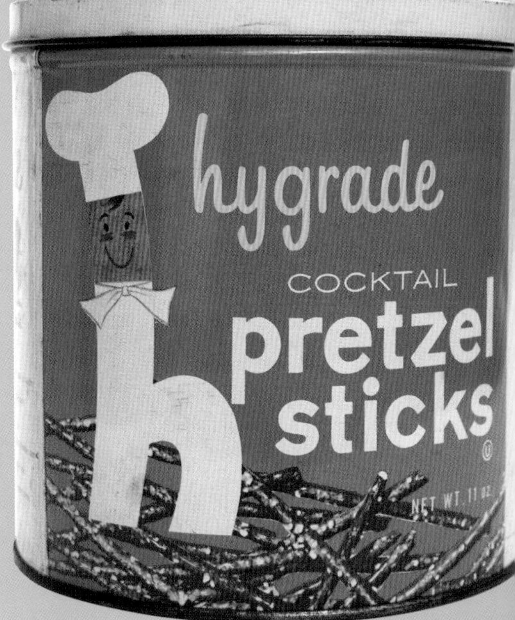

Hygrade Chef • c. 1960
Hygrade pretzel sticks
Container front

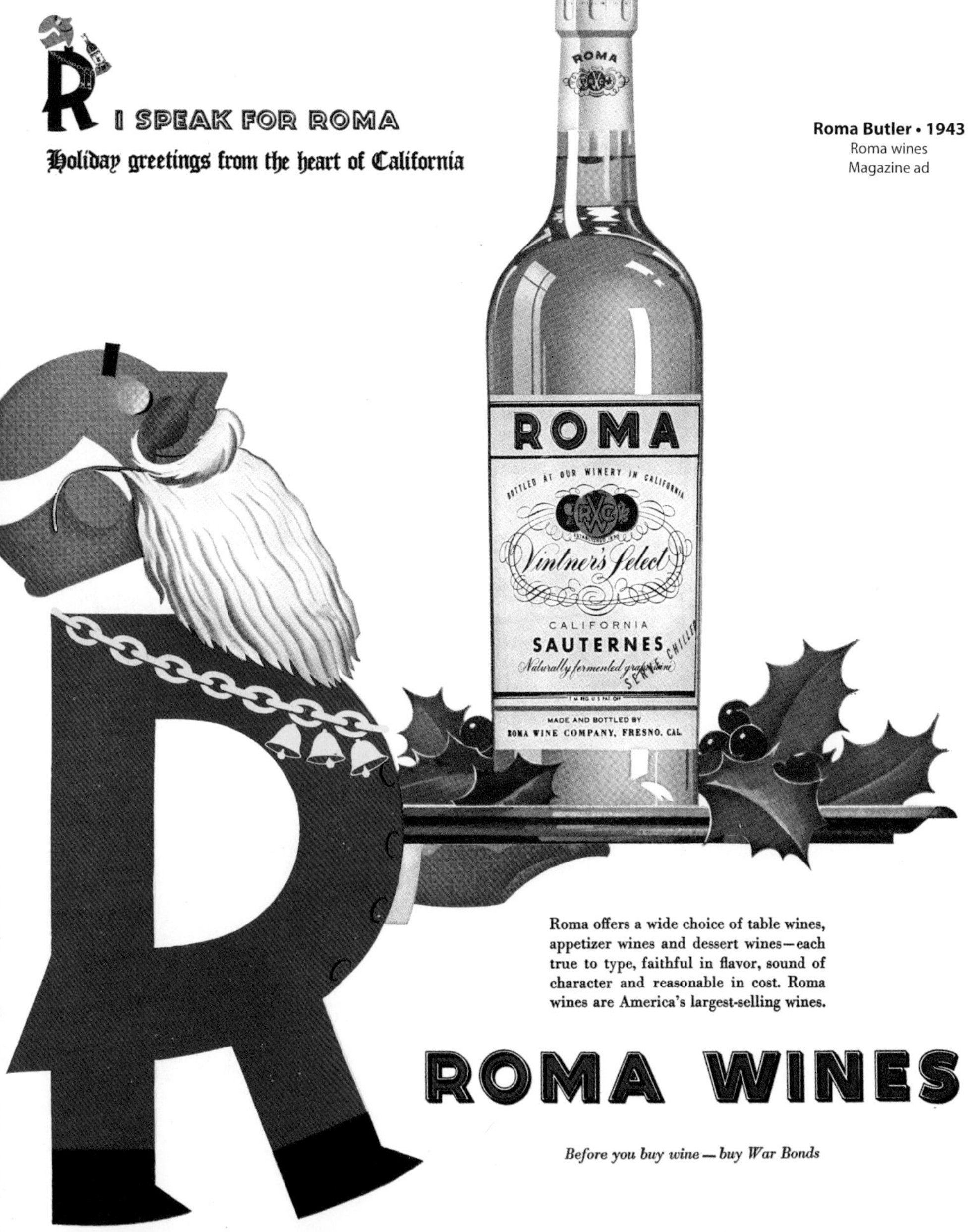

Roma Butler • 1943
Roma wines
Magazine ad

Artistically rendered alphabets have given illustrators free reign to breathe life into inanimate letters since the Dark Ages. The popularity of these lively renditions has never diminished, and a millennium after Medieval monks labored over their manuscripts, graphic artists and their clients were still drawn to these clever characterizations.

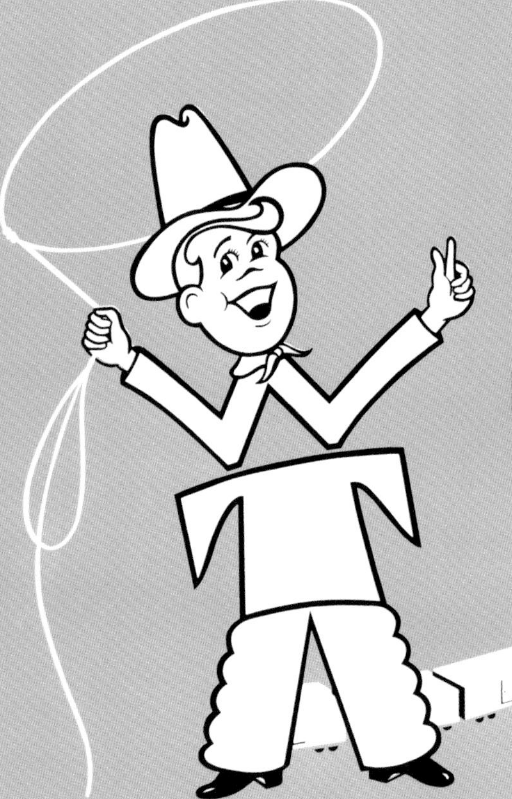

Whitey • c. 1956
White Tower restaurants
Store sign

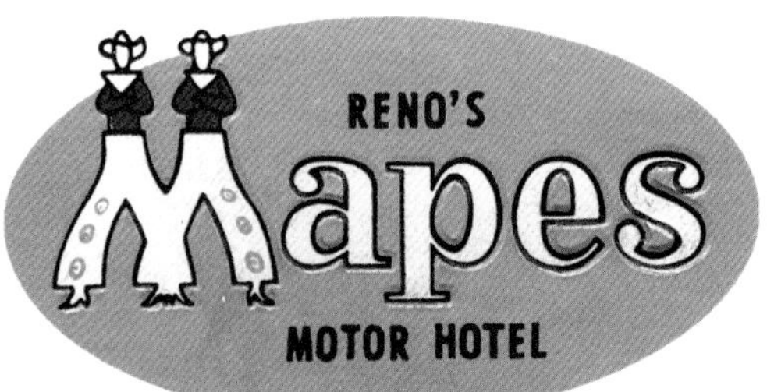

Mapes Cowboys • c. 1967
Mapes motor hotel
Matchbook cover

Suzuki Man • c. 1968
Suzuki motorcycles
Water decal

THE

Happy STEAK

Home of the Golden Spud

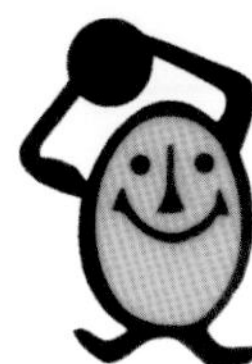

The Happy Steak • c. 1965
Happy Steak restaurants
Serving tray detail

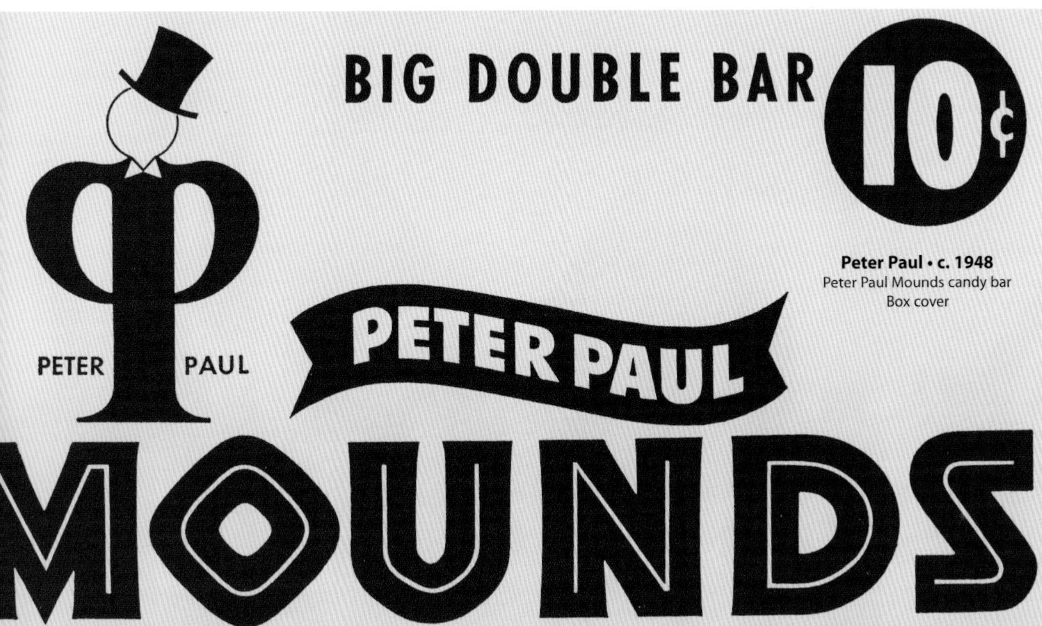

Peter Paul • c. 1948
Peter Paul Mounds candy bar
Box cover

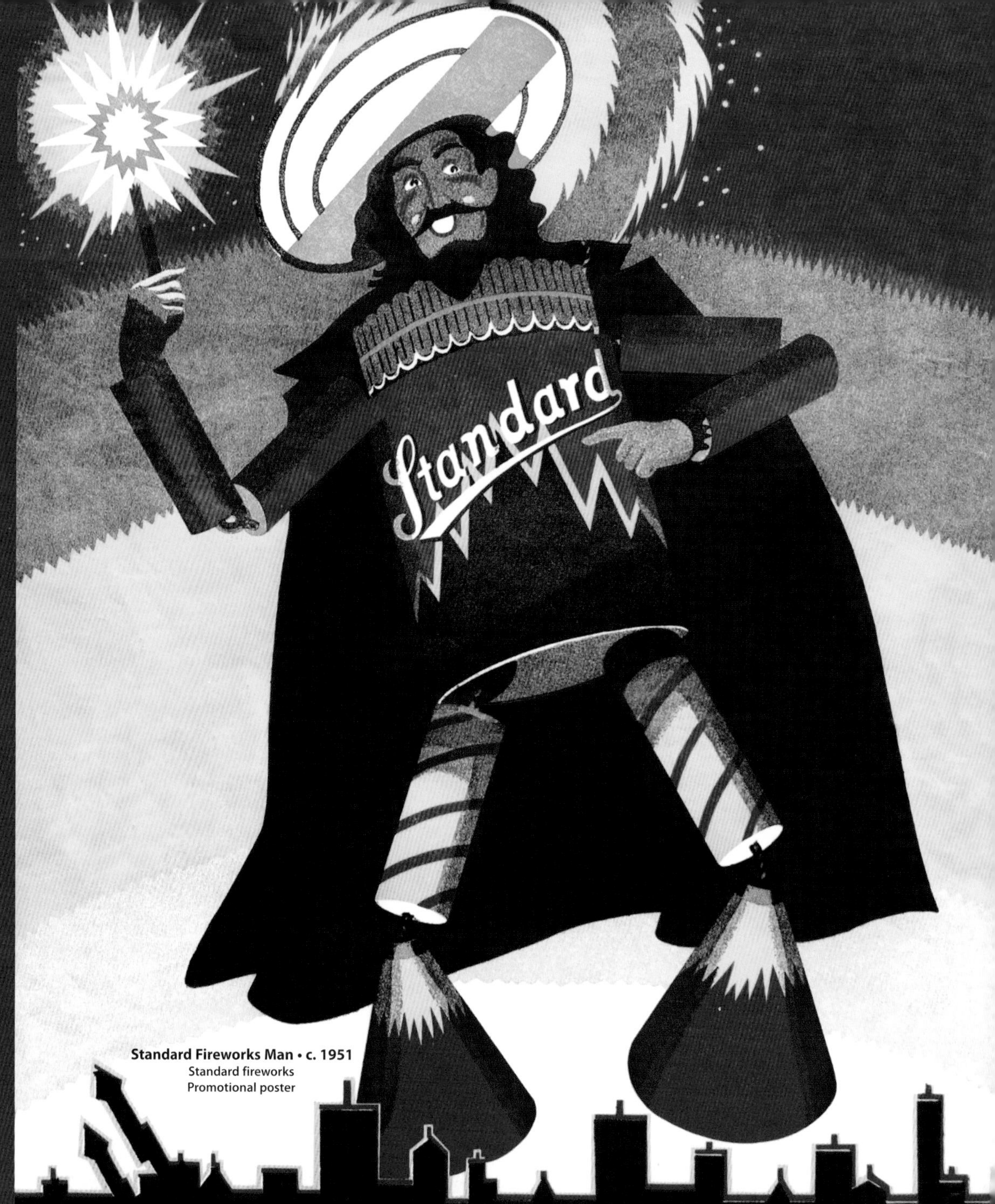

Standard Fireworks Man • c. 1951
Standard fireworks
Promotional poster

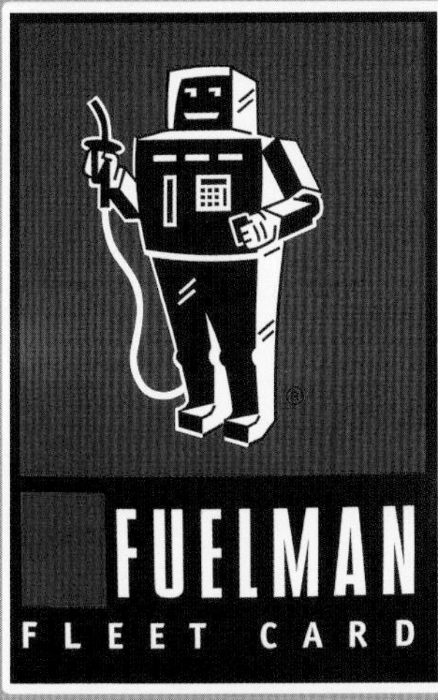

Fuelman • c. 1985
Fuelman fleet services
Store sign

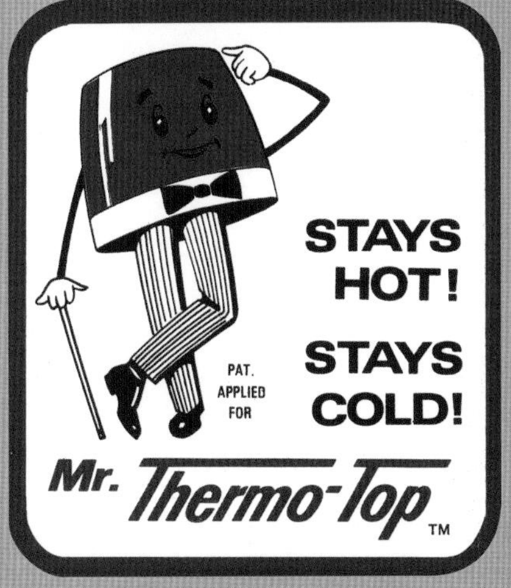

Mr. Thermo-Top • c. 1976
Thermo-Serv insulated beverage ware
Product label

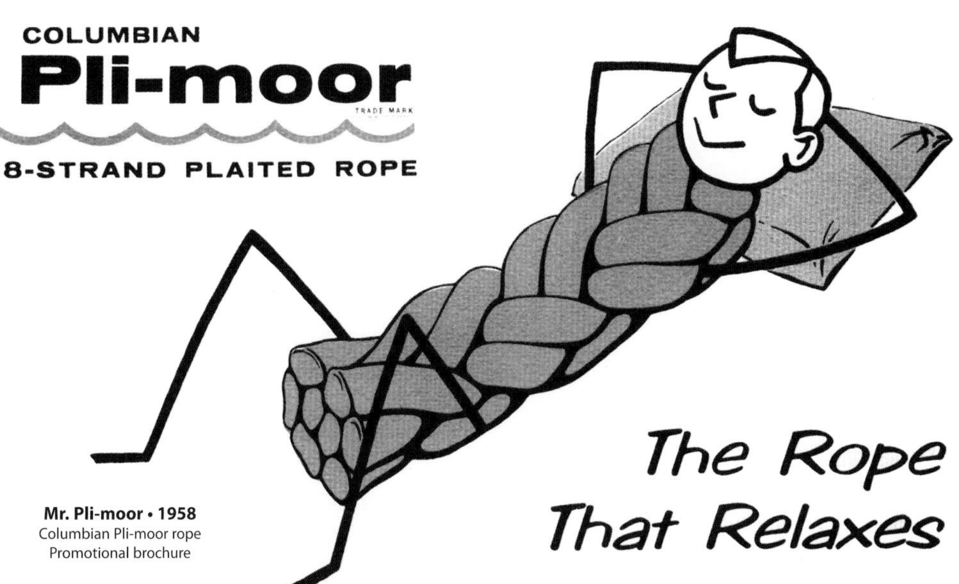

Mr. Pli-moor • 1958
Columbian Pli-moor rope
Promotional brochure

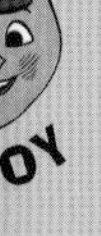

Give a product a face, arms, and legs and suddenly it becomes a personality! Over the years, hundreds of natural and manufactured objects—from fruits to fireworks—have been graphically "humanized" into more appealing, more accessible characters. Like the half-god, half-human beings of ancient mythology, our consumer culture's counterparts became half-human, half-product.

Miss Fluffy's

RICE COOK BOOK

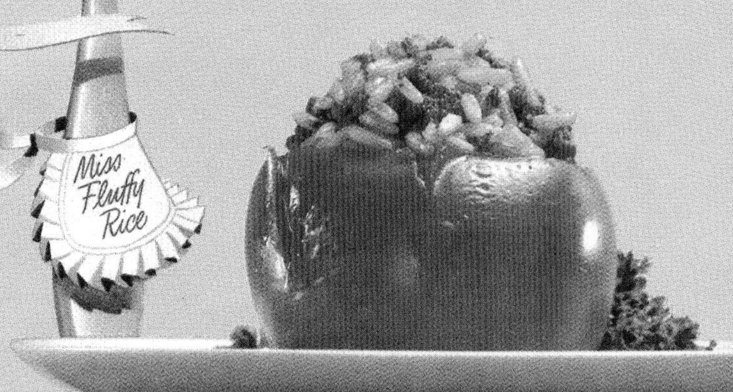

Miss Fluffy Rice • 1960
Rice Council for Market Development
Recipe booklet

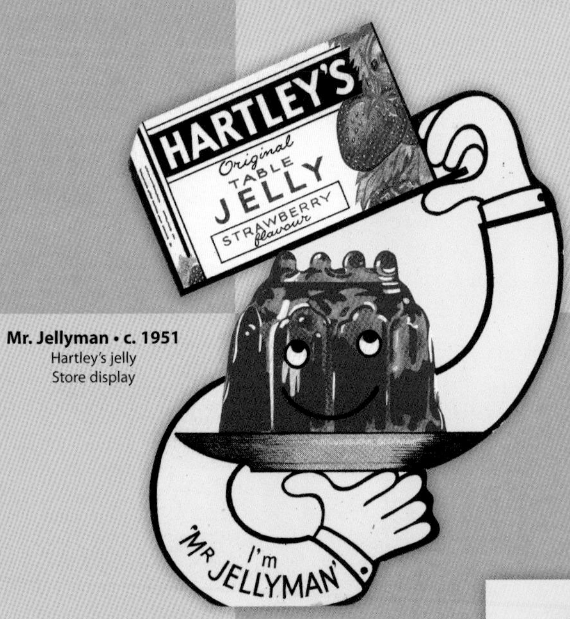

Mr. Jellyman • c. 1951
Hartley's jelly
Store display

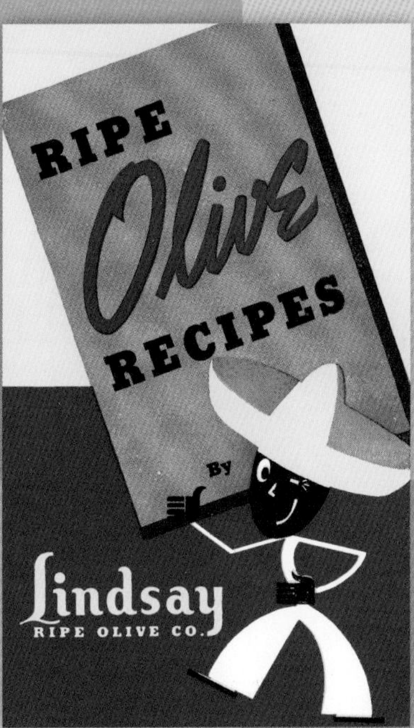

Lindsay Olive • c. 1951
Lindsay olives
Recipe pamphlet

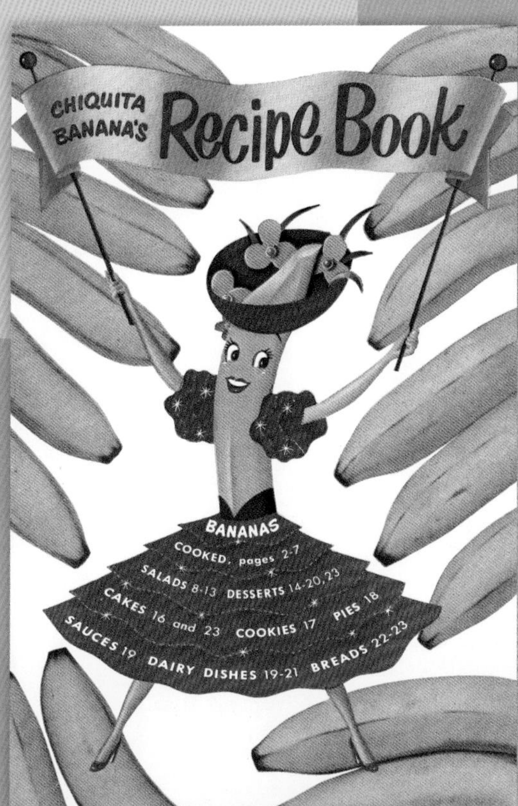

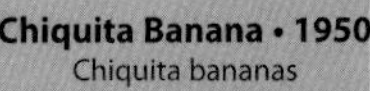

Chiquita Banana • 1950
Chiquita bananas
Recipe booklet

Mr. Weatherball • c. 1956
Citizens bank
Dime saver

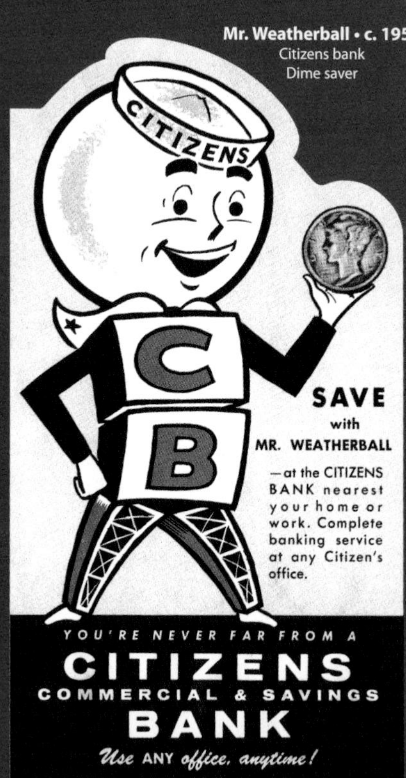

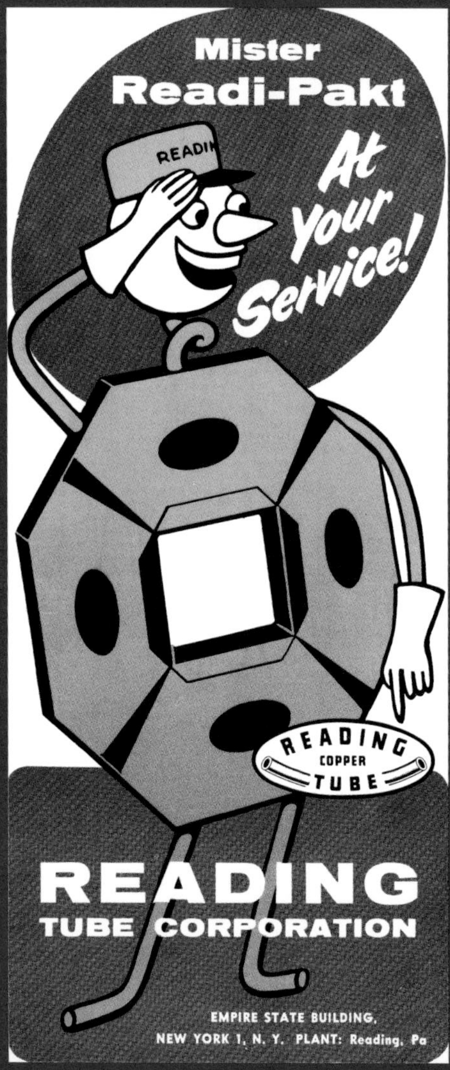

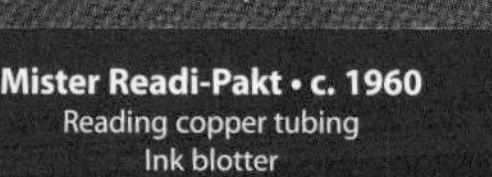
Mister Readi-Pakt • c. 1960
Reading copper tubing
Ink blotter

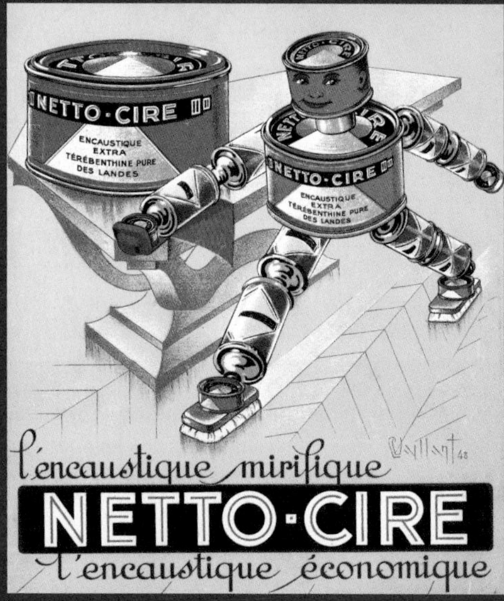

Netto-Cire Man • 1948
Netto-Cire floor polish
Store sign

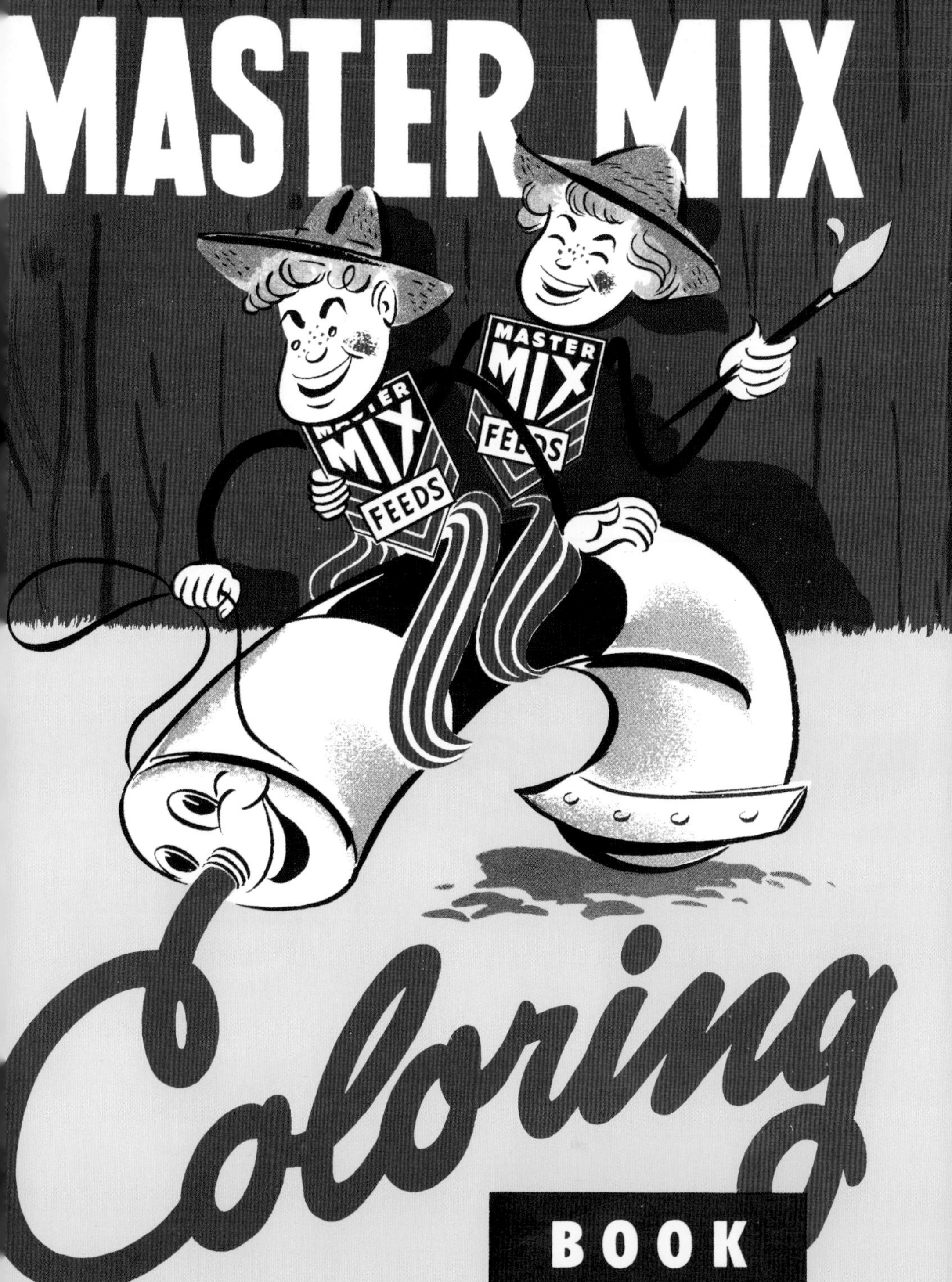

aster MIx Kids • c. 1948
Master Mix feeds
Coloring book cover

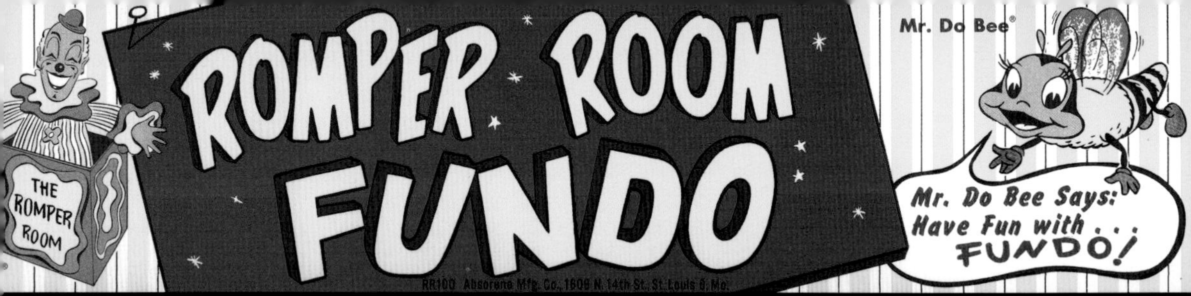

Mr. Do Bee • c. 1963
Fundo modeling clay
Store banner

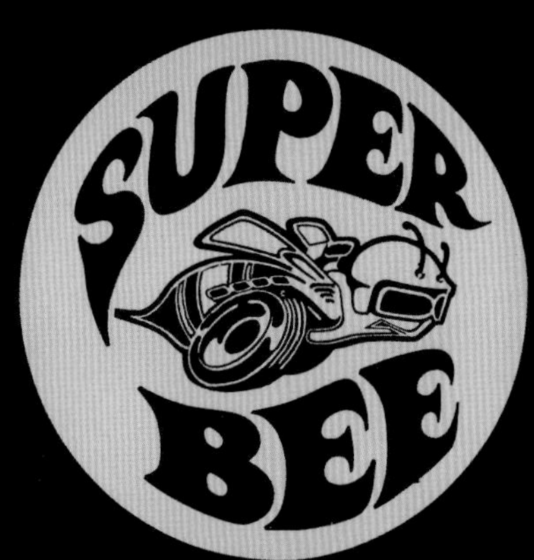

Super Bee • 1968
Dodge Super Bee
Tab button

the Beechcraft Busy Bee *

© WALT DISNEY —

CREATED by Walt Disney especially for Beechcraft, as a badge of merit and honor to be awarded to employees of any rank or station. To qualify for the award an employee must have demonstrated, by performance, the qualities of high efficiency, interest in his work and in training for further advancement, cheerful cooperation with others, and the constant determination to *"Kill 'em with Production."*

The Beechcraft Busy Bee, rampant on a field of blueprint paper shaped in the form of a Beech leaf, embodies these qualities. Although this Beechcraft Busy Bee is busy as can be, he's not too busy to look aside to see, if instead of two jobs, he can't do three. His flaunted Beechcraft winged insigne and his cheerful grin are indicative of his high morale, but his determination is written all over his face.

Most Beechcrafters will qualify for this award. With willing spirit and determination they are pushing production rates ever upward.

* Design copyrighted by Walt Disney

BEECH AIRCRAFT CORPORATION • WICHITA, KANSAS,

Beechcraft Busy Bee • c. 1943
Beechcraft aircraft
Promotional sheet

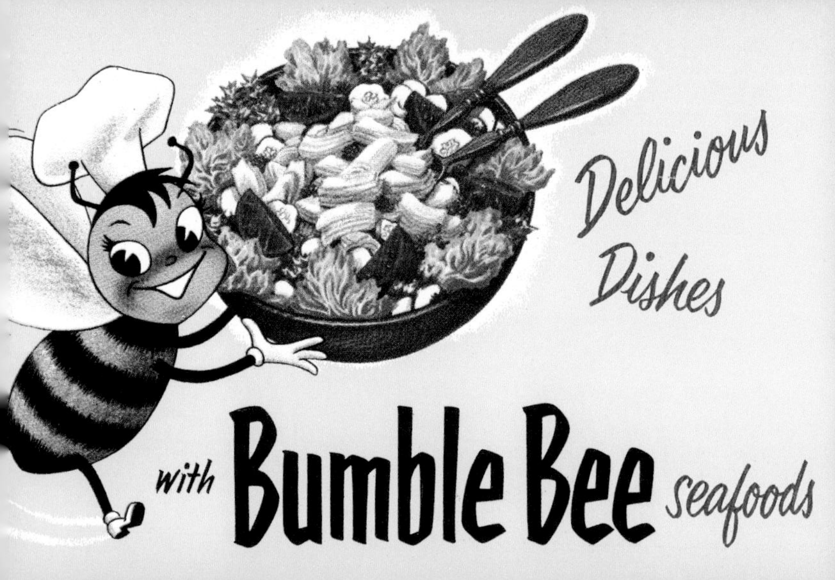

Bumble Bee • c. 1949
Bumble Bee seafoods
Recipe booklet

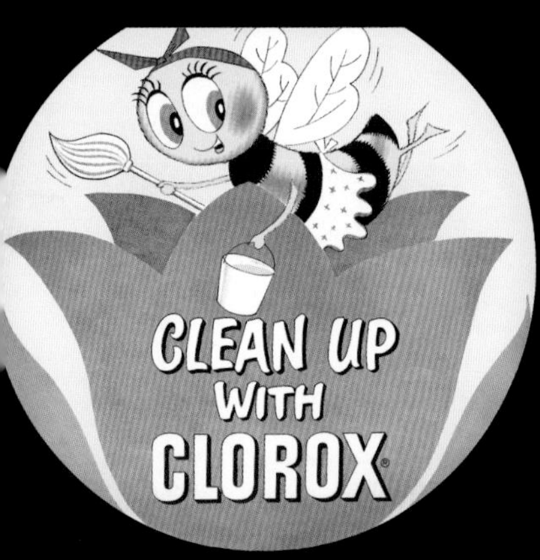

Busy Bee • c. 1958
Clorox bleach
Store banner

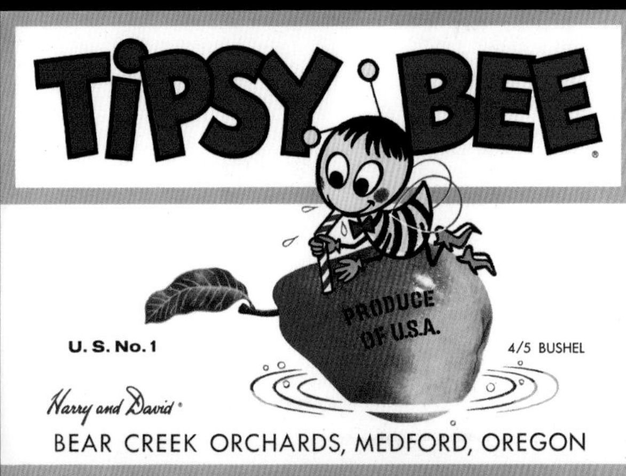

Tipsy Bee • c. 1947
Harry and David pears
Crate label

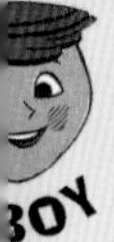

Like many ad characters, the Bumble Bee trademark began with a realistic rendering. But with each revision the insect got friendlier and more cartoon-like, and in his final evolution, he has no stinger! Bees enjoy a reputation for being energetic and diligent. Thus a company that selected a bee as a mascot showed how busily and conscientiously their employees worked for their shareholders and customers.

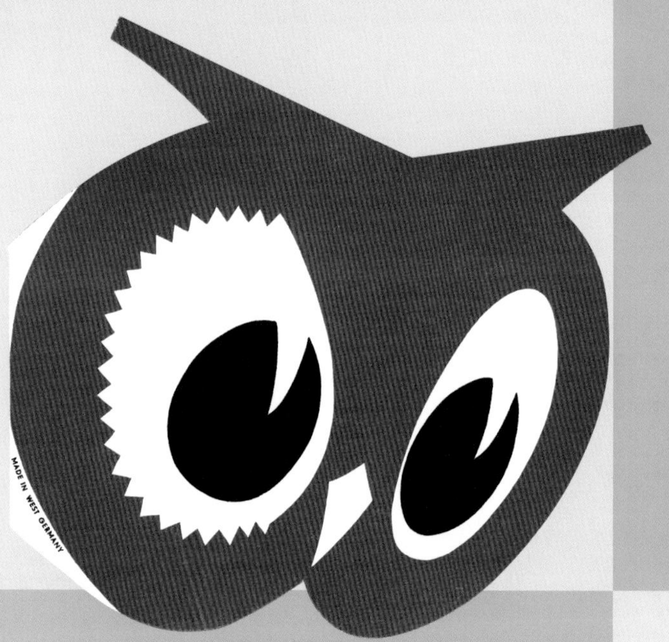

Red Owl • c. 1964
Red Owl food stores
Sewing kit cover

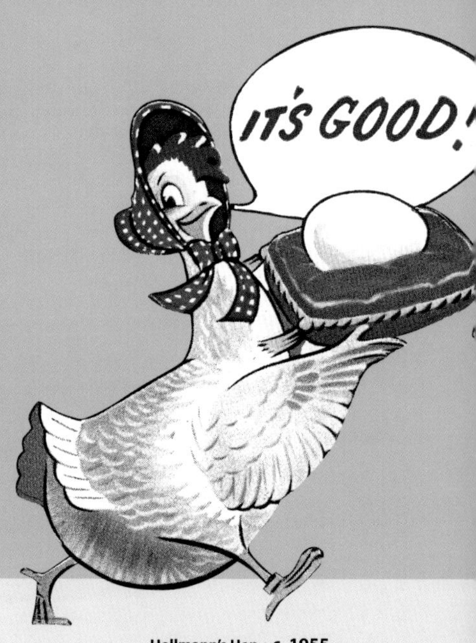

Hellmann's Hen • c. 1955
Hellmann's mayonnaise
Store display

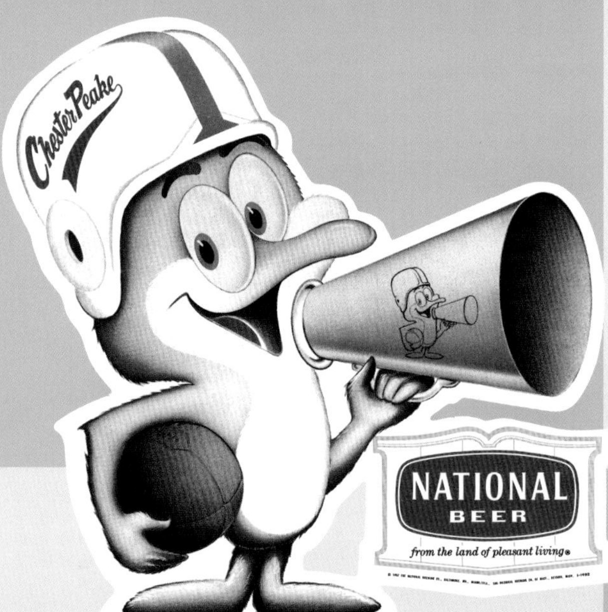

Chester Peake • 1962
National beer
Promotional sticker

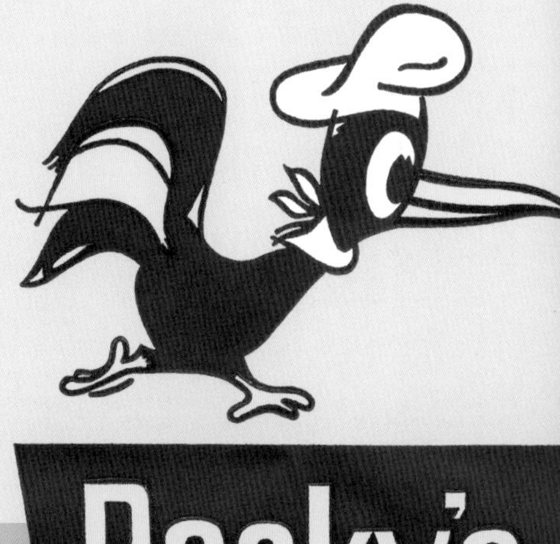

Beaky • c. 1968
Beaky's restaurant
Bag detail

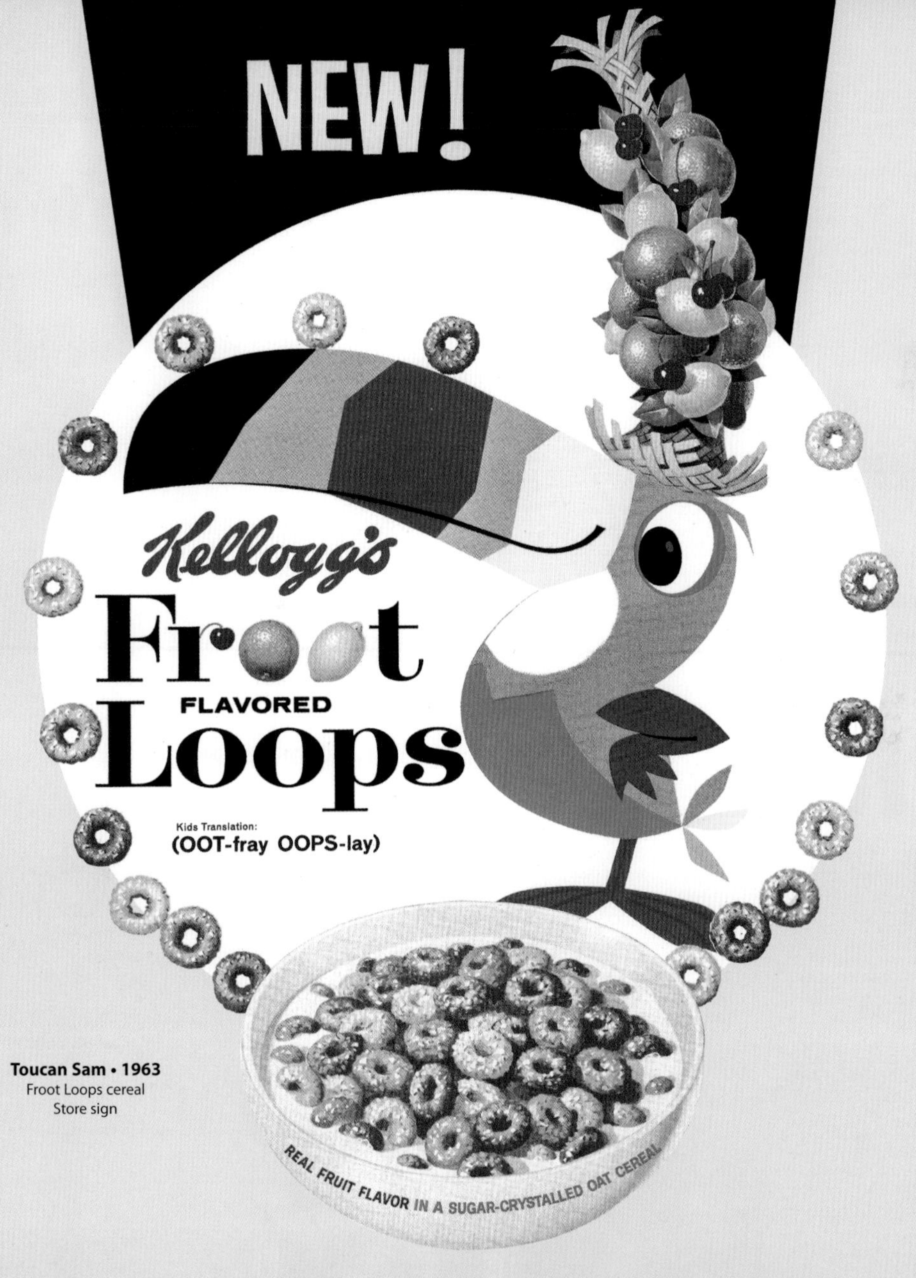

Toucan Sam • 1963
Froot Loops cereal
Store sign

Birds, in all their colorful varieties, have always been popular choices as ad characters. The Froot Loops mascot, Toucan Sam, was originally chosen for his striped beak with each color representing one of the flavors in the cereal. Owls have also been fashionable spokesbirds. The Red Owl logo reminded shoppers that they were wise to shop at that grocery store chain.

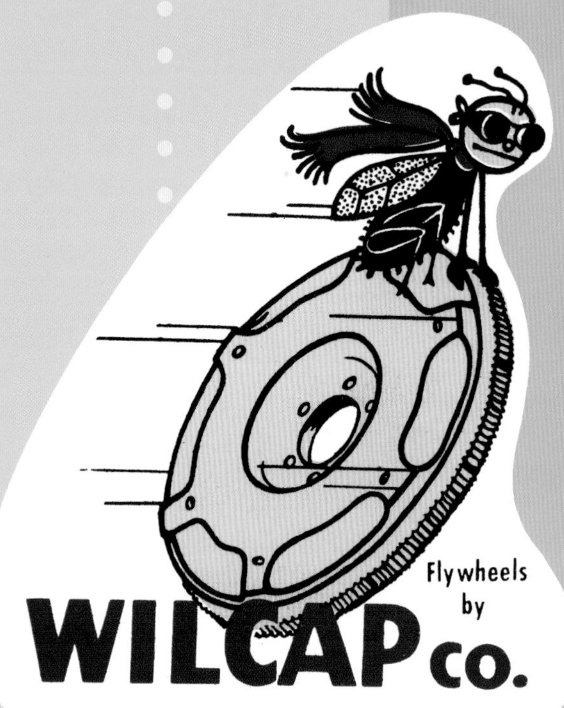

Wilcap Fly • c. 1965
Wilcap racing flywheels
Water decal

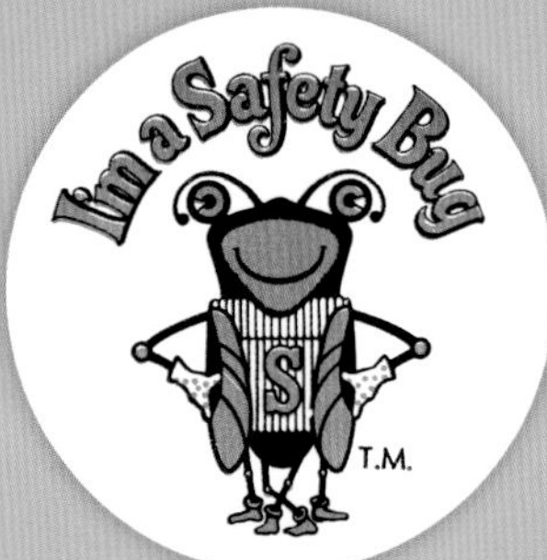

Safety Bug • 1968
Michigan Women's Club safety campaign
Tab button

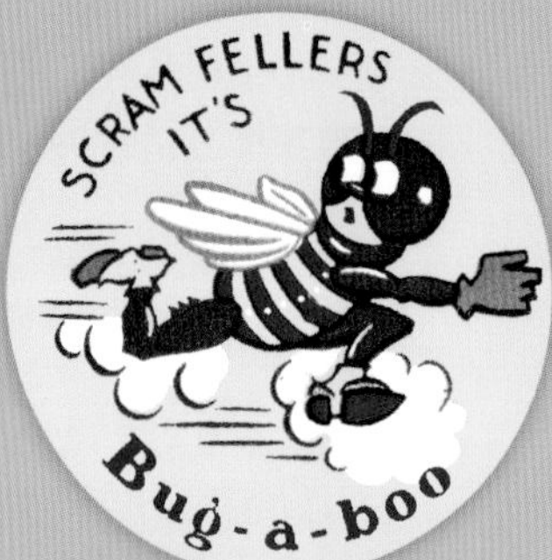

Bug-a-boo • c. 1941
Bug-a-boo insecticides
Pin-back button

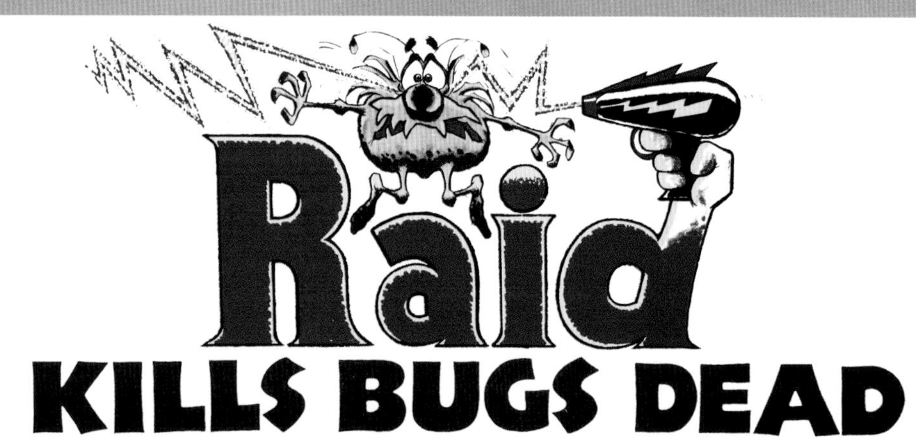

Raid Bug • c. 1977
Raid insecticides
Store sign

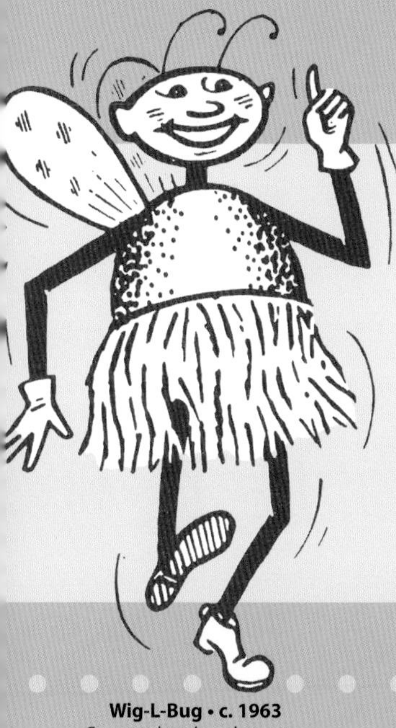

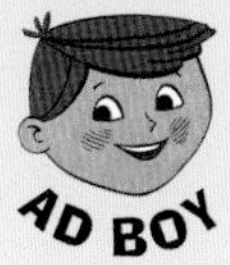

What's a Wig-L-Bug?

Bugs can be pesky pests, fleet flyers, or even cause an upset tummy. Because bugs also buzz, the vibrating machine used by dentists to mix cavity-filling metal amalgams was dubbed the Wig-L-Bug to make it seem less ominous to nervous young patients.

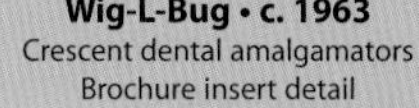

Wig-L-Bug • c. 1963
Crescent dental amalgamators
Brochure insert detail

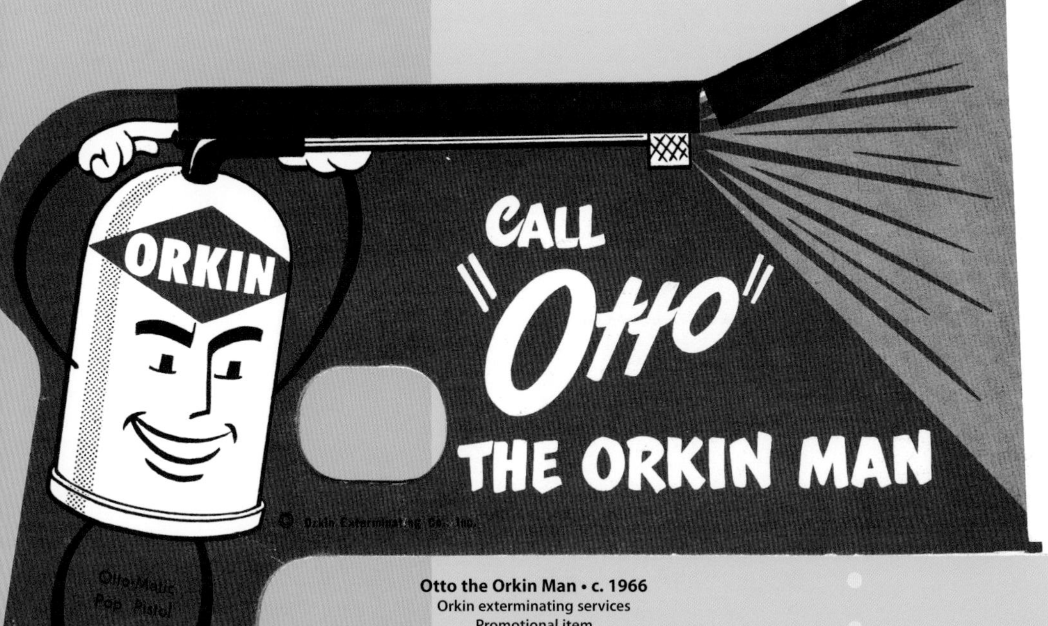

Otto the Orkin Man • c. 1966
Orkin exterminating services
Promotional item

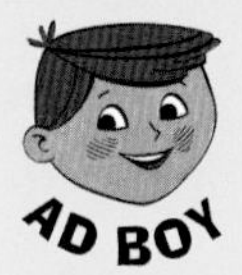

Burger joints not only named their menu items but also created "burger" characters to further promote their brands. The Red Barn chain had Big Barney, and A&W Restaurants invented a burger family: Papaburger, Mamaburger, Teenburger, and Babyburger. Bob's Pantry dubbed their double-decker cheeseburger Big Boy—a decision that proved so popular the diner was rechristened as the first Bob's Big Boy.

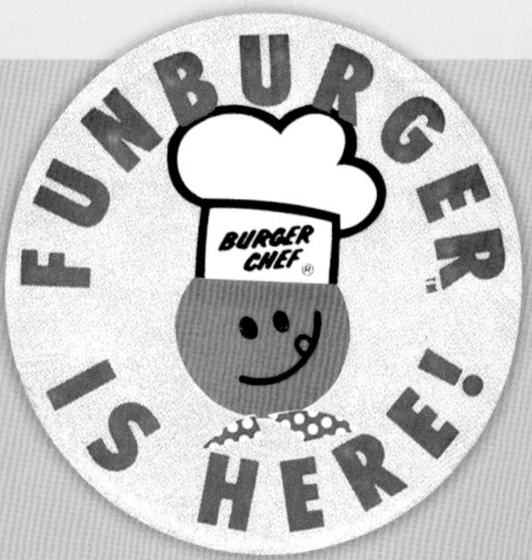

FUNBURGER IS HERE!
BURGER CHEF

Funburger • 1972
Burger Chef restaurants
Pin-back button

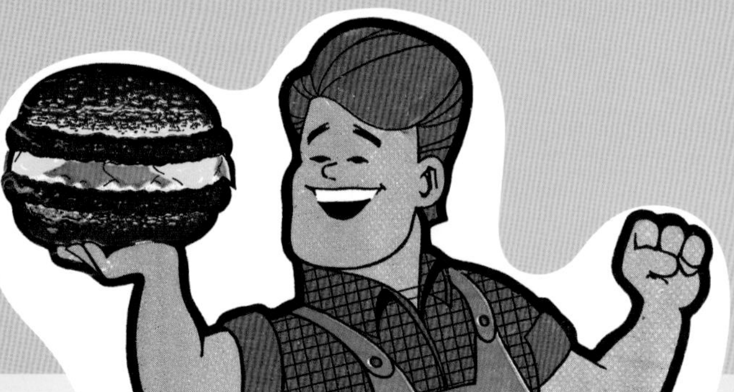

MEET BIG BARNEY AT THE
RED BARN

Big Barney • 1967
Red Barn restaurants
Hand puppet

©1957 W. GLEASON
Gleasons
RESTAURANTS
Home of the Hi-Burger
and FRESH STRAWBERRY PIE

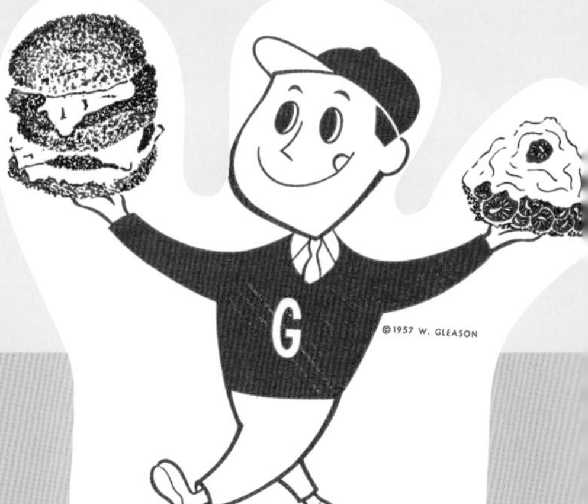

Hi-Burger Boy • 1957
Gleasons restaurants
Hand puppet

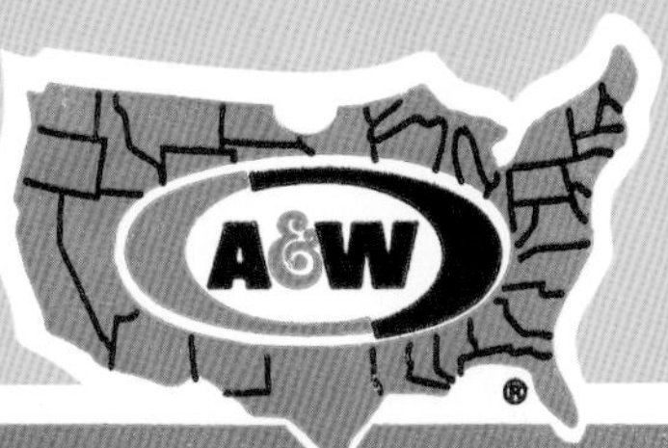

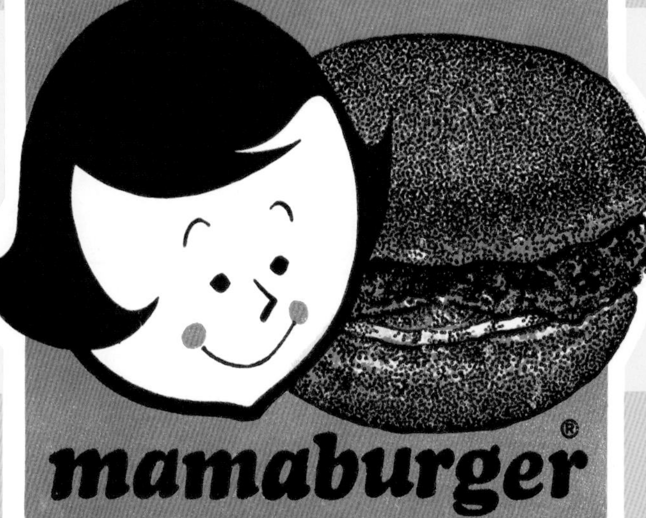

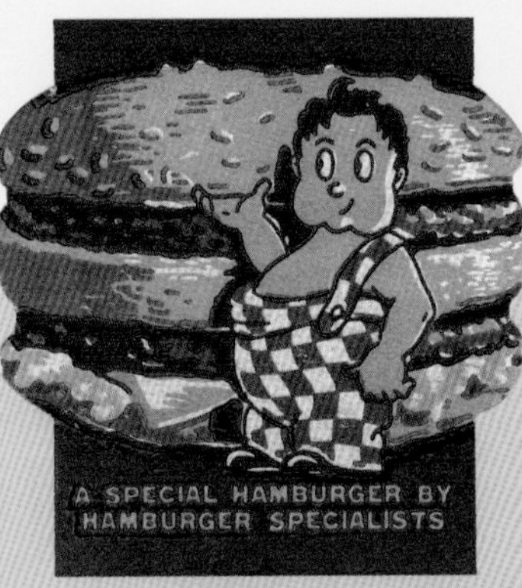

Mamaburger • c. 1974
A&W restaurants
Bag detail

Big Boy • c. 1949
Bob's Big Boy restaurants
Matchbook cover

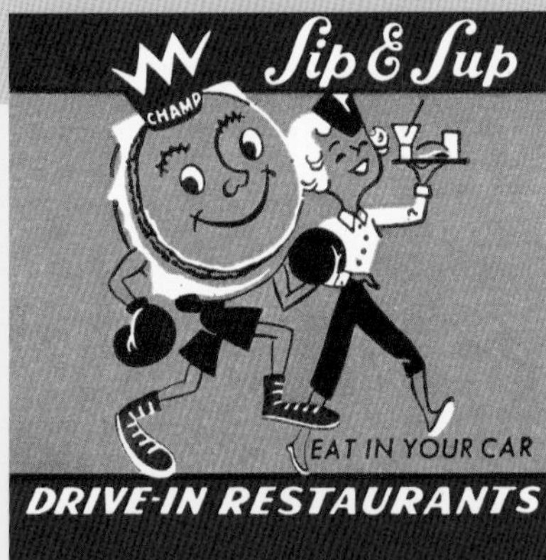

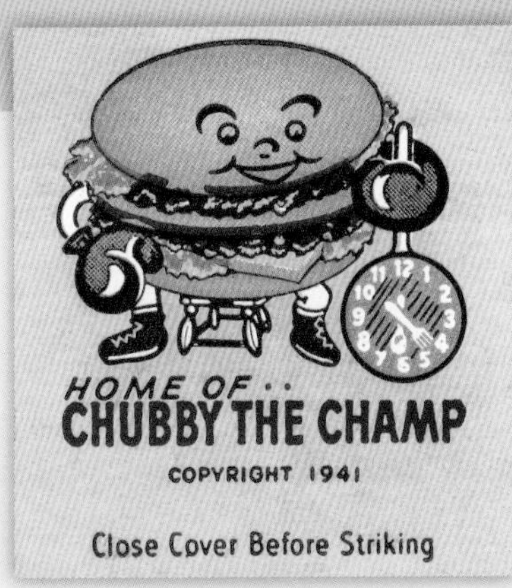

Champ • c. 1954
Sip & Sup restaurants
Matchbook cover

Chubby the Champ • 1941
The Clock restaurants
Matchbook cover

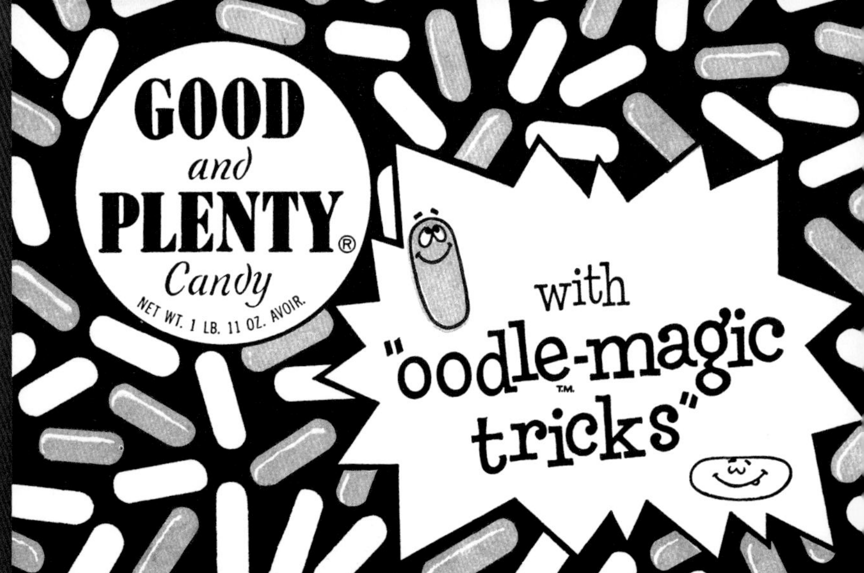

Oodle • 1965
Good and Plenty candy
Box front

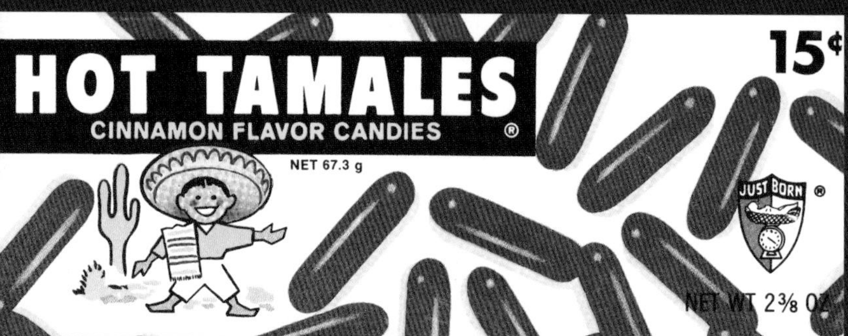

Hot Tamales Kid • c. 1965
Hot Tamales candy
Box front

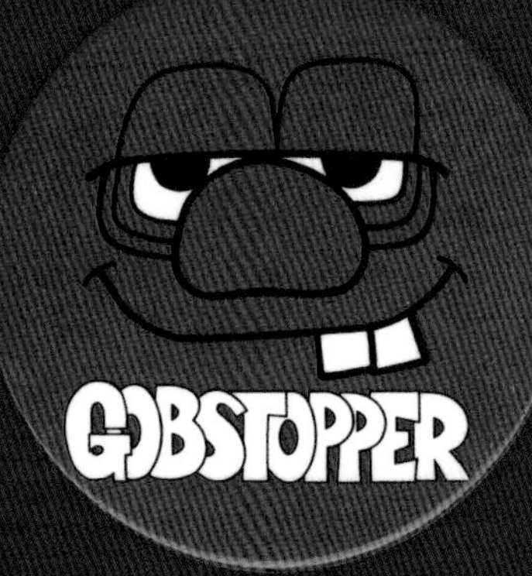

Everlasting Gobstopper • 1976
Everlasting Gobstopper candy
Pin-back button

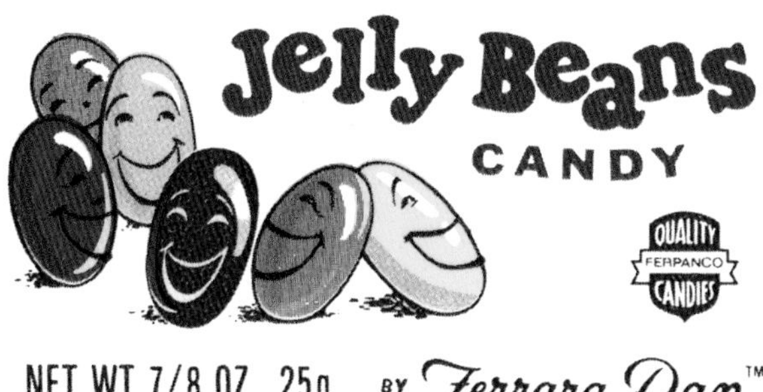

Jelly Beans • c. 1983
Jelly Beans candy
Box front

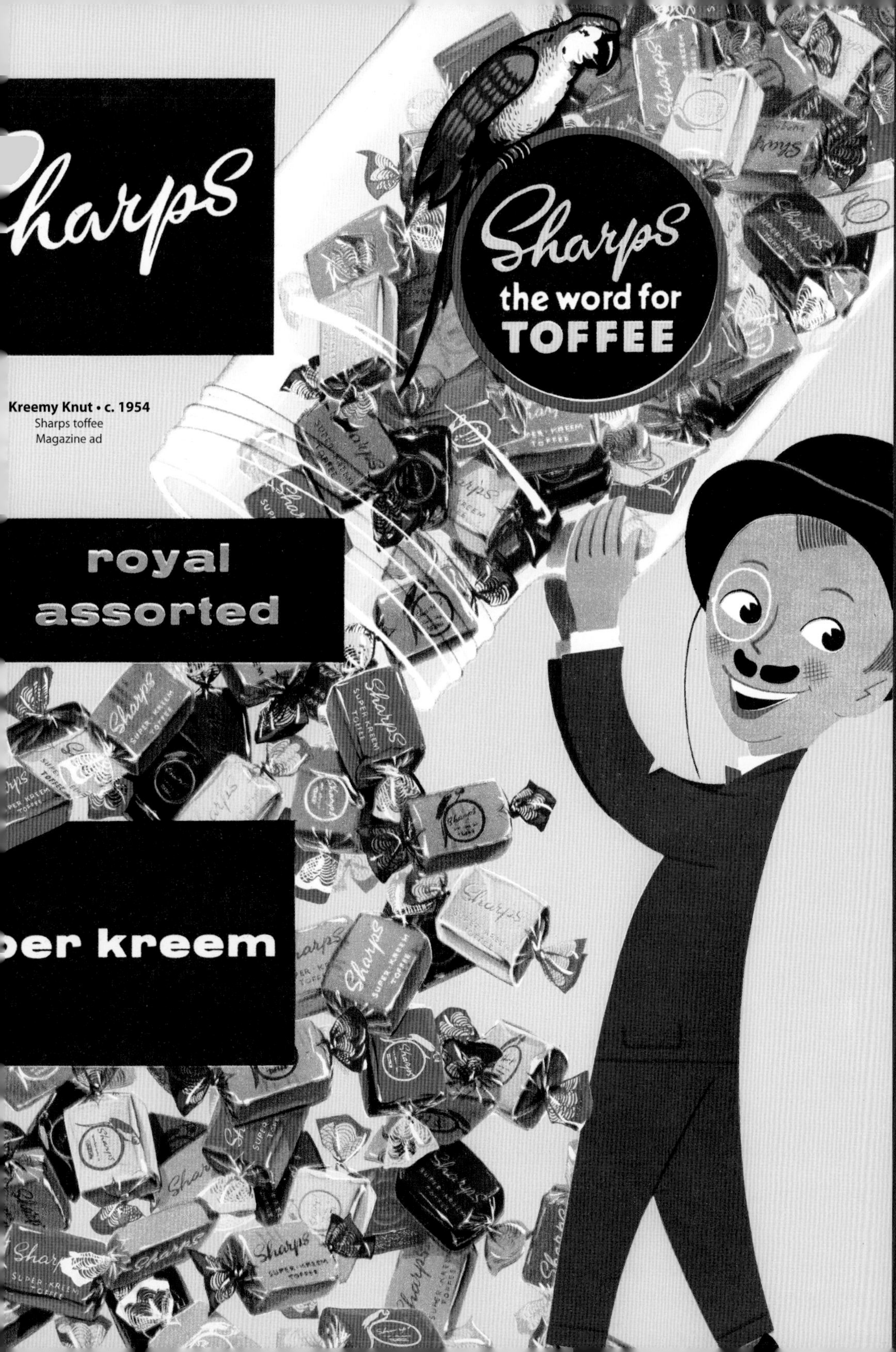

Sharps

Sharps
the word for
TOFFEE

Kreemy Knut • c. 1954
Sharps toffee
Magazine ad

royal
assorted

per kreem

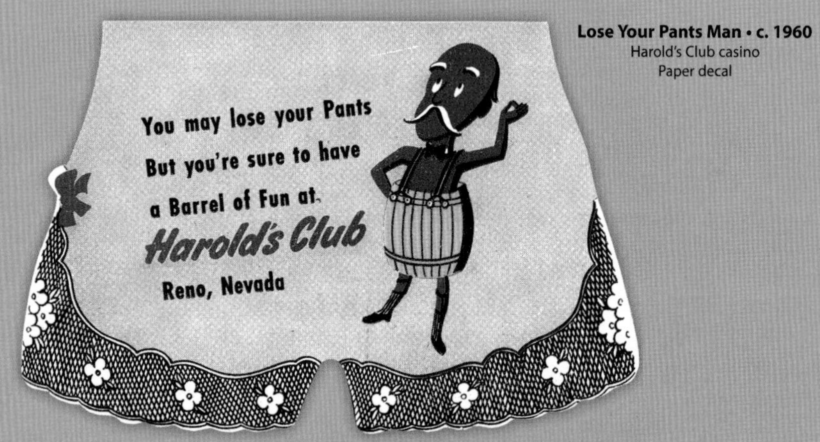

Lose Your Pants Man • c. 1960
Harold's Club casino
Paper decal

Wild Indian • c. 1962
Club Cal Neva casino
Slot machine sign

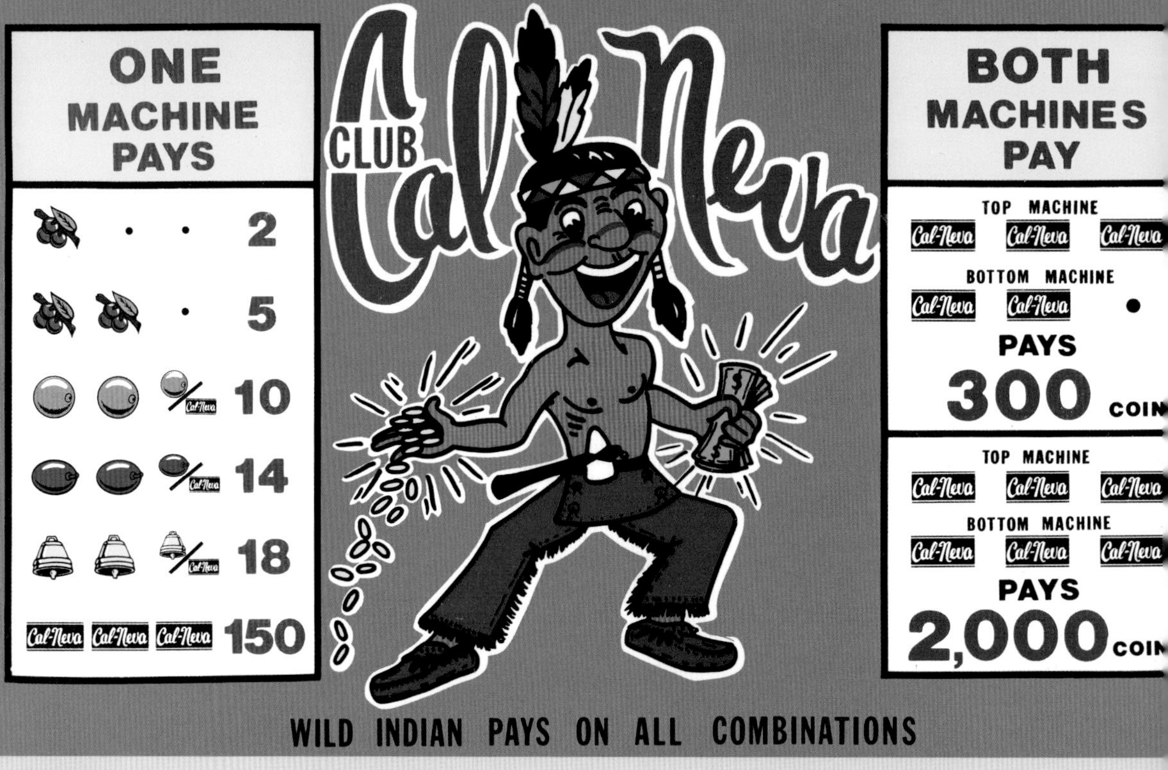

CLUB Cal Neva

ONE MACHINE PAYS			
cherry	•	•	2
cherry	cherry	•	5
orange	orange	orange / Cal-Neva	10
plum	plum	plum / Cal-Neva	14
bell	bell	bell / Cal-Neva	18
Cal-Neva	Cal-Neva	Cal-Neva	150

BOTH MACHINES PAY

TOP MACHINE
Cal-Neva Cal-Neva Cal-Neva
BOTTOM MACHINE
Cal-Neva Cal-Neva •
PAYS
300 COIN

TOP MACHINE
Cal-Neva Cal-Neva Cal-Neva
BOTTOM MACHINE
Cal-Neva Cal-Neva Cal-Neva
PAYS
2,000 COIN

WILD INDIAN PAYS ON ALL COMBINATIONS

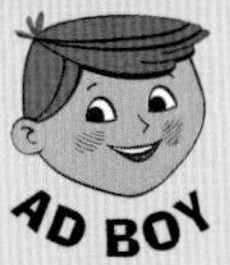

Prior to the 1950s, casinos were largely thought of either as seedy saloons for hard-c gamblers and gangsters, or as snooty, members-only clubs that were off limits to any one who wasn't a wealthy European aristocrat. But after World War II, Nevada's casinc owners began a campaign to change America's mind by portraying its establishment as fun, friendly places for grown-ups to play.

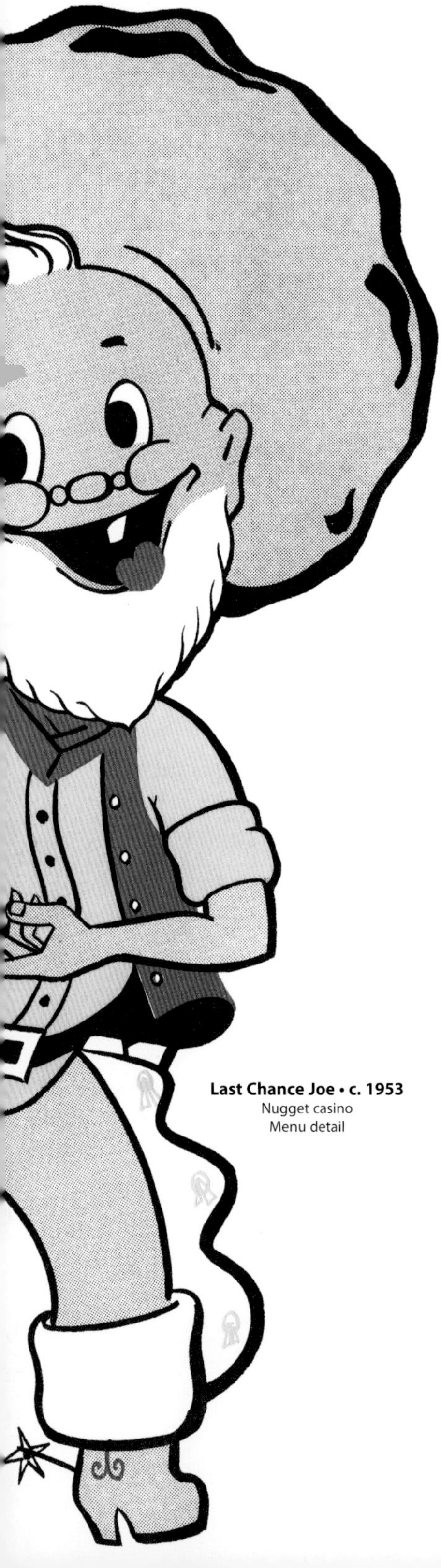

Last Chance Joe • c. 1953
Nugget casino
Menu detail

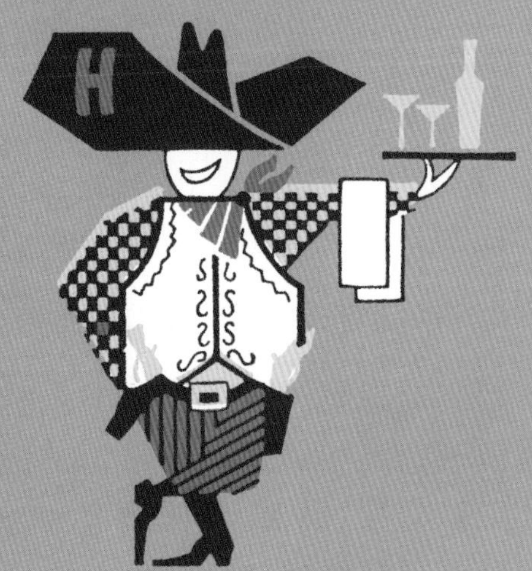

The ....

HOLIDAY

....HOTEL in Downtown Reno

Holiday Kid • c. 1961
Holiday Hotel casino
Paper napkin detail

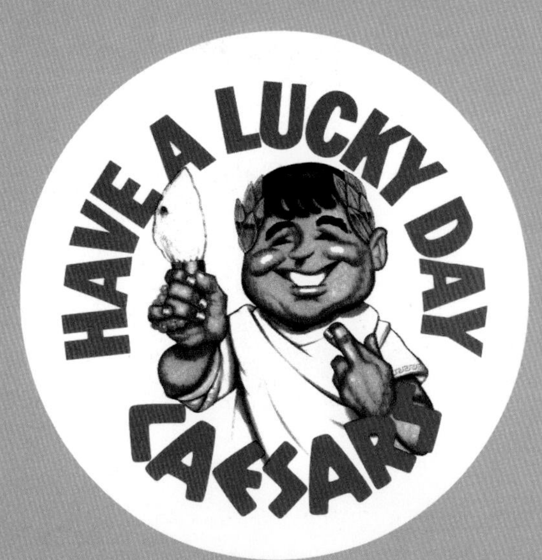

Caesar • c. 1979
Caesars Palace casino
Pin-back button

The Pink Pussy Cat • 1962
The Pink Pussycat College of Strip Tease
Matchbook cover

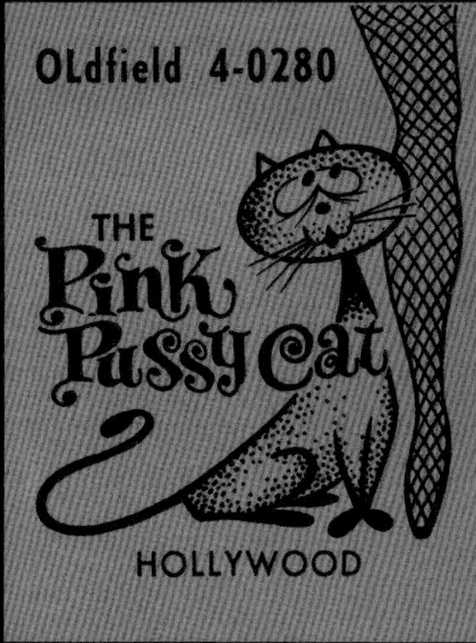

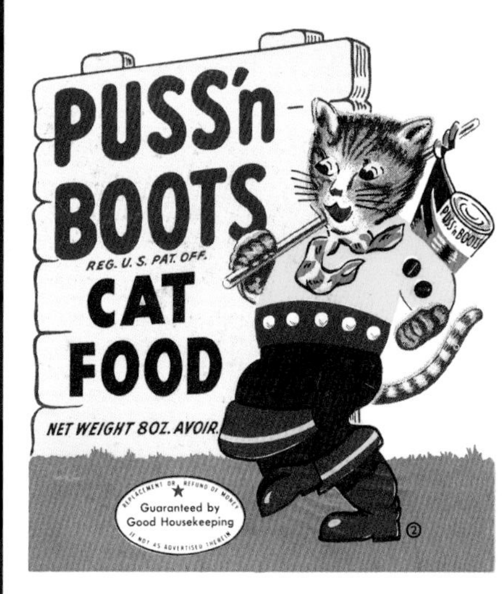

Puss'n Boots • c. 1955
Puss'n Boots cat food
Lens tissue pack cover

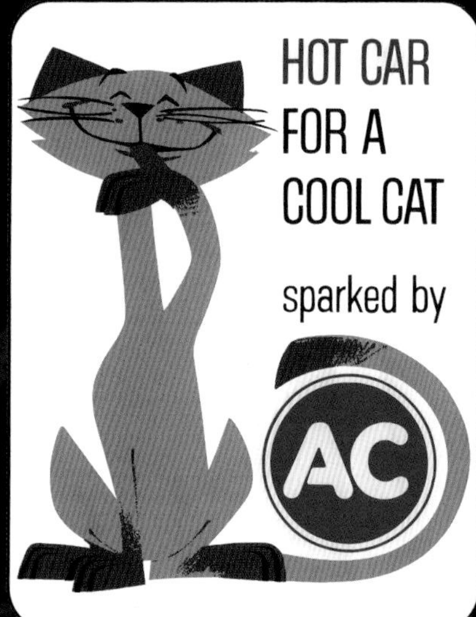

Cool Cat • c. 1968
AC spark plugs
Promotional sticker

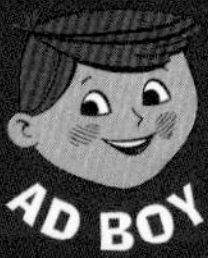

Instantly familiar as intimate members of millions of American households, cats and dogs have always been popular ad icons, and still are today. It is because they are so relatable to so many of us that they have been steadily employed to sell products not only within the pet industry but also items as diverse as batteries, chocolates, and even underwear!

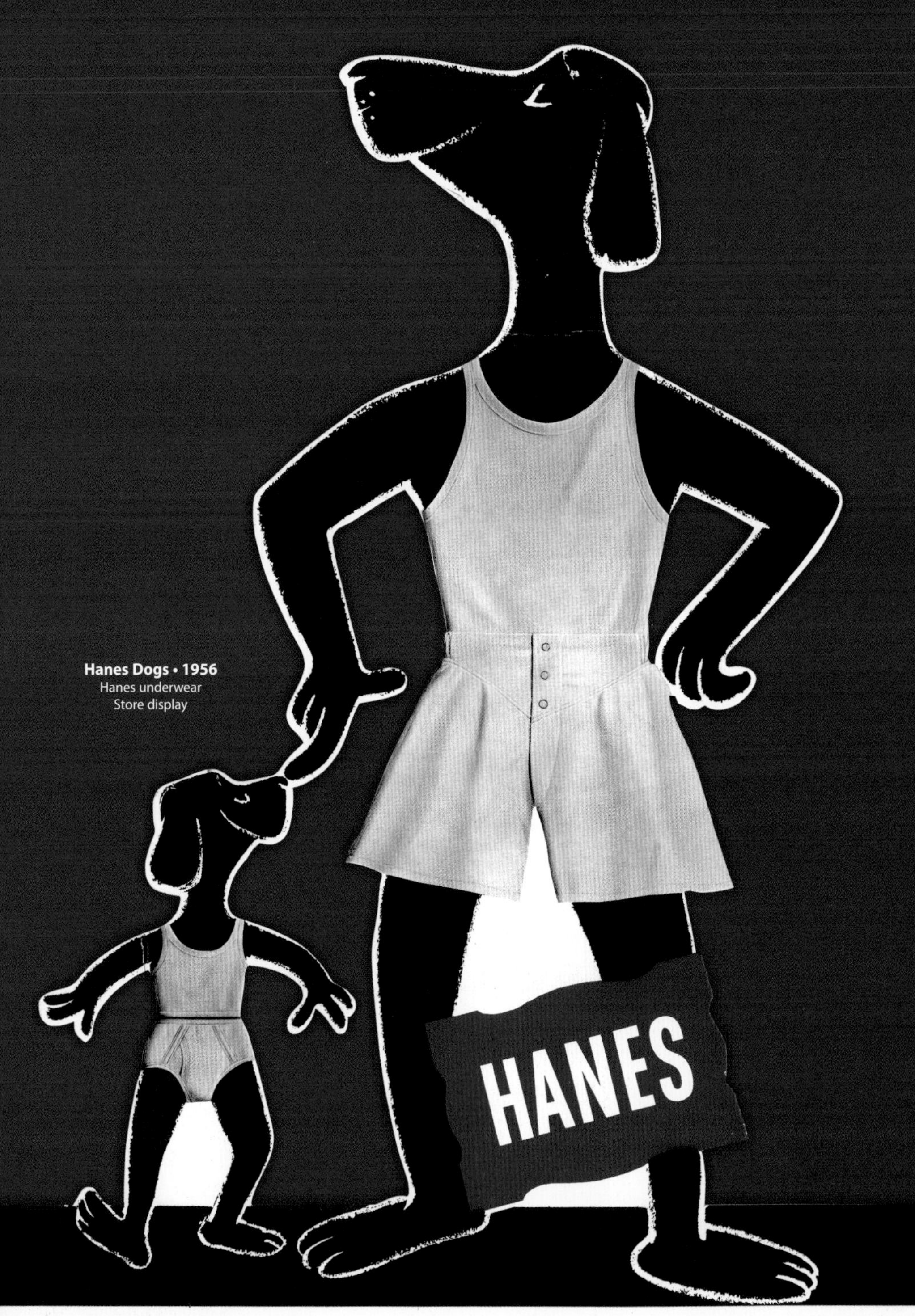

Hanes Dogs • 1956
Hanes underwear
Store display

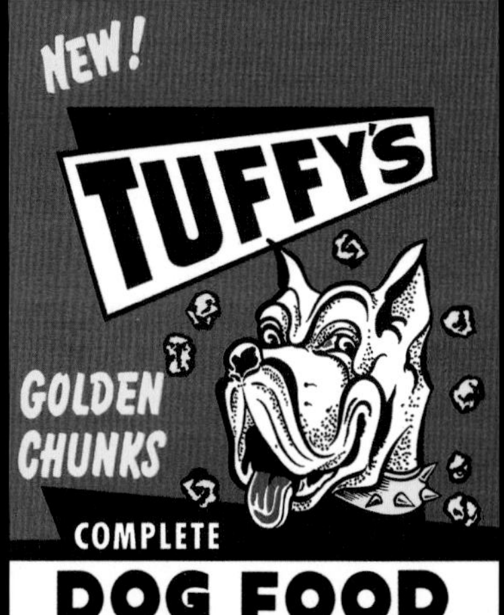

Tuffy • c. 1961
Tuffy's dog food
Playing card detail

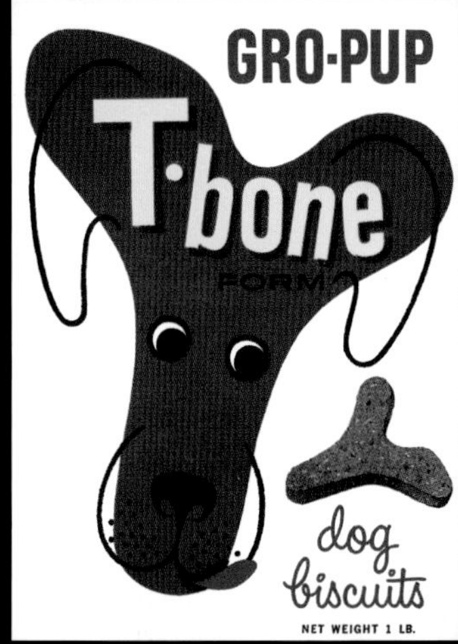

T•Bone • c. 1962
T•Bone dog biscuits
Box front

COOKED IN THE CAN

VACUUM PACKED

HOW I FEED MY DOG

1. "TRIM" (not table scraps) once daily and always at the same hour (he's becoming a clock watcher).

2. Give him sufficient time to comfortably eat all the food, but don't let him play over it.

3. Any food left in the dish is removed and that's that until the next meal.

4. Clean fresh water is always within his reach.

5. No feeding between meals.

6. Good eating habits of my dog depend on my self-discipline since he depends on me.

Other TRIM Products

Chicken
5 in 1
Beef Liver
Horsemeat

TRADE MARK REG. U.S. PAT. OFF.

KEEP YOUR DOG IN TRIM

Trim

BEEF
BEEF BY-PRODUCTS
DOG FOOD

INGREDIENTS

Beef, Beef by-products, ¾ of 1% wheat flour, 0.0045% sodium nitrite. Charcoal added.

ANALYSIS

Crude Protein, not less than 13%
Crude Fat, not less than... 4%
Crude Fibre, not more than 1%

NET WEIGHT 15 OZS.

HAS YOUR DOG SEEN HIS DOCTOR LATELY?

PACKED BY
B. A. BERNARD & CO., INC.
PHILADELPHIA 31, PA.

FED BY VETERINARIANS, BREEDERS—KENNEL AND PROFESSIONAL HANDLERS

Trim • c. 1958
Trim dog food
Can label

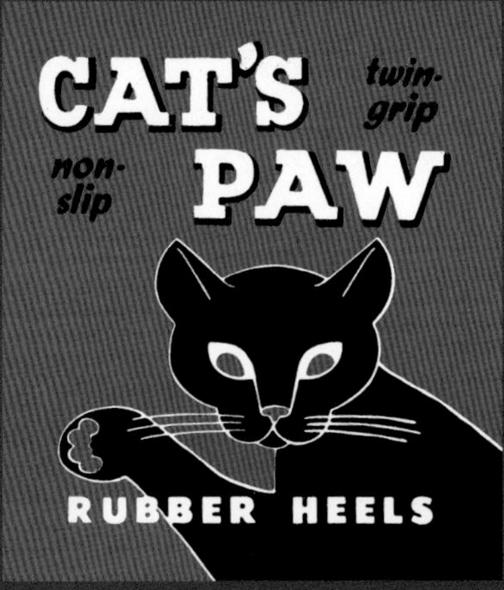

Blackie • 1951
Cat's Paw rubber heels
Box front

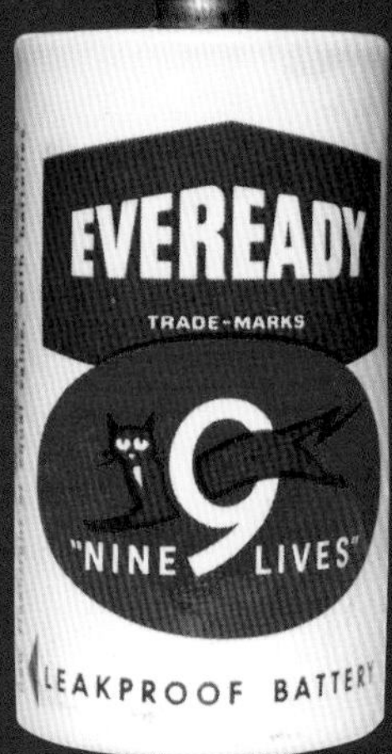

Eveready Cat • c. 1950
Eveready batteries
Dry cell battery

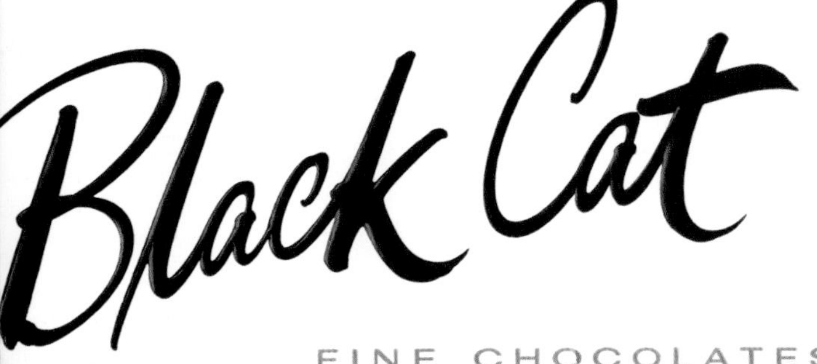

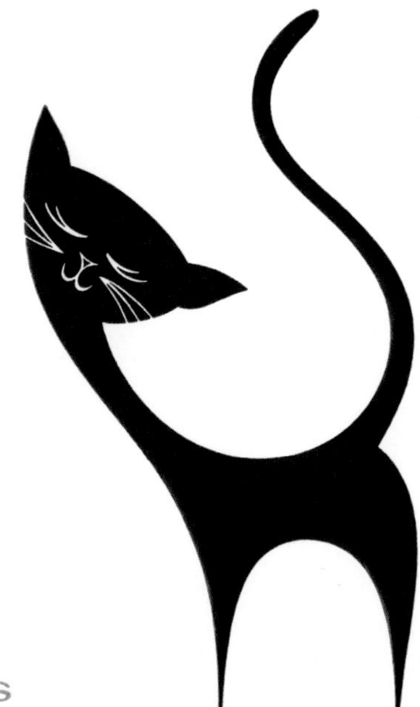

Black Cat • c. 1962
Cadbury's chocolates
Box cover

NEW from Battle Creek

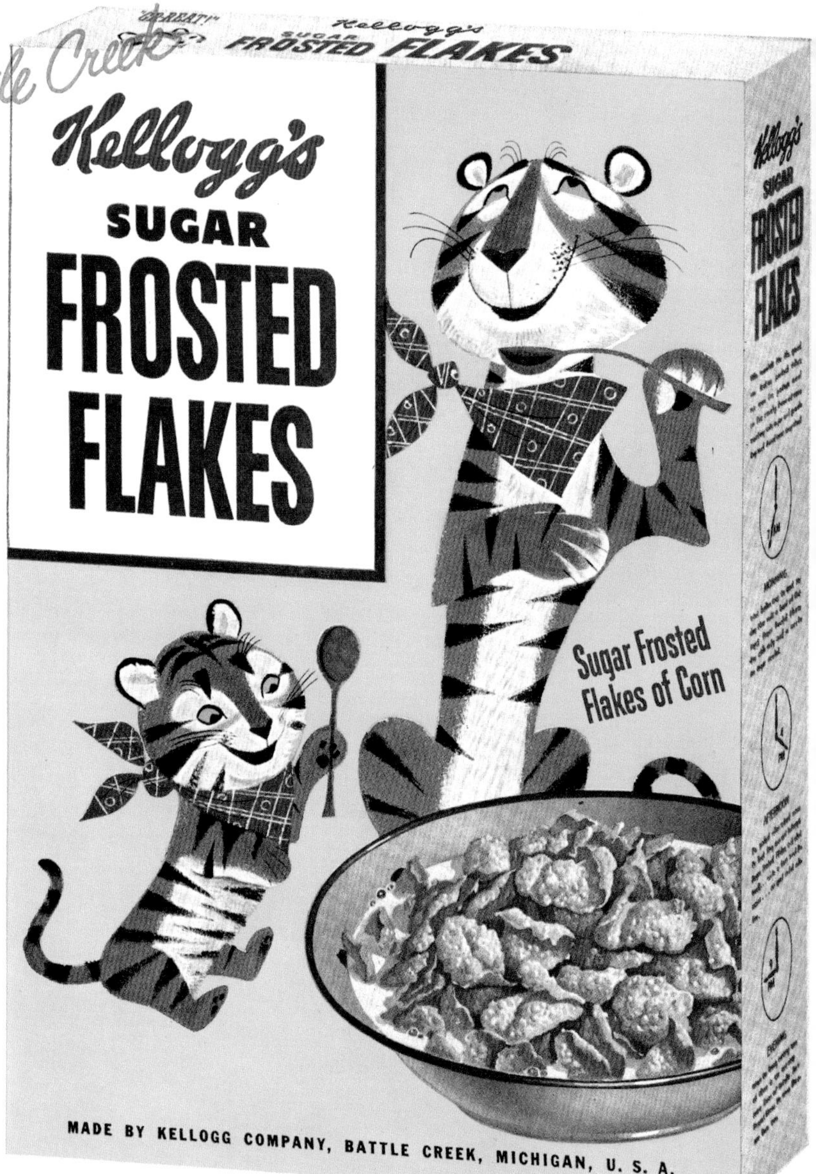

"GREAT!" Kellogg's SUGAR FROSTED FLAKES

Kellogg's

SUGAR

FROSTED

FLAKES

Sugar Frosted Flakes of Corn

MADE BY KELLOGG COMPANY, BATTLE CREEK, MICHIGAN, U. S. A.

Tony the Tiger,
Tony Jr.,
and Katy the Kangaroo • c. 1952
Sugar Frosted Flakes cereal
Magazine ad

Scared of tigers? We have Katy the Kangaroo, too. Both on your grocer's shelves now

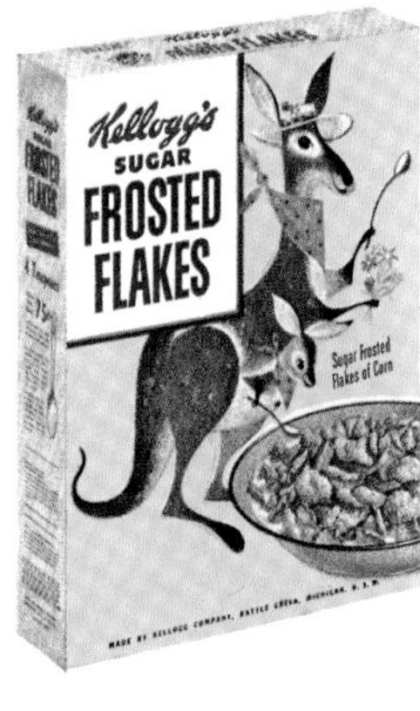

The biggest, sweetest thing that ever happened in cereals. Every crisp flake is sparkling all over with Kellogg's secret sugar frosting. Honest, folks . . . one taste is worth ten thousand words.

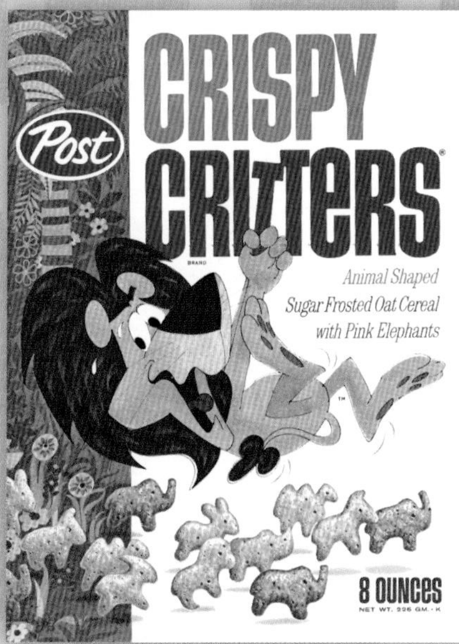

Linus • 1967
Crispy Critters cereal
Box front

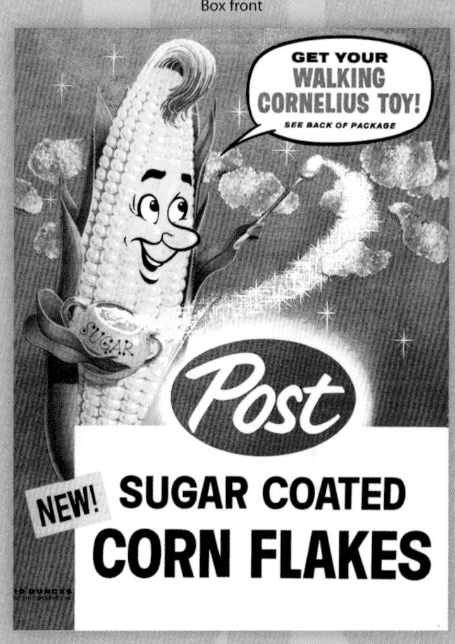

Cornelius • c. 1959
Sugar Coated Corn Flakes cereal
Box front

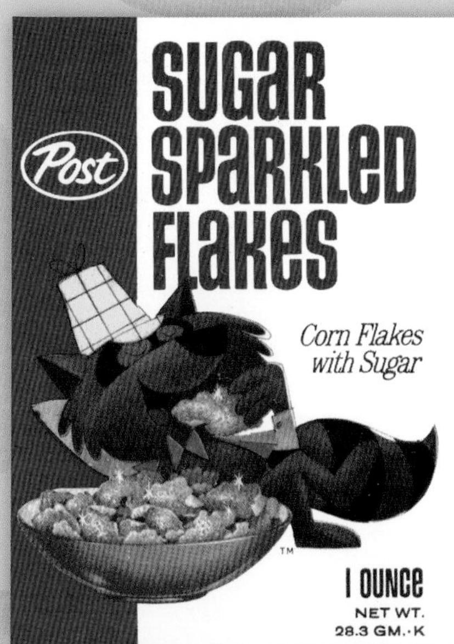

Rory Racoon • 1966
Sugar Sparkled Flakes cereal
Box front

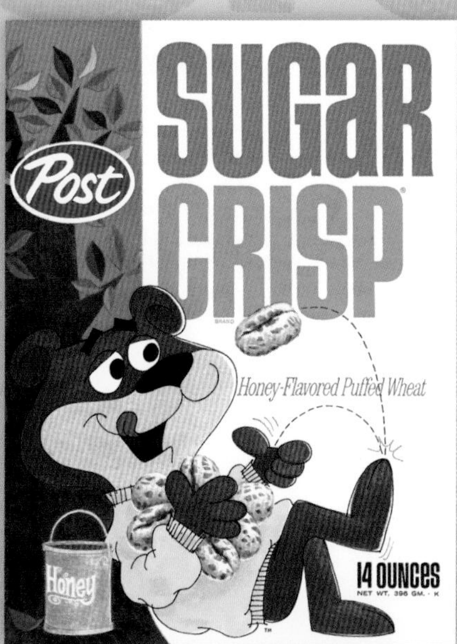

Sugar Bear • 1966
Sugar Crisp cereal
Box front

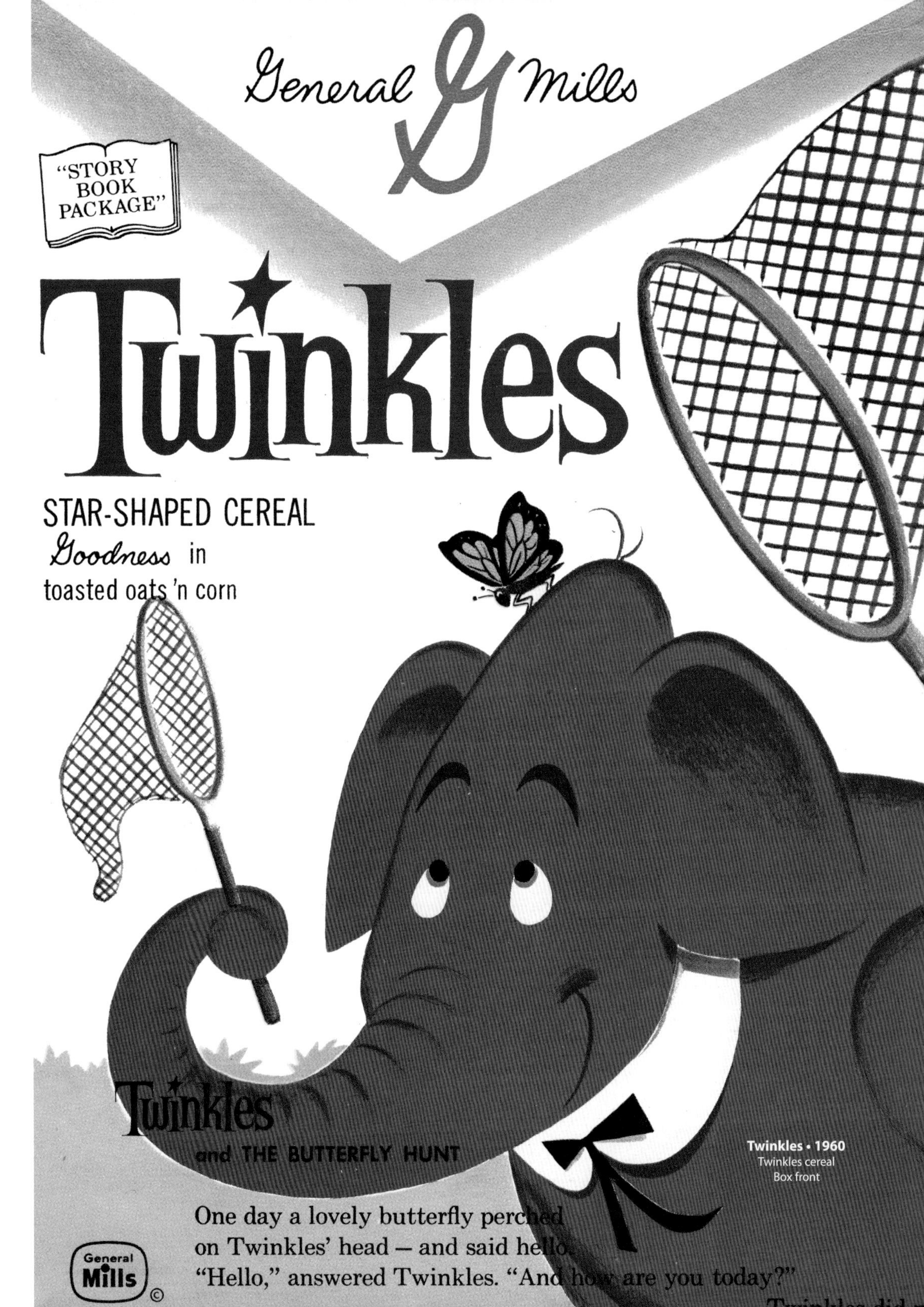

Twinkles • 1960
Twinkles cereal
Box front

Sir Grapefellow • 1973
Sir Grapefellow cereal
Box front

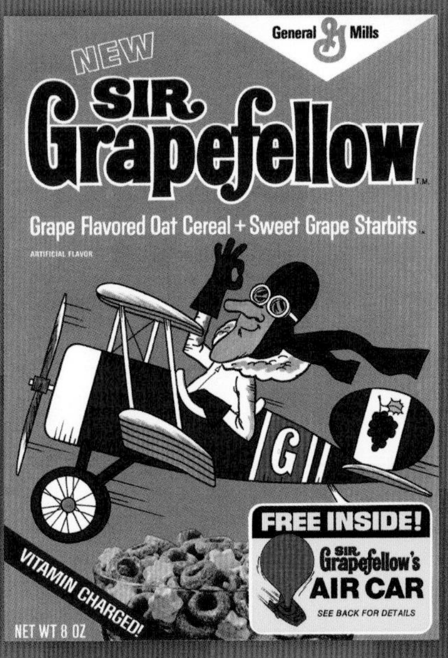

Sugar Pops Pete • 1959
Sugar Pops cereal
Box front

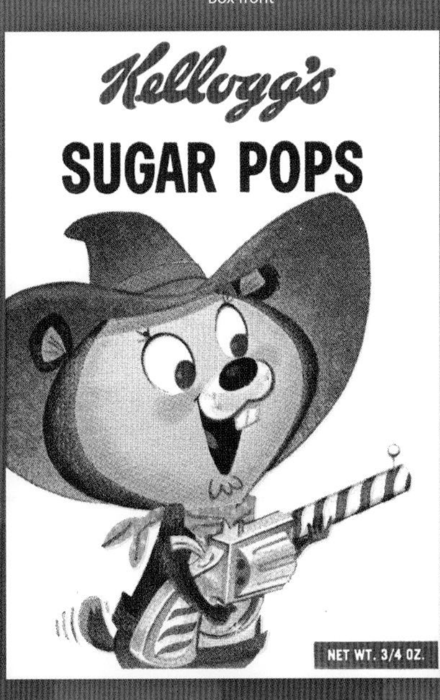

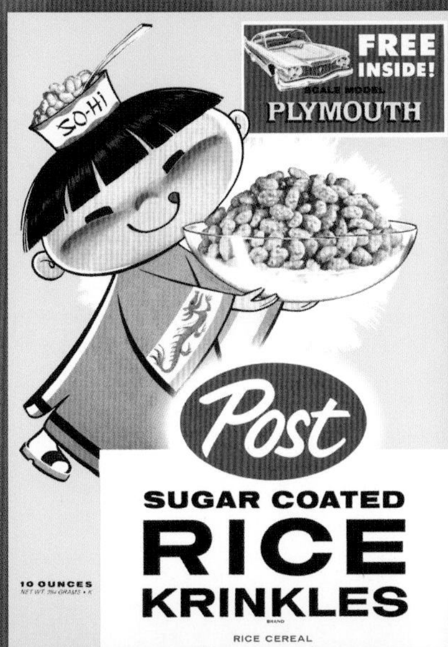

So-Hi • 1960
Sugar Coated Rice Krinkles cereal
Box front

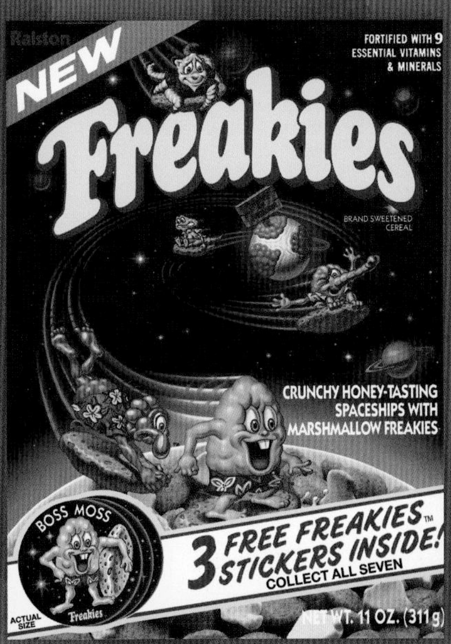

Freakies • 1987
Freakies cereal
Box front

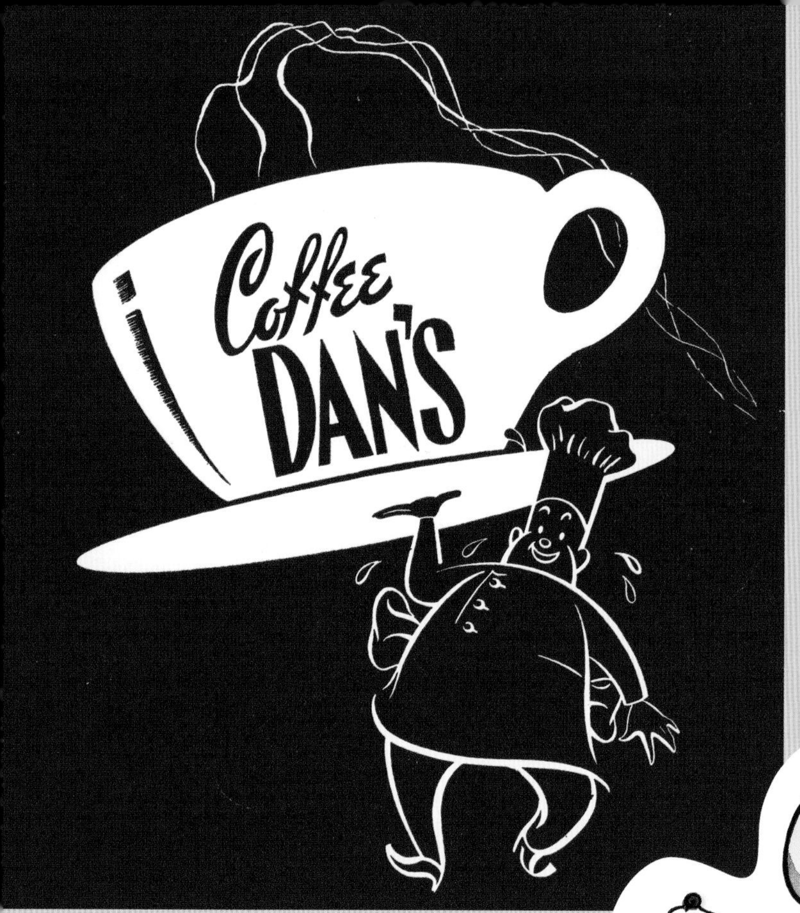

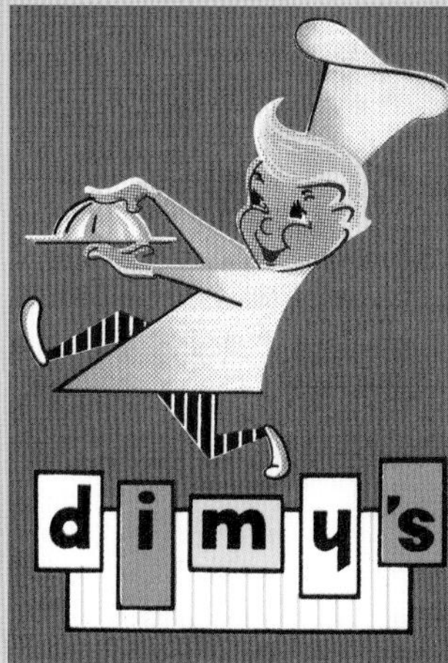

Dimy's Chef • c. 1967
Dimy's restaurant
Matchbook cover

Coffee Dan's Chef • 1956
Coffee Dan's restaurants
Menu cover

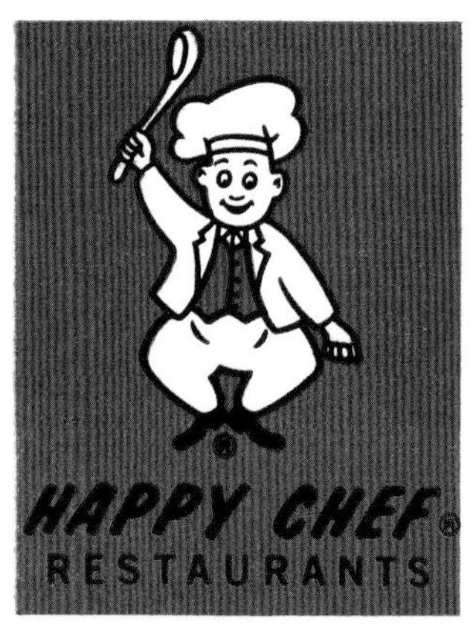

Happy Chef • 1976
Happy Chef restaurants
Matchbook cover

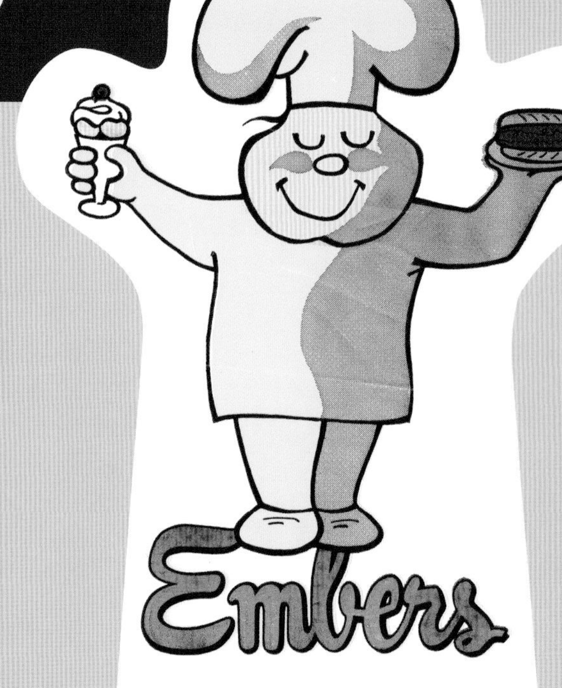

Embers Chef • c. 1967
Embers restaurants
Hand puppet

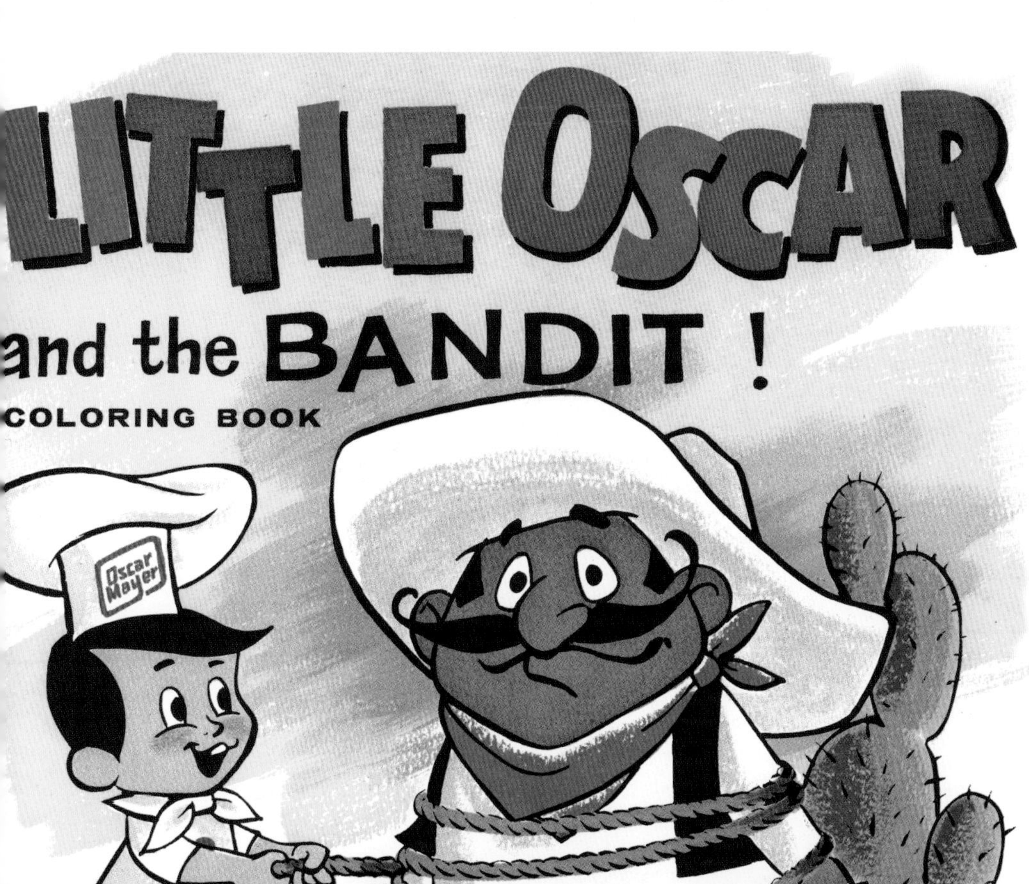

Little Oscar • 1962
Oscar Mayer wieners
Coloring book cover

The chefs of yesteryear were hardly the temperamental television celebrities many have become today. Most were portrayed as cheerful, hardworking line cooks anxious to please a hungry public. It didn't matter whether they were promoting a food brand, a neighborhood diner, or a restaurant chain. These bustling, service-oriented characters represented a comforting ideal of good cooking.

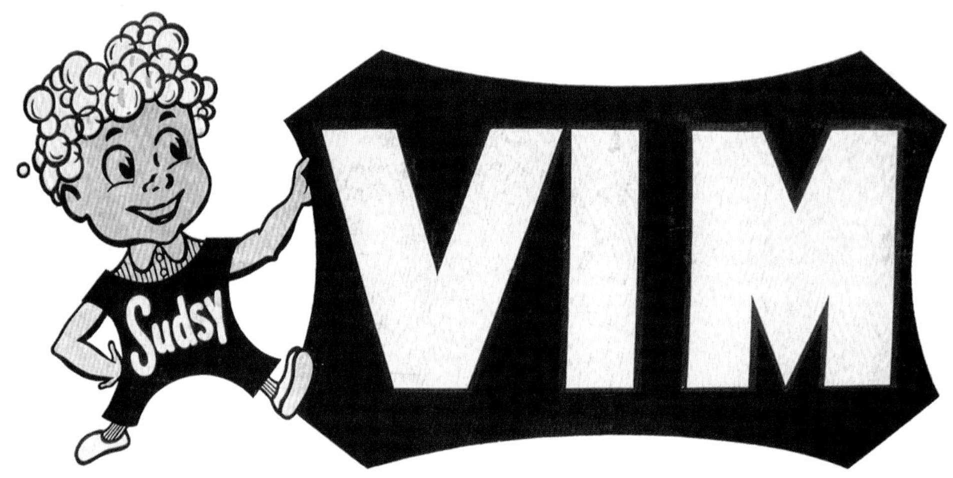

Sudsy • 1954
Vim cleanser
Box detail

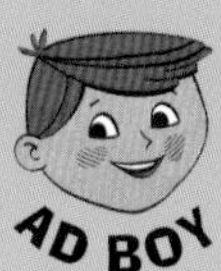

South of the equator he's the face of Don Maximo soap. In Canada he's called M. Net The French call him Mr. Propre. And in Italy he's Maestro Lindo. He's the Grime Fight The Man Behind the Shine. He's Mr. Clean! Ad characters can be put to work almost anywhere. The nattily attired Ty-D-Bol man could be found hailing inquisitive home makers while skippering his skiff inside a toilet tank.

Mr. Clean • c. 1974
Don Maximo soap
Soap bar wrapper

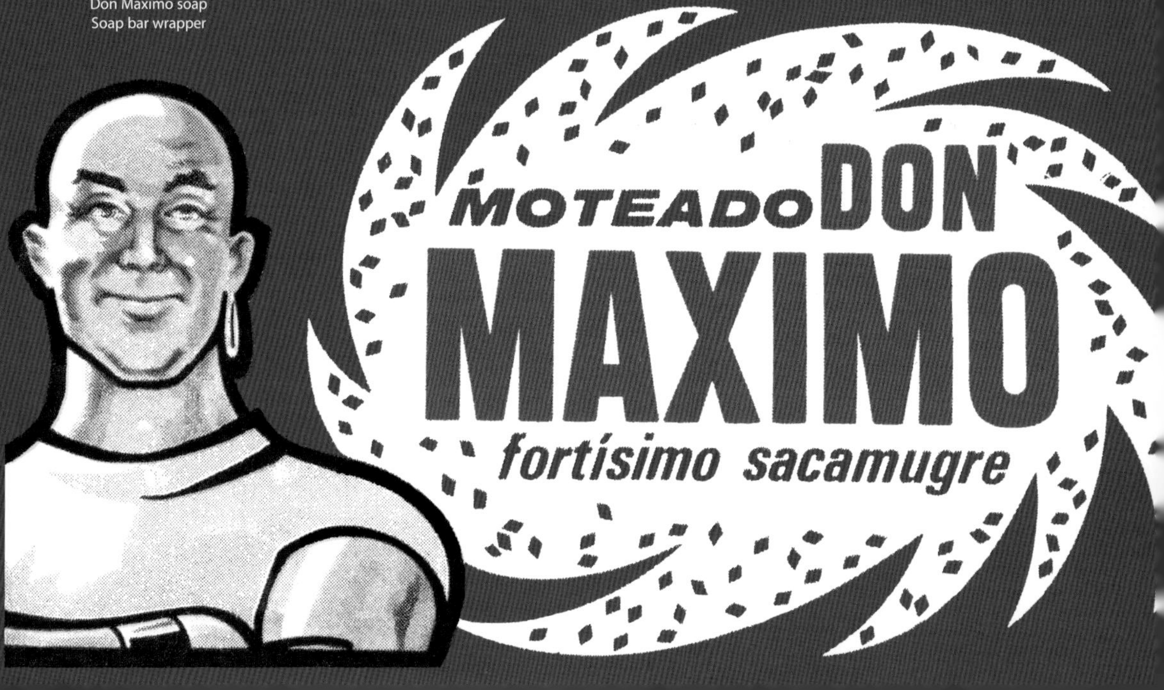

MOTEADO DON
MAXIMO
fortísimo sacamugre

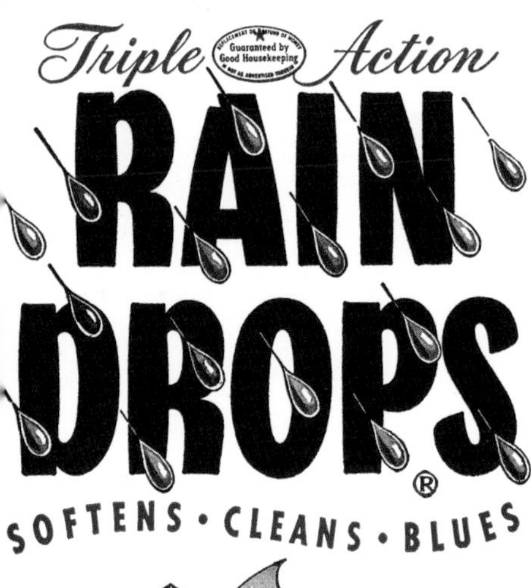

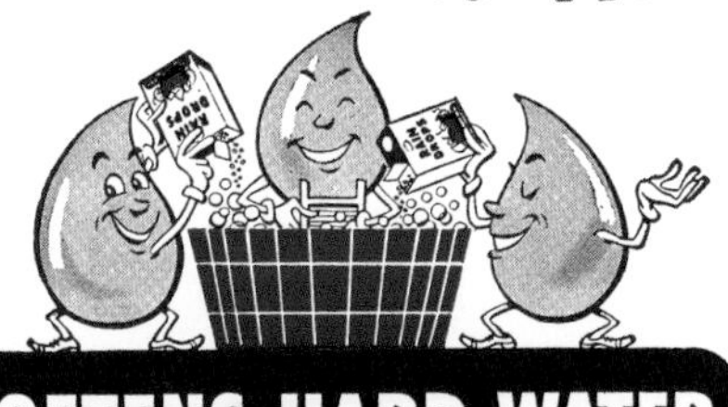

SOFTENS HARD WATER
BLUES • WHITENS • SAVES SOAP

Rain Drops • 1947
Rain Drops cleanser
Box front

NEW
BAB-O®
CLEANSER
BUBBLE ACTION
Cuts Grease 4 times as Quick!

Bab-O Bubble • 1953
Bab-O cleanser
Can label

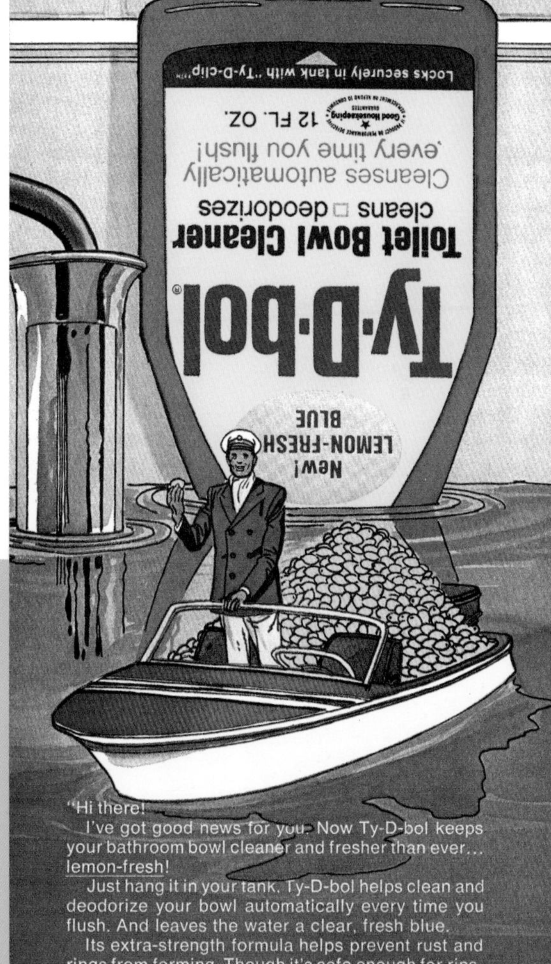

Ty-D-Bol Man • 1971
Ty-D-Bol toilet bowl cleanser
Magazine ad

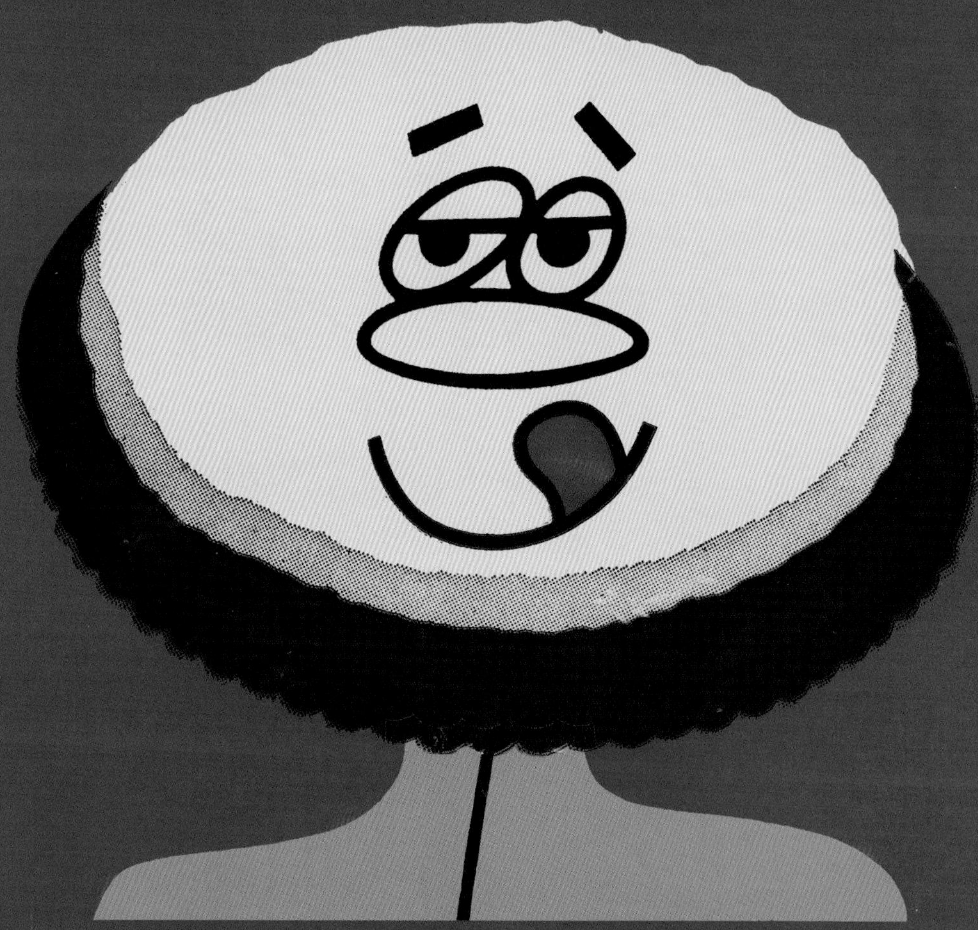

LICKITY

Lickity Splits

Lickity • c. 1971
Lickity Splits cookies
Hand puppet detail

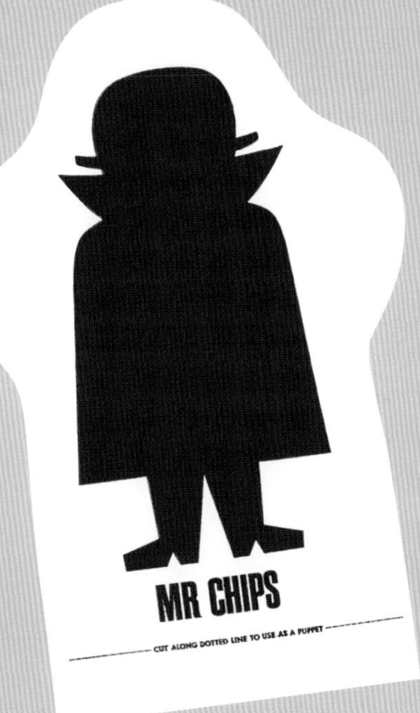

Mr Chips • c. 1971
Mr Chips cookies
Hand puppet

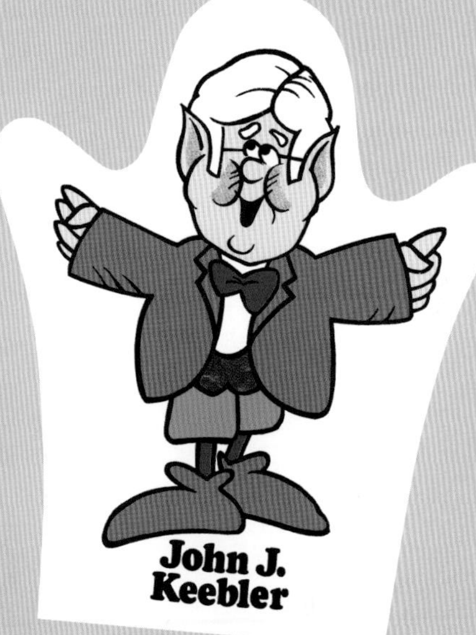

John J. Keebler • 1970
Keebler cookies
Hand puppet

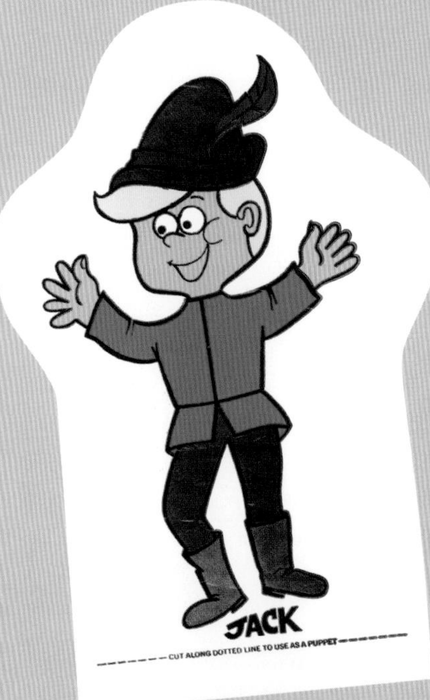

Jack • c. 1971
Scooter Pie snack pies
Hand puppet

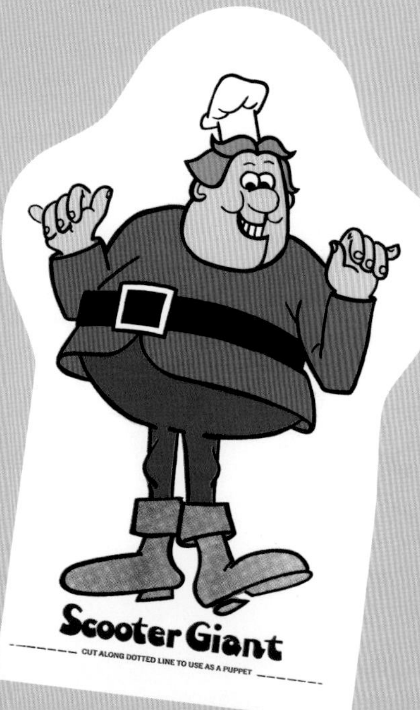

Scooter Pie Giant • c. 1971
Scooter Pie snack pies
Hand puppet

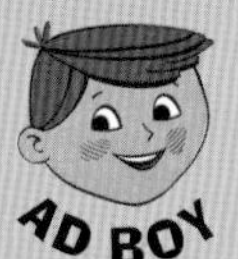

Fair promoters often adapted a distinctive local feature or natural landmark as a mascot. Butte county officials conceived the Golden Feather from the town's proxim to the Feather River waterfalls; Imperial hired an artist who blended agriculture and ranching in the character of Sunny Sol, a hybrid orange-headed cowboy; and Senor Diablo represented the town of Antioch nestled in the shadow of Mount Diablo.

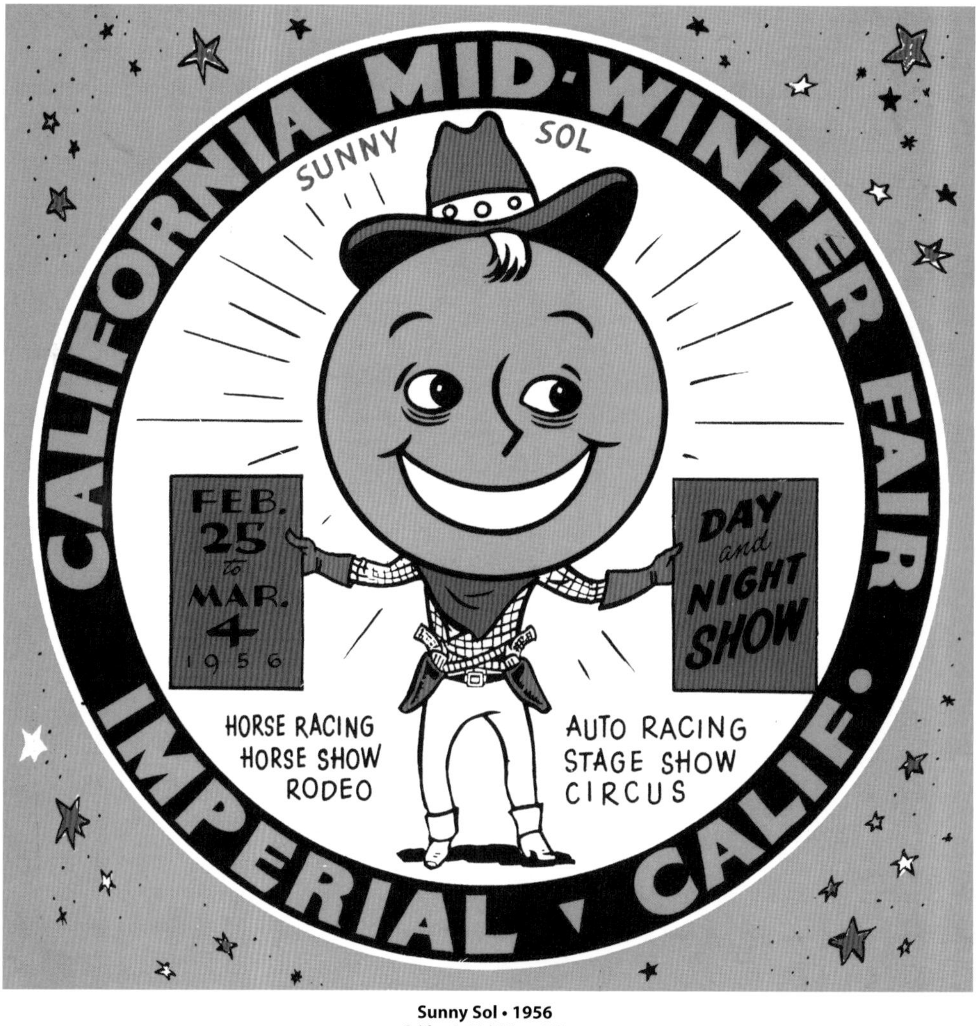

CALIFORNIA MID-WINTER FAIR

SUNNY SOL

FEB. 25 to MAR. 4 1956

DAY and NIGHT SHOW

HORSE RACING
HORSE SHOW
RODEO

AUTO RACING
STAGE SHOW
CIRCUS

IMPERIAL • CALIF.

Sunny Sol • 1956
California Mid-Winter Fair
Promotional sticker

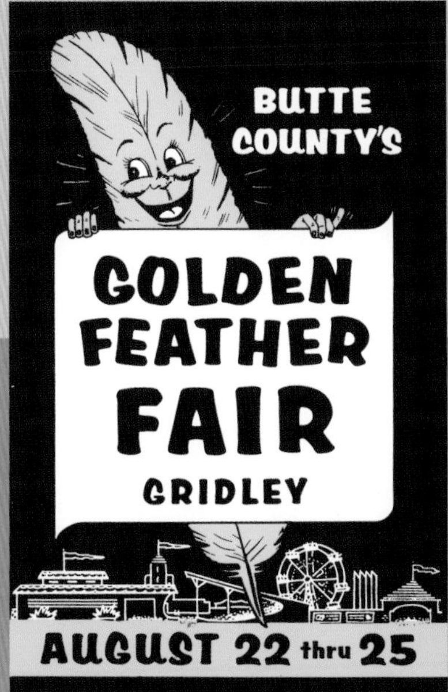

Golden Feather • c. 1957
Golden Feather Fair
Promotional sticker

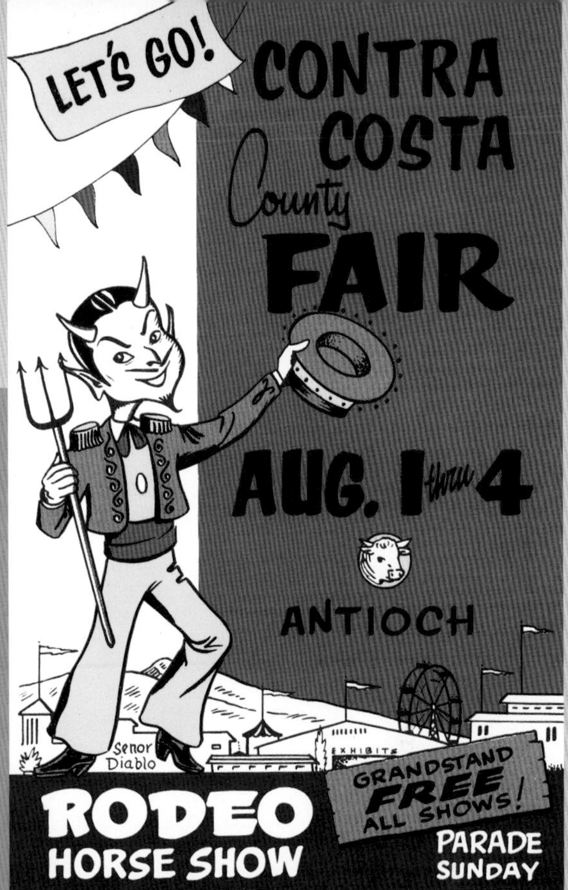

Senor Diablo • c. 1957
Contra Costa County Fair
Promotional sticker

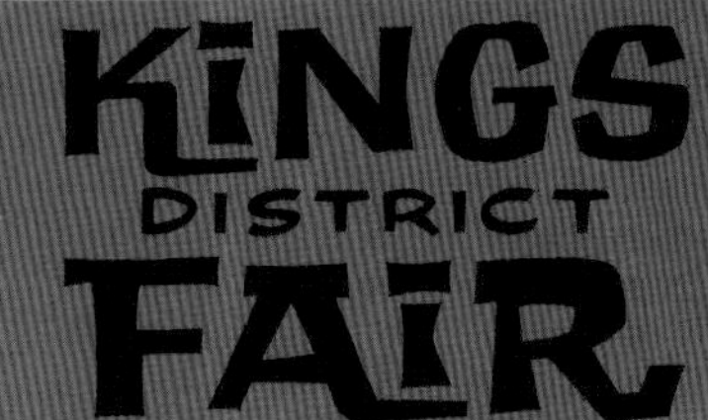

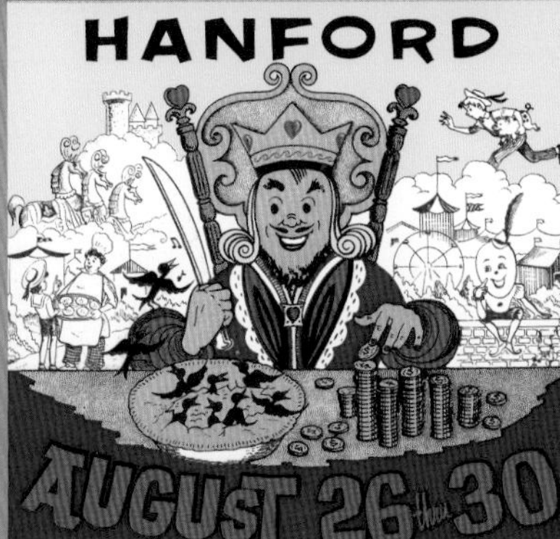

Hanford King • 1959
Kings District Fair
Promotional sign

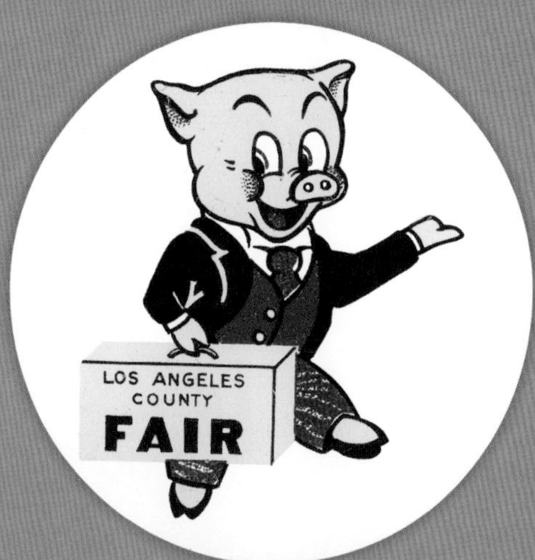

Thummer • c. 1960
Los Angeles County Fair
Pin-back button

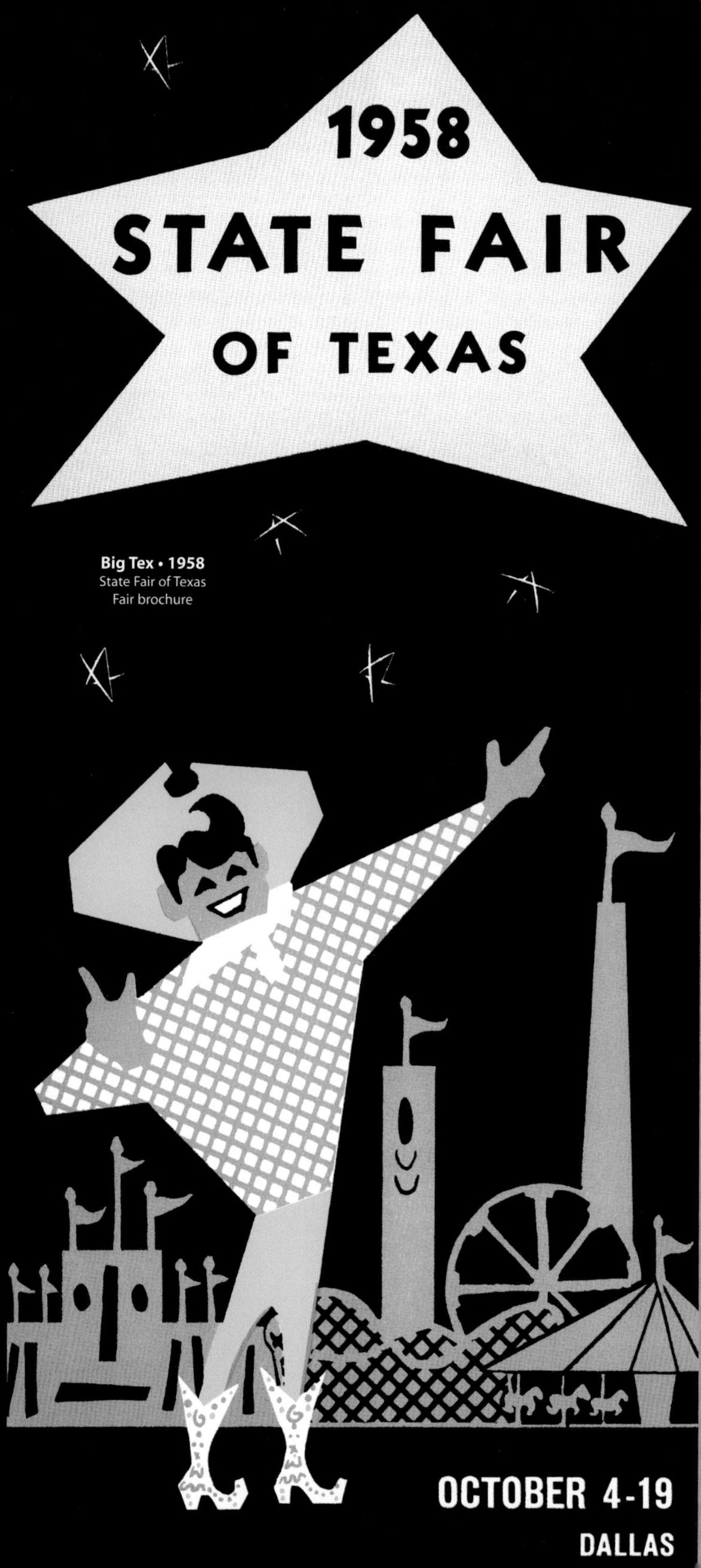

1958
STATE FAIR
OF TEXAS

OCTOBER 4-19
DALLAS

Big Tex • 1958
State Fair of Texas
Fair brochure

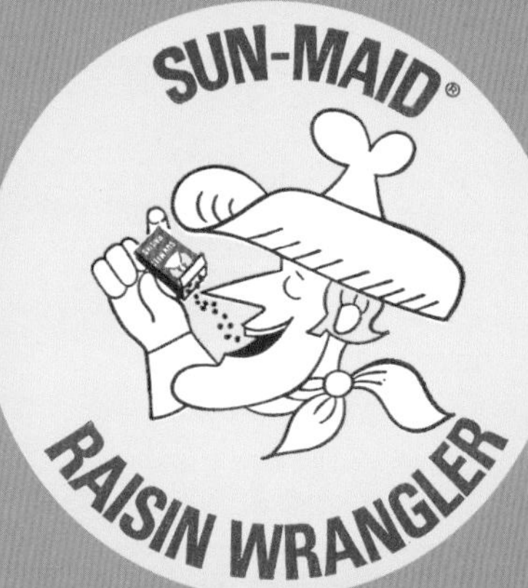

Raisin Wrangler • c. 1975
Sun-Maid raisins
Promotional sticker

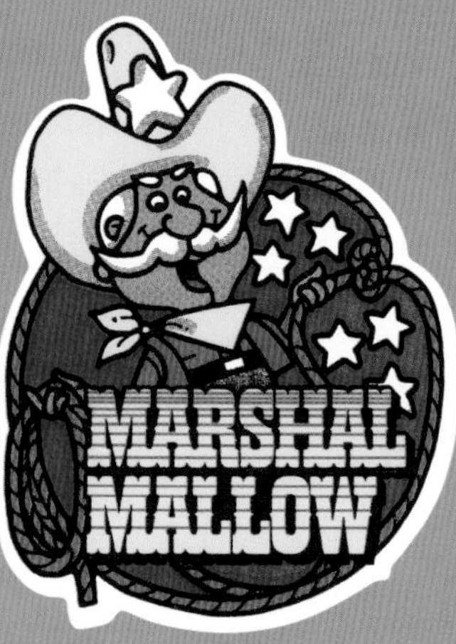

Marshal Mallow • c. 1980
Marshal Mallow hot cocoa mix
Promotional sticker

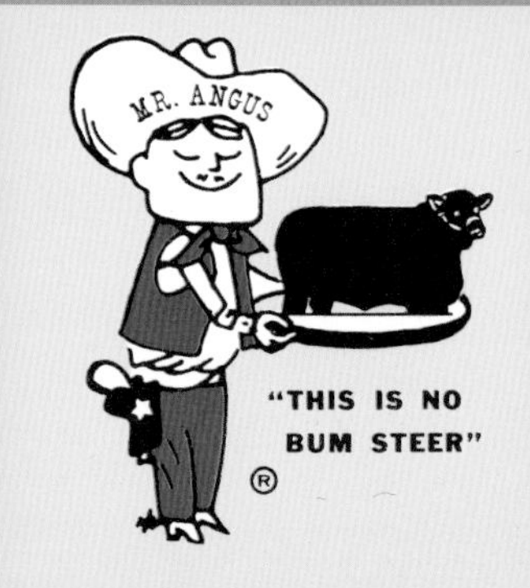

Mr. Angus • c. 1971
Black Angus restaurants
Matchbook cover

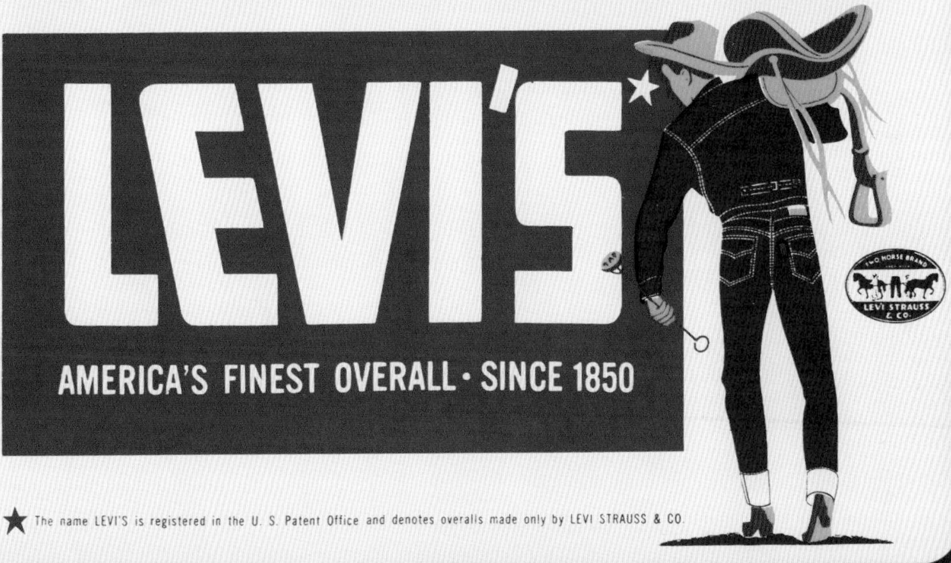

Levi's Cowboy • c. 1960
Levi's jeans
Water decal

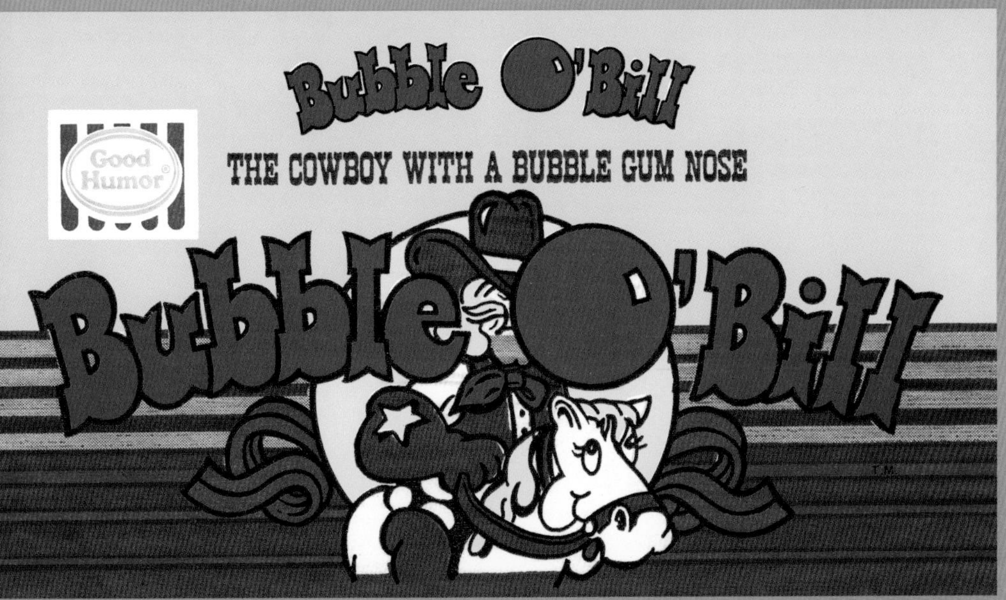

Bubble O'Bill • 1985
Good Humor ice cream
Ice cream bar wrapper

General Mills

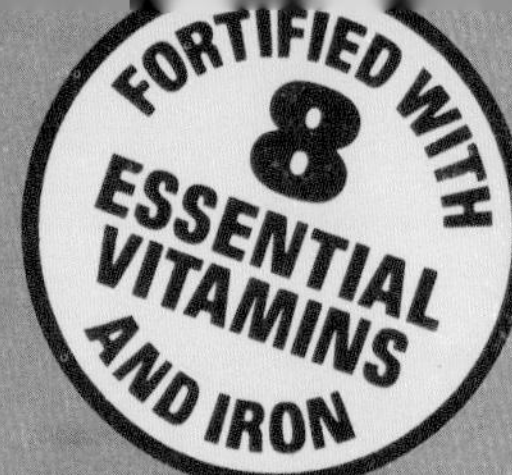

Crazy Cow • 1977
Crazy Cow cereal
Box front

Crazy COW®

THE FROSTED CORN CEREAL THAT
MAKES CHOCOLATE FLAVORED MILK

Just add milk!

INSIDE - one of 6
STAR WARS™ CARDS

SEE BACK PANEL

NET WT 12 OZ
(340 grams

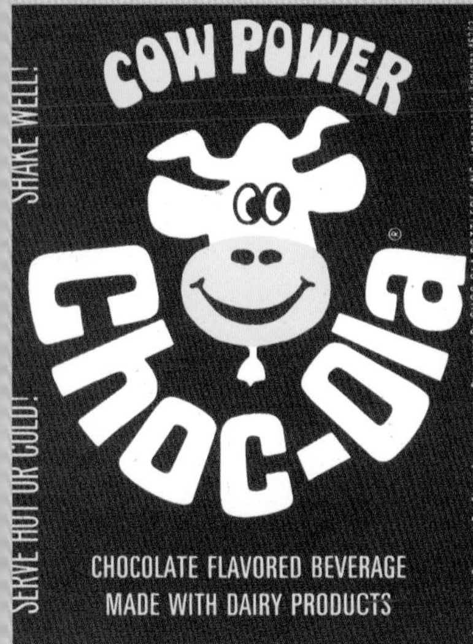

Choc-Ola Cow • c. 1971
Choc-Ola chocolate beverage
Can detail

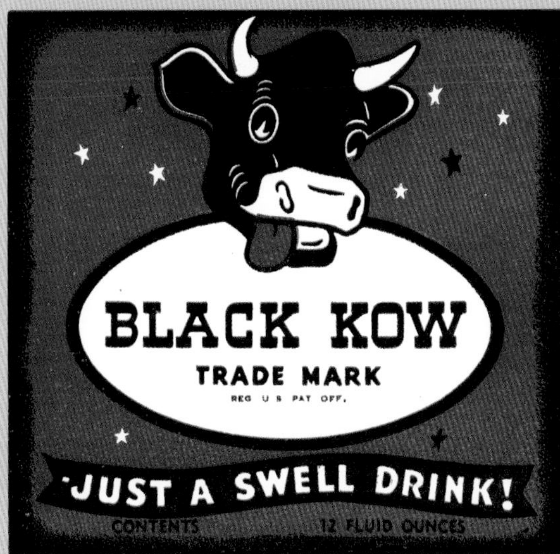

Black Kow • 1940
Black Kow soda
Paper label

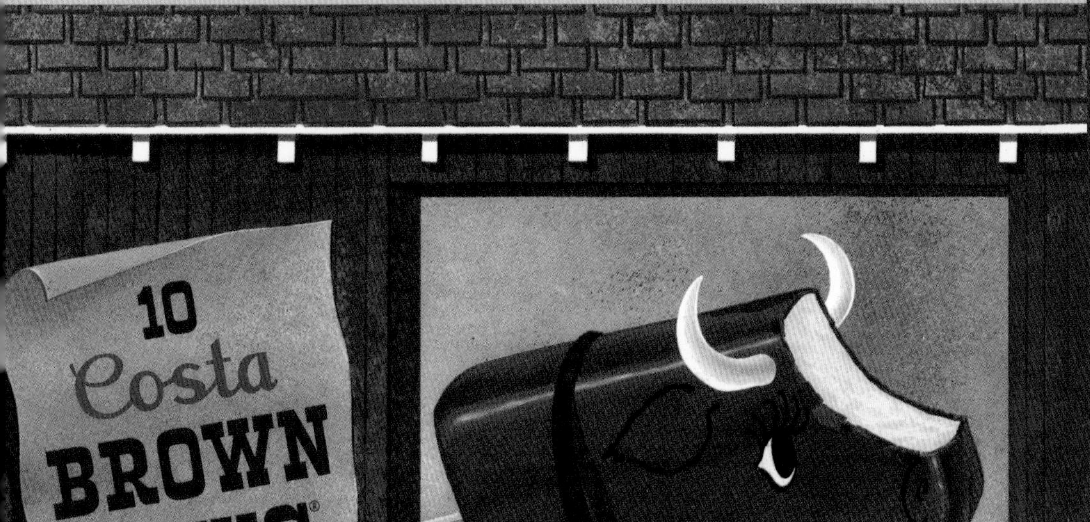

Brown Cow • 1963
Costa Brown Cows ice cream pops
Box front

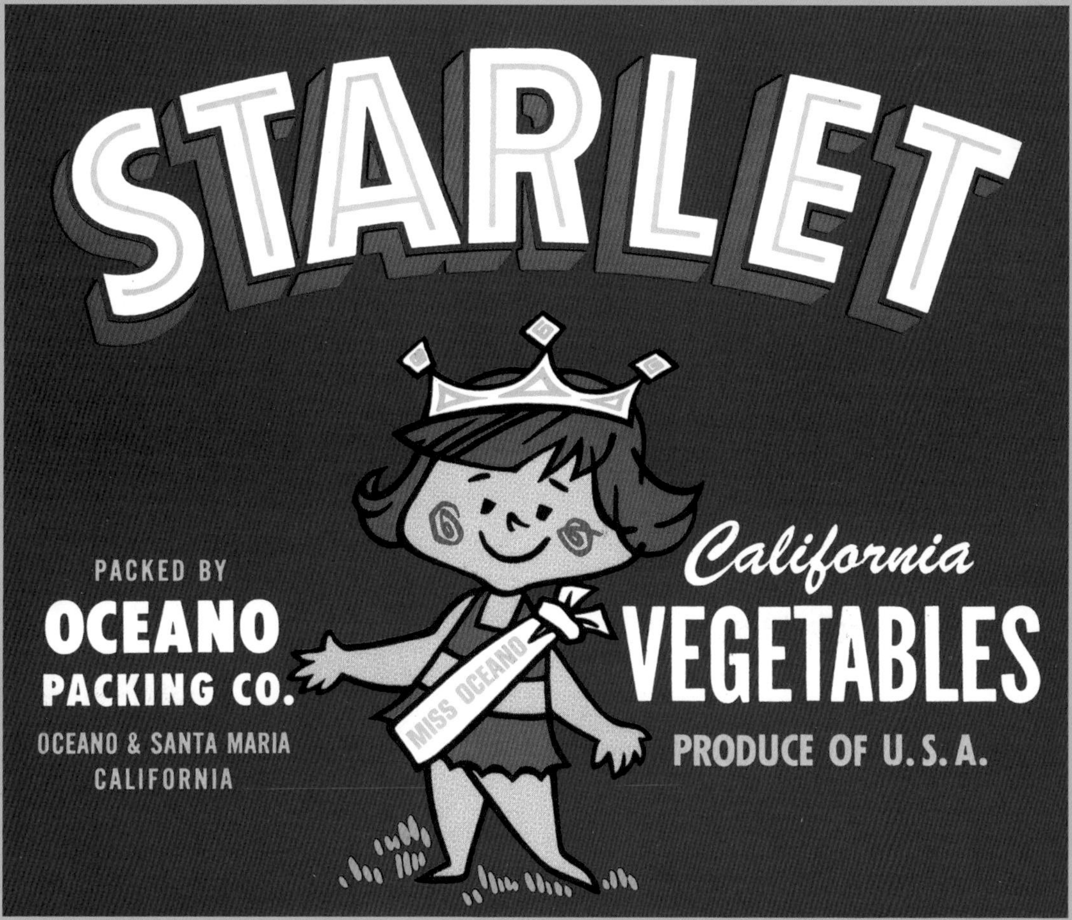

STARLET

PACKED BY
OCEANO
PACKING CO.
OCEANO & SANTA MARIA
CALIFORNIA

MISS OCEANO

California
VEGETABLES
PRODUCE OF U.S.A.

Miss Oceano • c. 1950
Starlet vegetables
Crate label

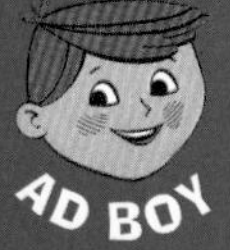

During the 1940s, wooden produce crates and their accompanying lithographic labe were largely replaced by preprinted cardboard boxes. Most of the labels were destro although some were consigned to storage where they remained undiscovered until t 1970s. Preserved was a legacy where from intense competition among vegetable an fruit growers bloomed eye-catching commercial art and colorfully inventive characte

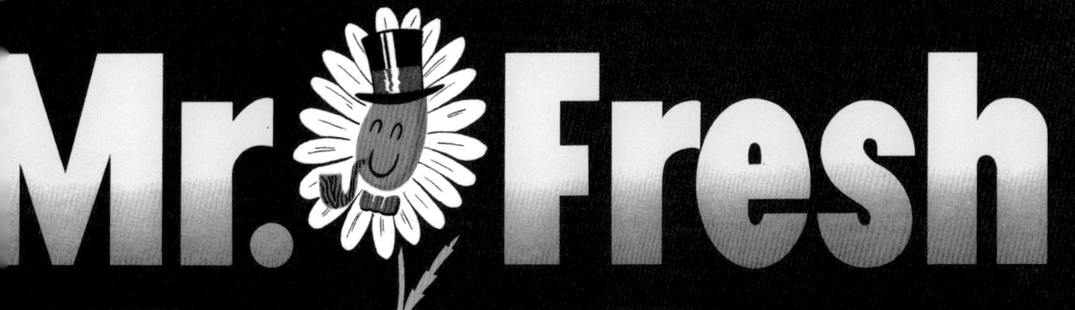

Mr. Fresh • c. 1960
Mr. Fresh fruits
Crate label

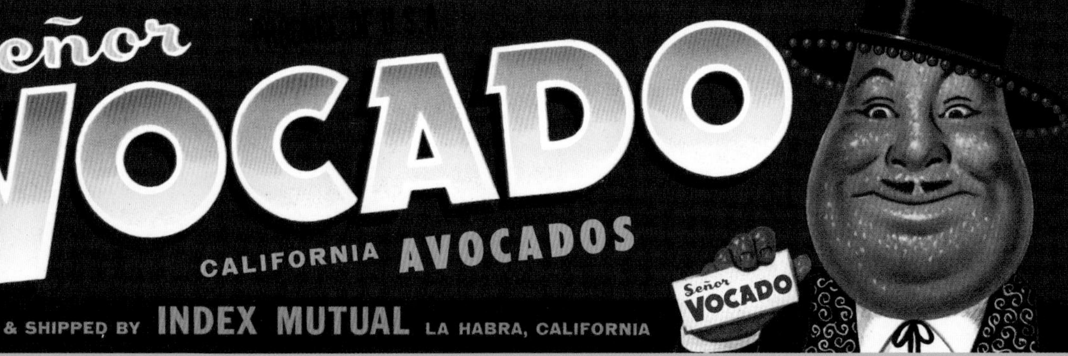

Señor Vocado • c. 1953
Señor Vocado avocados
Crate label

Pasha • c. 1953
Pasha grapes
Crate label

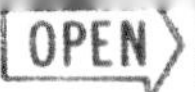

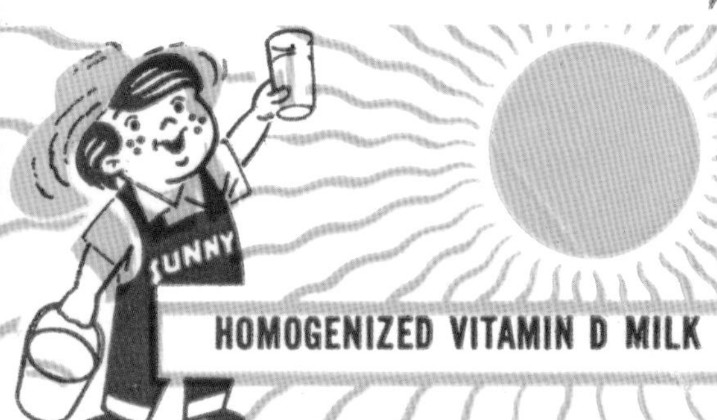

Sunny • c. 1970
Sunshine milk
Carton front

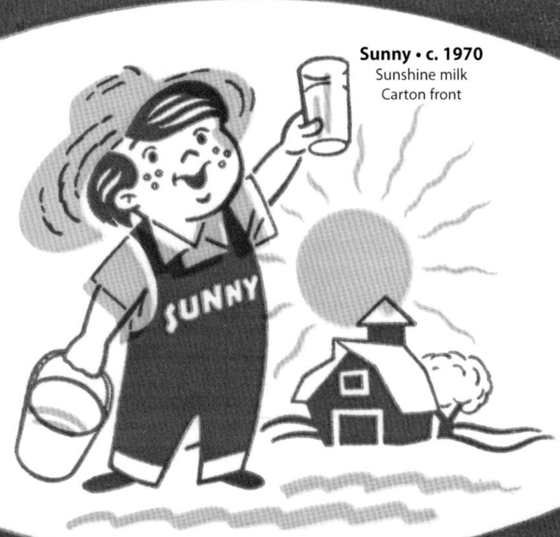

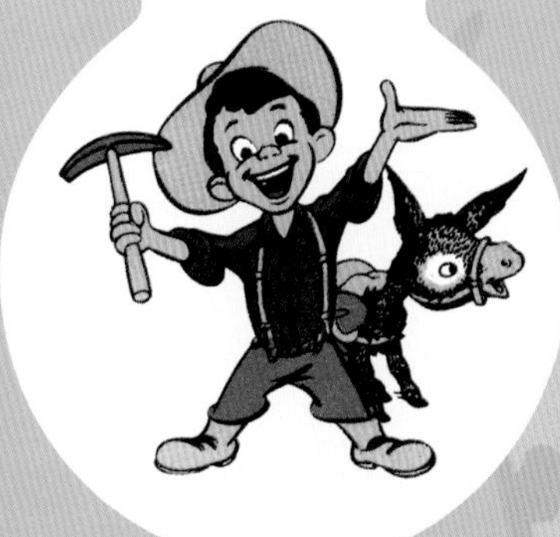

Golden State Kid • 1947
Golden State dairy products
Tab button

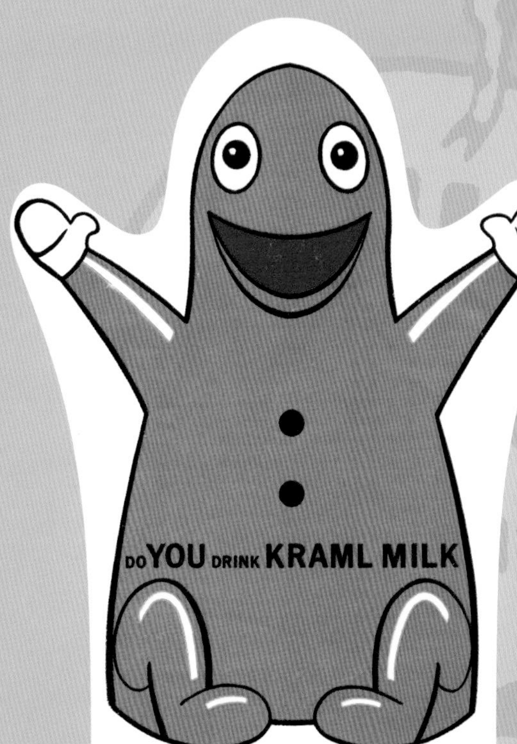

Wilkins • c. 1960
Kraml milk
Hand puppet

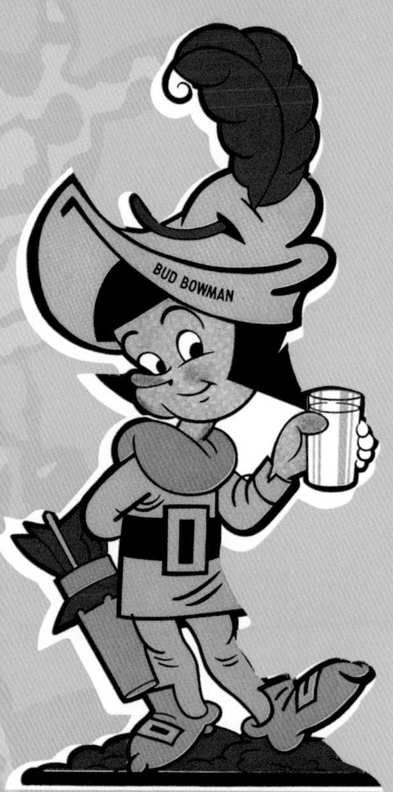

Bud Bowman • c. 1952
Bowman dairy products
Store display

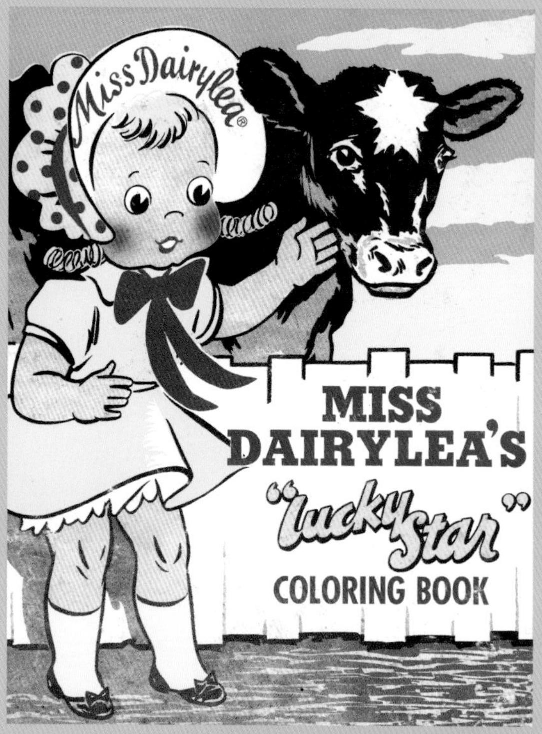

Miss Dairylea • c. 1958
Dairylea dairy products
Coloring book cover

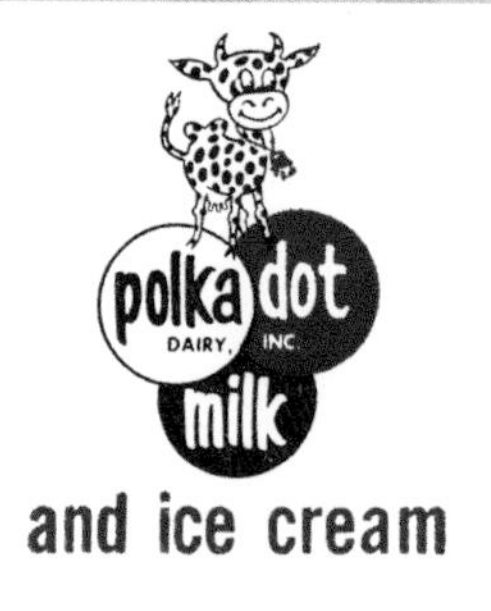

Polka Dot Cow • c. 1967
Polka Dot diary products
Matchbook cover

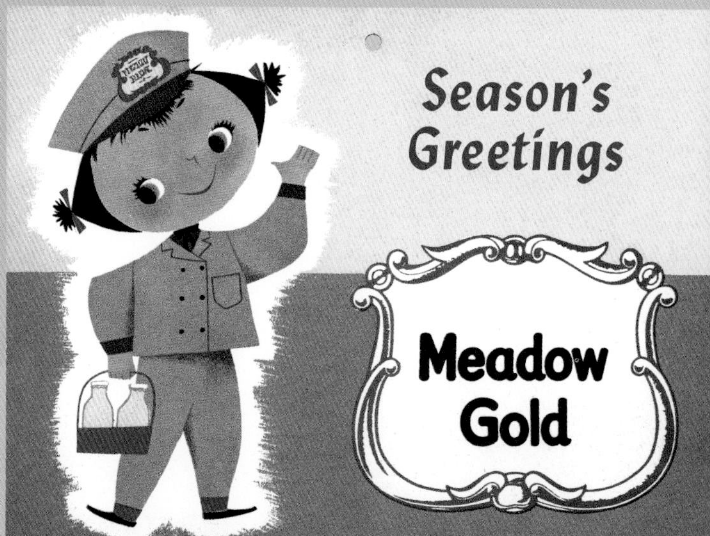

Meadow Gold Girl • 1956
Meadow Gold dairy products
Calendar cover

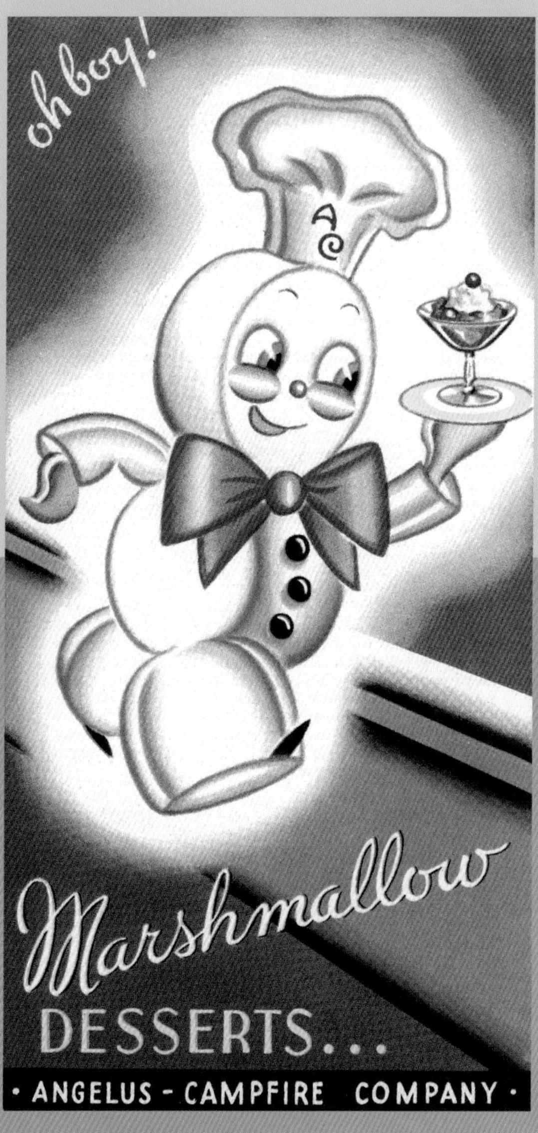

AC • 1936
Campfire marshmallows
Recipe booklet

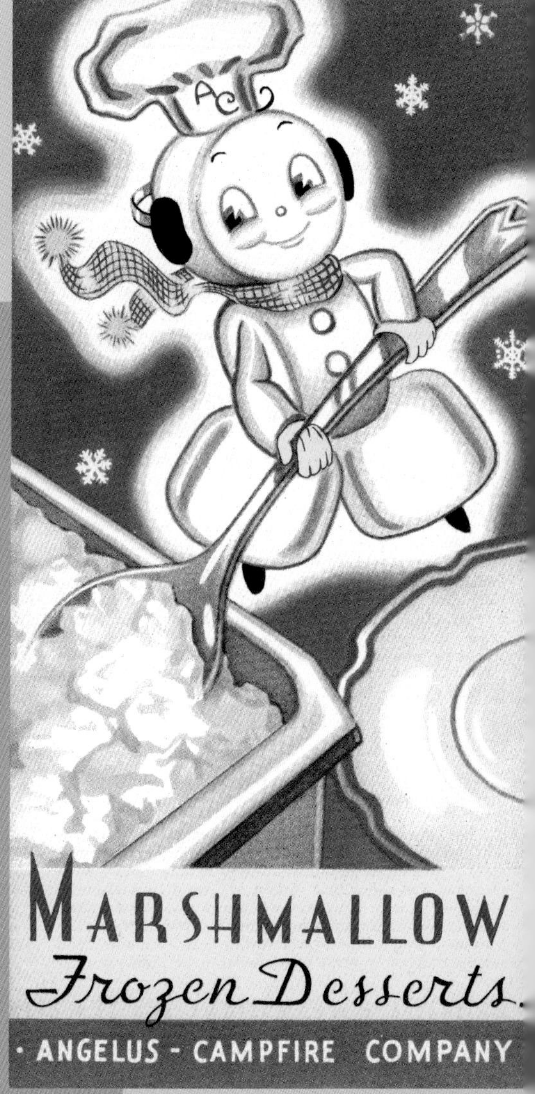

AC • 1936
Campfire marshmallows
Recipe booklet

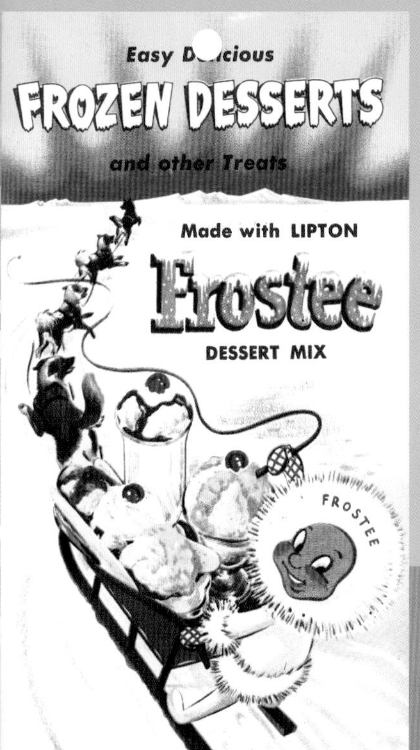

Frostee • 1960
Frostee dessert mix
Recipe pamphlet

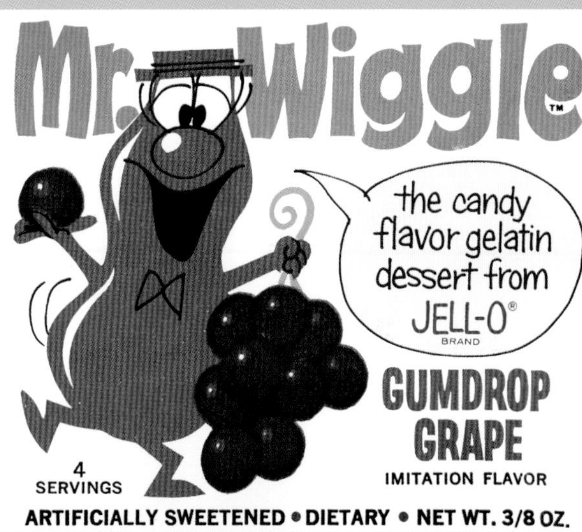

Mr. Wiggle • 1966
Mr. Wiggle gelatin dessert
Box front

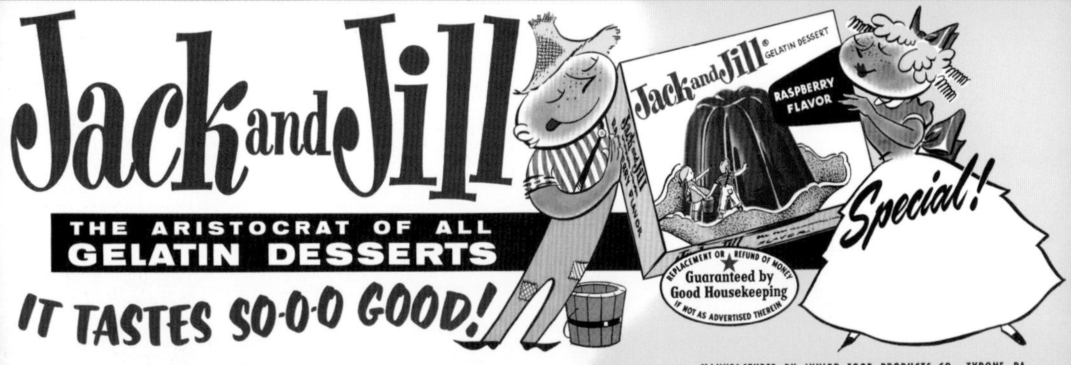

Jack and Jill • c. 1962
Jack and Jill gelatin dessert
Store banner

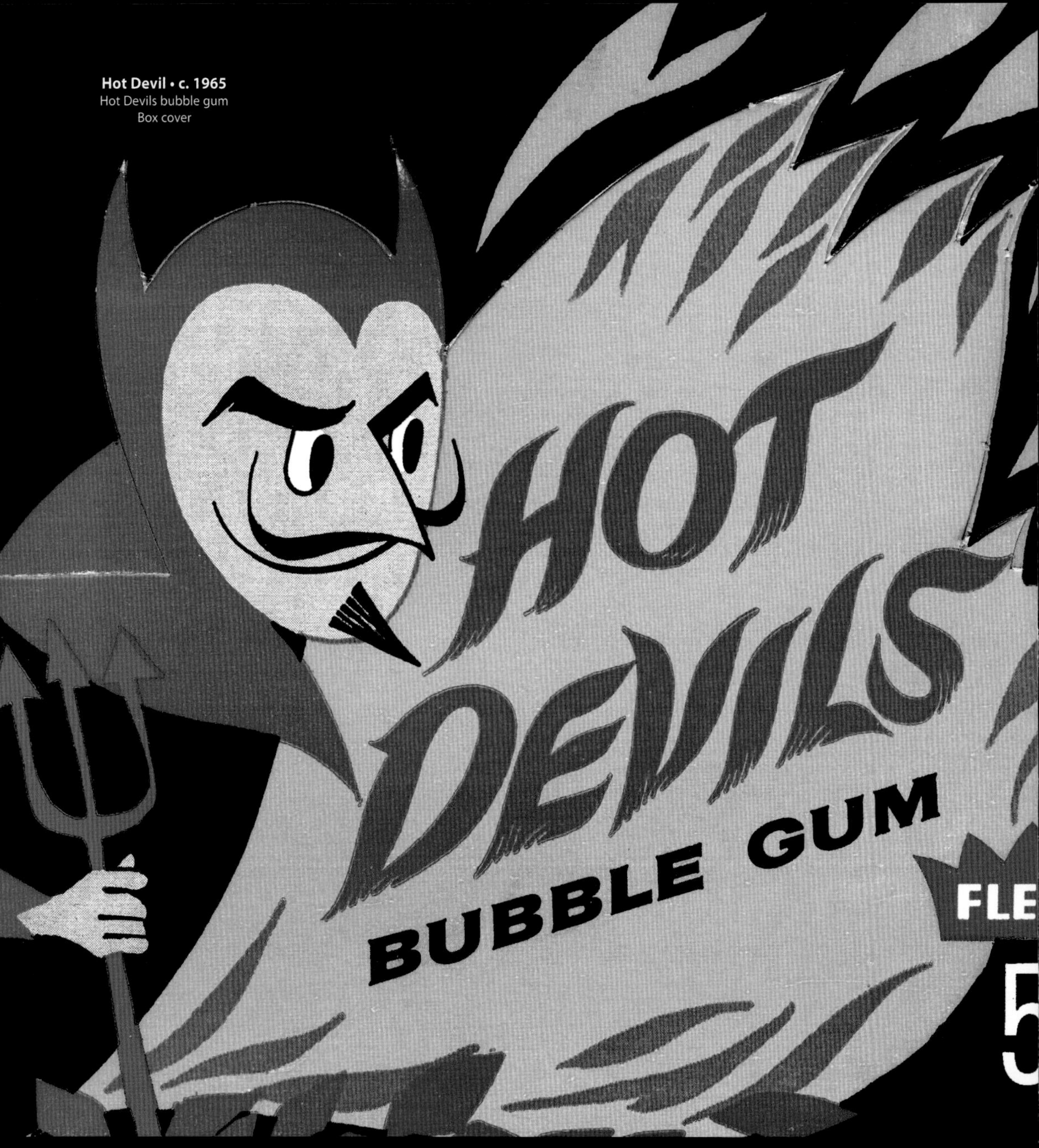

Hot Devil • c. 1965
Hot Devils bubble gum
Box cover

In early twentieth-century advertising, devils were rather menacing, whereas nowada they tend to be merely mischievous, carrying harmless looking tridents and sporting diabolical grins. In fact as time went on, most devil characters became almost pixie-li and were associated with boyish, devil-may-care activities such as exploding firecrac or chewing red-hot gum.

Li'l Red • c. 1974
Red Devil fireworks
Playing card

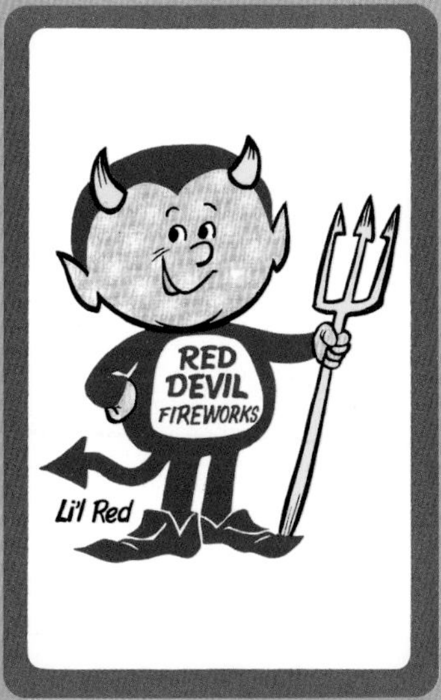

Little Devil • 1954
Hell's Half Acre, Wyoming
Water decal

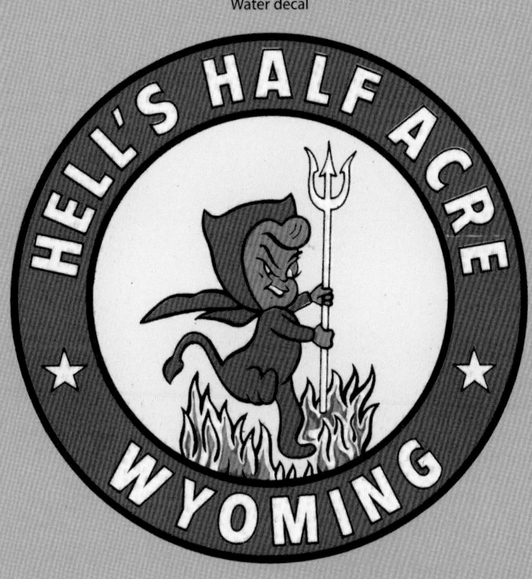

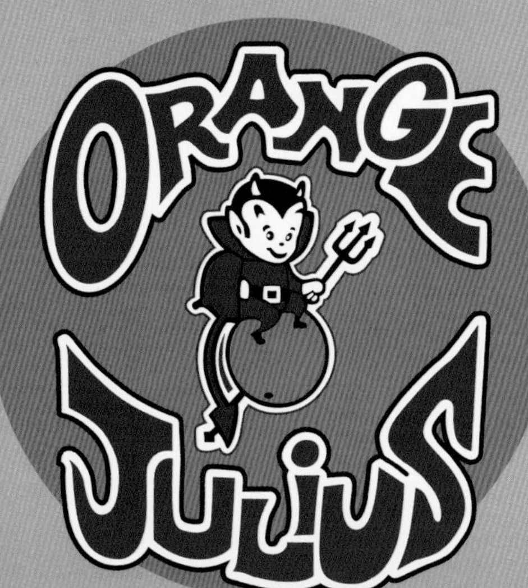

Orange Julius • c. 1968
Orange Julius orange smoothie
Iron-on decal

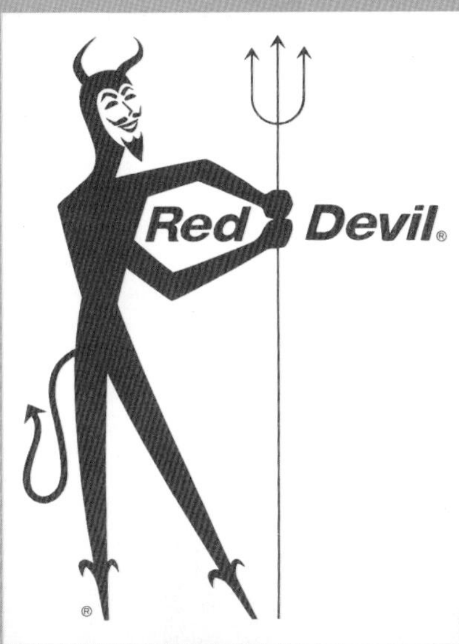

Red Devil • c. 1969
Red Devil paints
Information brochure detail

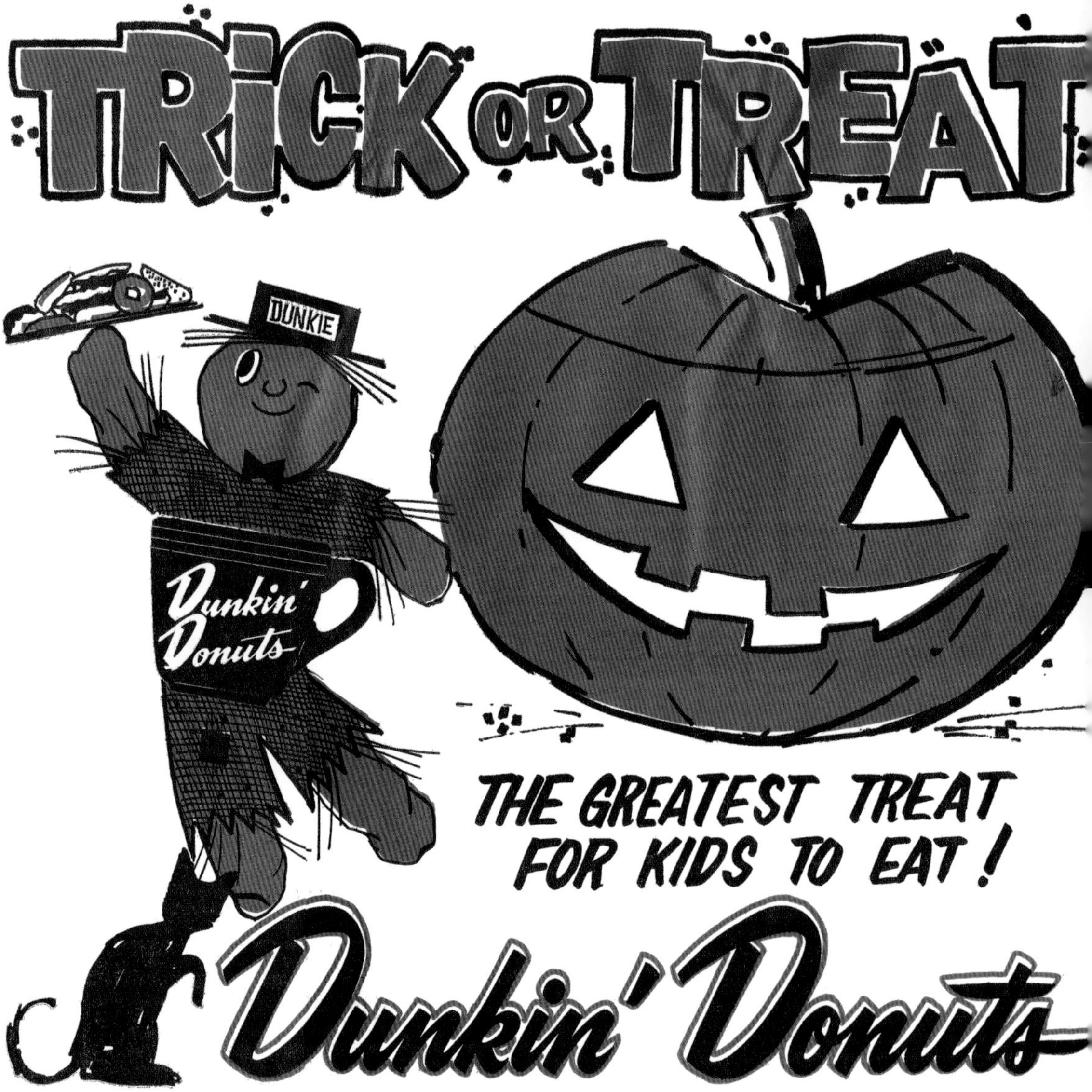

TRICK OR TREAT

DUNKIE

Dunkin' Donuts

THE GREATEST TREAT FOR KIDS TO EAT!

Dunkin' Donuts

Dunkie • c. 1966
Dunkin' Donuts donut shops
Bag detail

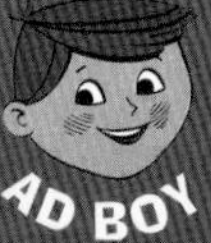

Was it the atypical shape or its all-too-healthy greaseless-ness that doomed the triangular donut from enduring popularity? We'll likely never know. But the delightfully oc Brown Bobby spokes-pastry is a charming legacy nonetheless. Dunkin' Donuts developed the now long-departed Dunkie, whose delightfully doughy cruller limbs were clothed, scarecrow-like, for a Halloween campaign.

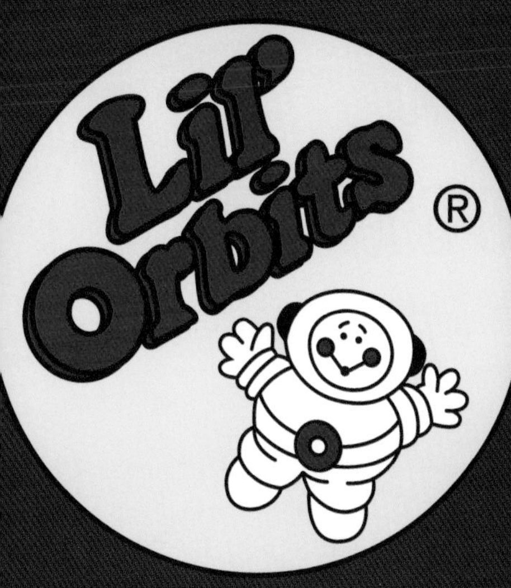

Lil' Orbits • 1974
Lil' Orbits, Inc. mini donuts
Promotional sign detail

Mister Donut • 1955
Mister Donut donut shops
Paper mask

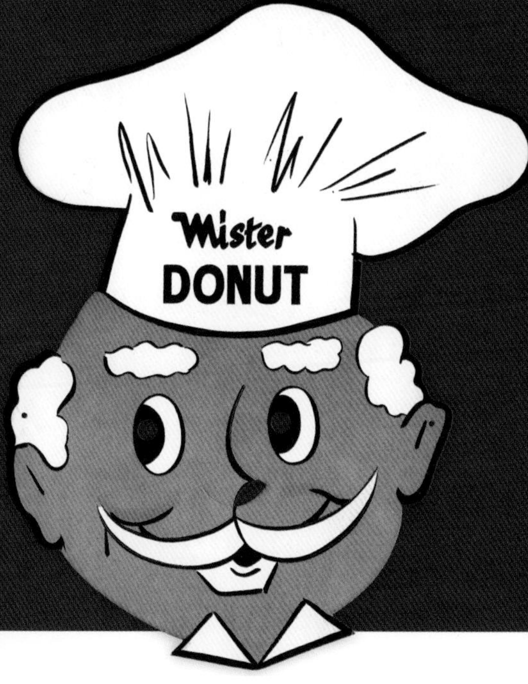

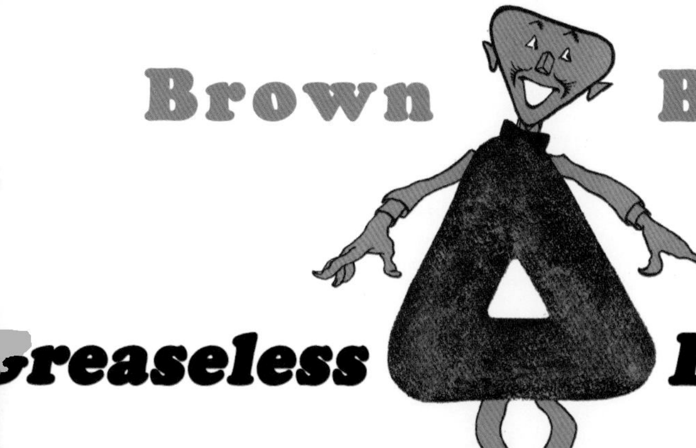

Brown Bobby • c. 1970
Brown Bobby greaseless doughnuts
Store banner

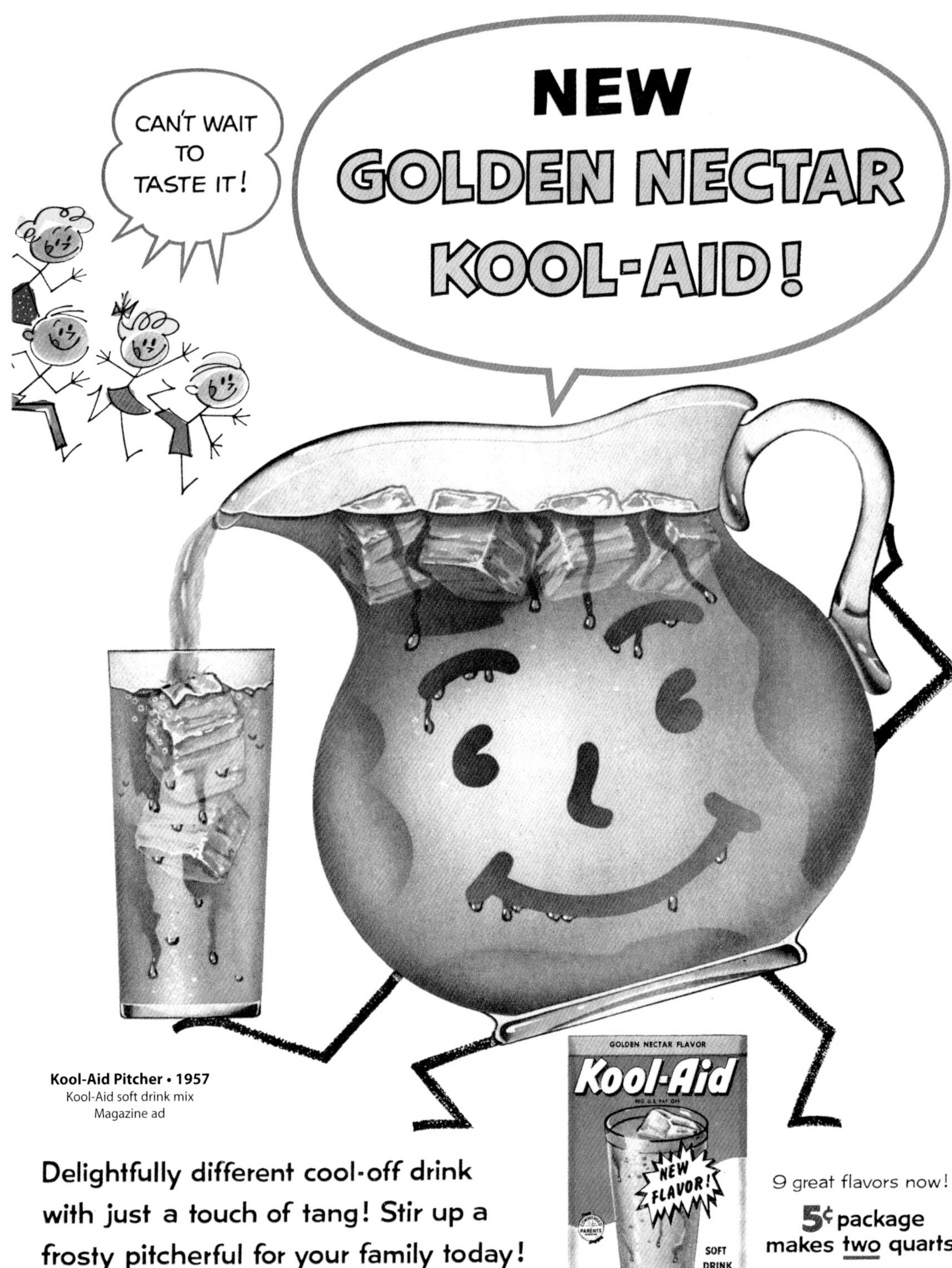

Kool-Aid Pitcher • 1957
Kool-Aid soft drink mix
Magazine ad

The Kool-Aid Kid, clad in lederhosen and pitching beverages from snowy Alpine mountaintops, was the brand's first ad character. In the 1960s, the smiling Kool-Aid Pitcher appeared in national magazines and became so popular that the pitcher itself became the new "pitchman." Walking, talking, and even wearing shades, the Kool-Aid Pitcher has evolved into the present-day Kool-Aid Man.

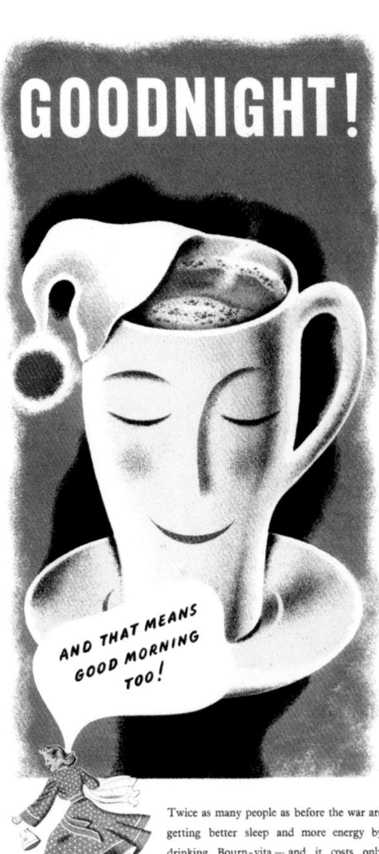

Bourn-vita Mug • 1950
Cadburys malted drink
Magazine ad

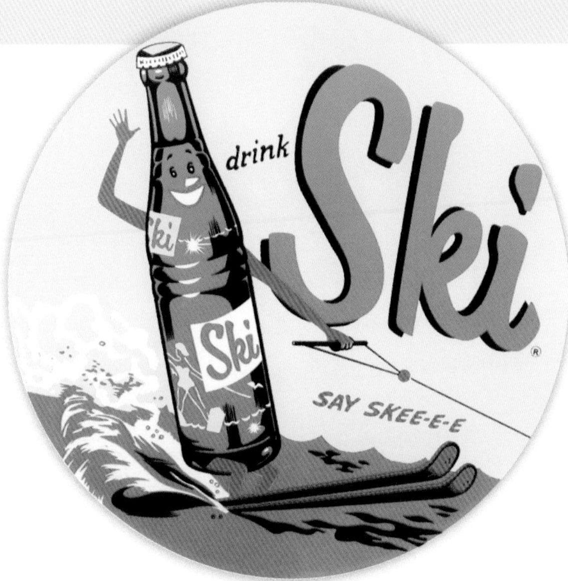

Ski • 1959
Ski soda
Store sign

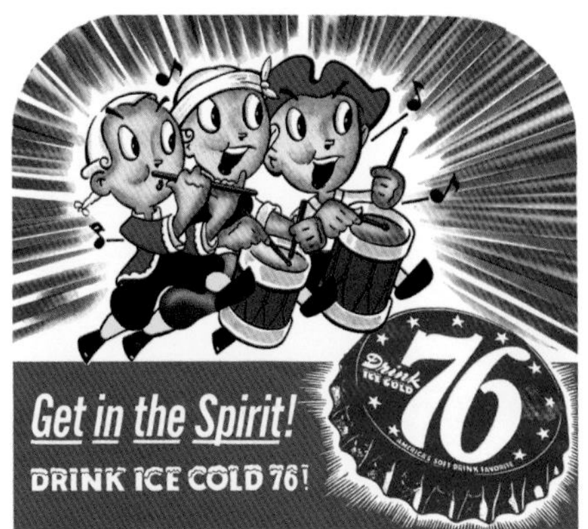

76 Kids • c. 1953
76 soda
Promotional sticker

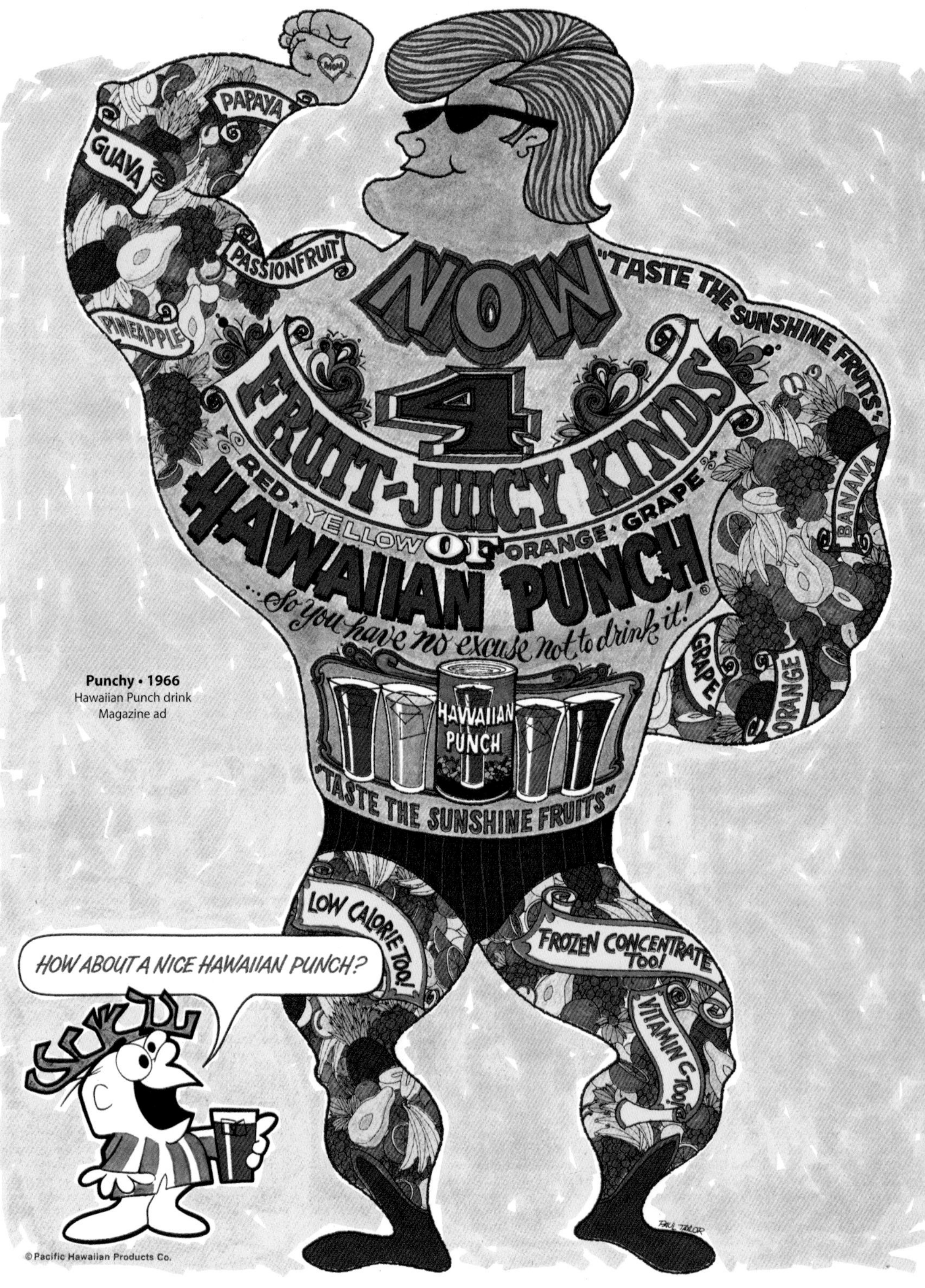

Punchy • 1966
Hawaiian Punch drink
Magazine ad

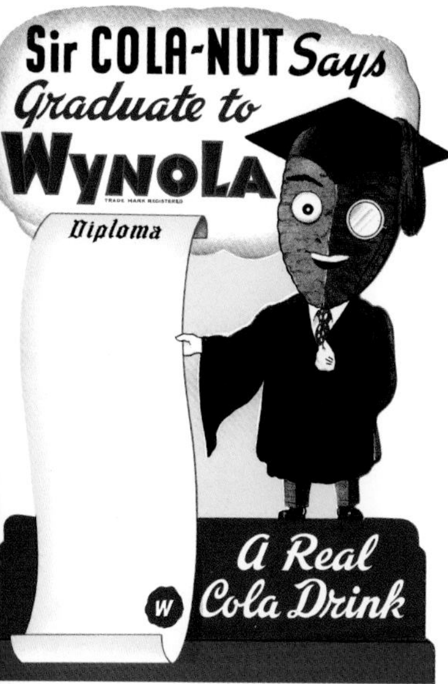

Sir Cola-Nut • c. 1949
Wynola soda
Store display

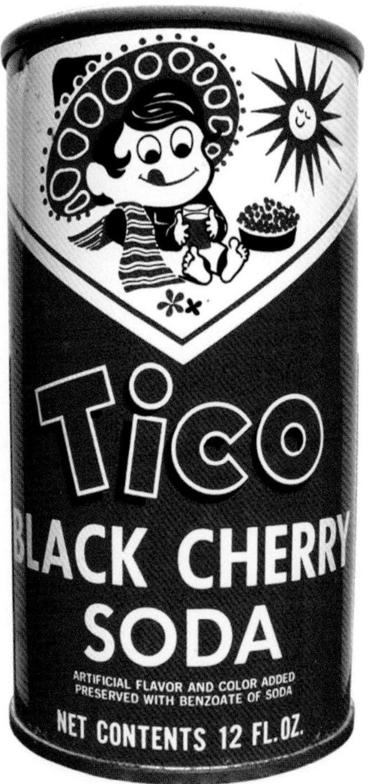

Tico • c. 1971
Tico soda
Soda can

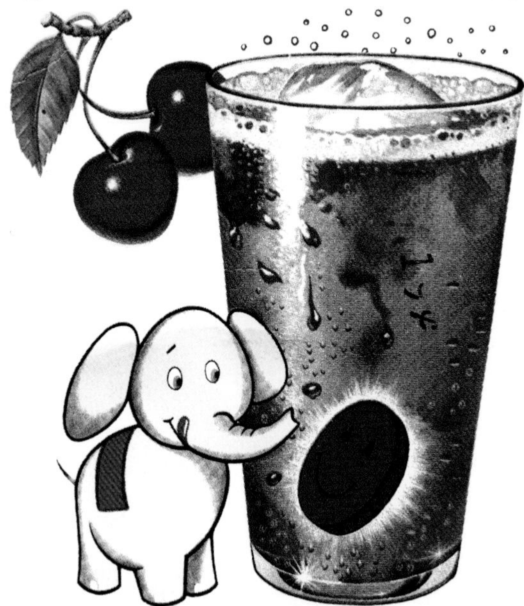

Fizzies Tablet • c. 1960
Fizzies soft drink tablets
Package front

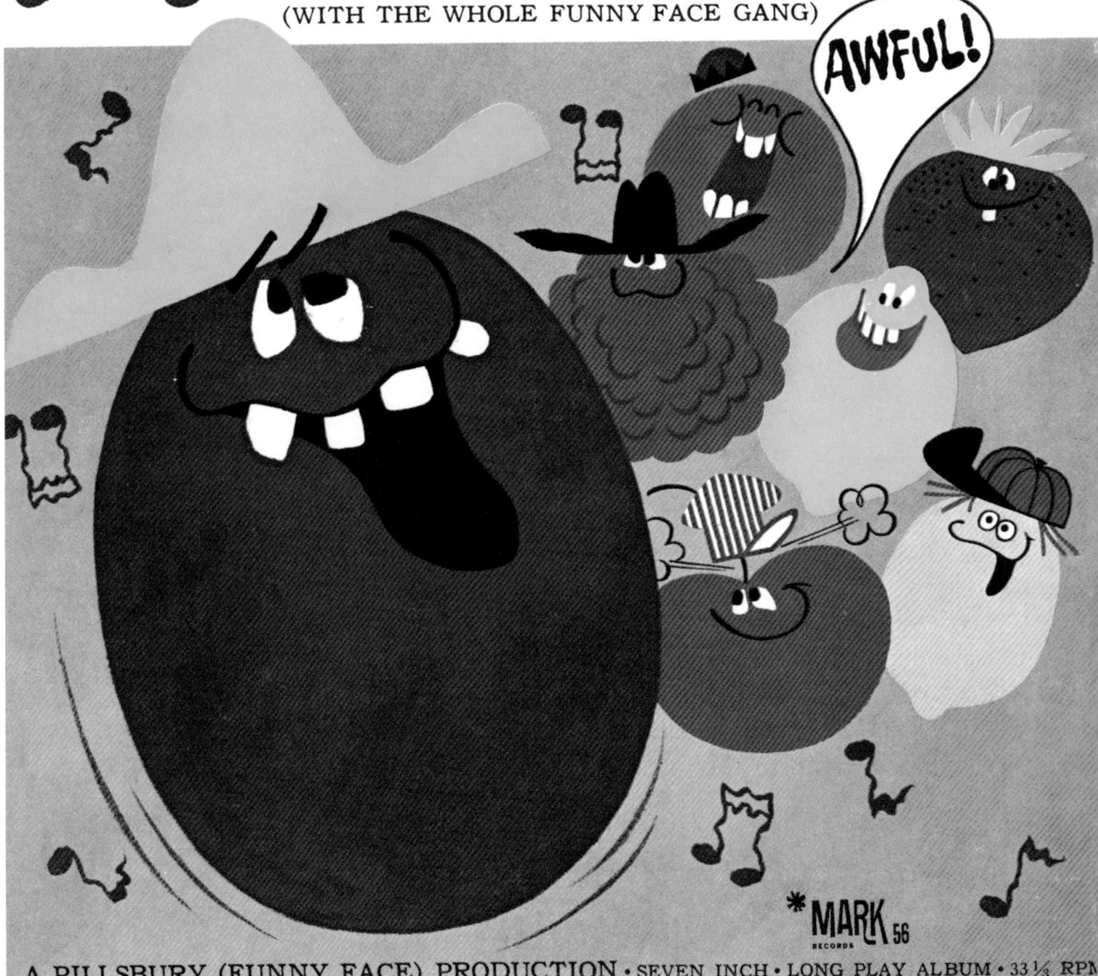

Goofy Grape • 1966
Funny Face drink mix
Record album cover

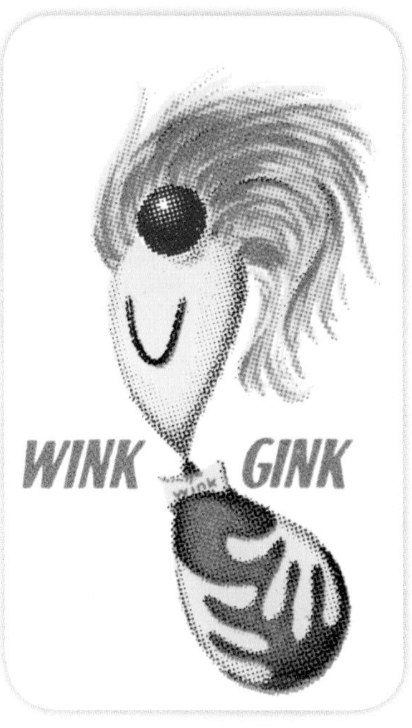

Wink Gink • 1965
Wink soda
Tab button

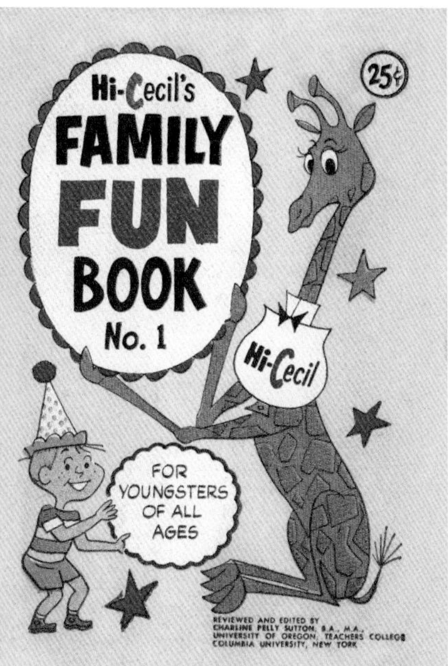

Hi-Cecil • 1958
Hi-C fruit drink
Promotional booklet

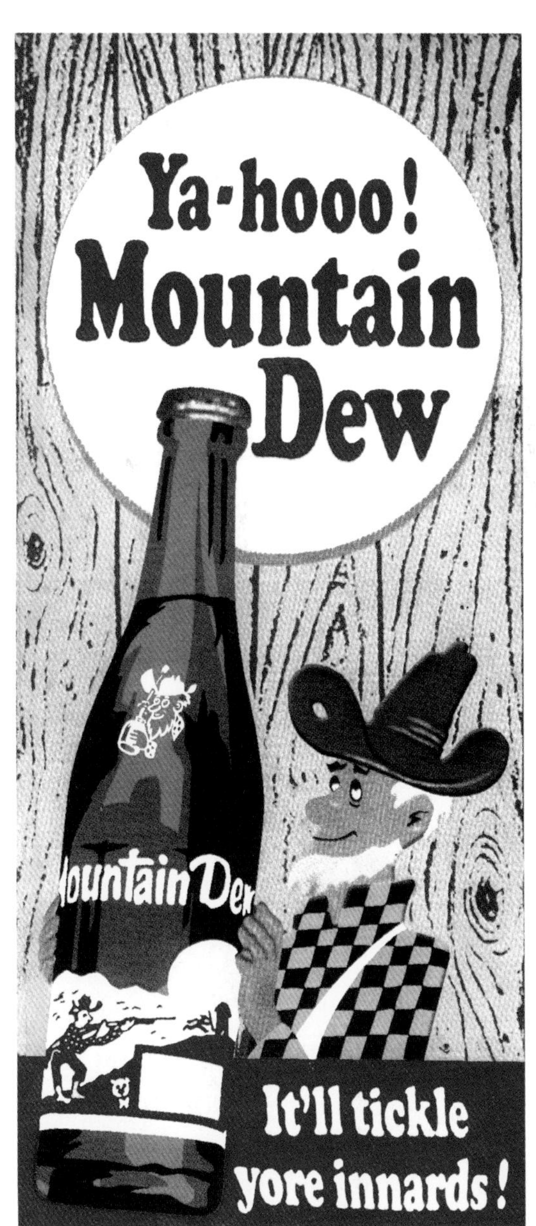

Gran' Pappy • c. 1966
Mountain Dew soda
Store sign

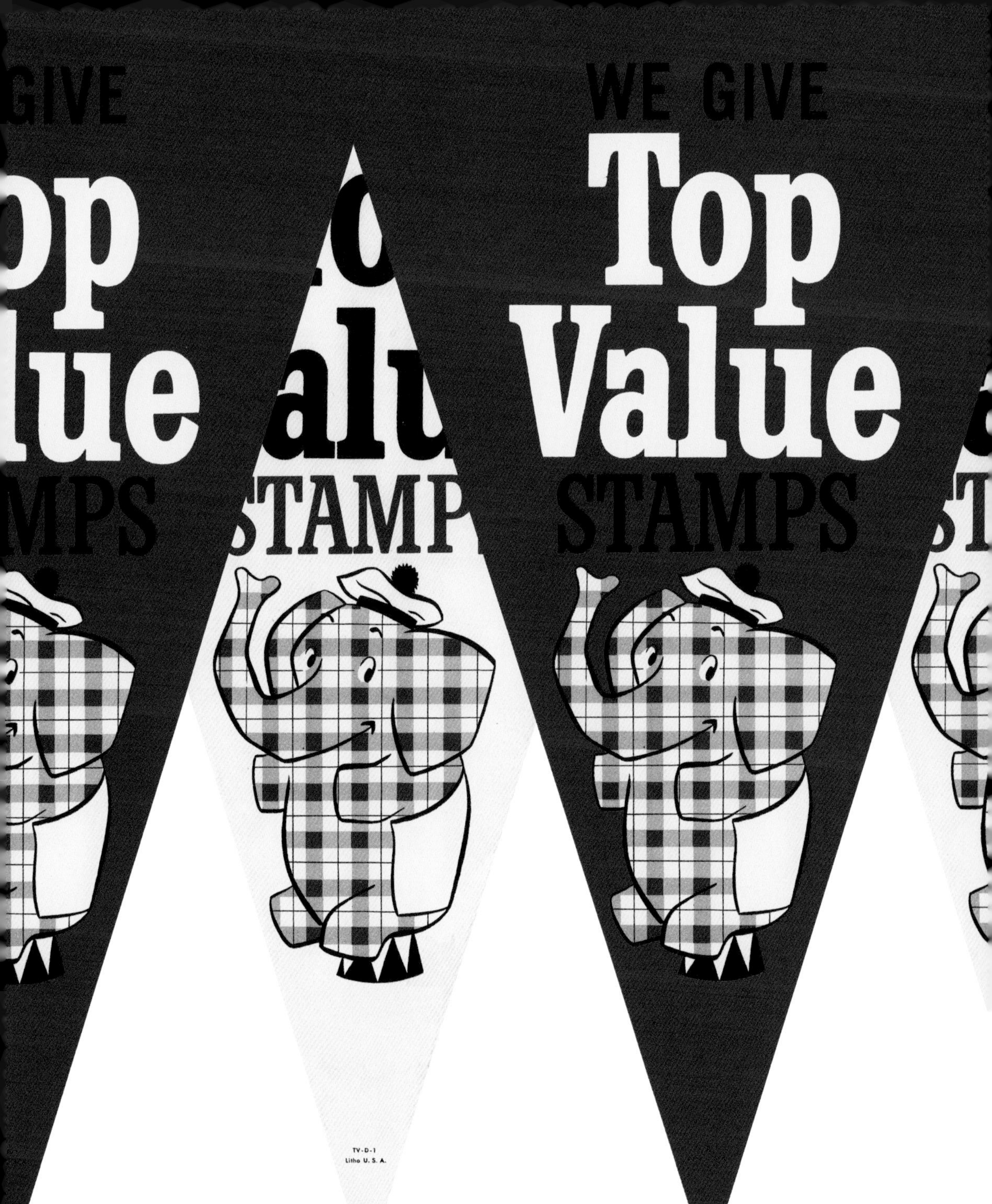

WE GIVE
Top
Value
STAMPS

TV-D-1
Litho U. S. A.

Toppie • 1958
Top Value savings stamps
Store banner

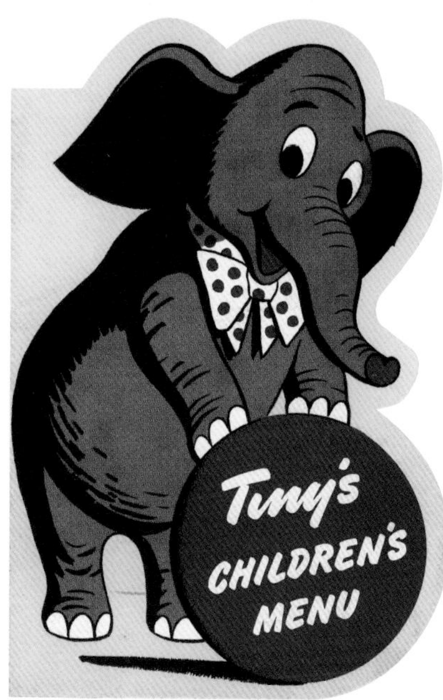

Tiny • c. 1955
Tiny's restaurant
Menu cover

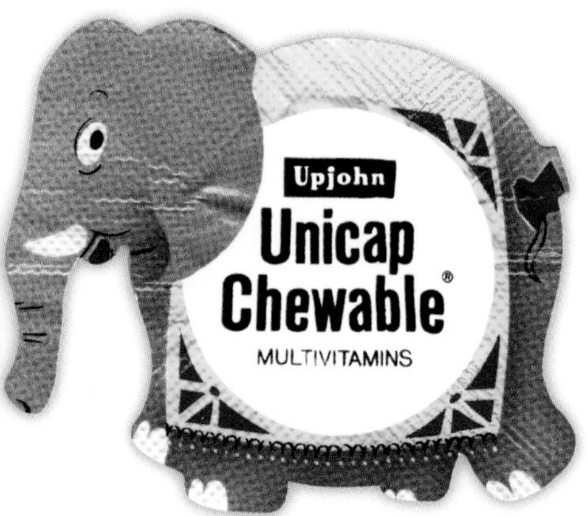

Elephant • 1969
Unicap chewable multivitamins
Package front

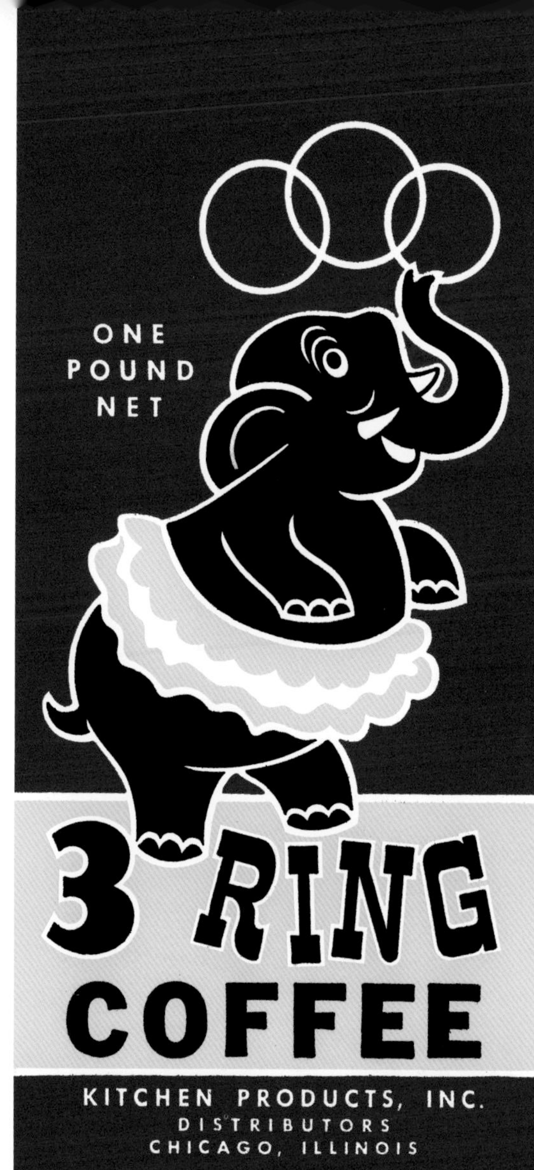

3 Ring Elephant • c. 1942
3 Ring coffee
Coffee bag

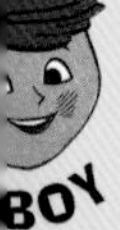

Throughout the 1940s, 50s, and 60s, circus elephants were used on a host of products directed at children, no doubt influenced by the popularity of Helen Aberson's 1939 creation of *Dumbo, the Flying Elephant,* and Disney's animated 1941 movie adaptation. Toppie, aptly named for both the Top Value brand and the Big Top circus tent, was the mascot for supermarket savings stamps.

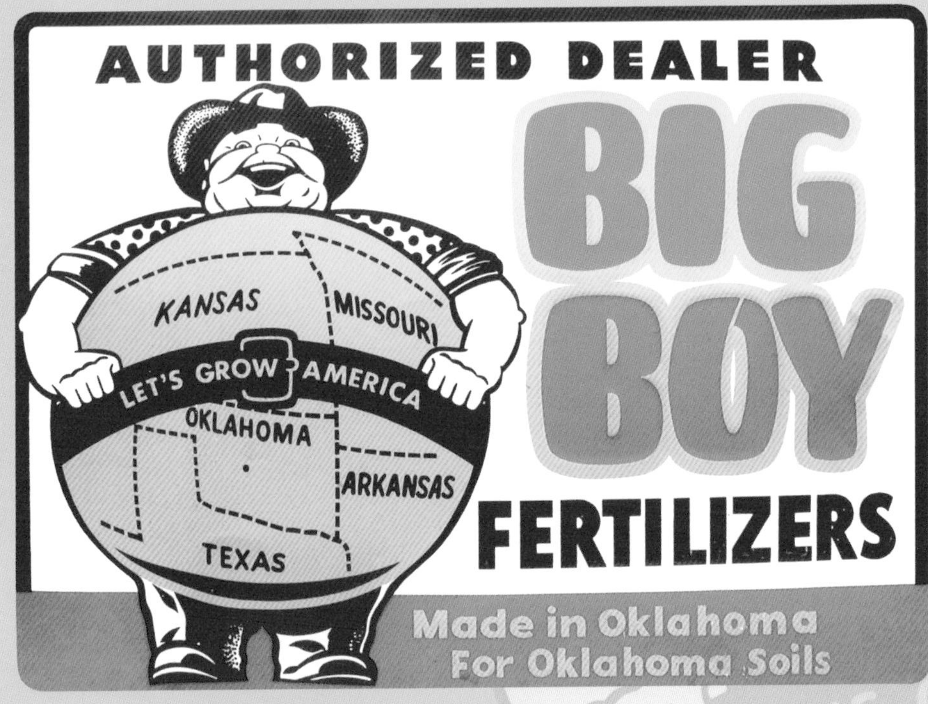

Big Boy • c. 1940
Big Boy fertilizers
Store sign

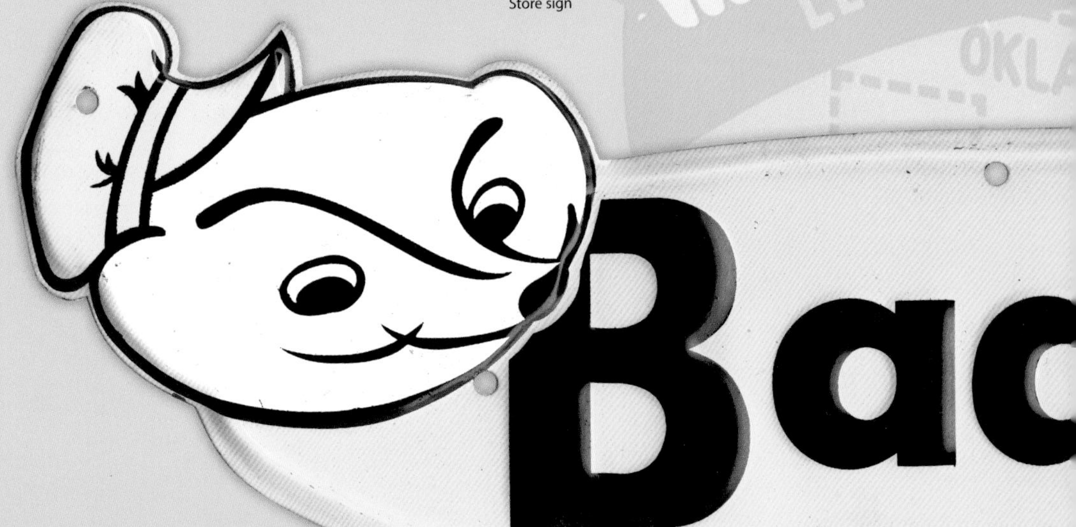

Buddy Badger • c. 1957
Badger farm equipment
Promotional sign

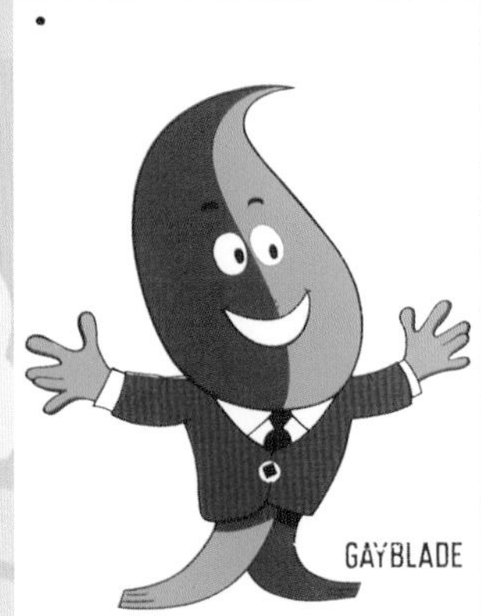

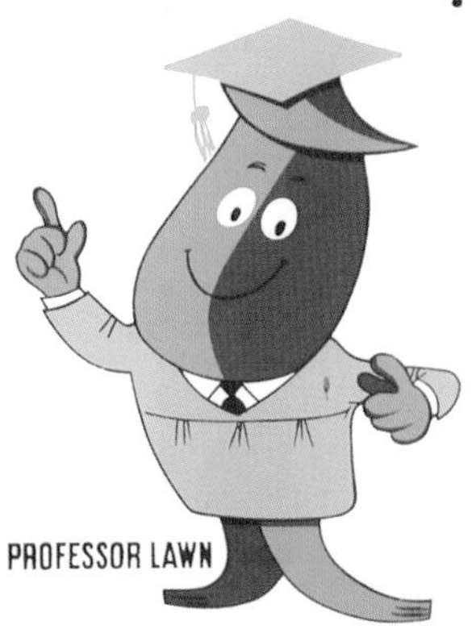

SPECIAL

AGRICO® a Better Lawn In Every Bag

Gayblade and Professor Lawn • c. 1961
Agrico fertilizers
Store sign

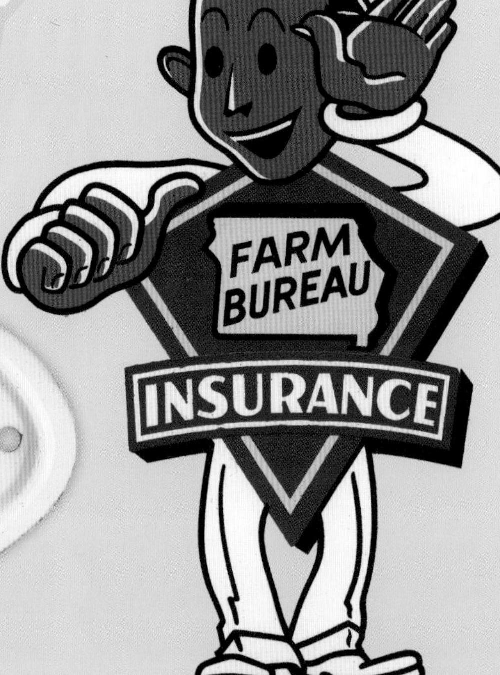

Mr. Insurance • 1952
Farm Bureau insurance
Water decal

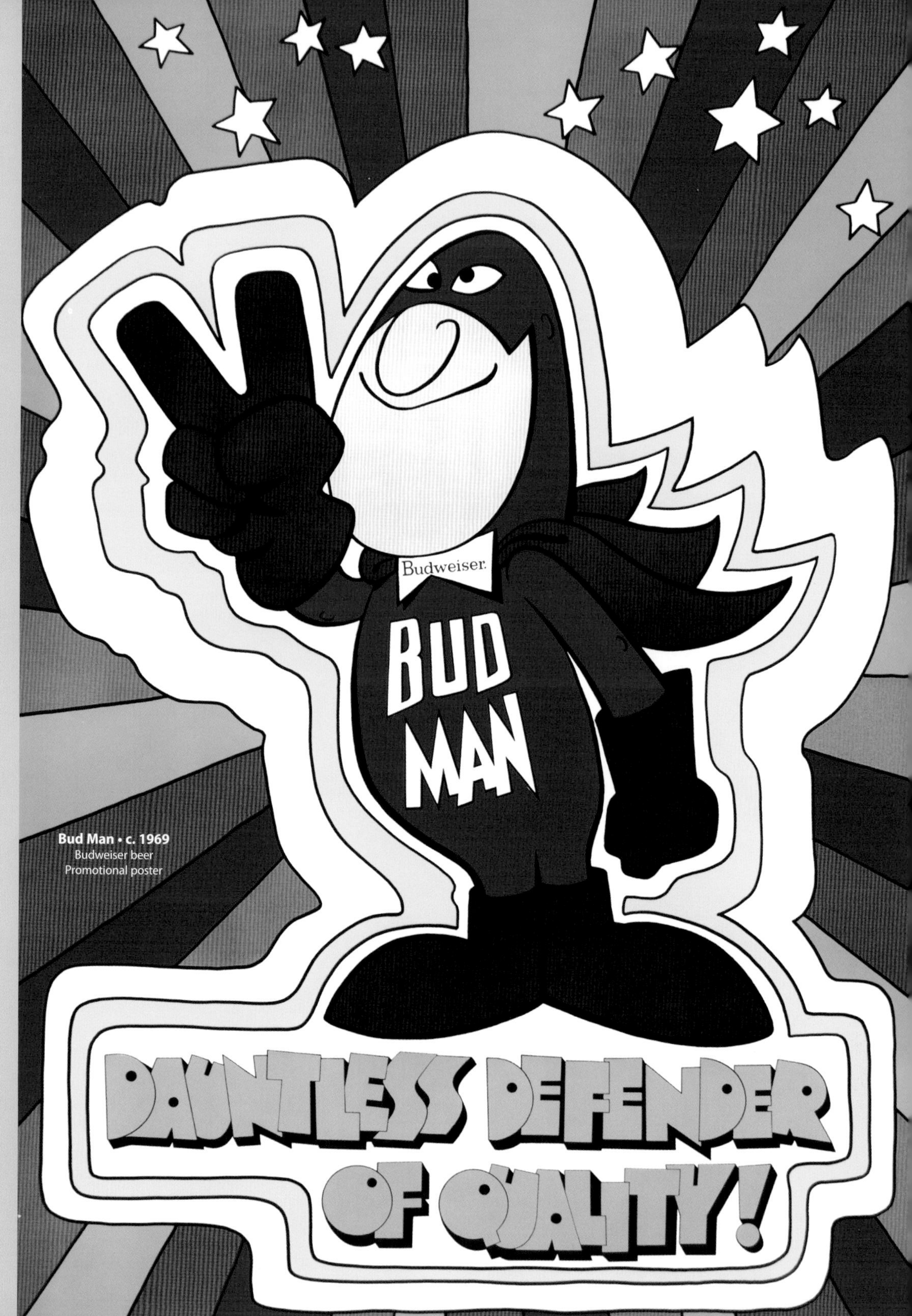

Bud Man • c. 1969
Budweiser beer
Promotional poster

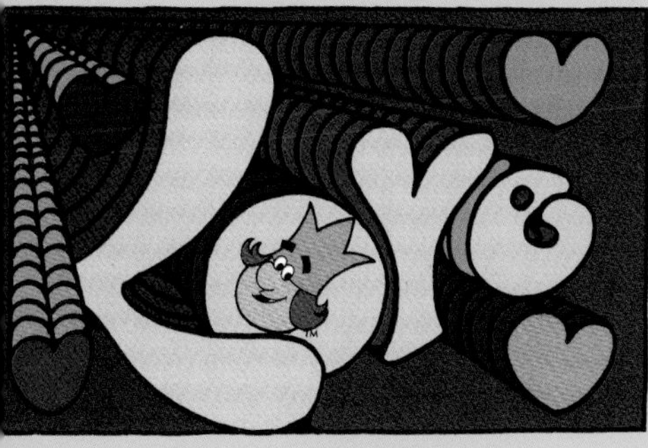

The Burger King • 1972
Burger King restaurants
Promotional postcard

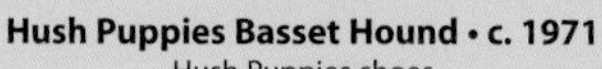

Hush Puppies Basset Hound • c. 1971
Hush Puppies shoes
Store display

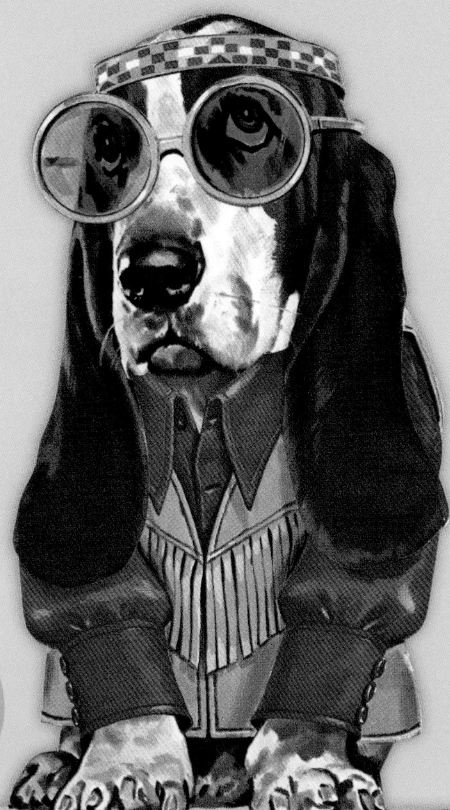

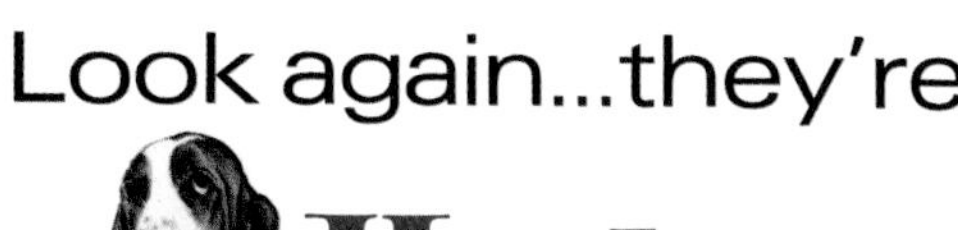

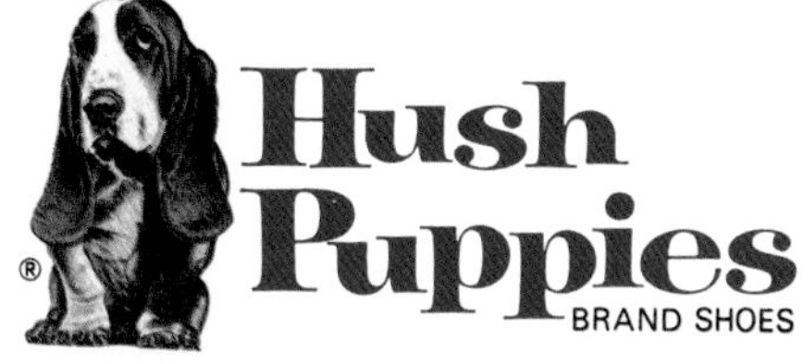

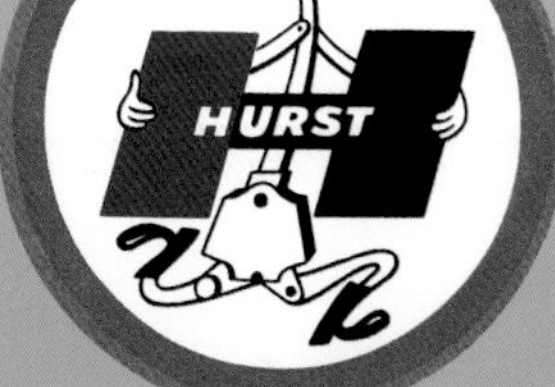

Mr. Shifter • c. 1969
Hurst shifters
Promotional sticker

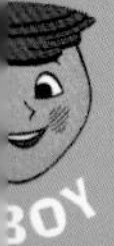

The late 1960s and early 70s hosted the counterculture revolution amid an explosion of day-glow colors and psychedelic graphics. Advertisers were quick to incorporate this fresh imagery to suggest that their products were hip and happening. Even the usually conservative Hush Puppies brand jumped on the rock 'n' roll bandwagon and got into the groove.

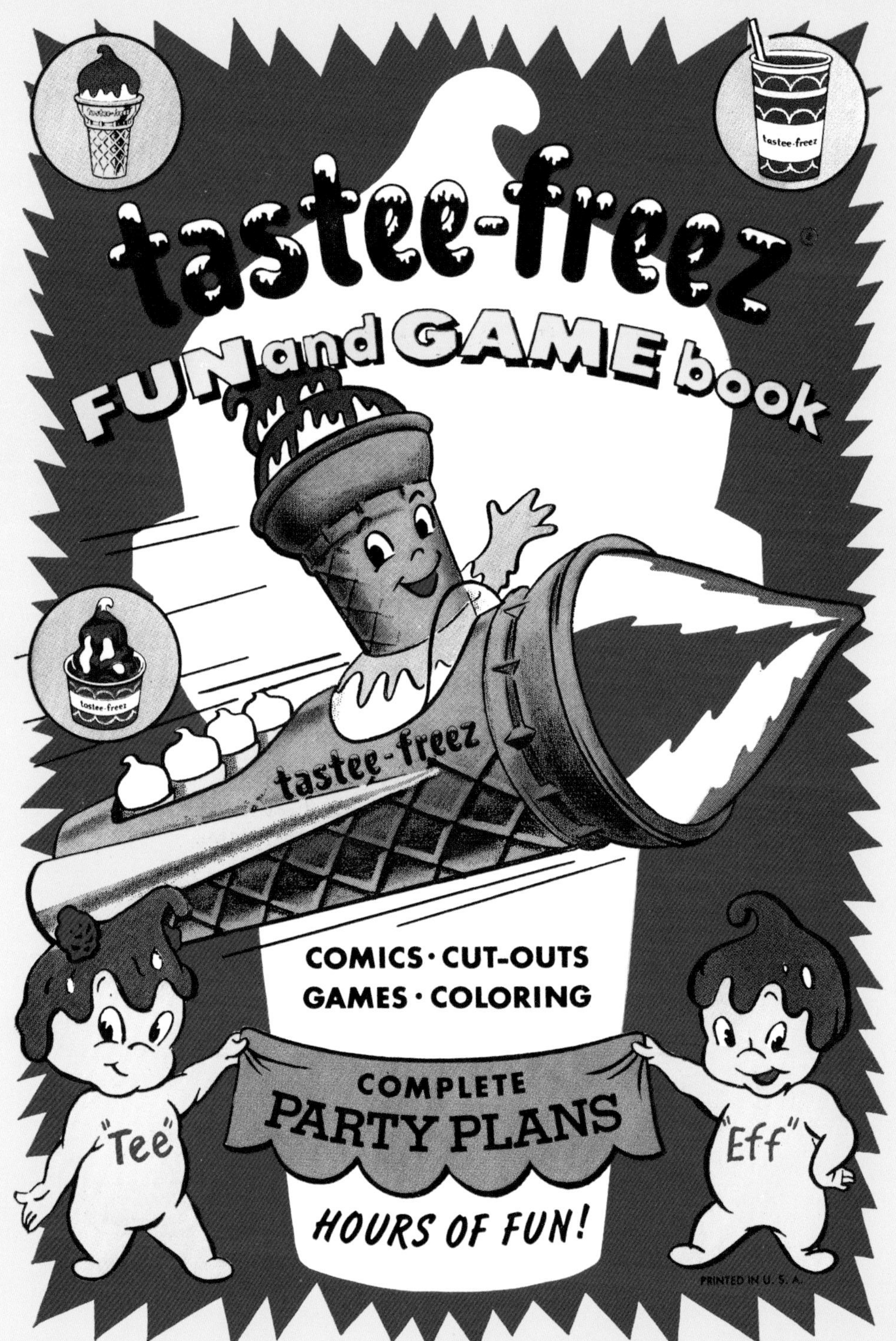

Tee and Eff • 1957
Tastee-Freez frozen desserts
Comic book cover

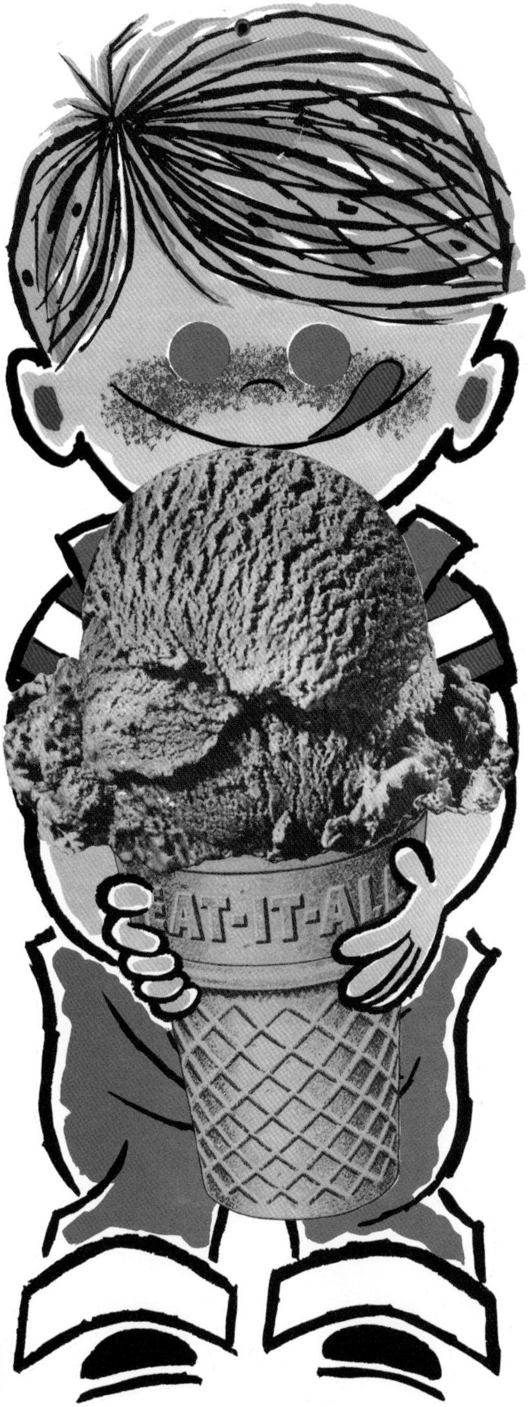

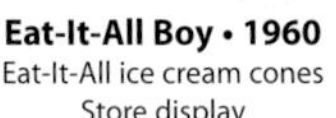

Eat-It-All Boy • 1960
Eat-It-All ice cream cones
Store display

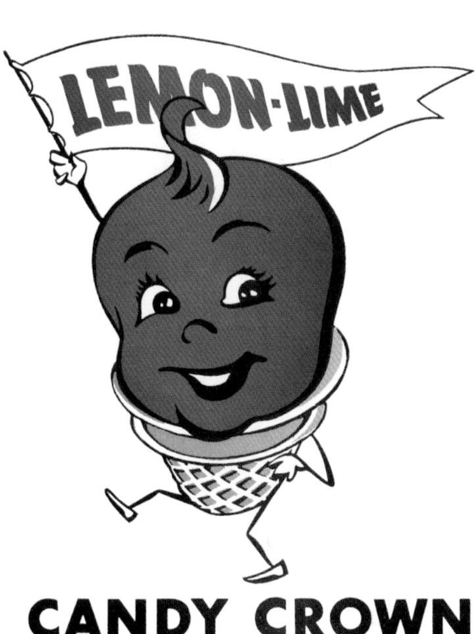

Lemon-Lime • c. 1967
Candy Crown ice cream cone coatings
Store sign

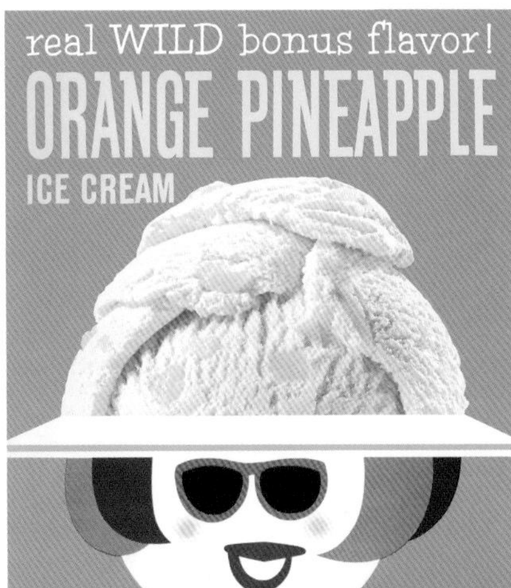

Orange Pineapple Girl • c. 1968
Breyers ice cream
Store poster

Wish-Bone Genie • 1957
Wish-Bone salad dressing
Magazine ad

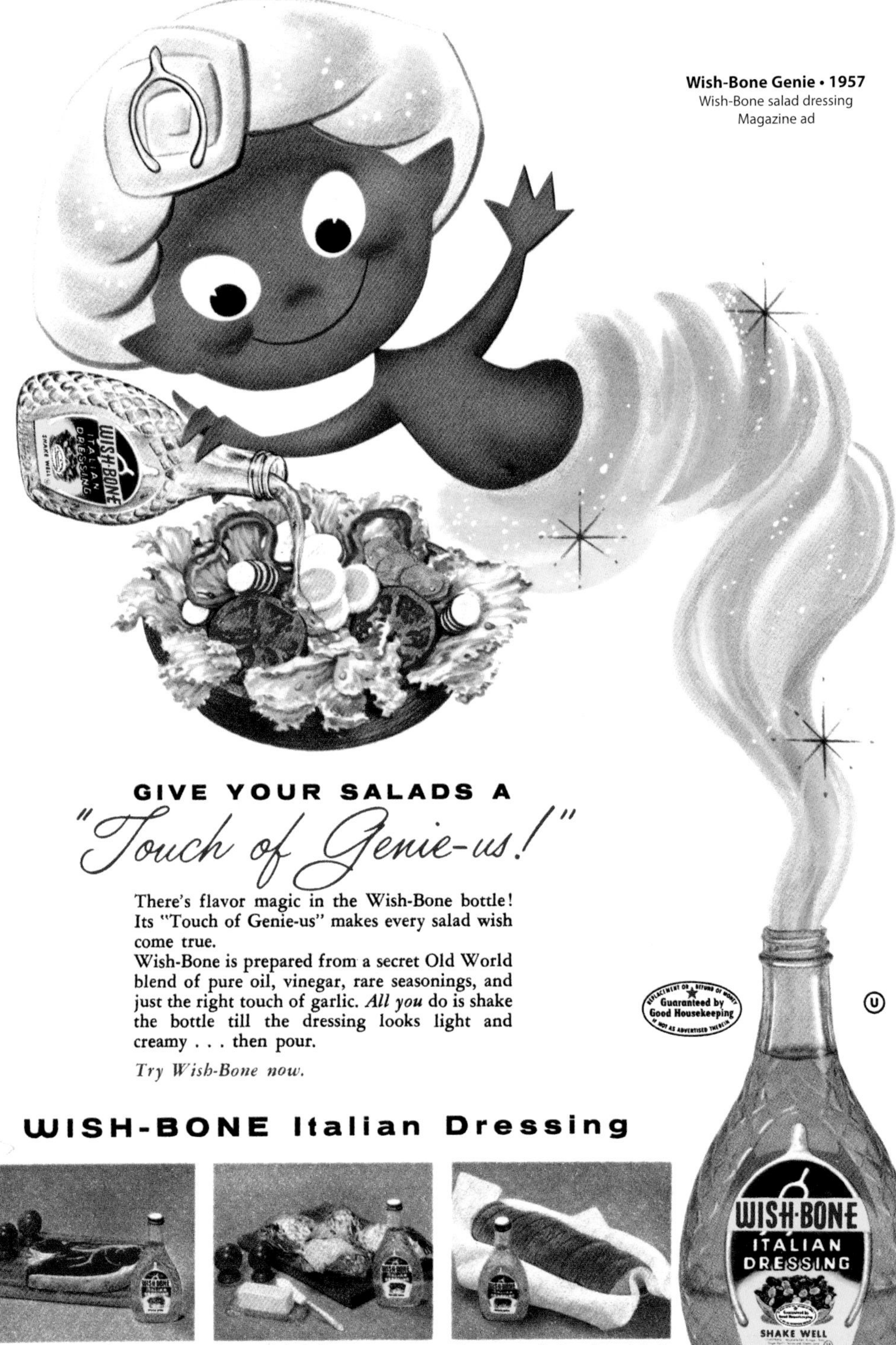

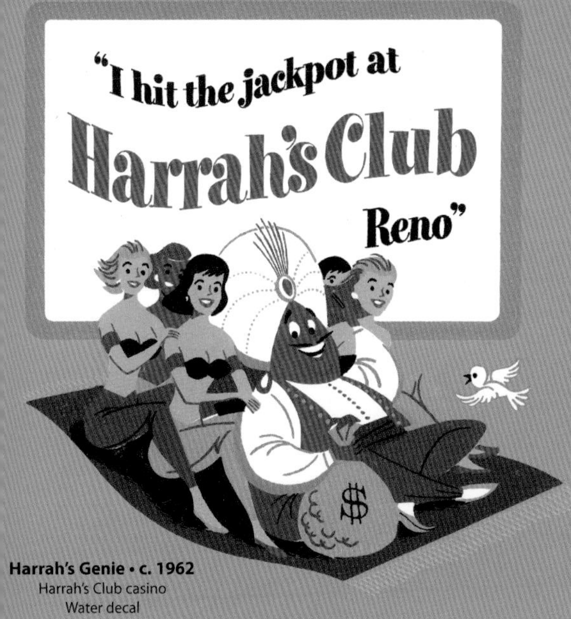

Harrah's Genie • c. 1962
Harrah's Club casino
Water decal

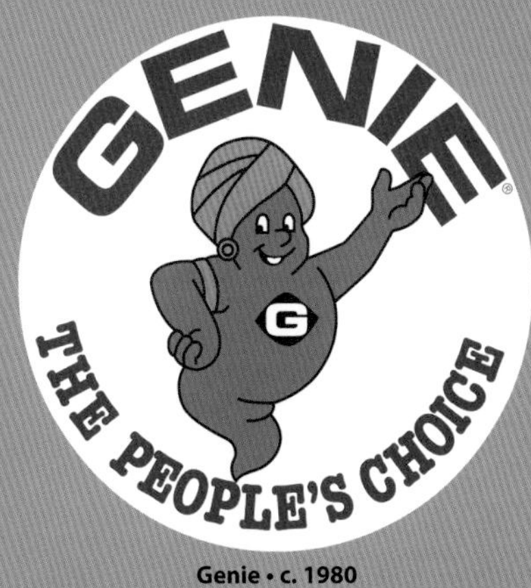

Genie • c. 1980
Genie garage door openers
Pin-back button

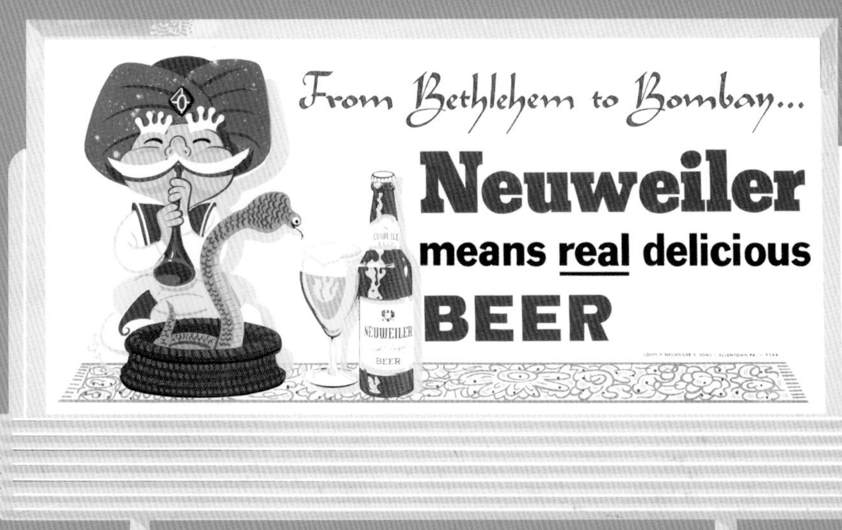

Neuweiler Genie • c. 1962
Neuweiler beer
Store sign detail

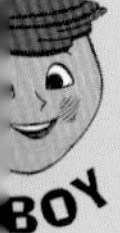

The 1950s saw a host of Aladdin-inspired genies promising that your wish was their command. It was the decade that saw the introduction of both television and garage door remote controls as well as many other electronic products with automatic features. Innovations in food processing lead to "instant" products, like fully prepared and seasoned salad dressings, ready to pour with a shake of the bottle.

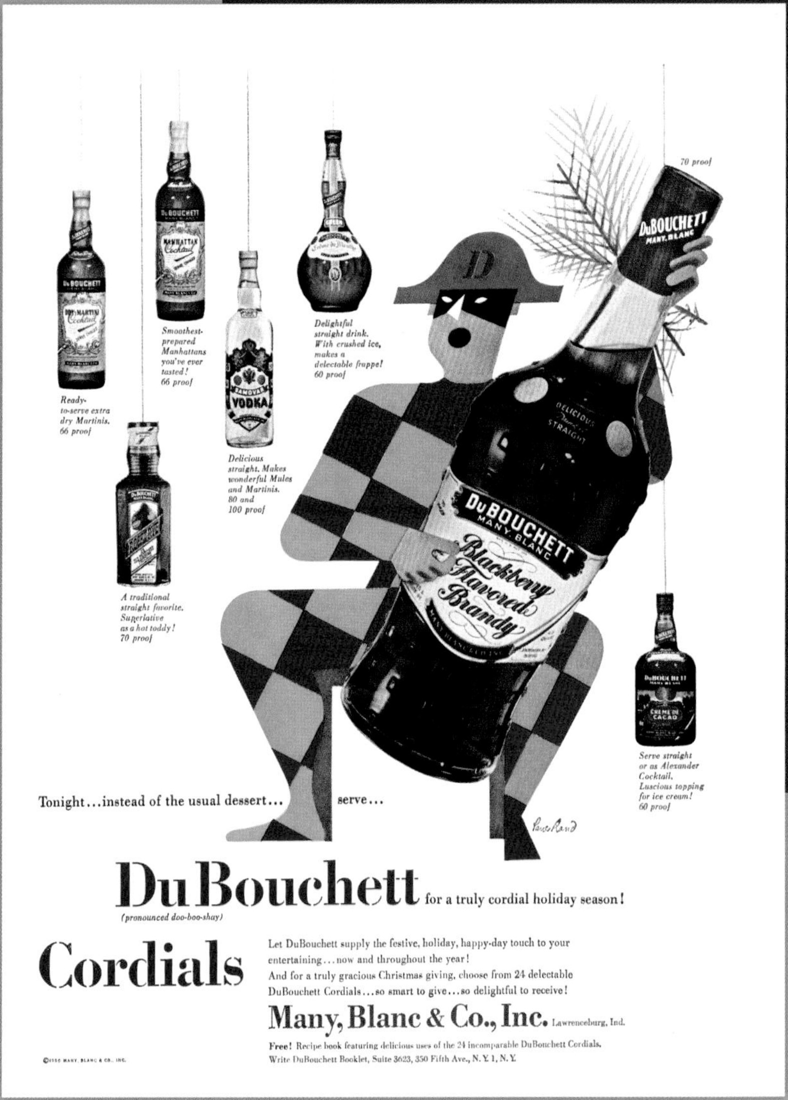

70 proof

Ready-to-serve extra dry Martinis. 66 proof

Smoothest-prepared Manhattans you've ever tasted! 66 proof

Delicious straight. Makes wonderful Mules and Martinis. 80 and 100 proof

Delightful straight drink. With crushed ice, makes a delectable frappe! 60 proof

A traditional straight favorite. Superlative as a hot toddy! 70 proof

Serve straight or as Alexander Cocktail. Luscious topping for ice cream! 60 proof

Tonight...instead of the usual dessert... serve...

DuBouchett for a truly cordial holiday season!

(pronounced doo-boo-shay)

Cordials

Let DuBouchett supply the festive, holiday, happy-day touch to your entertaining...now and throughout the year!
And for a truly gracious Christmas giving, choose from 24 delectable DuBouchett Cordials...so smart to give...so delightful to receive!

Many, Blanc & Co., Inc. Lawrenceburg, Ind.

Free! Recipe book featuring delicious uses of the 24 incomparable DuBouchett Cordials.
Write DuBouchett Booklet, Suite 3623, 350 Fifth Ave., N. Y. 1, N. Y.

DuBouchett Harlequin • 1950
DuBouchett cordials
Magazine ad

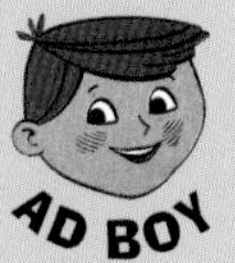

European fine art influenced these print ads created by American graphic designer, P Rand. The Dubonnet Man was Rand's take on a character conceived by the Ukrainian-French artist Cassandre. By 1950, Picasso had reached the peak of his popularity and stylized whimsy is also clear in Rand's work. In a playful yet elegant way, brandy snift and champagne bottles were transformed into witty and colorful characters.

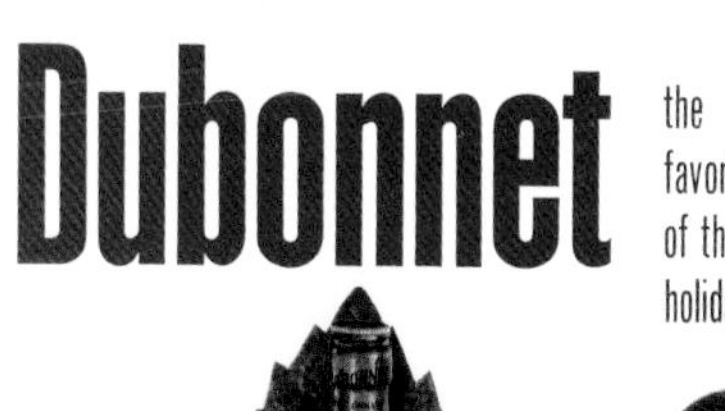

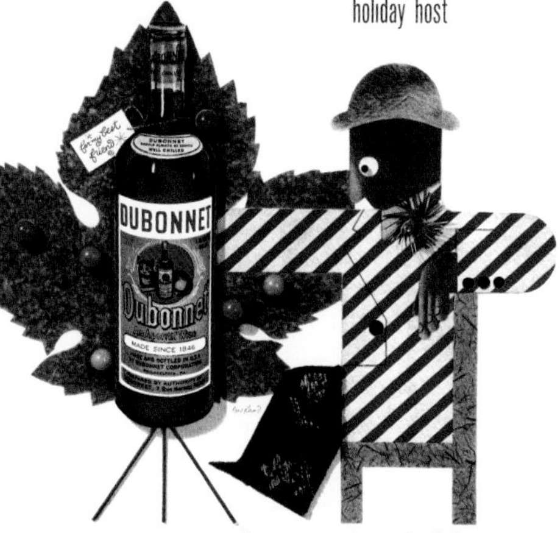

Dubonnet Man • 1951
Dubonnet aperitif wine
Magazine ad

Coronet Brandy Man • 1943
Coronet V.S.Q. brandy
Magazine ad

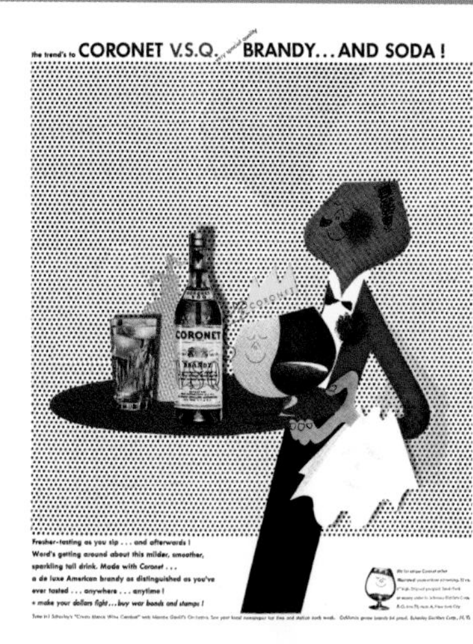

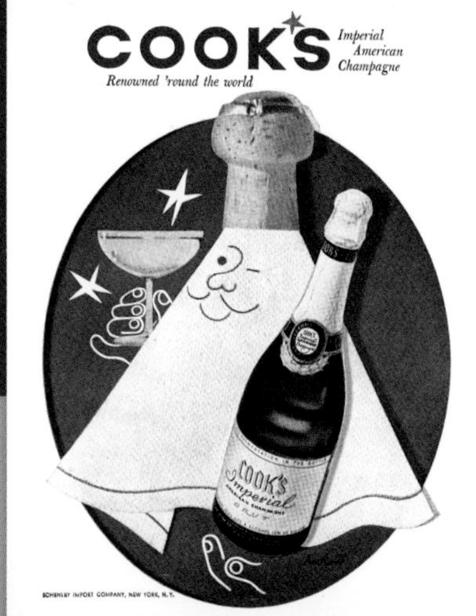

Cook's Champagne Man • 1955
Cook's champagne
Magazine ad

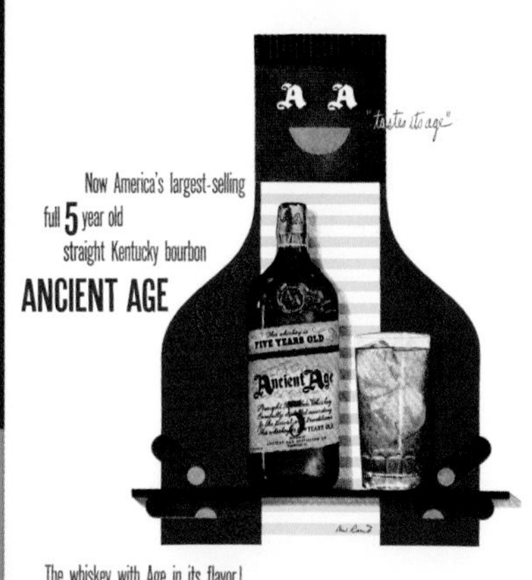

Double A • 1949
Ancient Age bourbon
Magazine ad

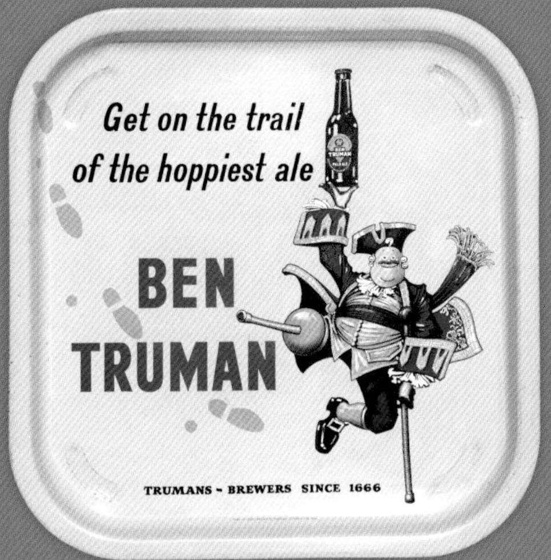

Ben Truman • c. 1962
Ben Truman ale
Serving tray

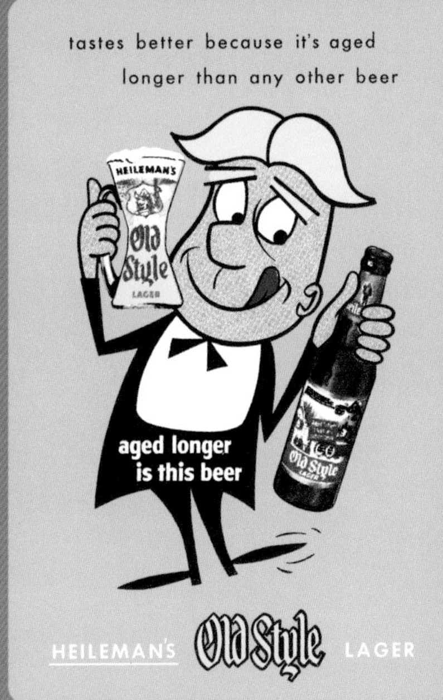

Old Style • c. 1956
Old Style larger
Playing card

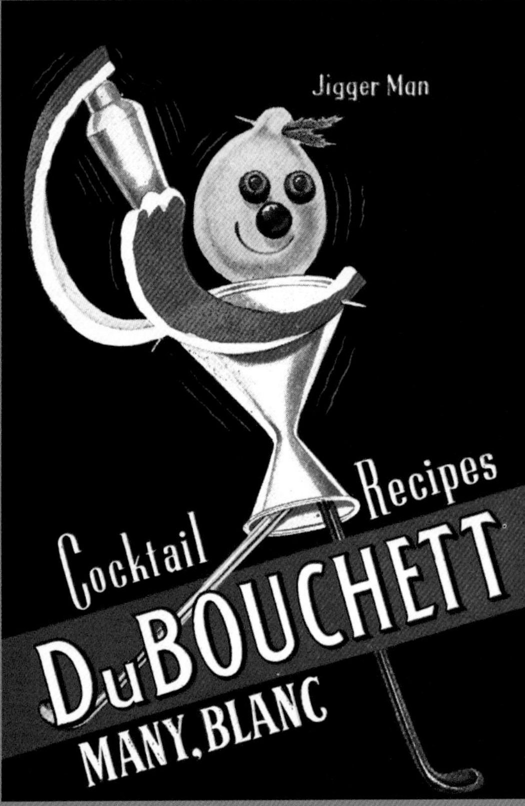

Jigger Man • c. 1947
DuBouchett cordials
Recipe booklet

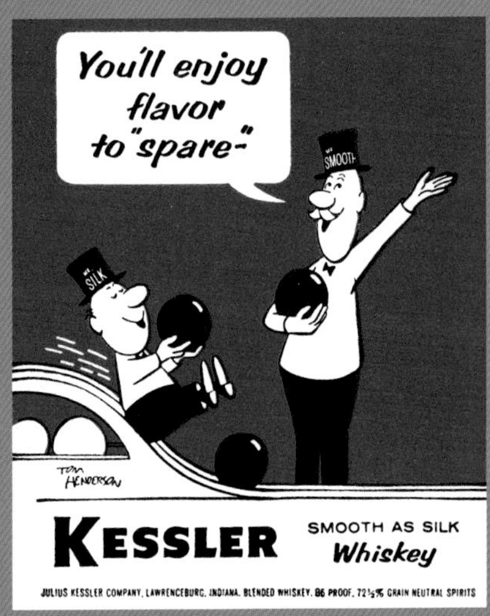

Mr. Silk and Mr. Smooth • c. 1944
Kessler whiskey
Matchbook back

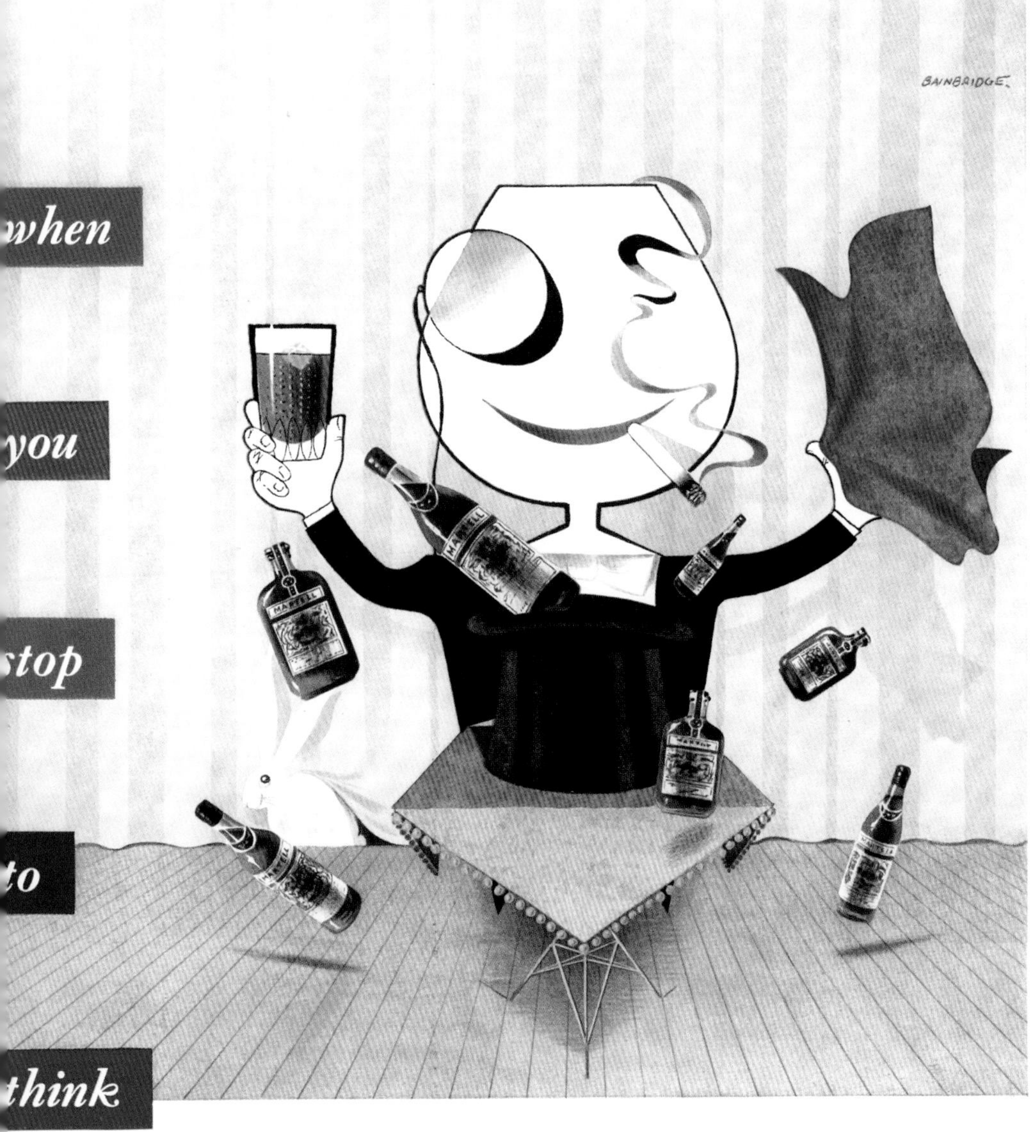

there's nothing like a long Martell

THE LONG DRINK WITH GINGER ALE OR SODA

Brandyman • 1959
Martell brandy
Magazine ad

make friends with MARTELL

COGNAC BRANDY AT ITS BEST

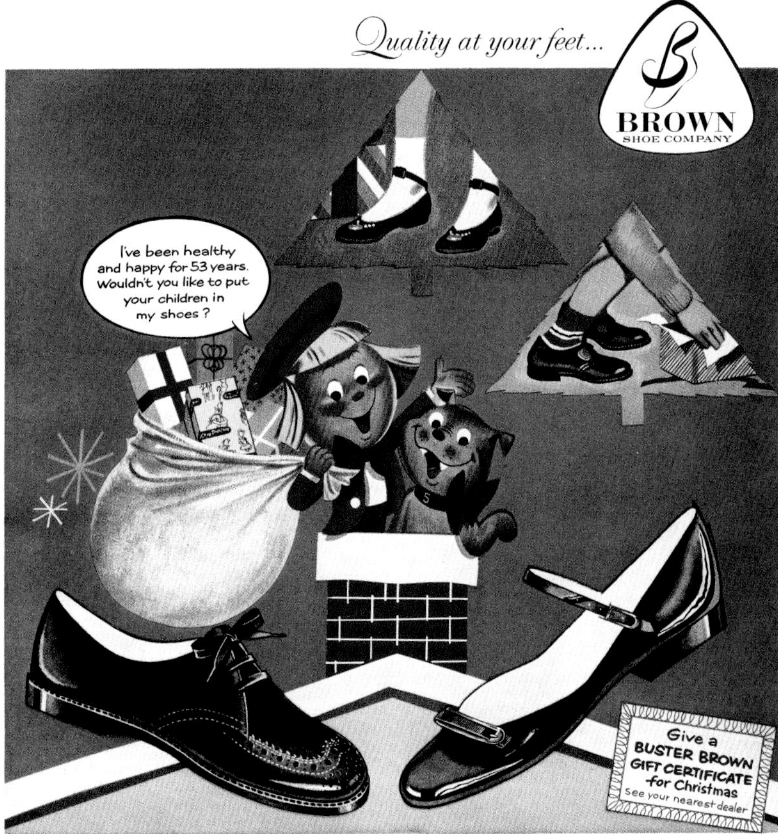

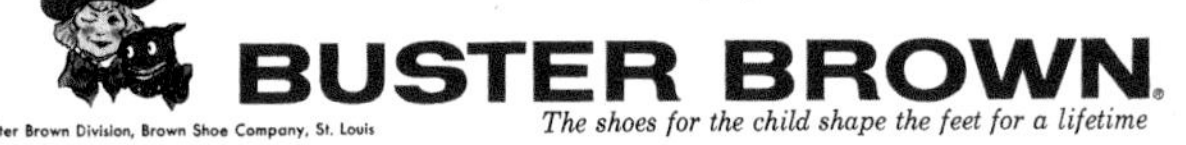

Buster Brown and Tige • 1957
Buster Brown shoes
Magazine ad

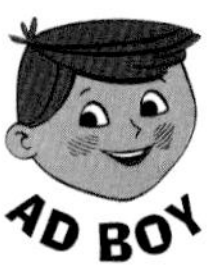

Many successful ad characters have been with us since the 1950s and some are over a century old. Besides being immediately identifiable, characters could be customized to suit the marketing occasion at hand. During the holiday season advertisers often presented their mascots as old family friends, singing Christmas carols in the snow like the Blatz Men or becoming chimney shimmying Santa's helpers like Buster Brown and Tige.

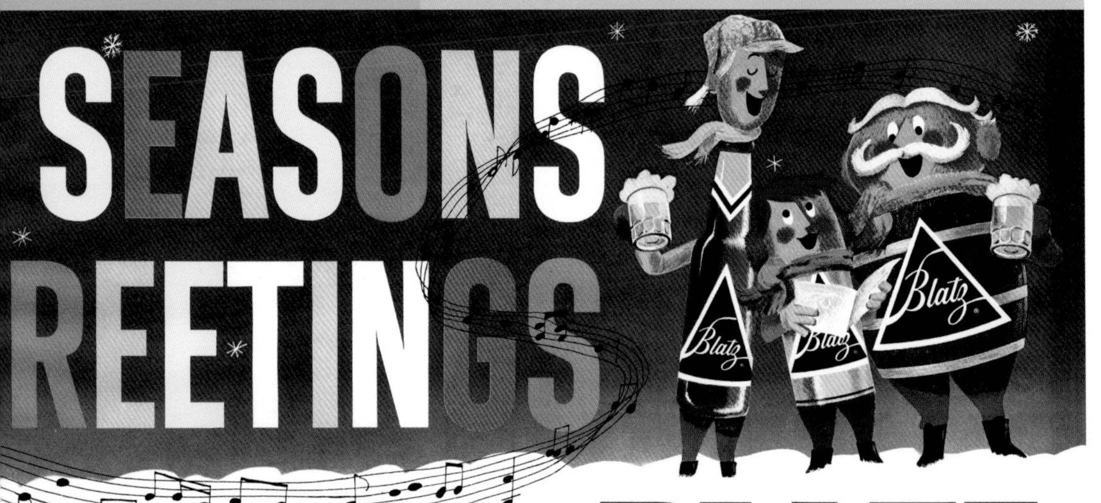

Blatz Men • 1960
Blatz beer
Store sign

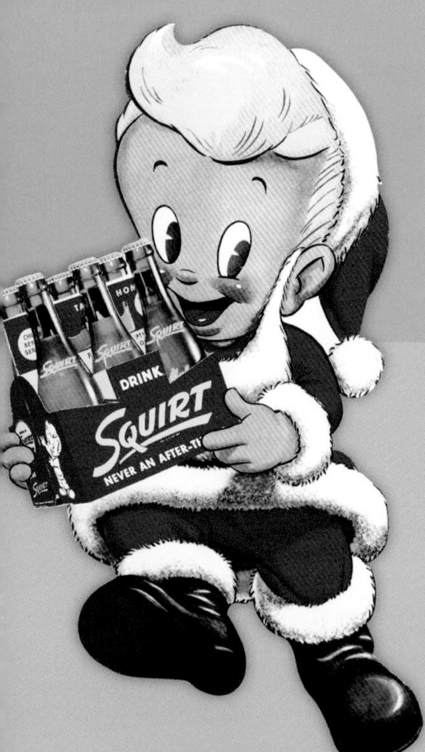

Squirt • c. 1948
Squirt soda
Store display

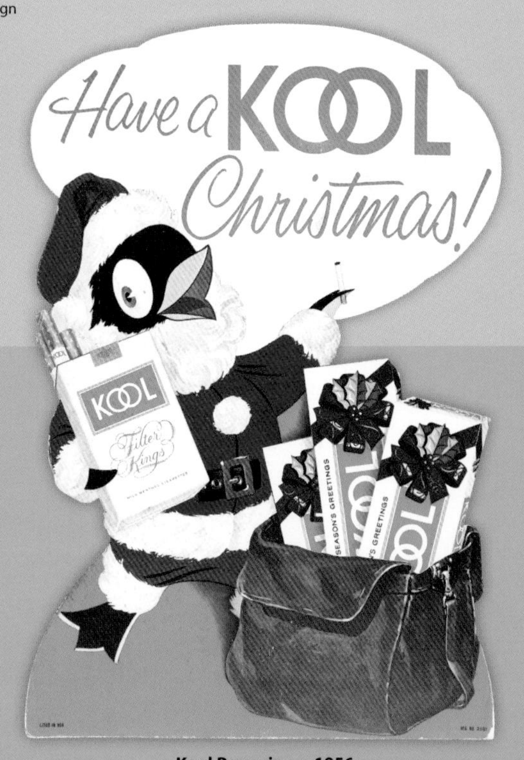

Kool Penguin • c. 1956
Kool cigarettes
Store display

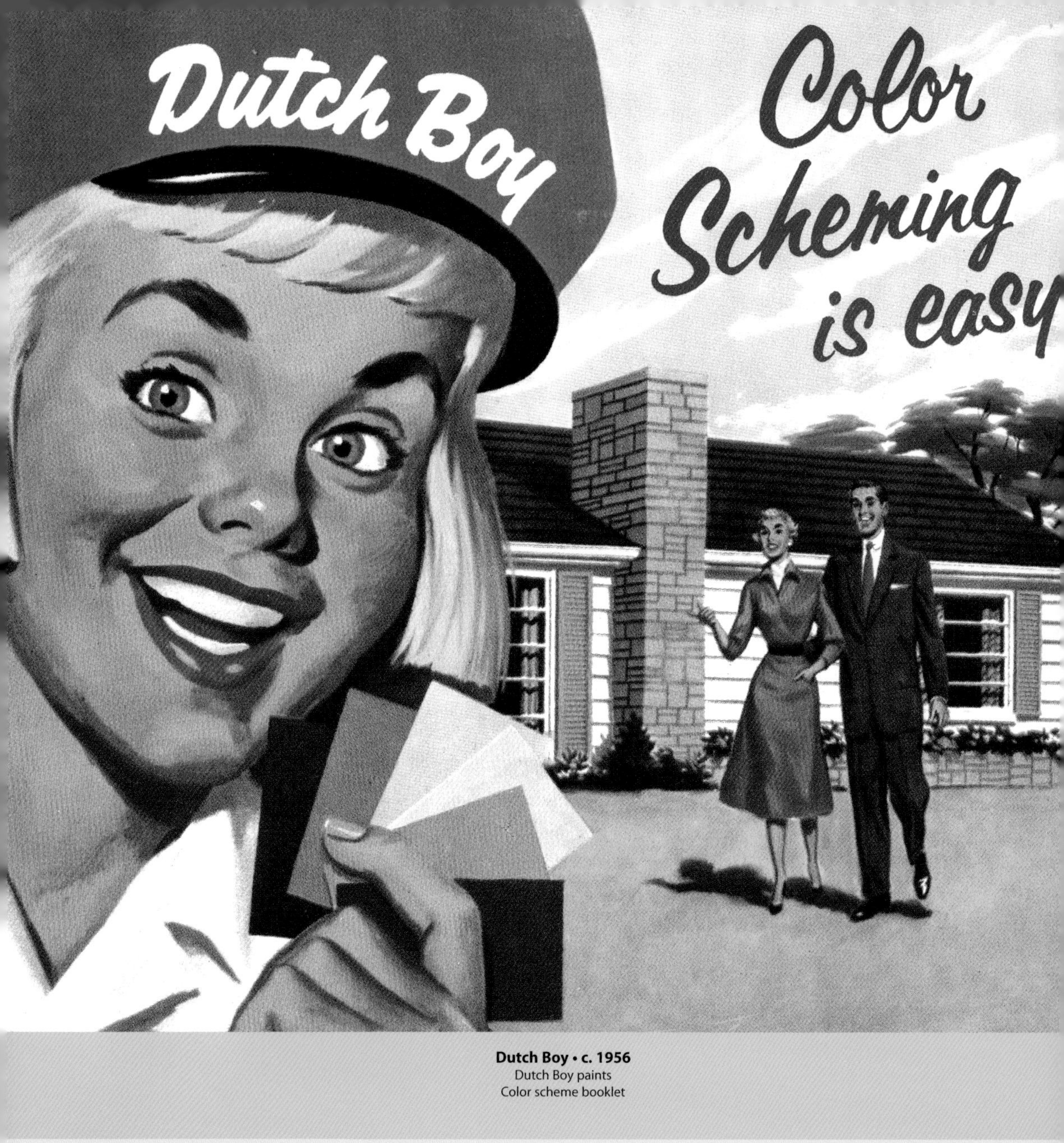

Dutch Boy

Color Scheming is easy

Dutch Boy • c. 1956
Dutch Boy paints
Color scheme booklet

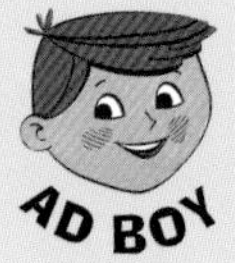

Thanks to today's sprawling hardware havens, it's easy to assume that the do-it-yoursel home-improvement phenomenon is relatively new but it really began in earnest durin postwar, baby-boom years. Dutch Boy paint is one brand that's still going strong, due a in part to its highly recognizable mascot. Who wouldn't associate long-wearing, superic quality and the famous myth about the lad who held back the sea with just one finger?

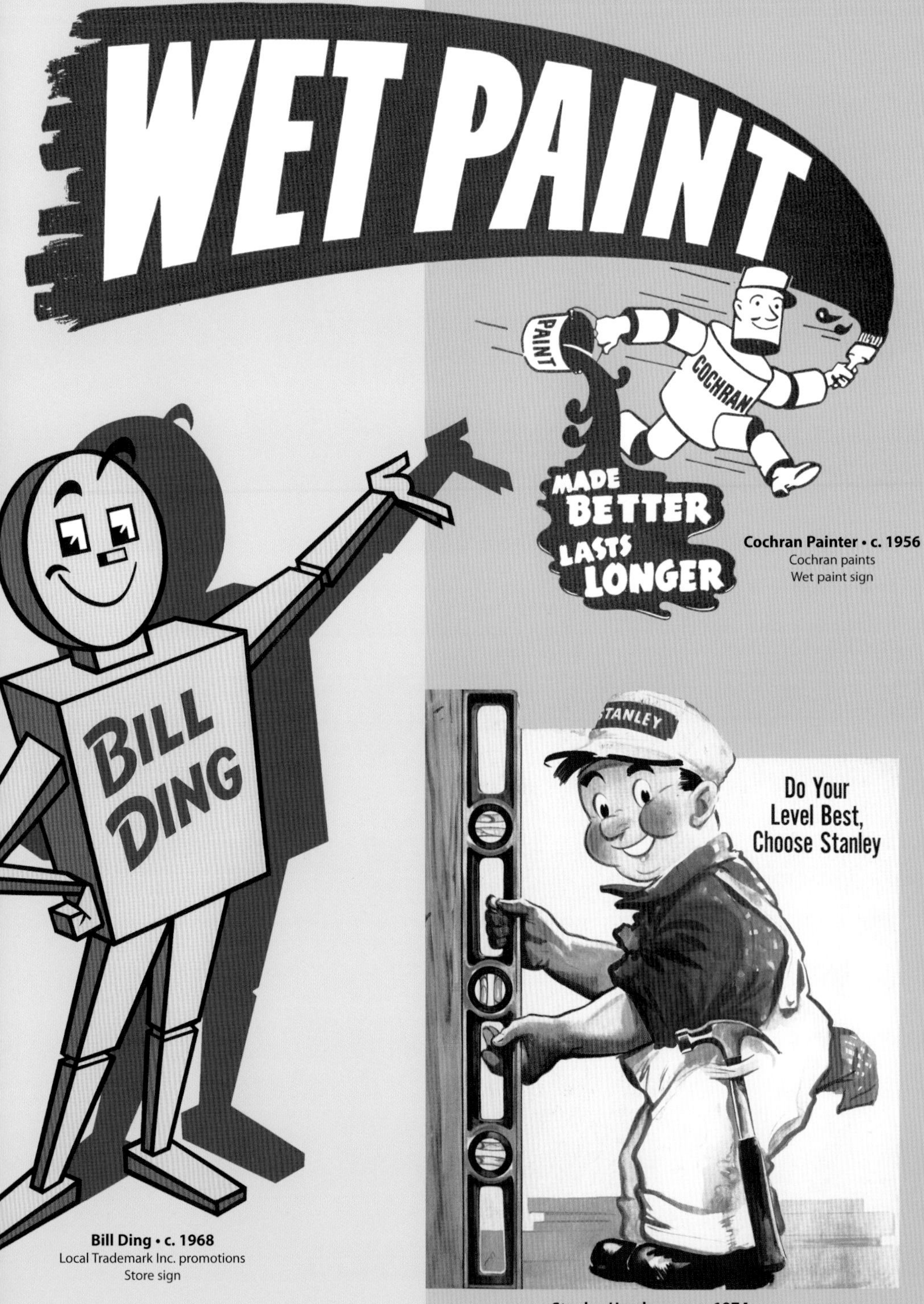

Cochran Painter • c. 1956
Cochran paints
Wet paint sign

Bill Ding • c. 1968
Local Trademark Inc. promotions
Store sign

Stanley Handyman • c. 1974
Stanley tools
Store display

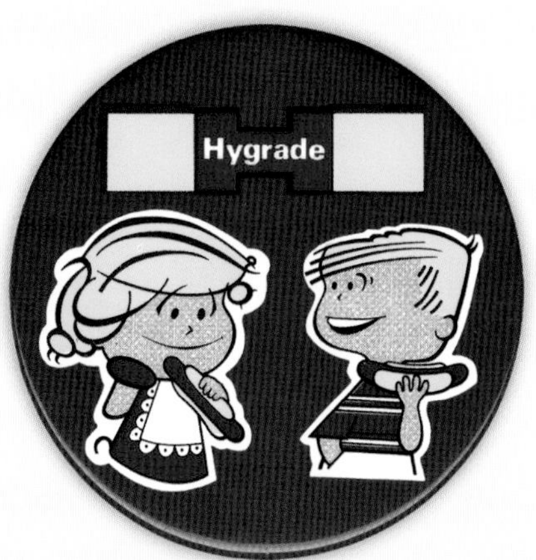

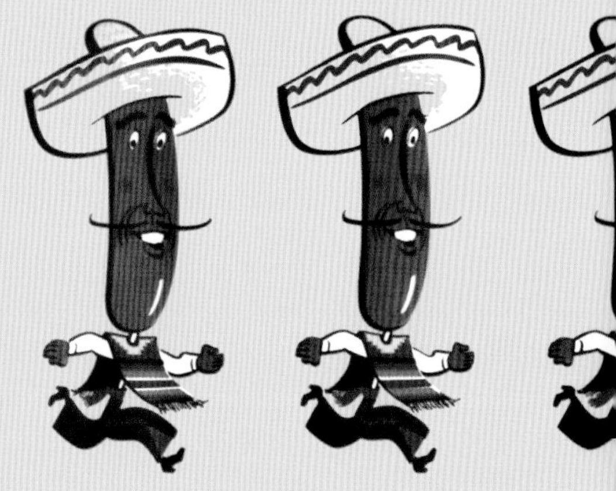

Hygrade Kids • c. 1976
Hygrade hot dogs
Pin-back button

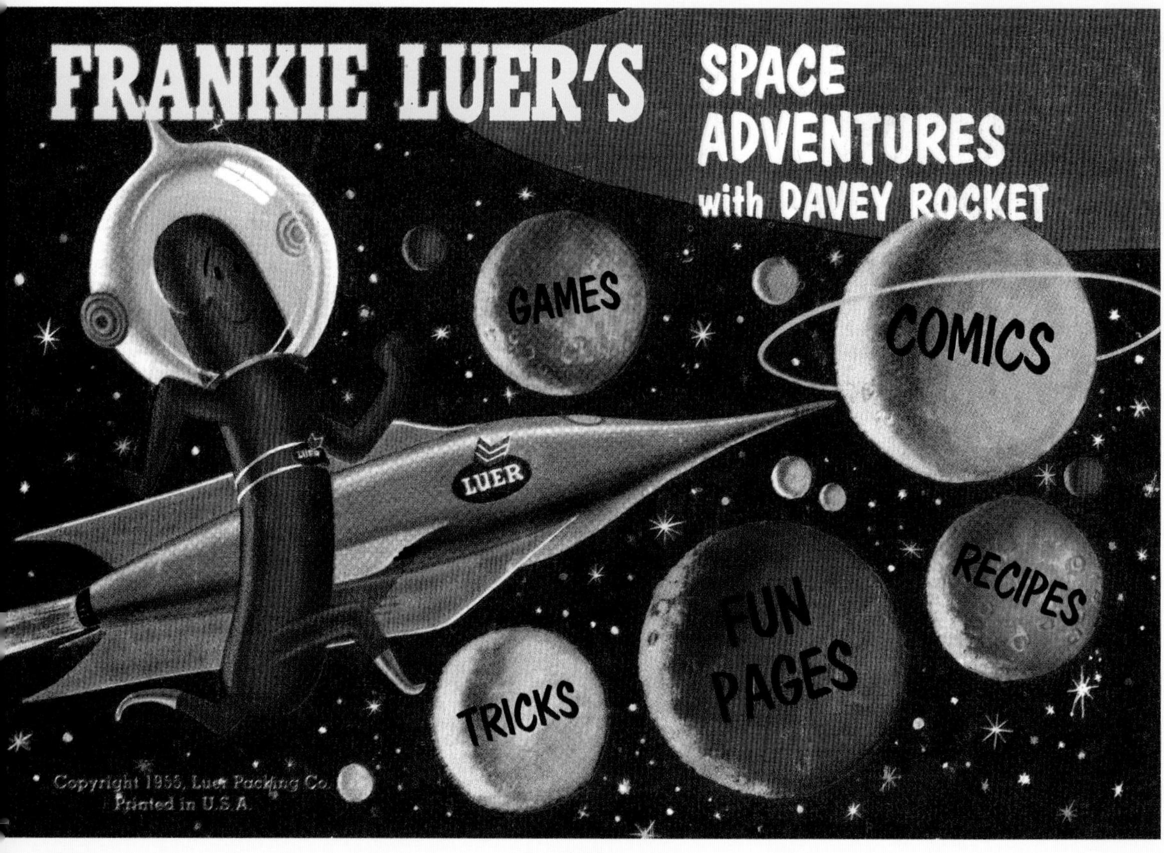

FRANKIE LUER'S SPACE ADVENTURES with DAVEY ROCKET
GAMES
COMICS
LUER
RECIPES
FUN PAGES
TRICKS
Copyright 1955, Luer Packing Co.
Printed in U.S.A.

Frankie Luer • 1955
Luer hot dogs
Promotional booket

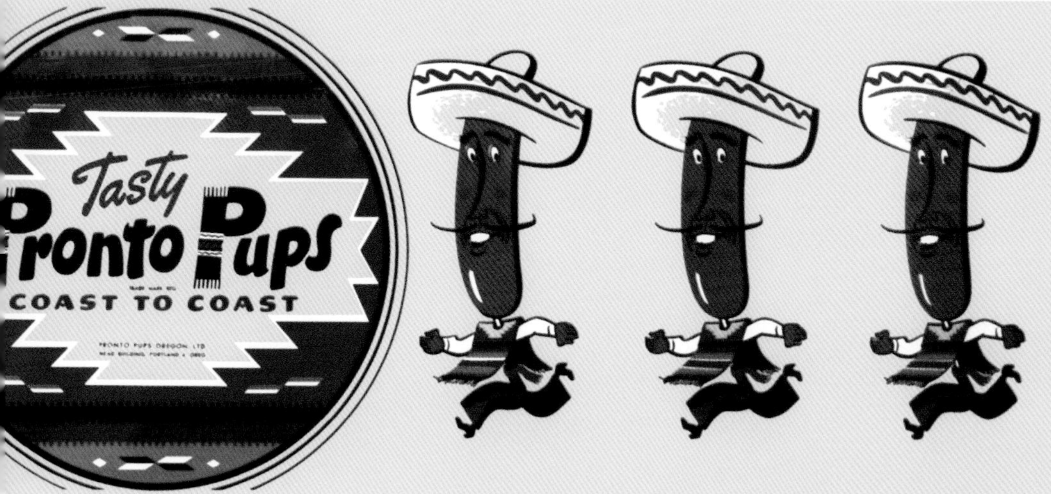

Pronto Pups Señor • c. 1958
Pronto Pups hot dog on a stick
Water decal

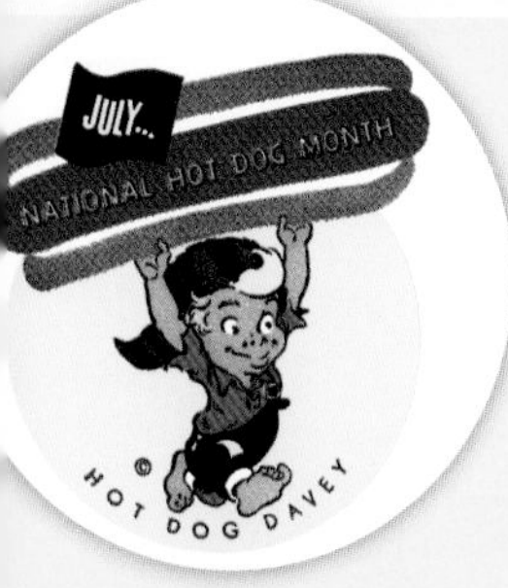

Hot Dog Davey • c. 1955
National Hot Dog Month promotion
Pin-back button

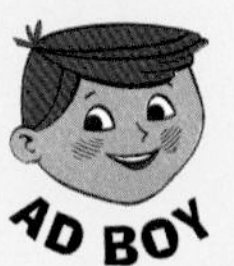

It's no surprise that many of the frankfurter industry's top dog personalities are anthropomorphic wieners. Nathan's of Coney Island has Frankie, Frankie Luer of Luer Meat Products became an astronaut in the 1950s at the dawn of the space race, and Pronto Pups corn dogs has a serape-wearing señor.

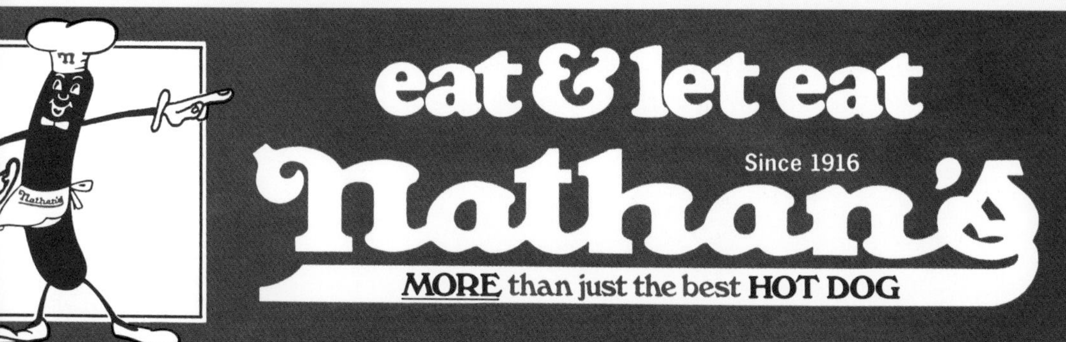

Frankie • c. 1977
Nathan's Famous hot dogs
Bumper sticker

Emperor Nero • c. 1957
Puppy Palace restaurant
Store sign

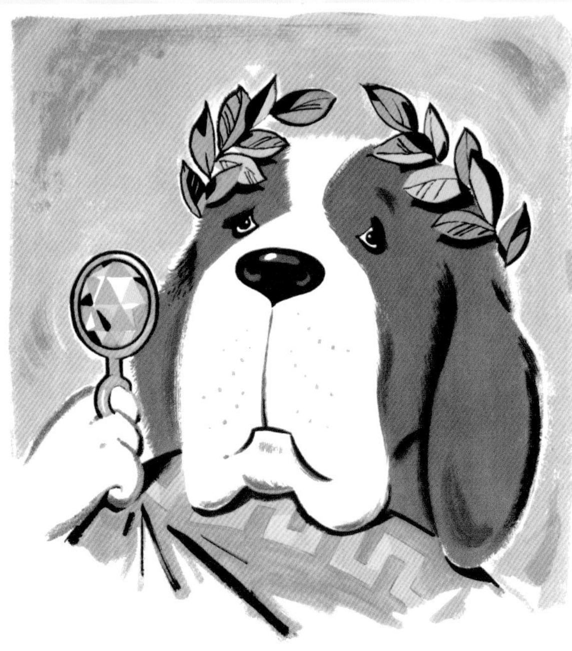

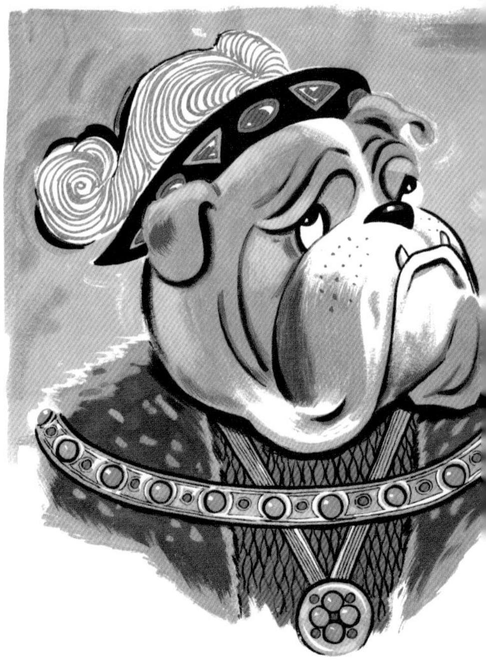

King Henry • c. 1957
Puppy Palace restaurant
Store sign

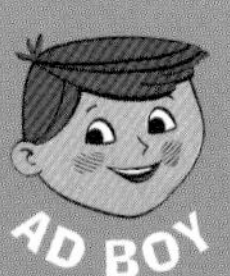

When did the frankfurter become known as a "dog"? This is debatable. But without q tion the wiener is shaped like a dachshund. Hot dog vendors have always relished co clever names for the franks on their menus. At the Puppy Palace, each hot dog had it canine character. Ordering a Kaiser Willie got you a dog with mustard and sauerkraut while the lei-draped King Koko dog came with Hawaiian pineapple, and so on.

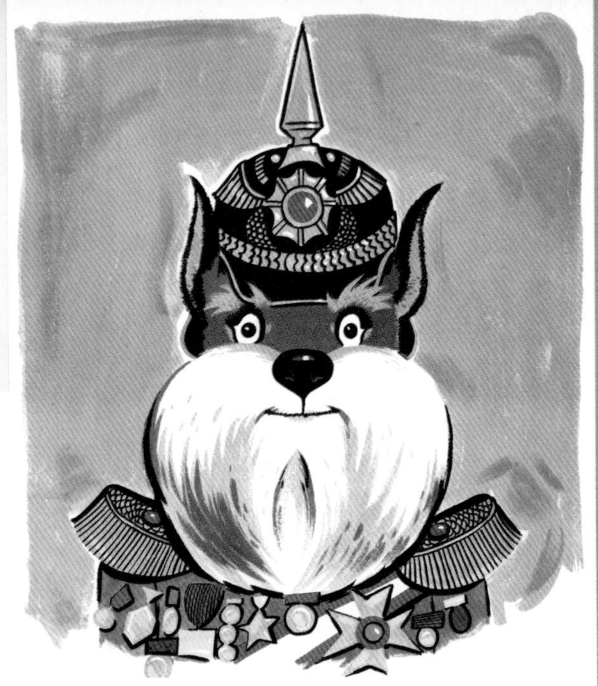

Kaiser Willie

mustard, sauerkraut

HOT DOG *from* PUPPY PALACE

Kaiser Willie • c. 1957
Puppy Palace restaurant
Store sign

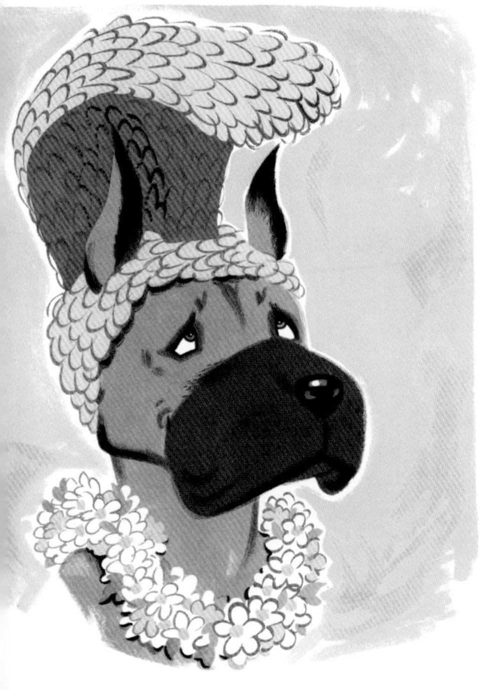

King Koko

catsup, bacon and pineapple

HOT DOG *from* PUPPY PALACE

King Koko • c. 1957
Puppy Palace restaurant
Store sign

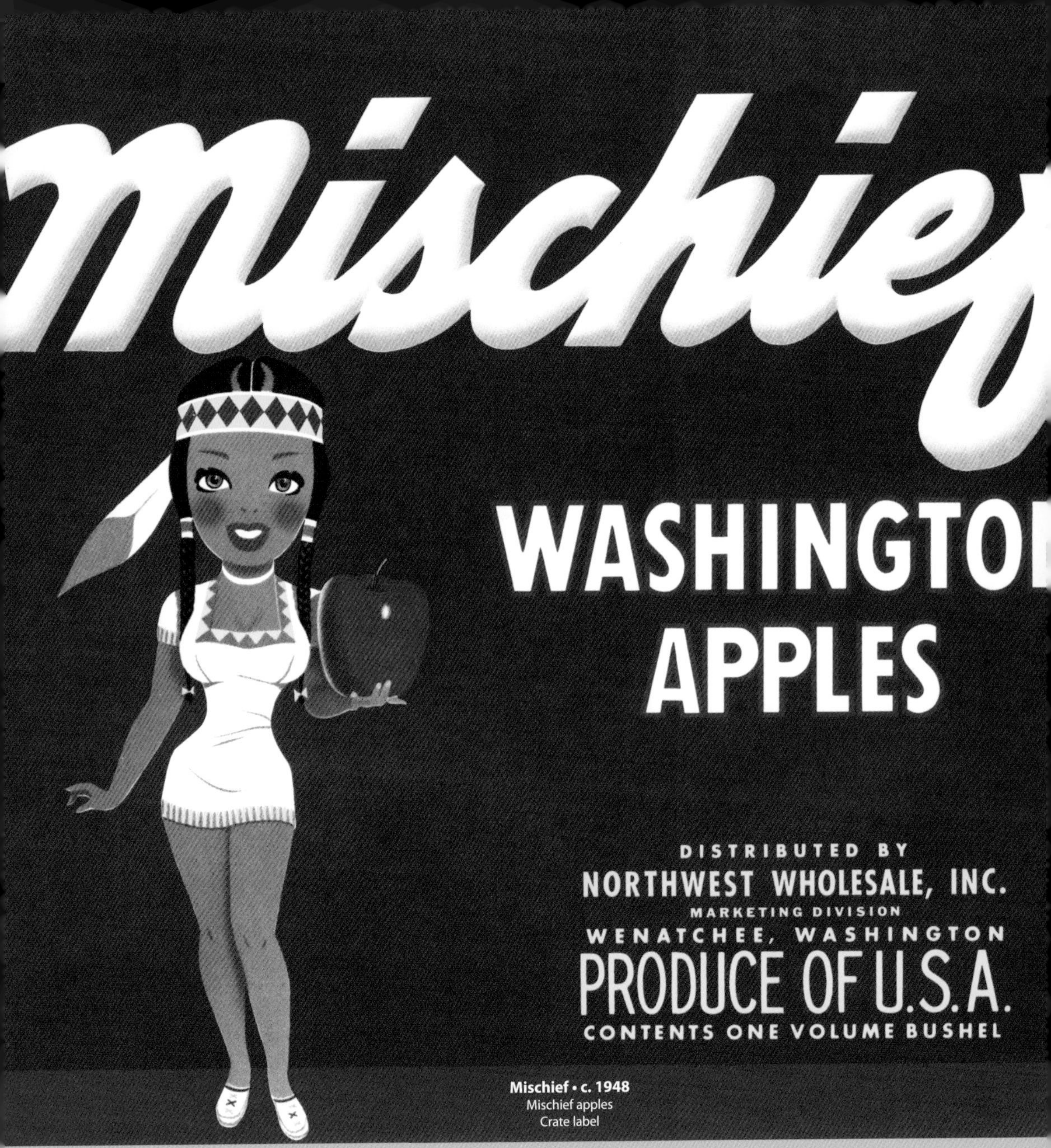

Mischief

WASHINGTON

APPLES

DISTRIBUTED BY

NORTHWEST WHOLESALE, INC.

MARKETING DIVISION

WENATCHEE, WASHINGTON

PRODUCE OF U.S.A.

CONTENTS ONE VOLUME BUSHEL

Mischief • c. 1948
Mischief apples
Crate label

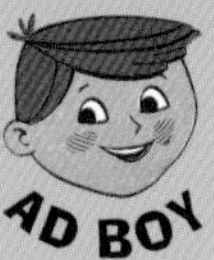

Throughout the twentieth century, Native American women and girls have been usec to represent nature's wholesome bounty. These exotic, sensual creatures were usuall portrayed in a pristine wilderness with come-hither expressions, scantily clad in buck with a jaunty feather and two long braids. It's no wonder that the subliminal messag "forbidden fruit" made them popular choices for fruit crate labels.

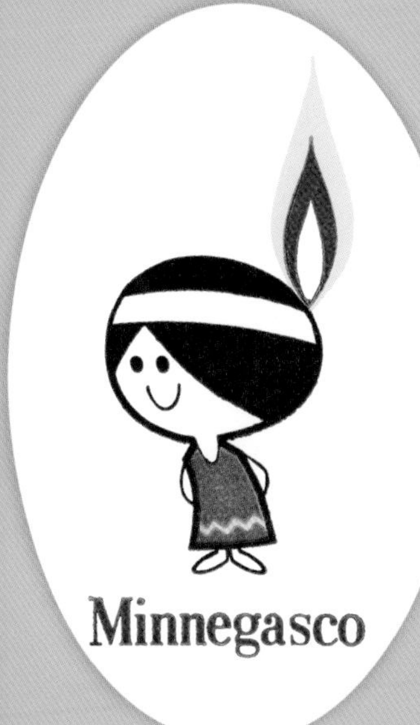

Minnegasco Minnie • 1959
Minneapolis Gas Company
Pin-back button

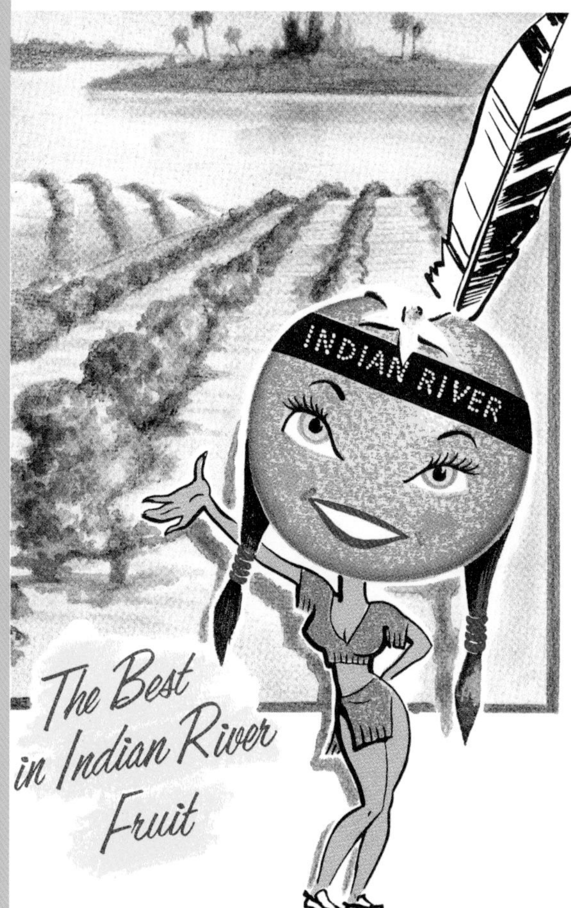

Indian River Maiden • 1957
Chester Groves fruits
Catalog cover detail

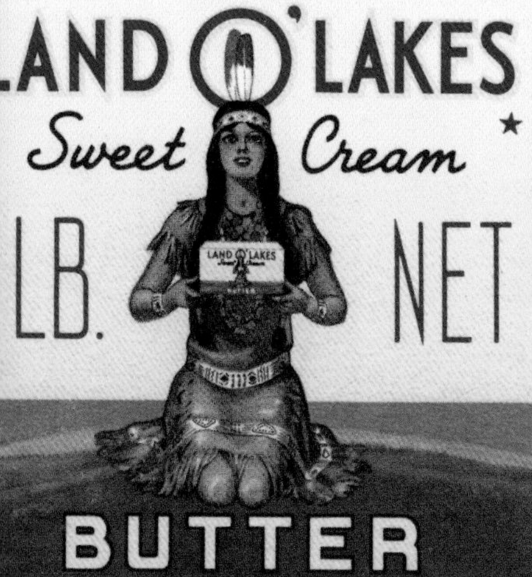

Land O' Lakes Maiden • c. 1959
Land O' Lakes butter
Box side

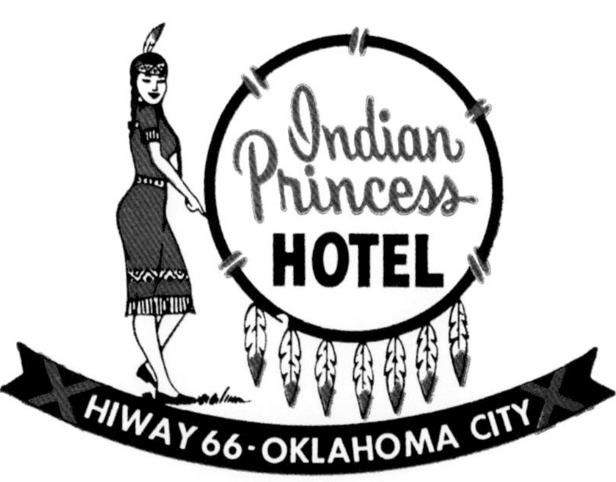

Indian Princess • c. 1959
Indian Princess hotel
Matchbook cover

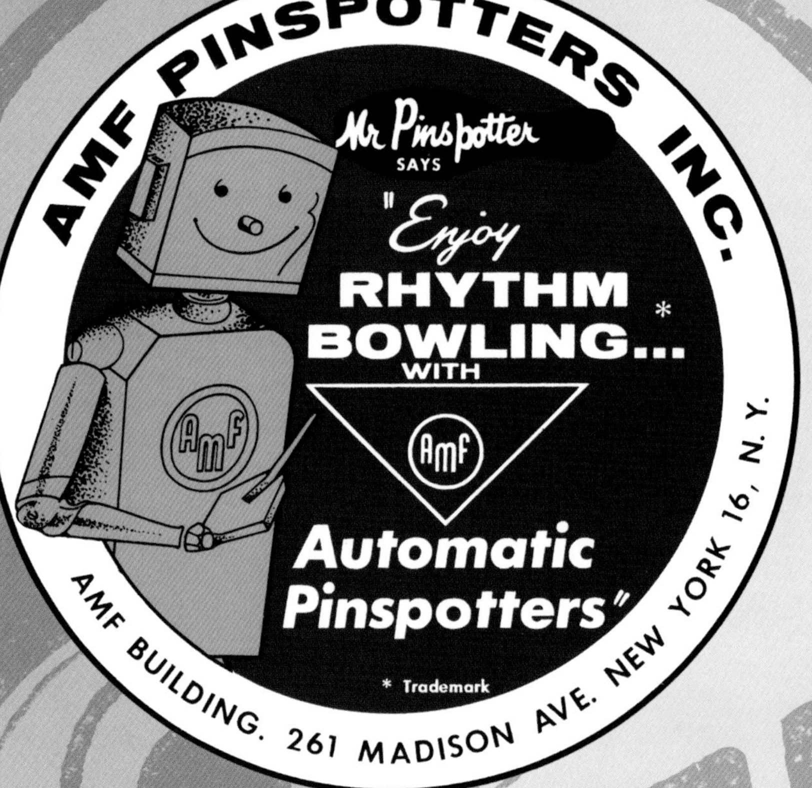

AMF PINSPOTTERS INC.

Mr Pinspotter SAYS

"Enjoy RHYTHM* BOWLING... WITH AMF Automatic Pinspotters"

* Trademark

AMF BUILDING. 261 MADISON AVE. NEW YORK 16, N. Y.

Mr. Pinspotter • c. 1959
AMF automatic bowling pinspotters
Promotional decal

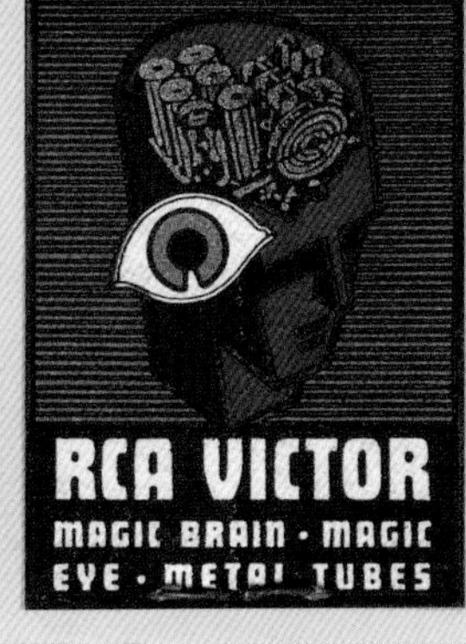

Magic Brain and Magic Eye • 1935
RCA Victor tubes
Matchbook back

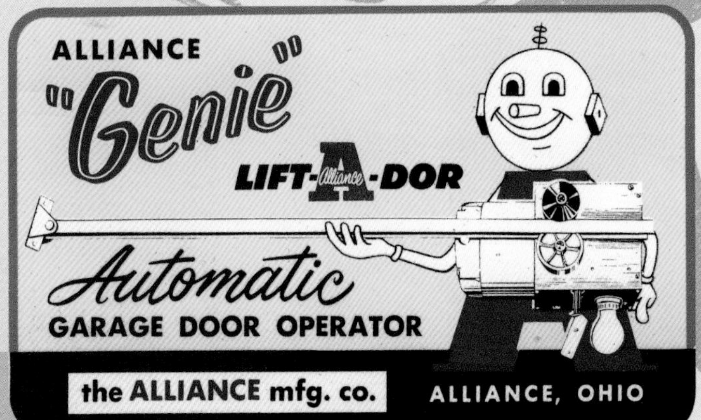

Genie • c. 1958
Genie garage door openers
Water decal

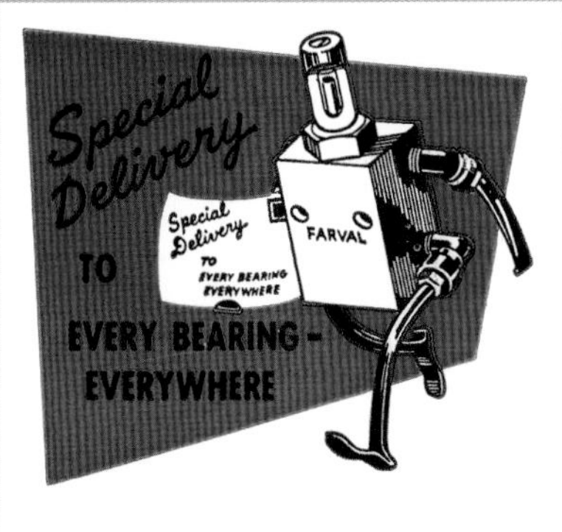

Farval Man • c. 1956
Farval lubrication equipment
Matchbook back

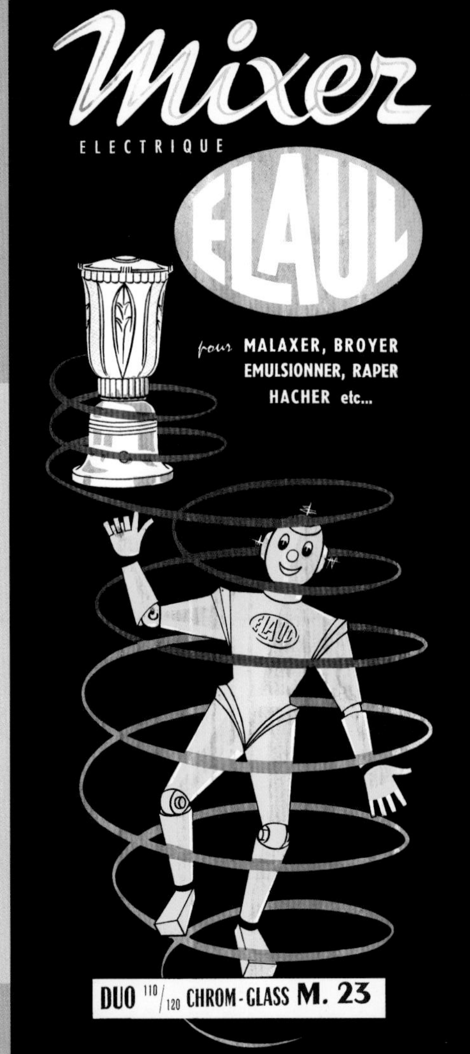

Elaul Robot • c. 1958
Elaul electric mixers
Box cover

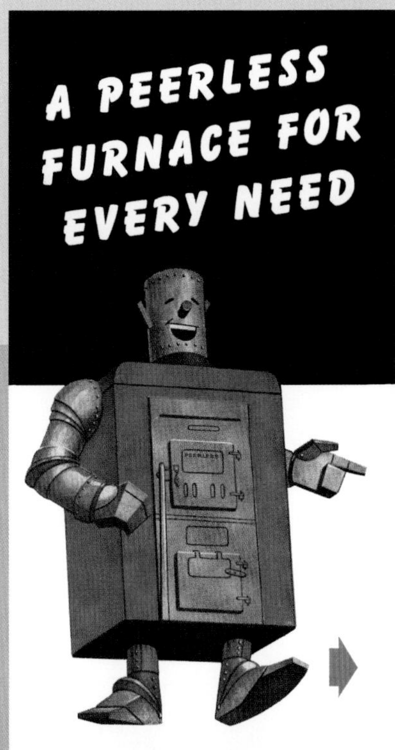

Furnace Man • c. 1947
Peerless furnaces
Promotional brochure

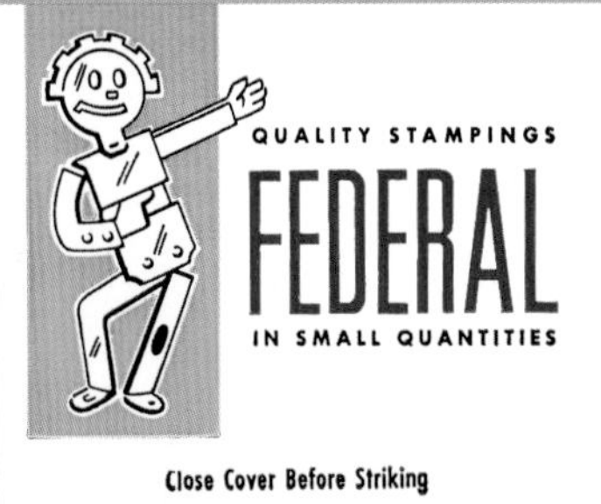

Federal Man • c. 1966
Federal stamping services
Matchbook cover

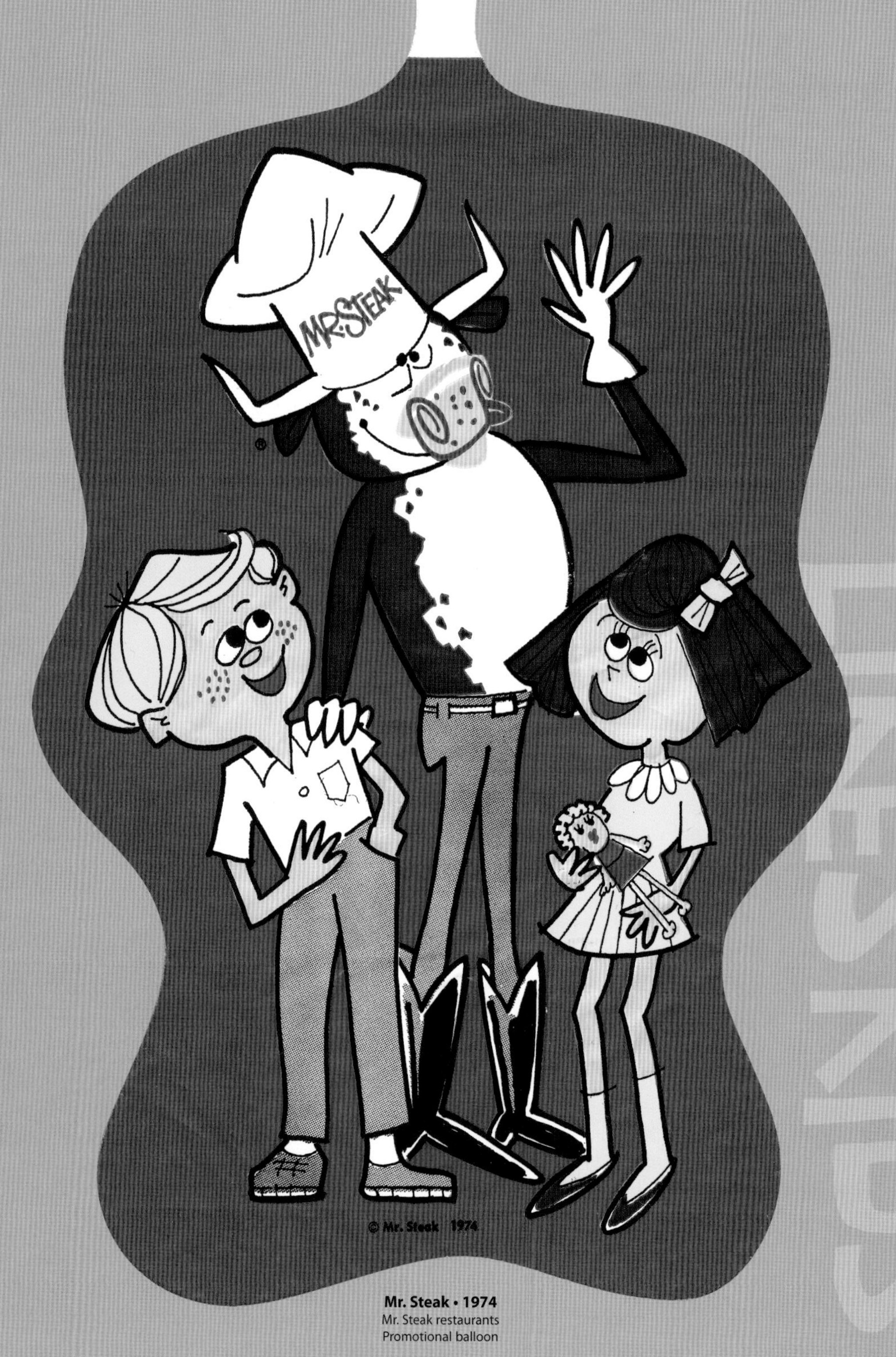

Mr. Steak • 1974
Mr. Steak restaurants
Promotional balloon

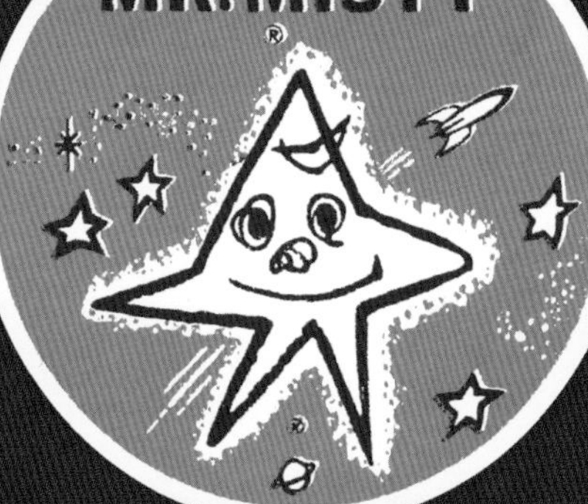

Mr. Misty • c. 1969
Mr. Misty frozen beverage
Container cap

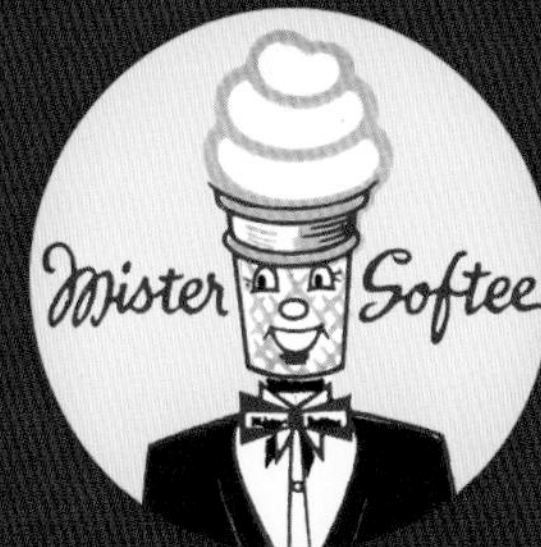

Mister Softee • c. 1965
Mister Softee ice cream
Pin-back button

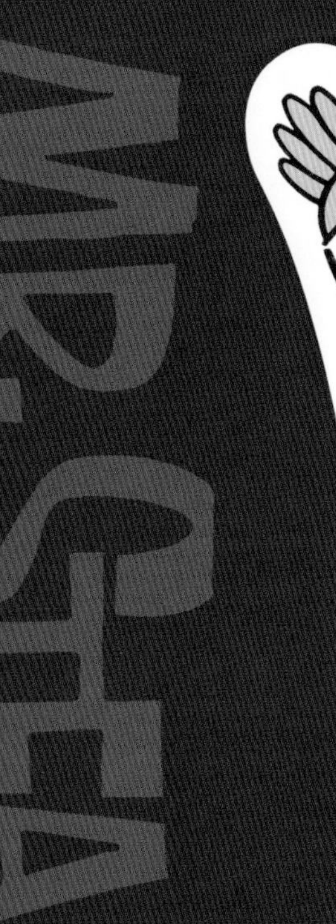

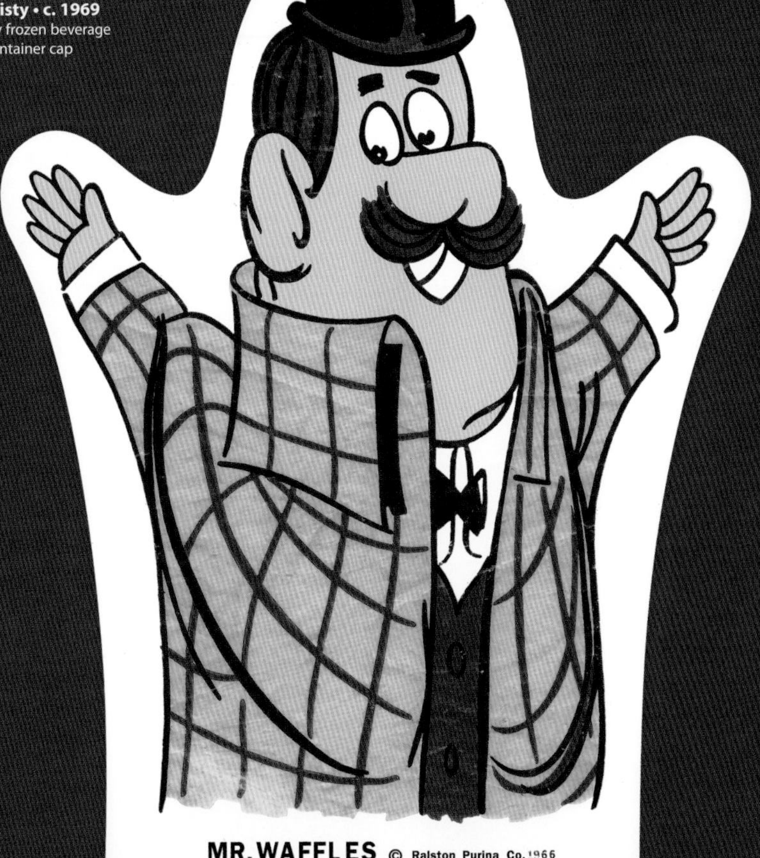

Mr. Waffles • 1966
Mr. Waffles cereal
Hand puppet

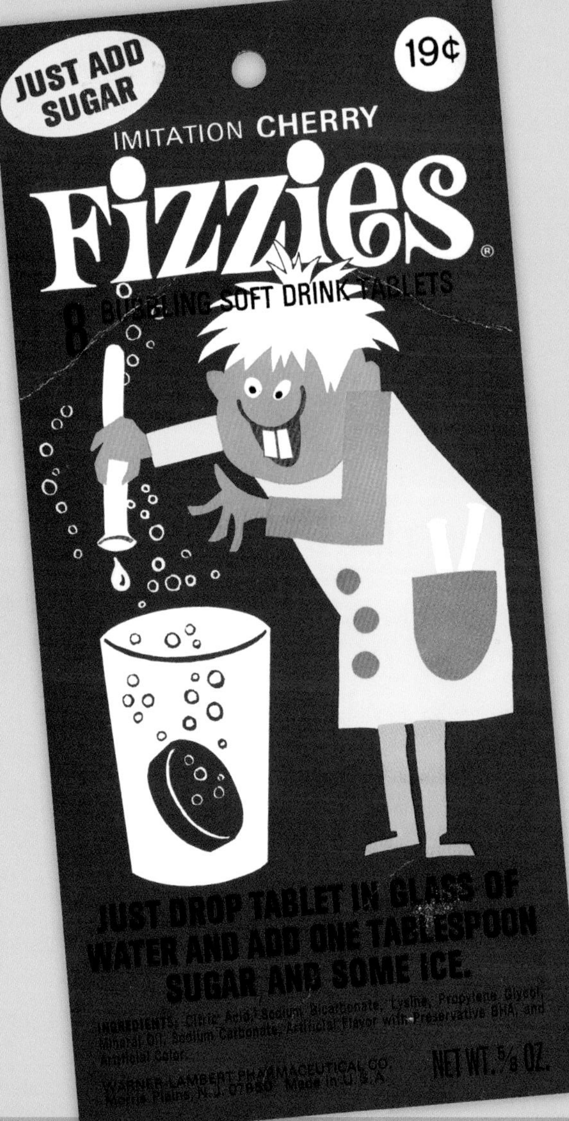

Mad Scientist • c. 1965
Fizzies soft drink tablets
Package front

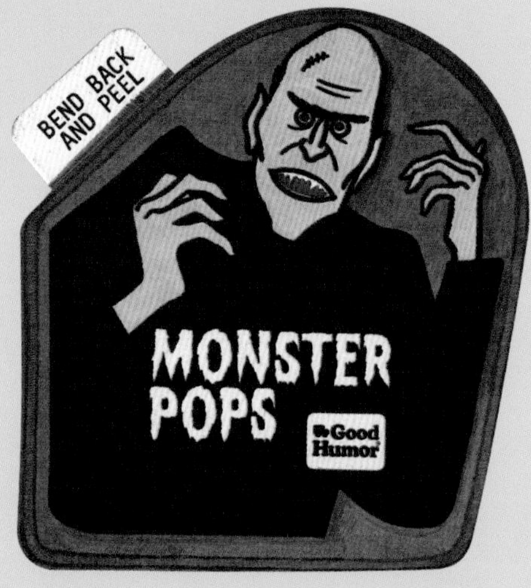

Monster Pops • c. 1974
Good Humor ice cream
Promotional sticker

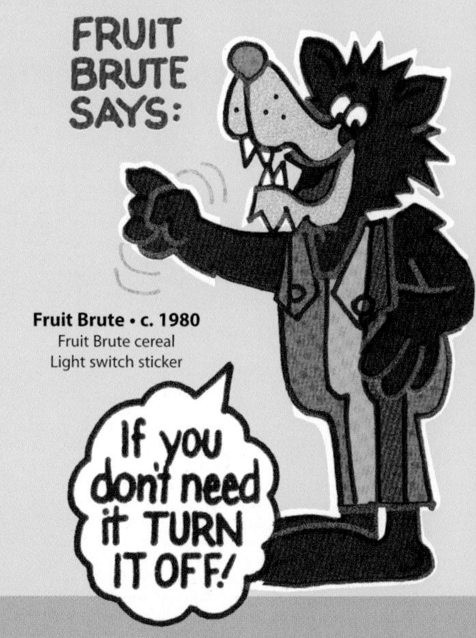

Fruit Brute • c. 1980
Fruit Brute cereal
Light switch sticker

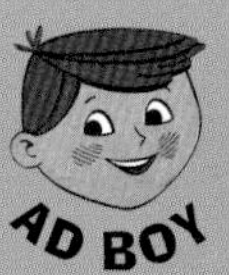

The 1960s ushered in the era of the friendly, family-oriented ghoul thanks to two tele sion shows: *The Munsters* and *The Addams Family*. In the 70s the enormous success of children's cereal characters, Count Chocula and Franken Berry, made Madison Avenu take notice. Kiddie monster brands and products have been popular with both adver ers and consumers ever since.

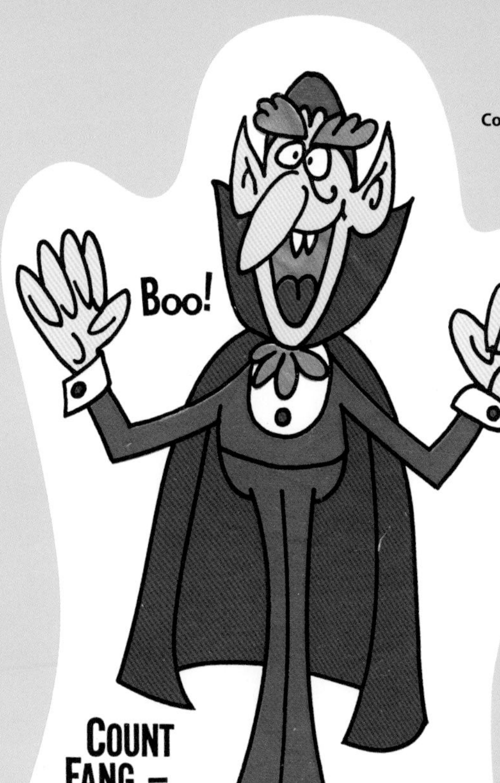

Count Fang Burger • 1977
Burger Chef restaurants
Hand puppet

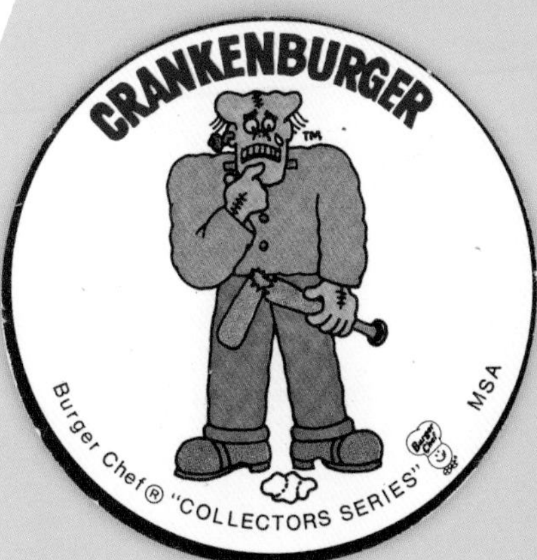

Crankenburger • 1977
Burger Chef restaurants
Collectible card

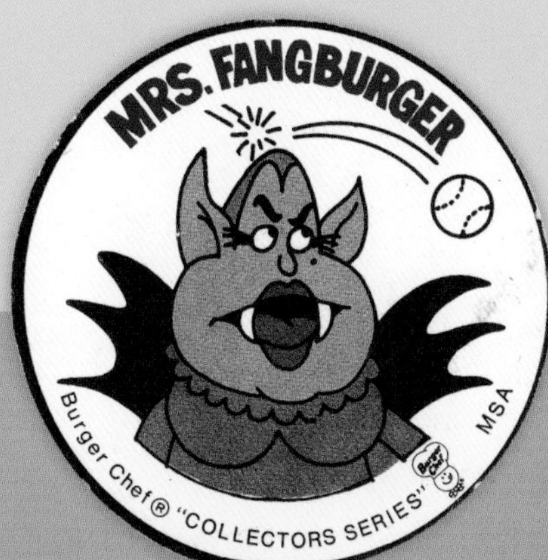

Mrs. Fangburger • 1977
Burger Chef restaurants
Collectible card

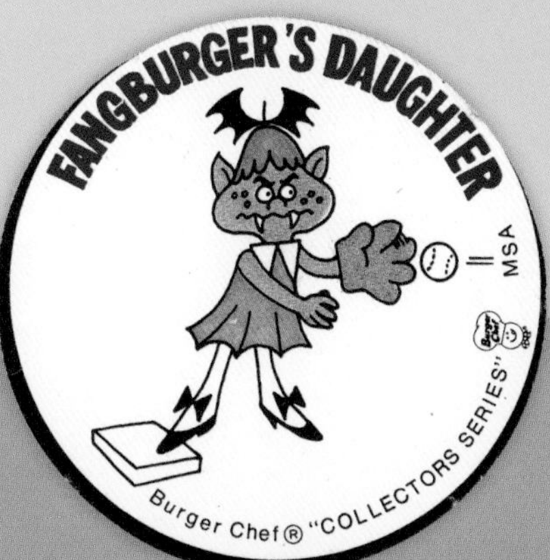

Fangburger's Daughter • 1977
Burger Chef restaurants
Collectible card

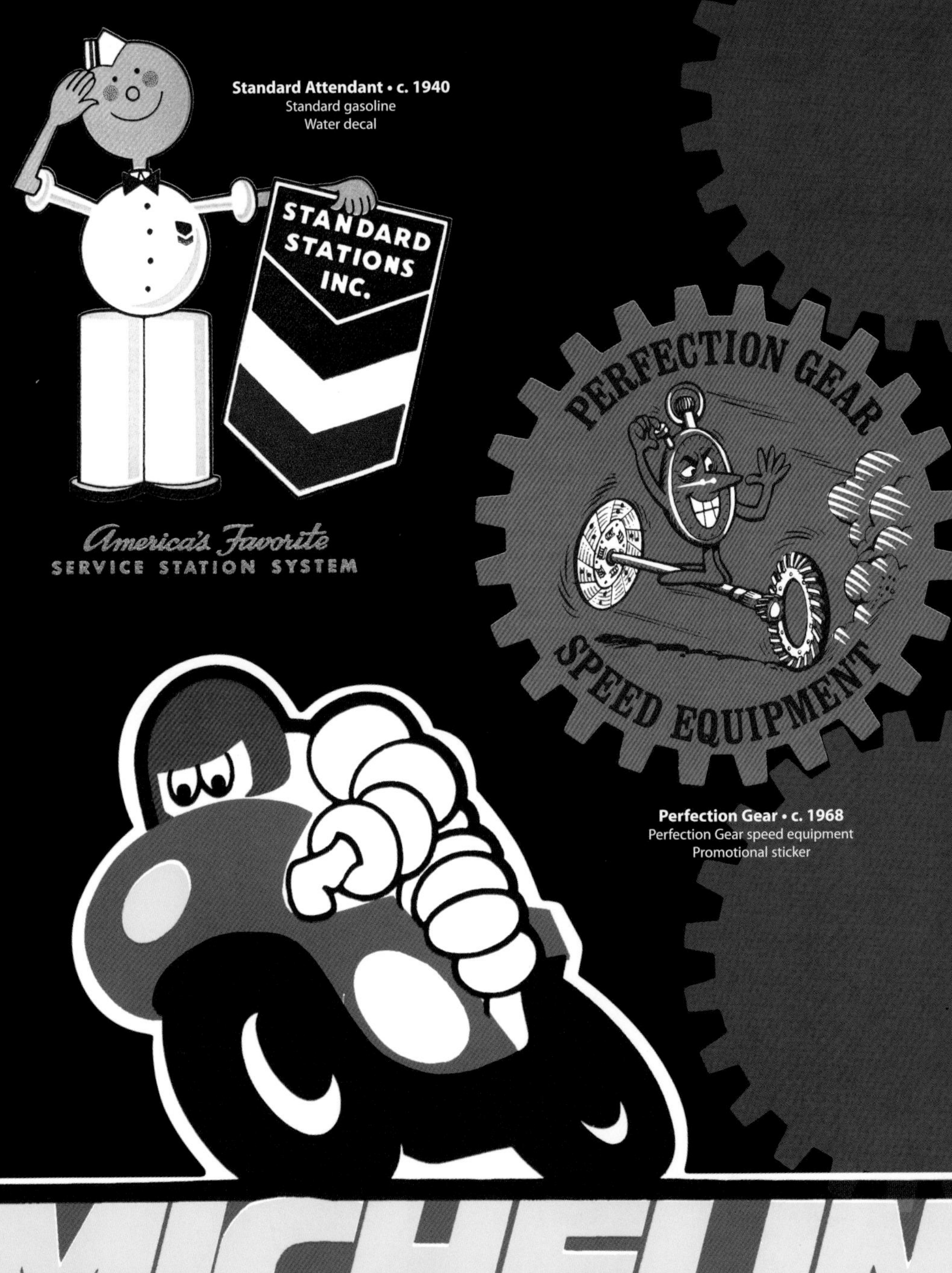

Standard Attendant • c. 1940
Standard gasoline
Water decal

Perfection Gear • c. 1968
Perfection Gear speed equipment
Promotional sticker

MOTOR AGE

A CHILTON PUBLICATION

SEPTEMBER 1961

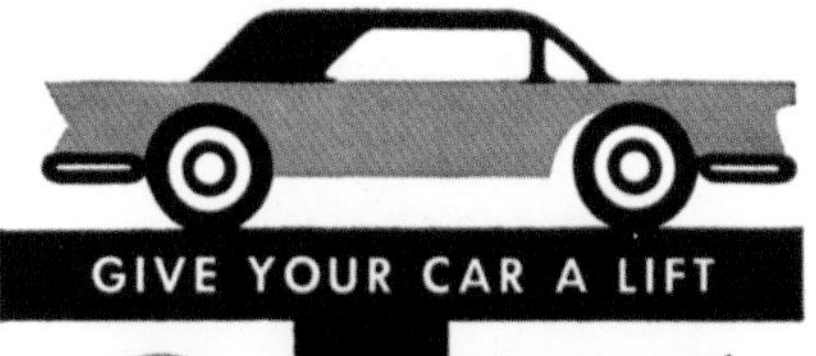

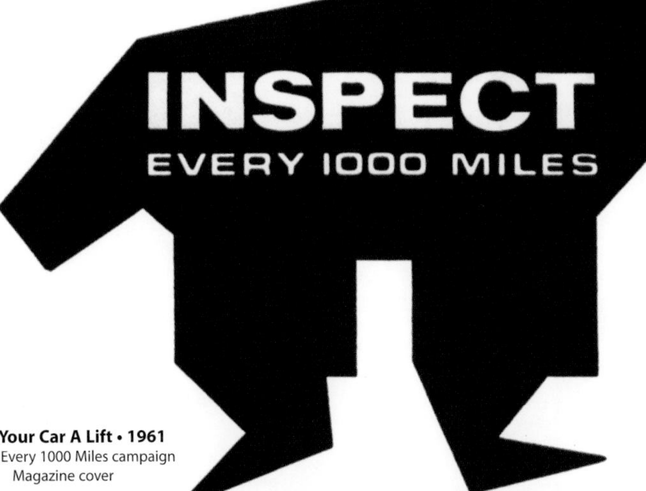

Give Your Car A Lift • 1961
Inspect Every 1000 Miles campaign
Magazine cover

For the last century the automobile industry has capitalized on remarkable creativity in advertising and has inspired an array of affable ad characters. Oil companies promoted the image of friendly gas station attendants and crisp auto mechanics. From grinning grillwork to the tire-bodied Michelin Man, car models and auto parts were recast as memorable mascots by their manufacturers.

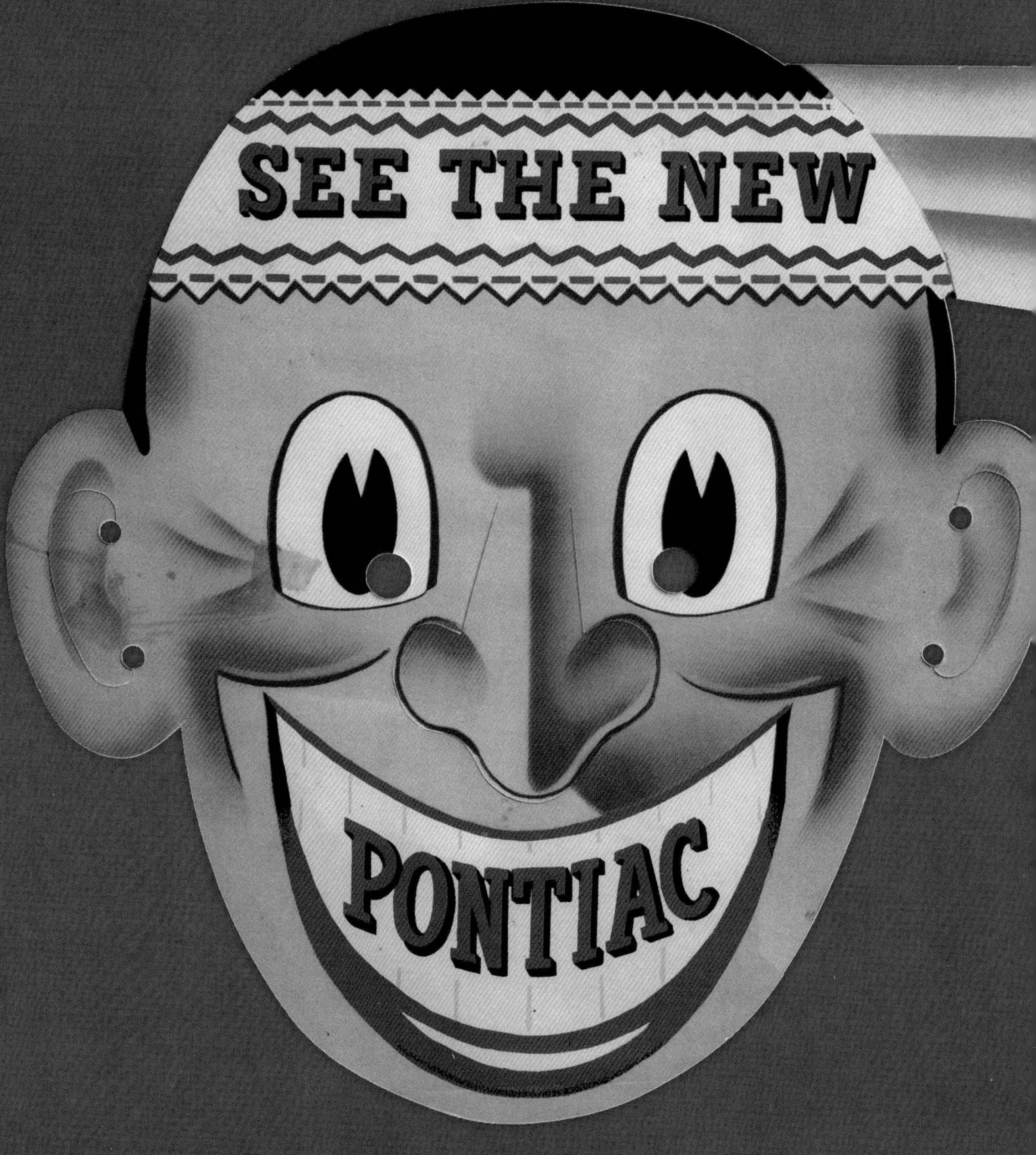

SEE THE NEW

PONTIAC

Chief Pontiac • c. 1941
Pontiac automobiles
Paper mask

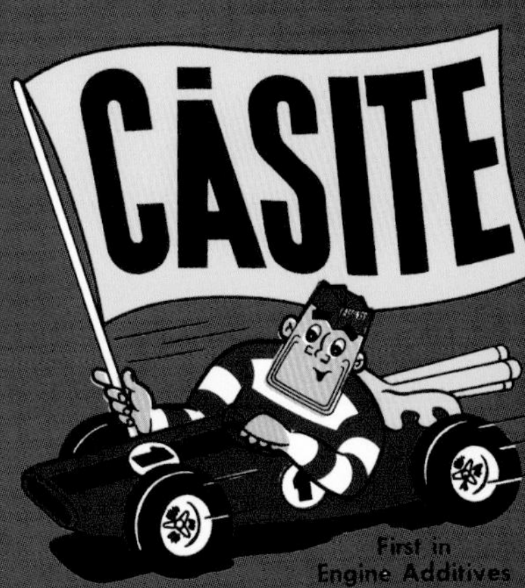

Hastings Man • c. 1958
Casite engine additives
Promotional sticker

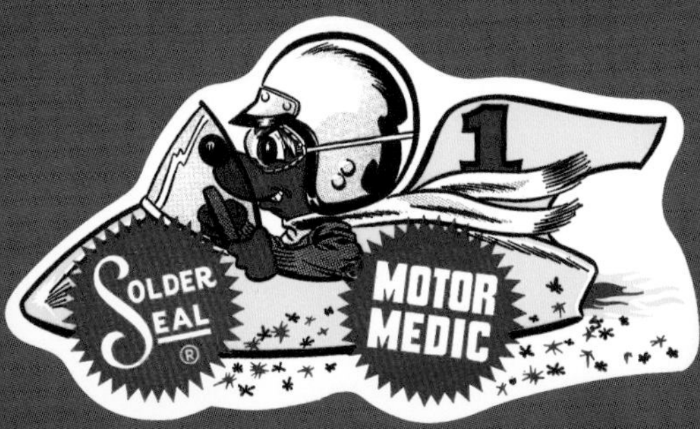

Motor Medic • c. 1969
Solder Seal motor oil
Promotional sticker

NGK
EXPO'70
OSAKA

Spark Boy • 1970
NGK spark plugs
Promotional sticker

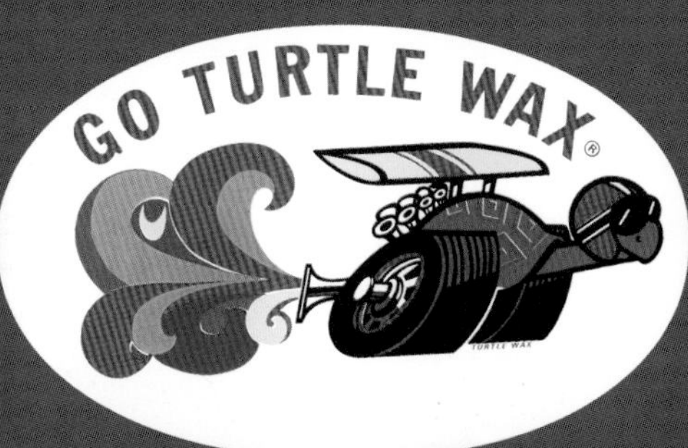

Tommy the Turtle • c. 1968
Turtle Wax car wax
Promotional sticker

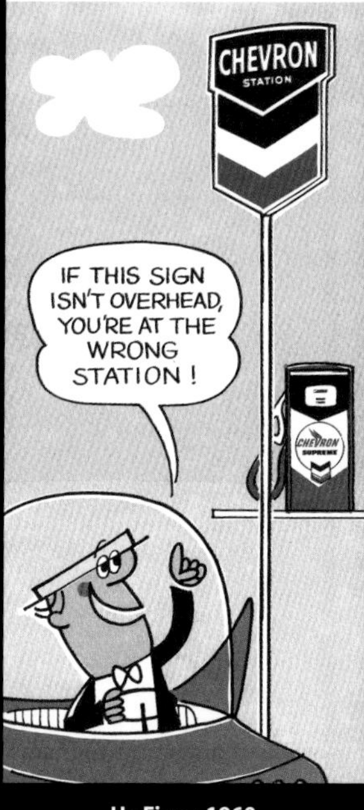

Hy Finn • 1960
Chevron gasoline
Road map

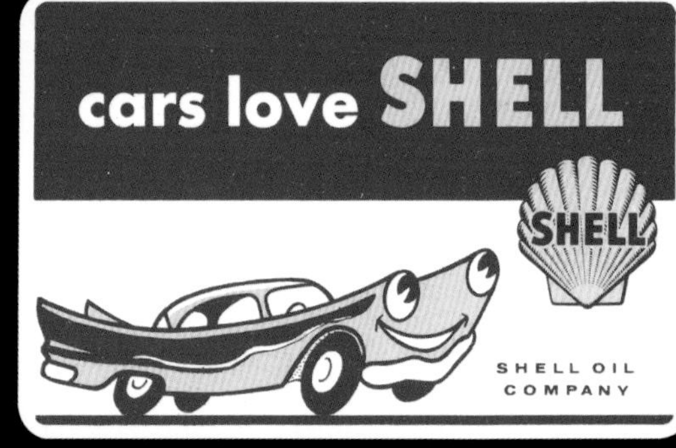

Cars Love Shell • 1960
Shell gasoline
Wallet calendar

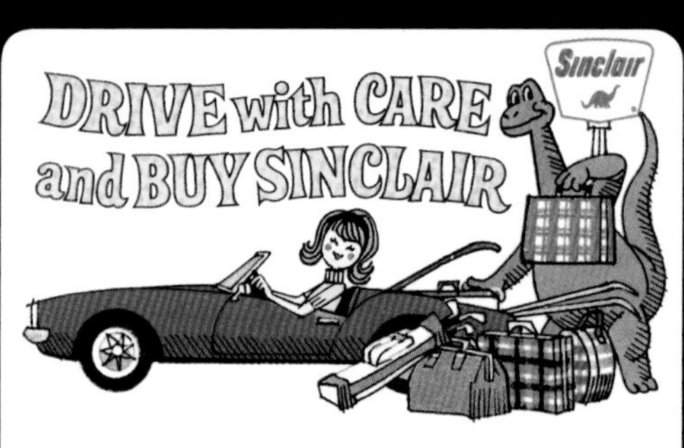

Dino • 1968
Sinclair gasoline
Wallet calendar

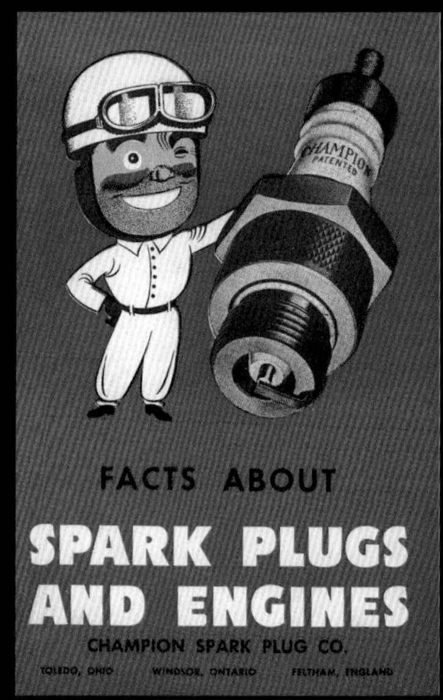

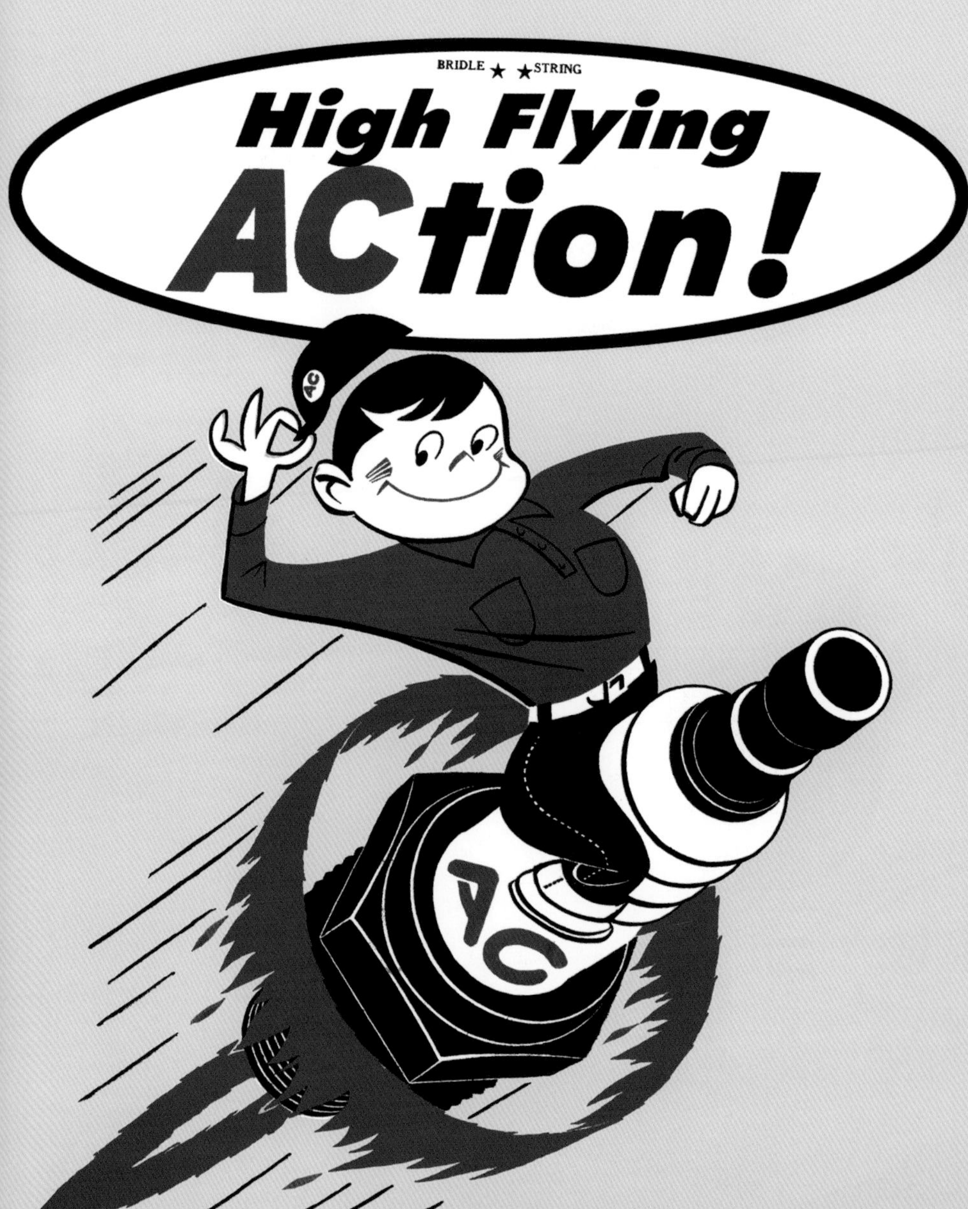

AC Boy • 1961
AC spark plugs
Promotional kite detail

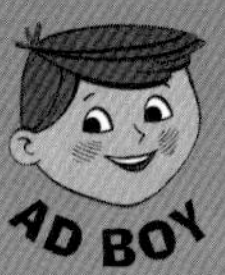

The late 1960s and early 70s saw a whole pack of sporty muscle cars, hatchbacks, and subcompacts with cool names and cartoon-inspired mascots. Plymouth's Road Runne was so-called after the popular television cartoon character and there was the AMC Gremlin and Dodge Demon, among others. The Demon was later renamed the Dart S in response to complaints from religious groups about the devil-with-pitchfork logo.

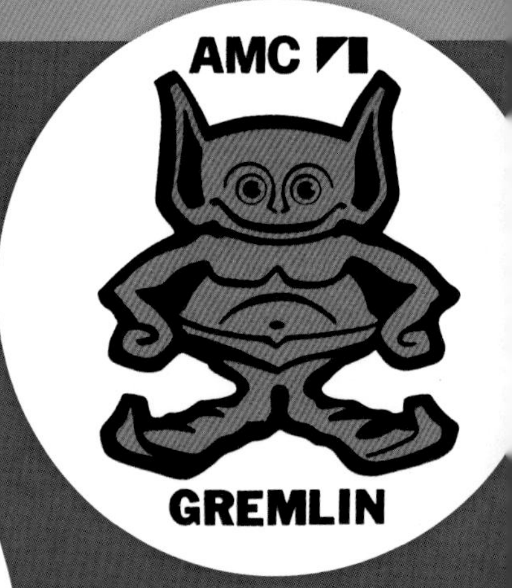

AMC
GREMLIN

Gremlin • c. 1970
AMC Gremlin
Pin-back button

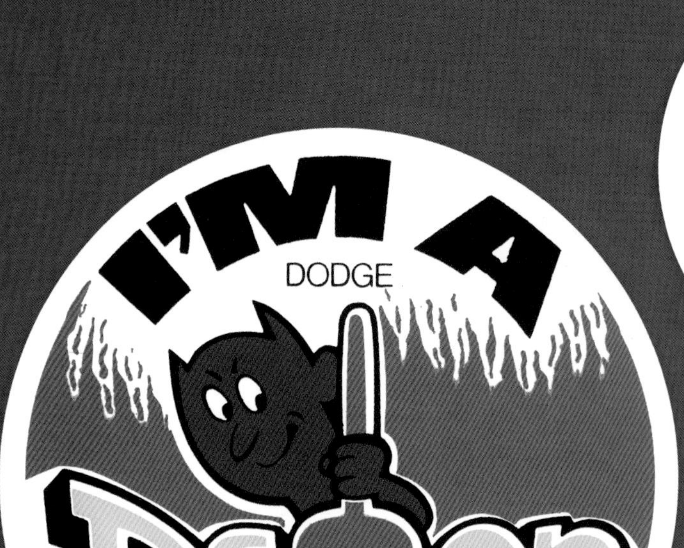

I'M A
DODGE
Demon
LOVER

Demon • 1972
Dodge Demon
Promotional sticker

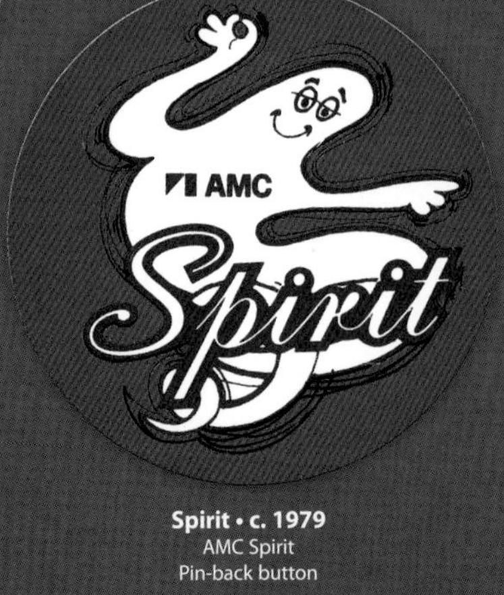

AMC
Spirit

Spirit • c. 1979
AMC Spirit
Pin-back button

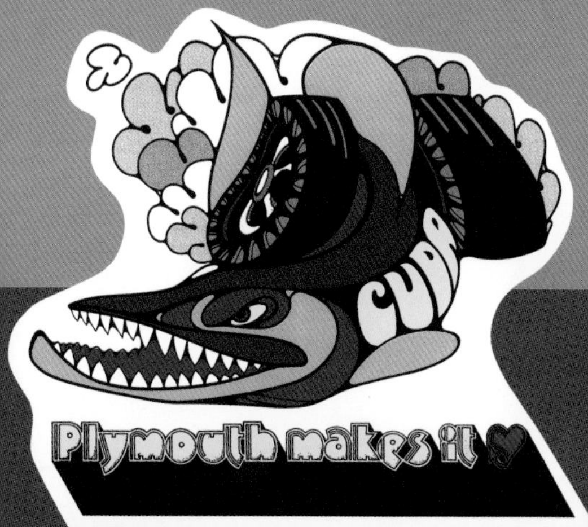

Cuda • c. 1970
Plymouth Cuda
Promotional sticker

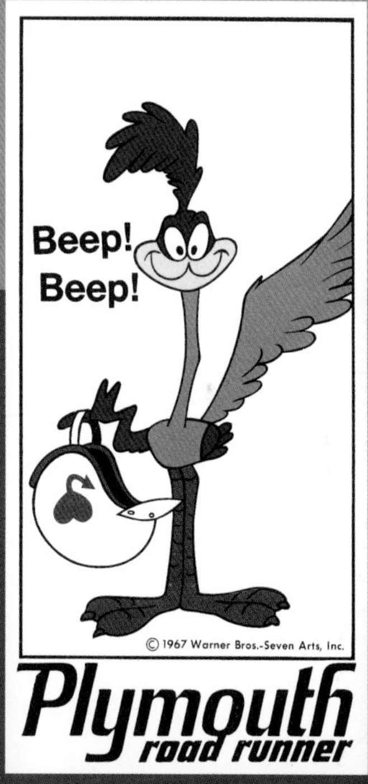

Road Runner • 1967
Plymouth Road Runner
Promotional sticker

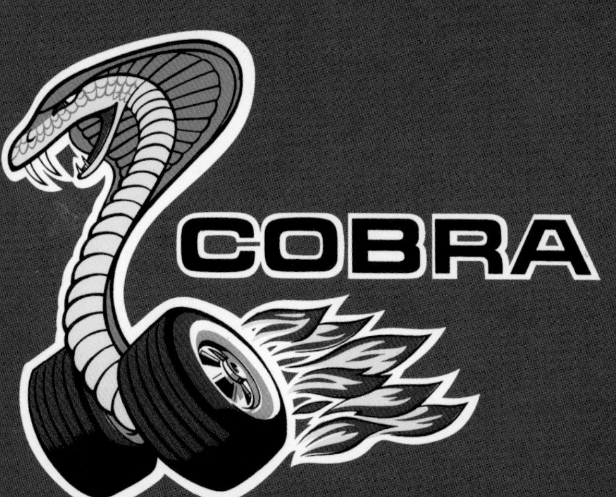

Cobra • c. 1968
Shelby Cobra
Water decal

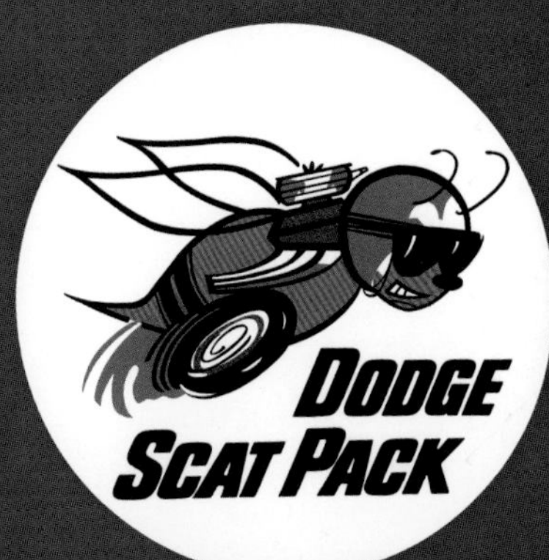

Scat Pack • 1969
Dodge Scat Pack
Water decal

Going all out—
or feeling all in?

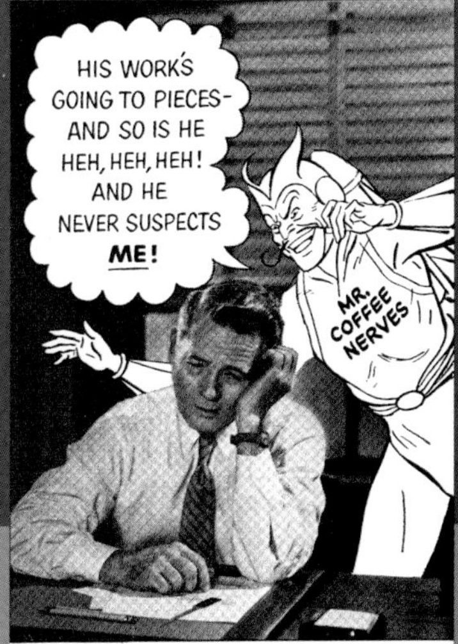

SWITCH TO POSTUM
Sleep better—feel better!

No need to put up with the troubles "Mr. Coffee Nerves" can bring. If the caffein in coffee or tea keeps you restless all night, listless all day, simply SWITCH TO CAFFEIN-FREE POSTUM. While many people can handle caffein, others—perhaps *you*—suffer sleepless nights, upset nerves, indigestion. So switch to delicious INSTANT POSTUM—and *sleep!* Then see if you don't do better—look and feel like a million! And cup for cup, POSTUM costs only about 1/3 as much as coffee. That's INSTANT POSTUM—made instantly in your cup!

A Product of General Foods

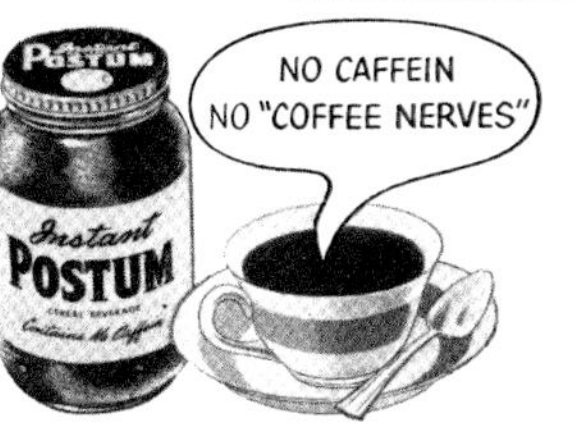

Mr. Coffee Nerves • 1954
Instant Postum hot beverage
Magazine ad

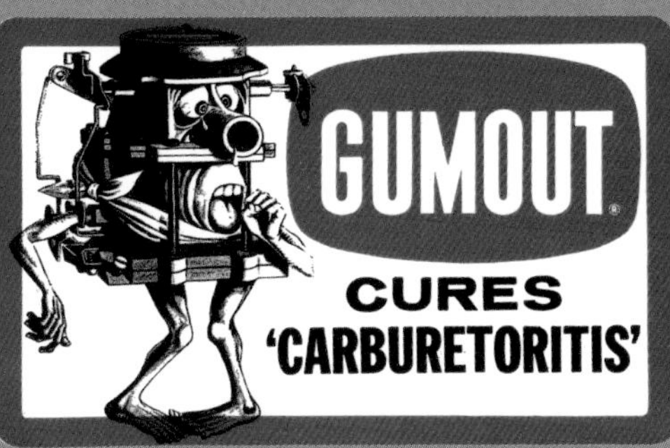

Carburetoritis • c. 1971
Gumout fuel additives
Promotional sticker

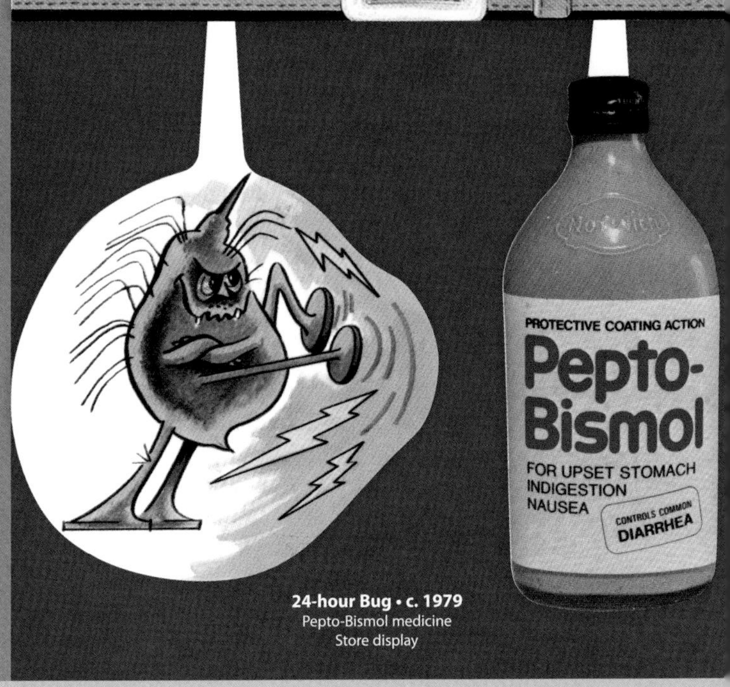

24-hour Bug • c. 1979
Pepto-Bismol medicine
Store display

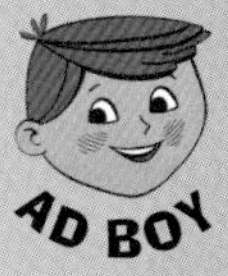

They get on your nerves, make your carburetor choke, your stomach ache, and your toaster break. They are the Nasties: tricksters, trouble-makers, and tormentors that torture innocent consumers. At the same time, these anti-hero icons underscored the special product that could repair the problem, soothe your stress, and make your household havoc-free.

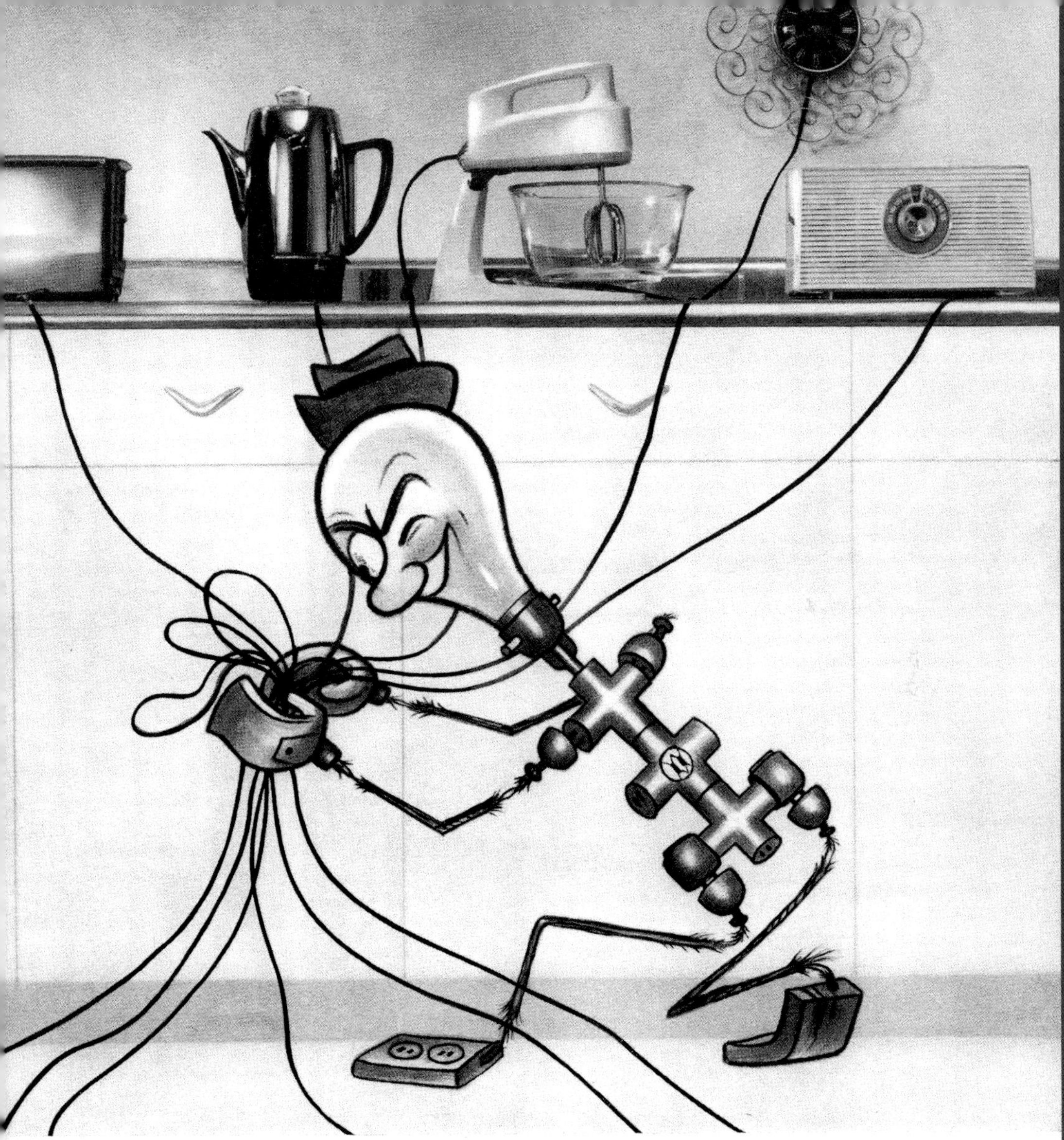

Don't let "Skimpy Wiring" tie up your kitchen

This could never happen in a Medallion Home. Yet many houses, old and new, are still plagued by Skimpy Wiring.

With his weak, undersized wires and overloaded circuits, Skimpy can slow down even the finest appliances . . . keep you from installing new ones. With Skimpy around, you just can't *live better electrically*.

So to bring your whole house up to modern Medallion standards, replace Skimpy Wiring with full-powered *copper* wiring. Ask an electrical contractor or power company man to check your HOUSEPOWER today.

Make sure any home you build, buy or rent bears the Medallion Home symbol – sign of *no* Skimpy Wiring!

Skimpy Wiring • 1959
Kennecott copper wire
Magazine ad

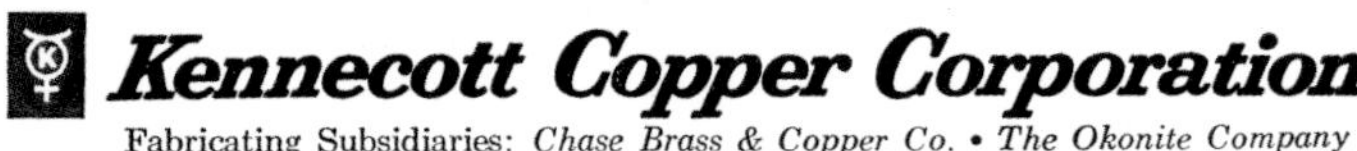

Blacky Carbon • 1955
Bardahl motor oil
Store poster

BEWARE
Blacky Carbon
Call For
BARDAHL
ADD IT TO YOUR MOTOR OIL

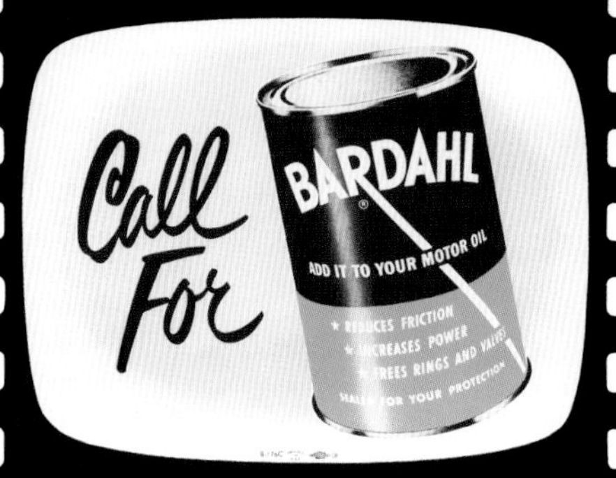

Dirty Sludge • 1955
Bardahl motor oil
Store poster

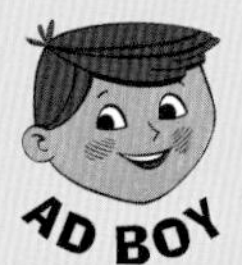

Some companies pitted their Nasties against a heroic foil or Nemesis, often personifie by a superhero or private investigator. The gang of Blacky Carbon, Dirty Sludge, Stick Valves, and Gummy Rings was thwarted by the engine oil grime-fighter, Bardahl. The Raid Bugs met their match with Captain Raid. The Creeping Pound was trailed by the Ry-Krisp Weight-Watcher, and tooth decay was vanquished by Colgate's Tuffy Tooth.

Sticky Valves • 1955
Bardahl motor oil
Store poster

BEWARE
Sticky Valves

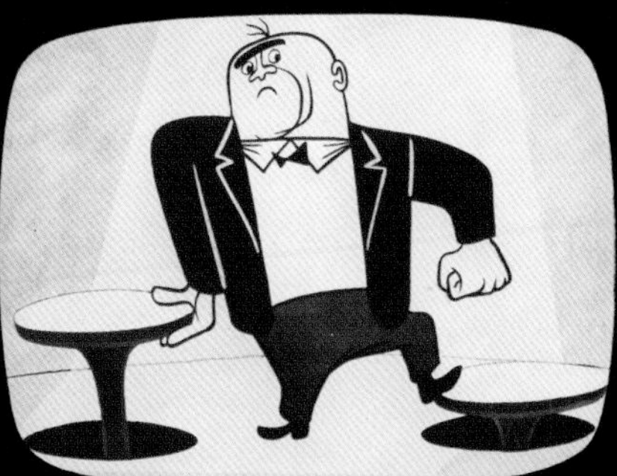

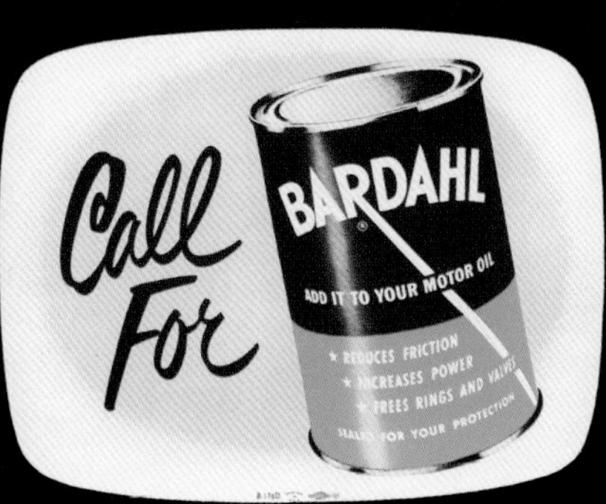

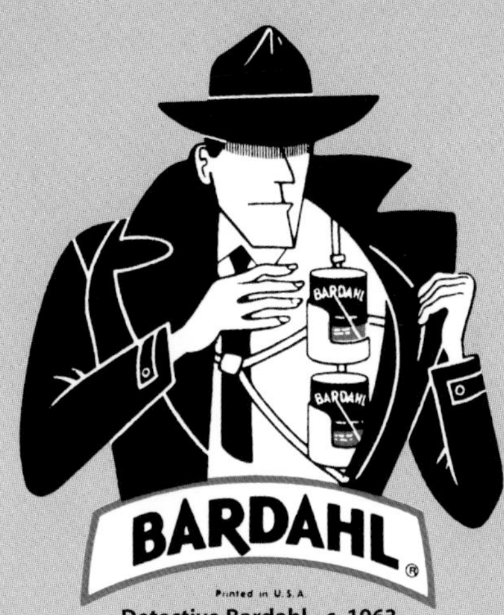

Detective Bardahl • c. 1963
Bardahl motor oil
Water decal

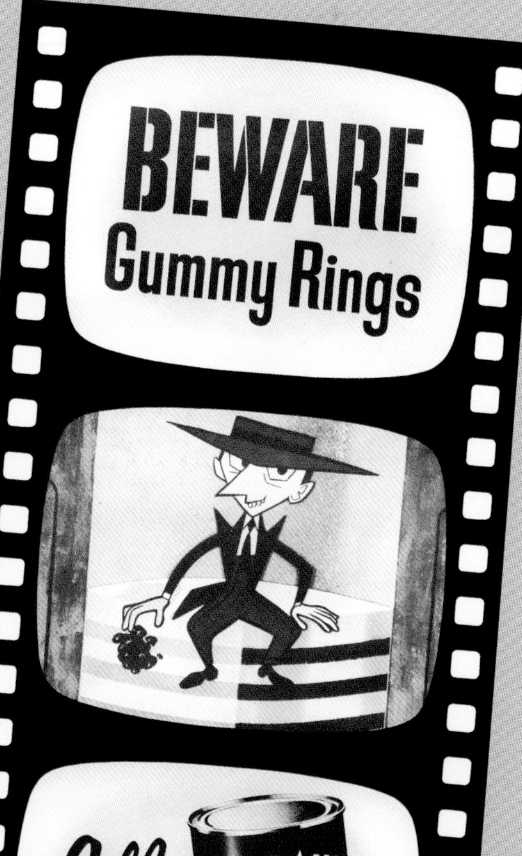

Gummy Rings • 1955
Bardahl motor oil
Store poster

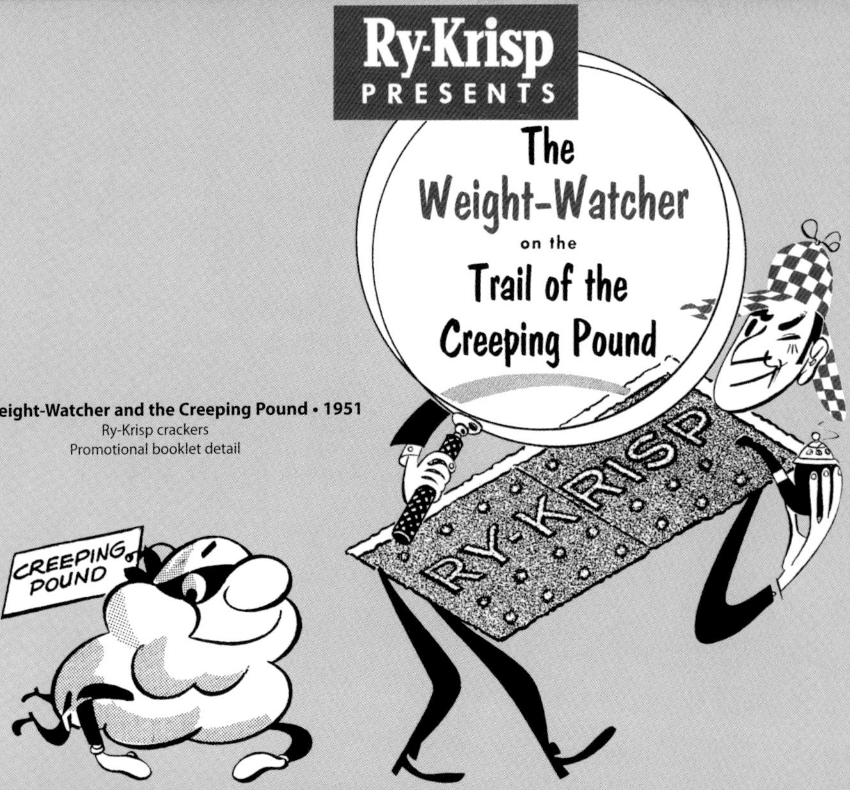

Ry-Krisp
PRESENTS

The Weight-Watcher on the Trail of the Creeping Pound

CREEPING POUND

RY-KRISP

The Weight-Watcher and the Creeping Pound • 1951
Ry-Krisp crackers
Promotional booklet detail

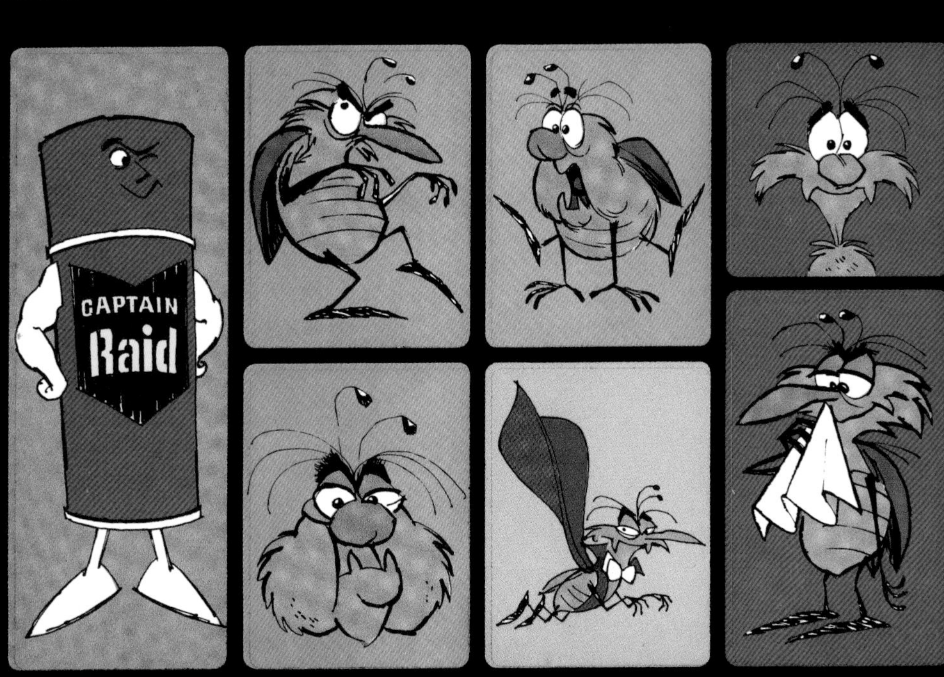

Captain Raid and the Raid Bugs • c. 1977
Raid insecticide
Promotional stickers

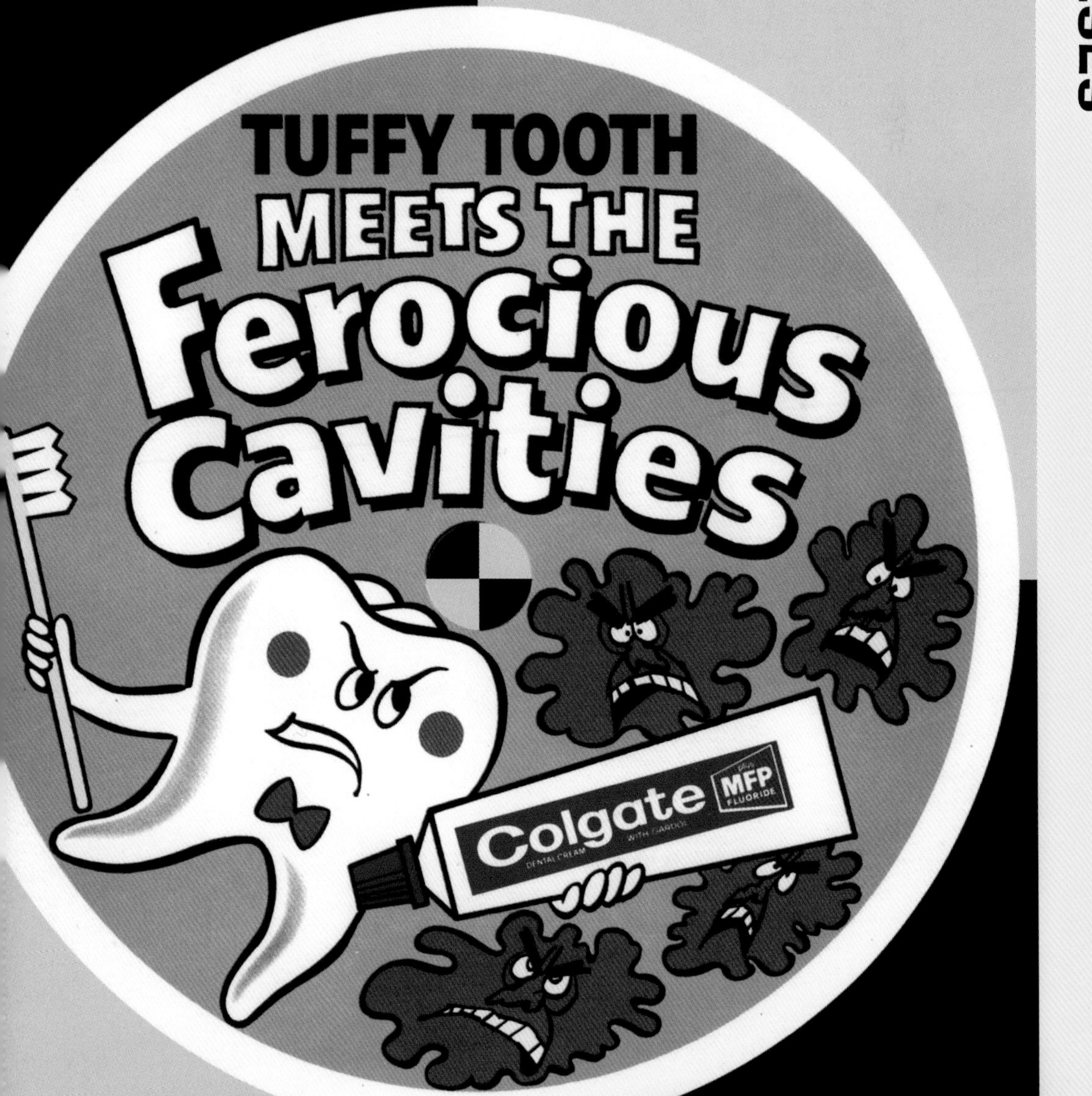

TUFFY TOOTH
MEETS THE
Ferocious
Cavities

Colgate
MFP FLUORIDE

Tuffy Tooth and the Ferocious Cavities • 1969
Colgate toothpaste
Phonograph record

Super Nut • c. 1971
Luden's Super Nut bar
Pin-back badge

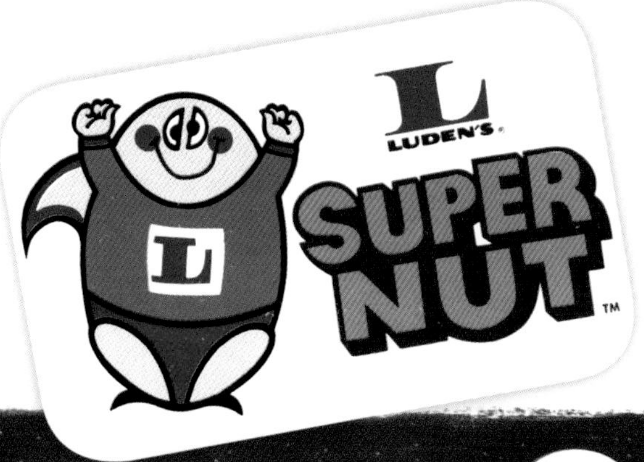

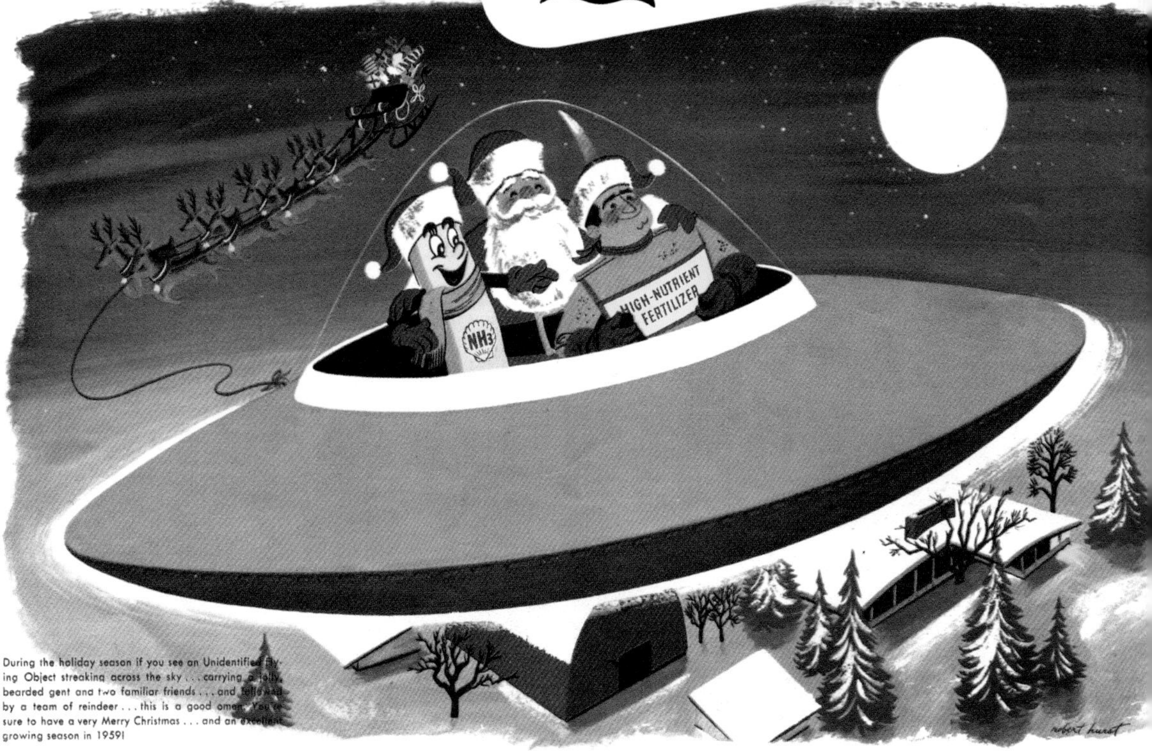

During the holiday season if you see an Unidentified Fly-ing Object streaking across the sky . . . carrying [illegible] bearded gent and two familiar friends . . . and [illegible] by a team of reindeer . . . this is a good [illegible] sure to have a very Merry Christmas . . . and an [illegible] growing season in 1959!

NH3 and High-Nutrient Fertilizer Man • 1958
Shell fertilizers
Promotional calendar detail

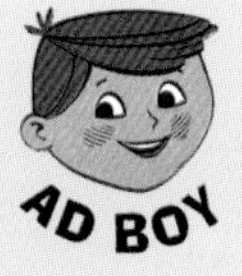

America's fascination with westerns, outer space, and private eyes inspired a long list similarly themed ad characters throughout the 1950s and 60s. Comic book superherc also made their mark. The Cheerio Kid could be found flexing his cereal-fortified bice while rescuing his girlfriend Sue. Dress an otherwise mundane product or legume in cape or a costume and suddenly you had Super Nut or High-Nutrient Fertilizer Man.

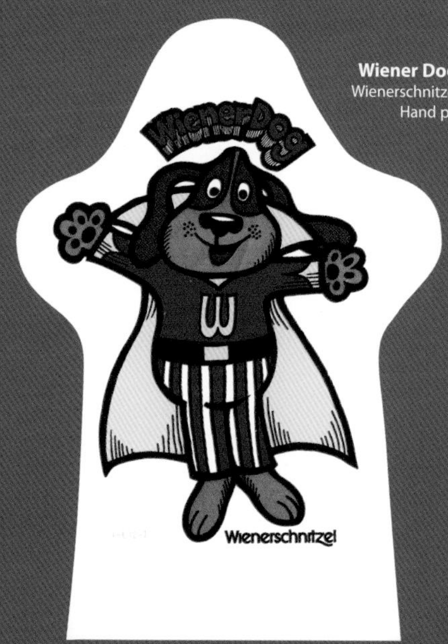

Wiener Dog • c. 1977
Wienerschnitzel restaurants
Hand puppet

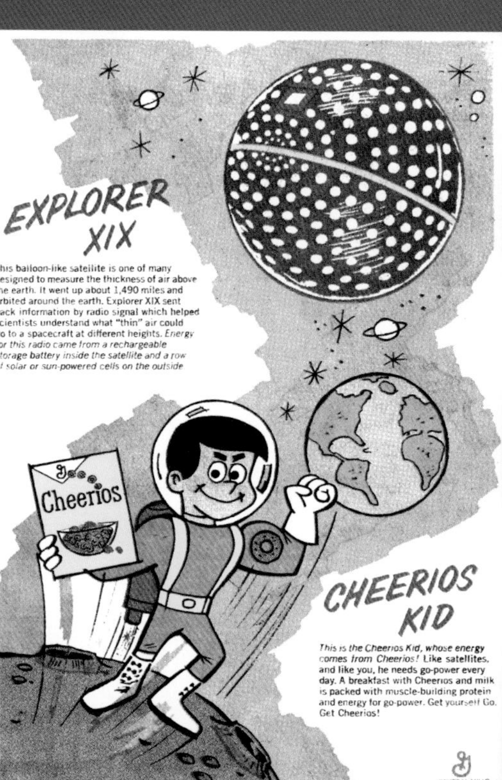

Cheerios Kid • 1968
Cheerios cereal
Comic book ad

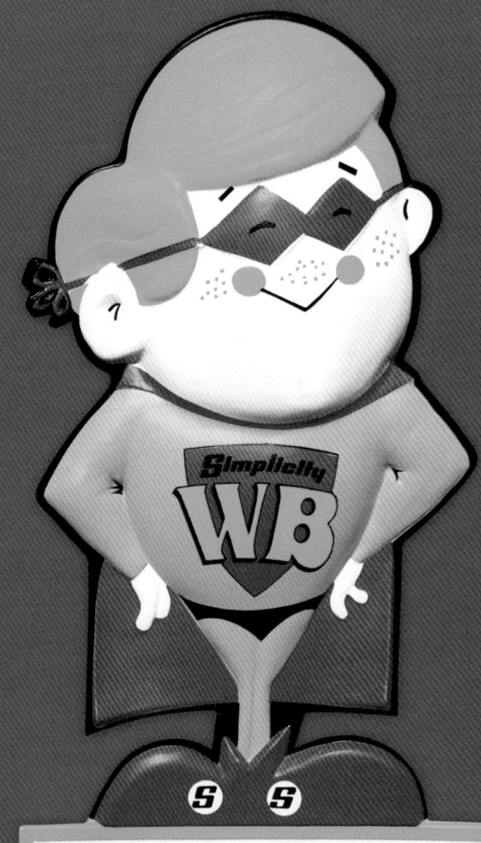

Wonder Boy • c. 1971
Simplicity lawn mowers
Store display

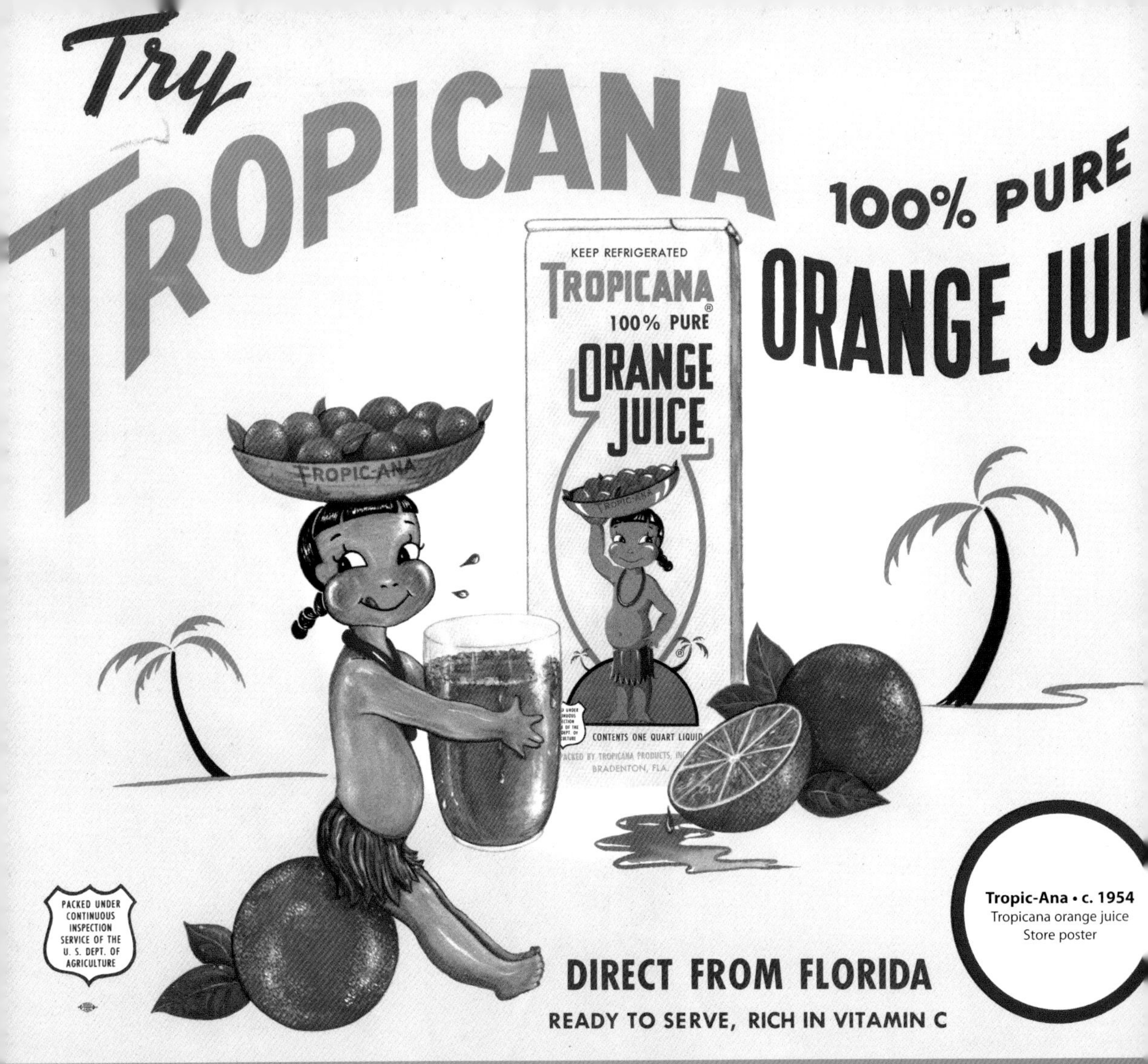

Try
TROPICANA
100% PURE
ORANGE JUI

KEEP REFRIGERATED
TROPICANA
100% PURE
ORANGE
JUICE
CONTENTS ONE QUART LIQUID
BRADENTON, FLA.

TROPIC-ANA

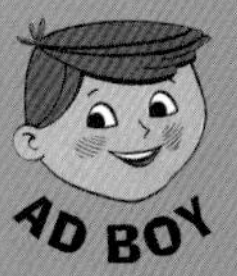

DIRECT FROM FLORIDA
READY TO SERVE, RICH IN VITAMIN C

Tropic-Ana • c. 1954
Tropicana orange juice
Store poster

AD BOY

Advances in food packaging, storage, and delivery led to a host of new, once-perishable products. Orange juice and frozen juice concentrates were two that led the way. Manufacturers often chose wholesome, youthful, even juvenile ad characters such as Teddy Snow Crop and the Minute Maid to promote their technological breakthrough Once the center of attention on every Tropicana juice carton, Tropic-Ana currently exi solely as a subject of historic interest on the company's website.

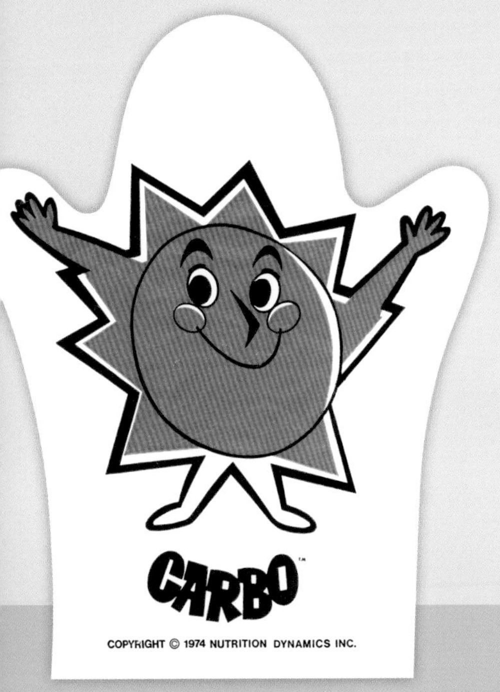

Carbo • 1974
Carbo drink
Hand puppet

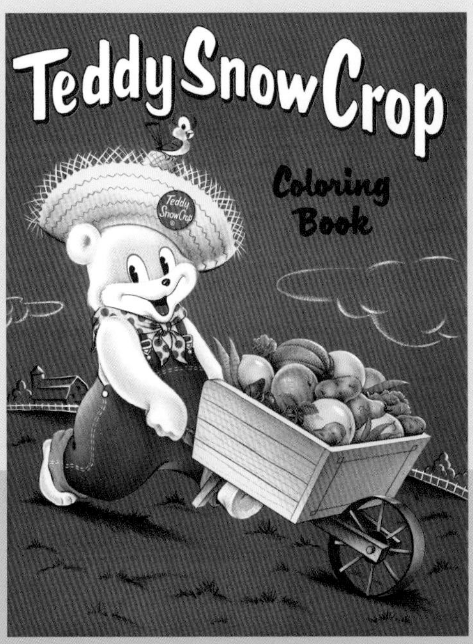

Teddy Snow Crop • 1956
Snow Crop frozen orange juice
Coloring book cover

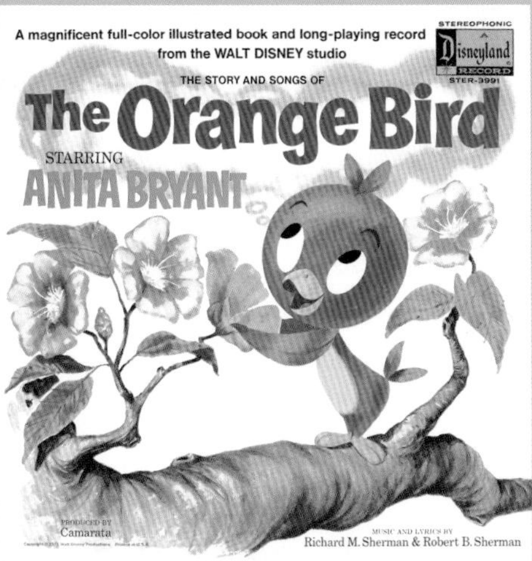

The Orange Bird • 1971
Disneyland record
Record album cover

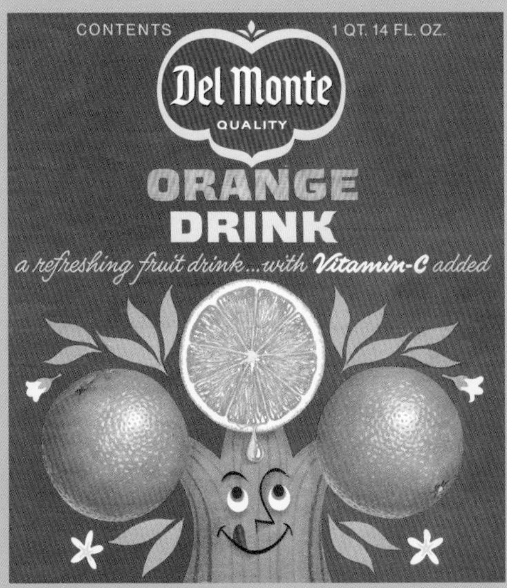

Orange Tree • c. 1968
Del Monte orange drink
Can label

Ferocious Lion • c. 1970
Ferocious Lion orange drink
Carton front

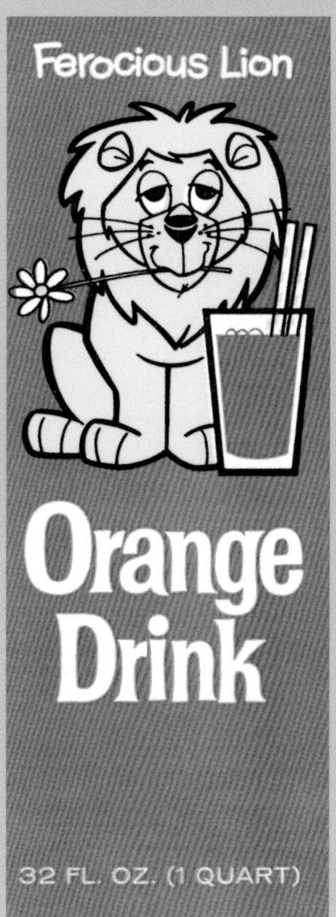

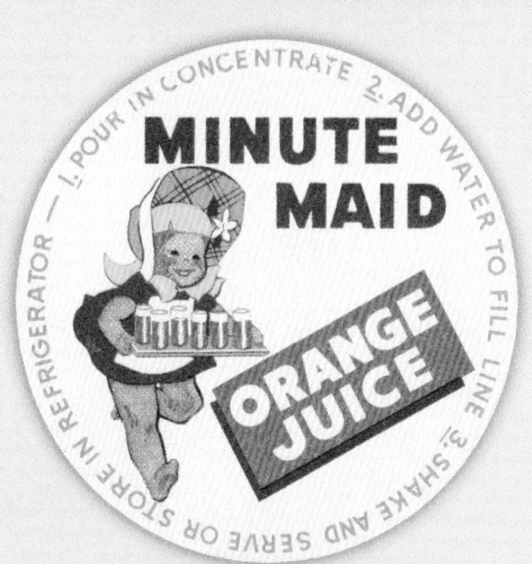

Minute Maid • c. 1955
Minute Maid orange juice
Container lid

BRIGH
ORANG
FLAVO

rich and true
in taste

FANTA:
FROM THE SAME COMPANY THAT BOTTLES COCA-COL

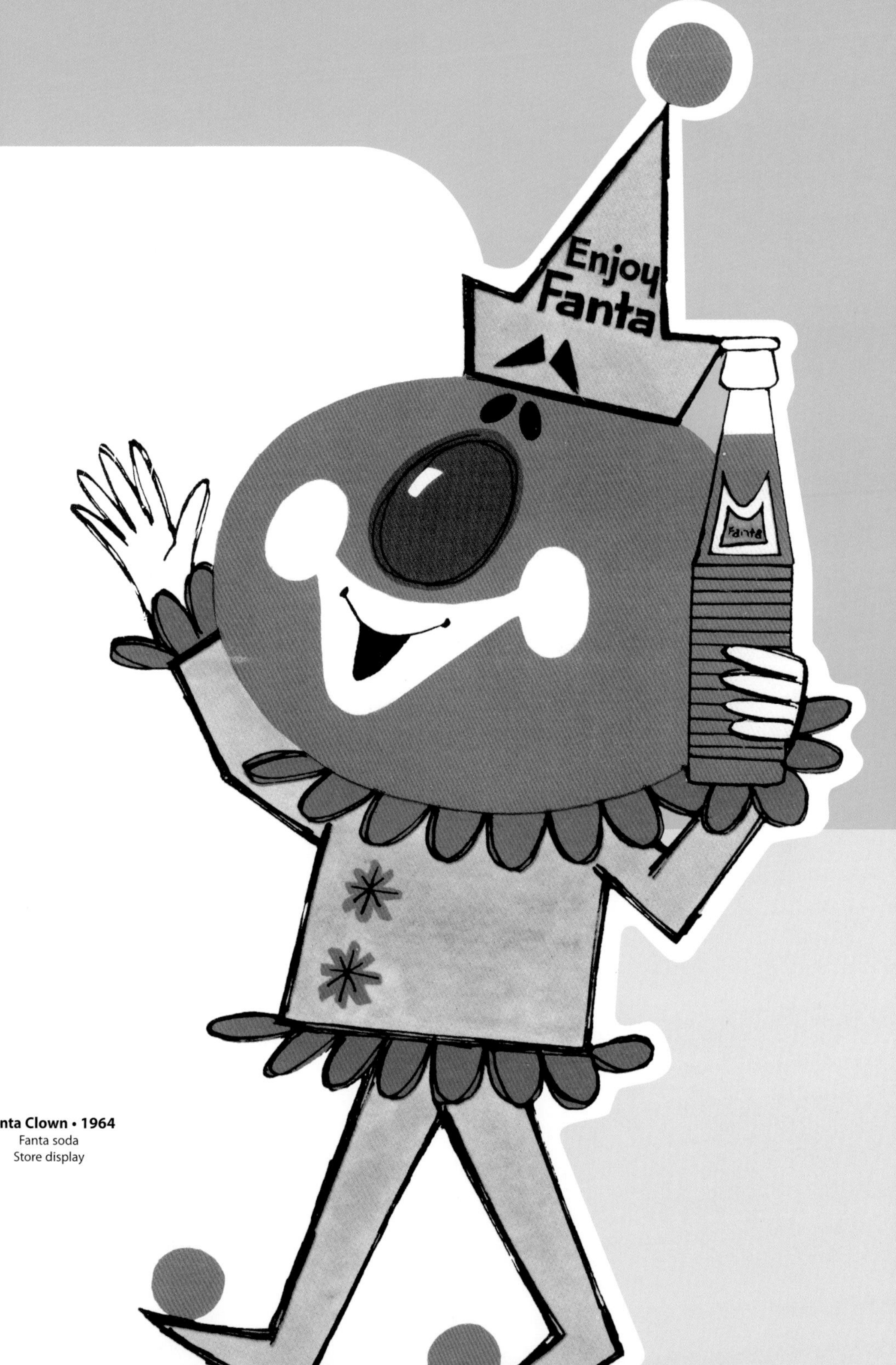

Fanta Clown • 1964
Fanta soda
Store display

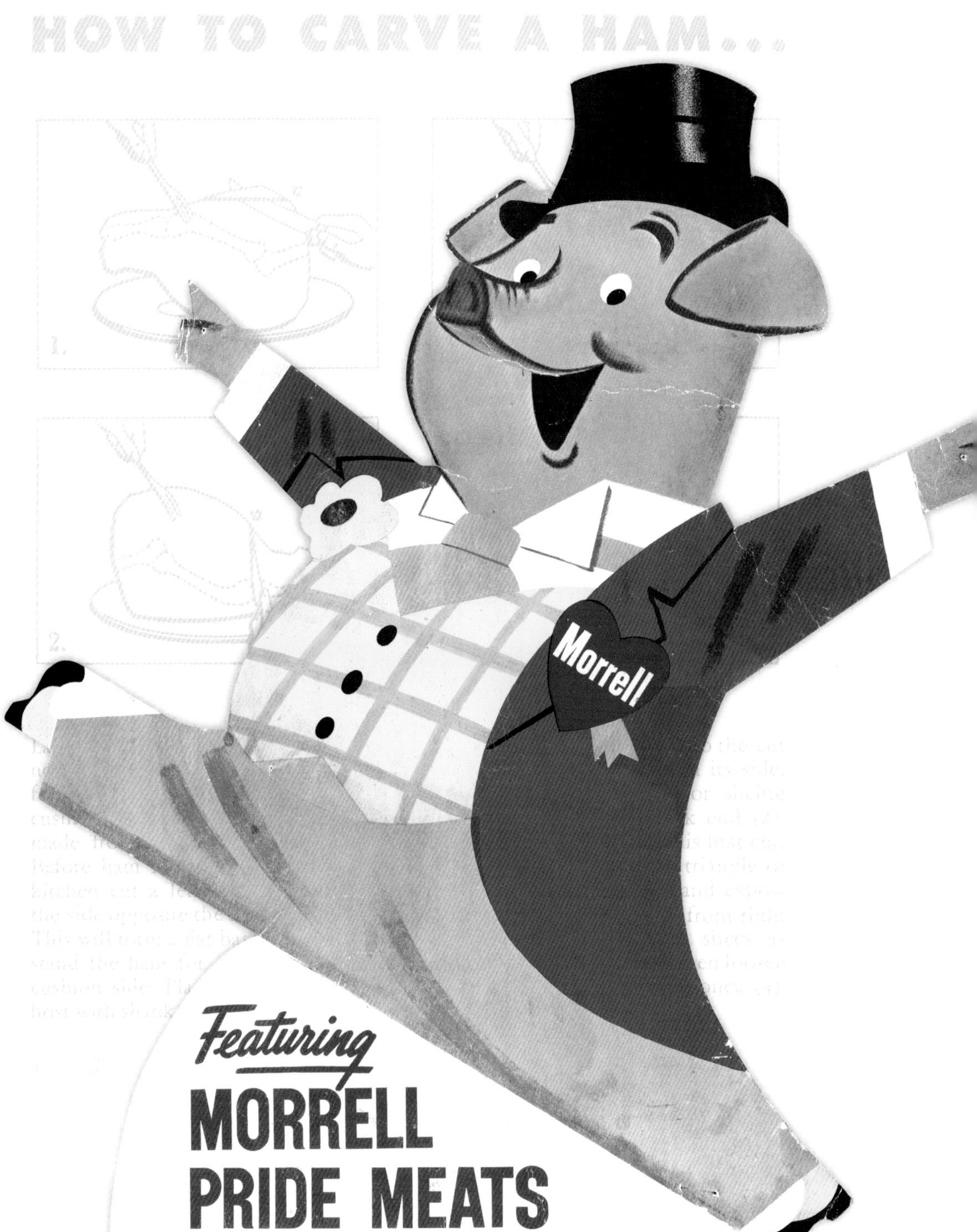

HOW TO CARVE A HAM...

Morrell

Featuring

MORRELL
PRIDE MEATS

Mr. Ham • c. 1952
Morrell meats
Store sign

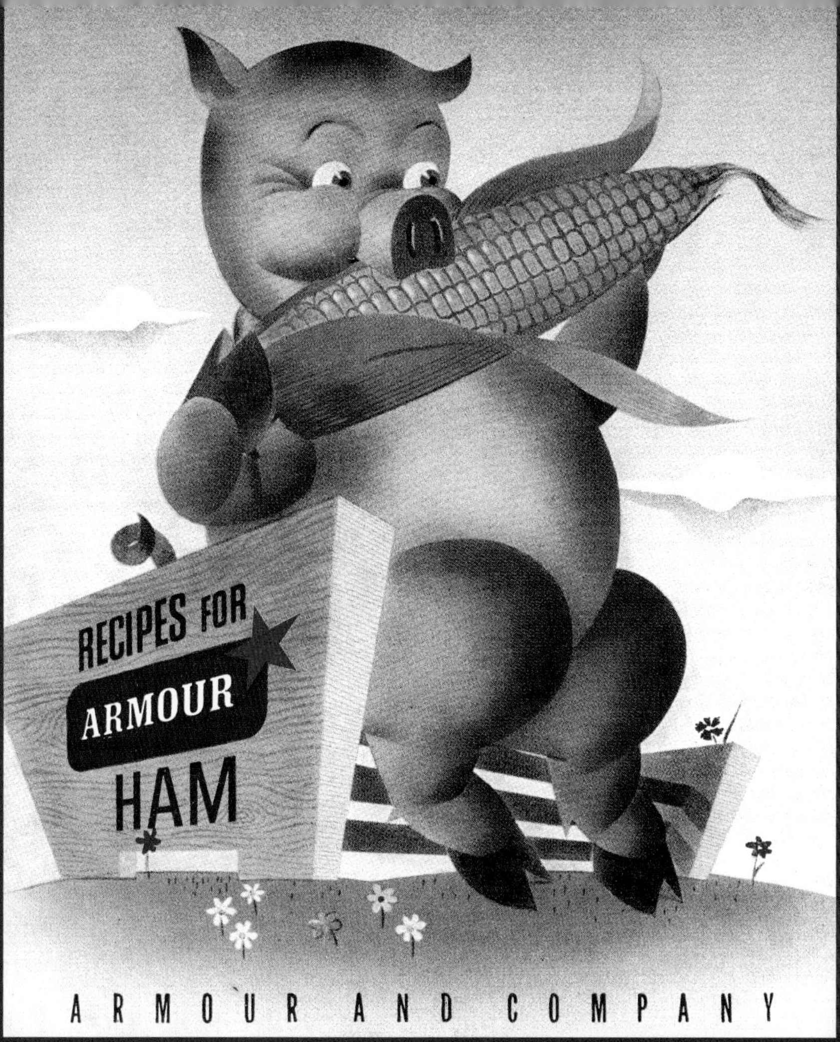

RECIPES FOR
ARMOUR
HAM
ARMOUR AND COMPANY

Armour Pig • c. 1958
Armour ham
Recipe booklet

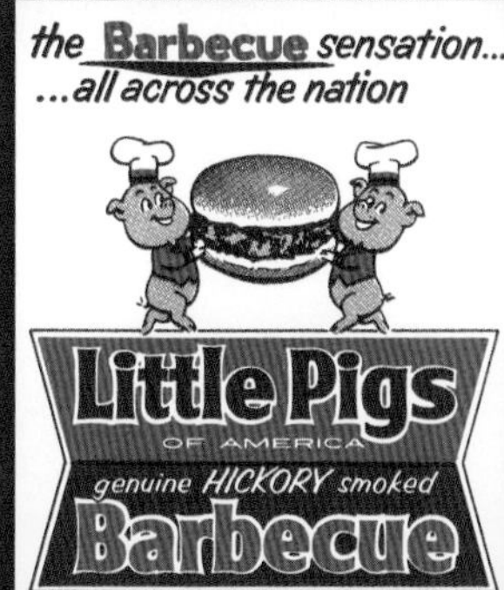

Little Pigs • c. 1967
Little Pigs restaurants
Matchbook cover

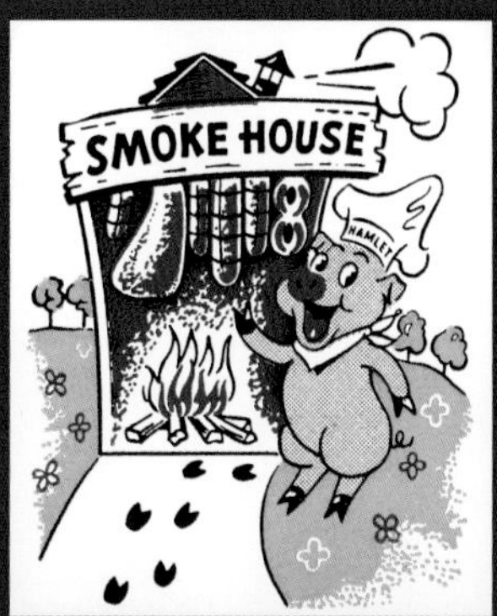

Hamlet • c. 1961
Sugardale meats
Matchbook cover

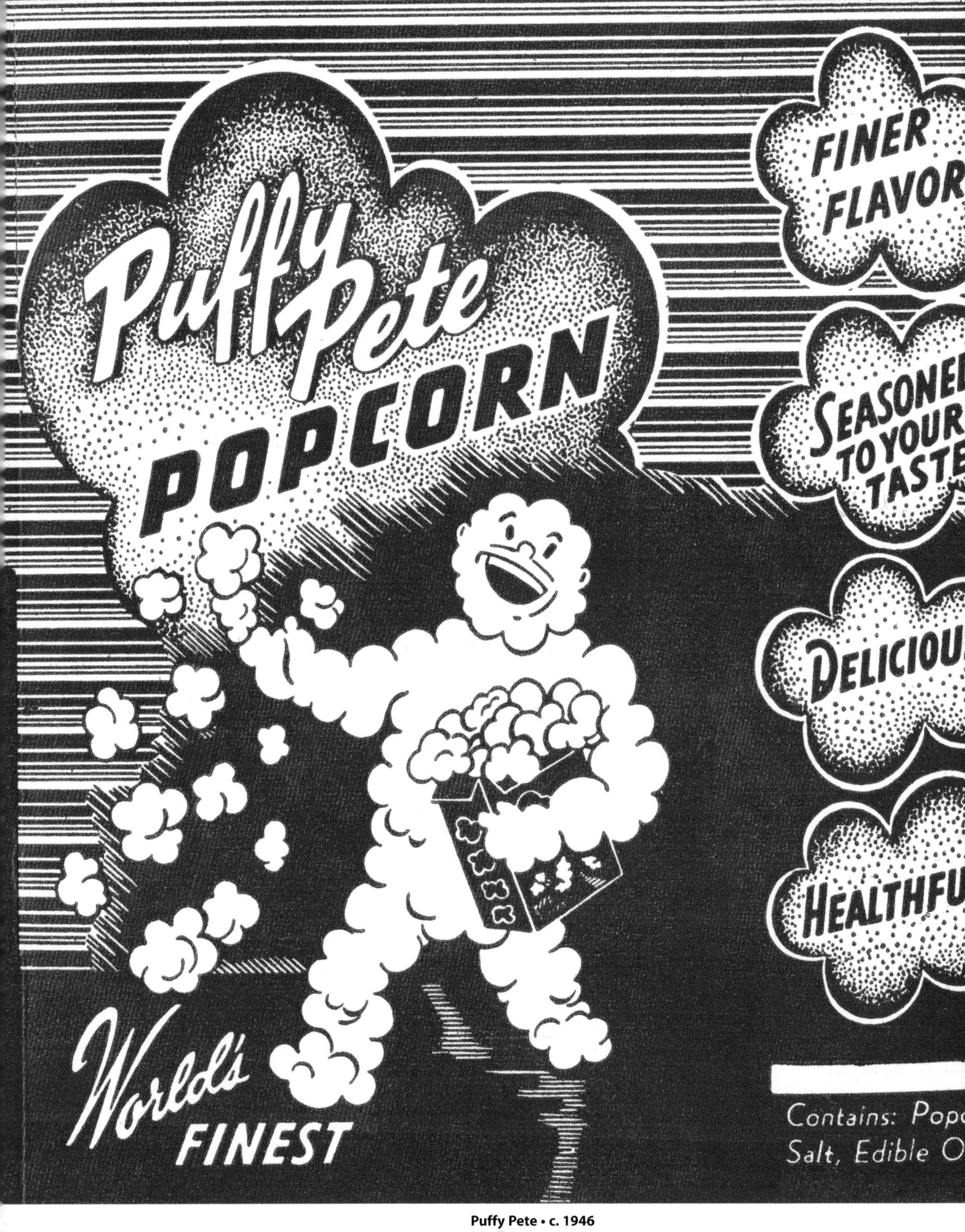

Puffy Pete • c. 1946
Puffy Pete popcorn
Box front

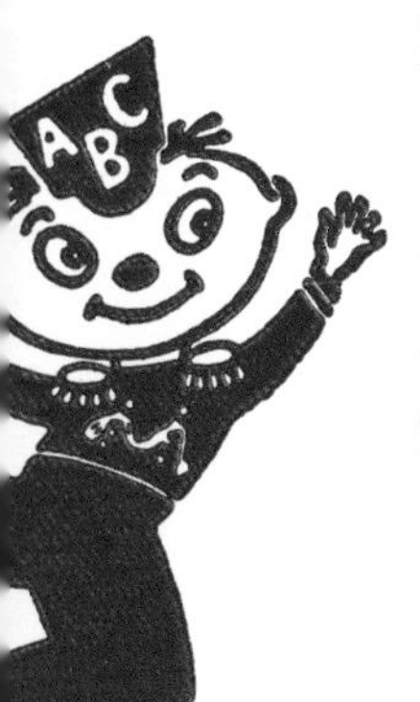

Mr.
e-lish

OP
ORN

REDIENTS
rn, Salt, Edible Oil,
al and Artificial Col-
, Flavoring

ABC

Mr.
Dee-lish

POP
CORN

fresh
crispy
so good

15¢

Mr. Dee-lish • c. 1950
Mr. Dee-lish popcorn
Box front

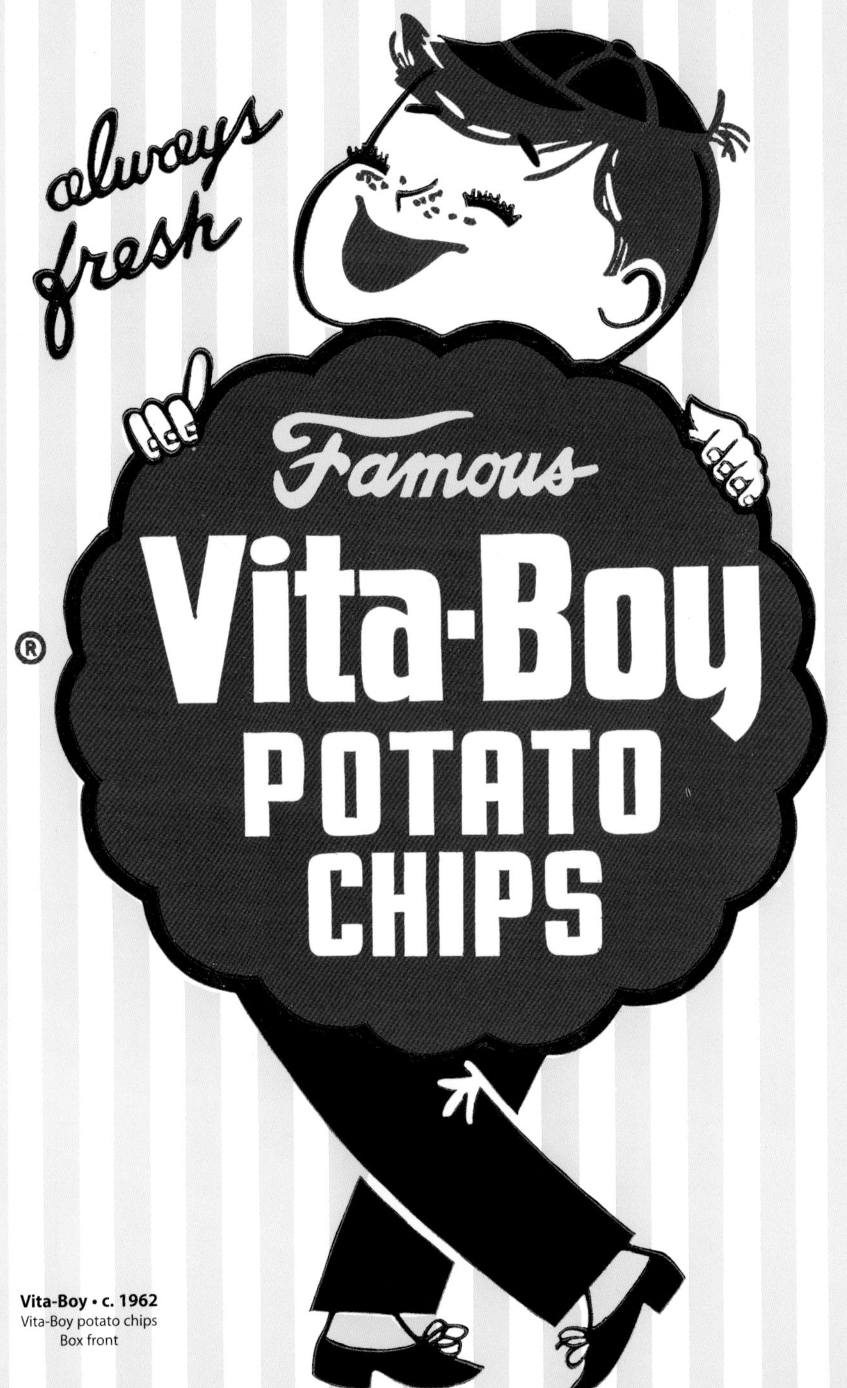

Vita-Boy • c. 1962
Vita-Boy potato chips
Box front

Lay's Potato • 1961
Lay's potato chips
Football schedule detail

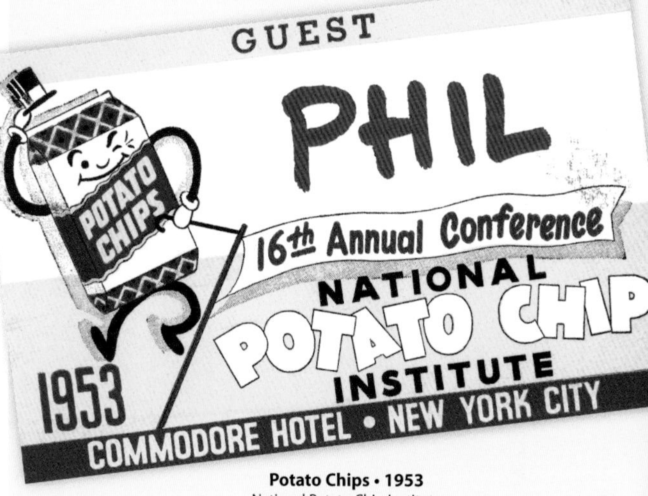

Potato Chips • 1953
National Potato Chip Institute
Guest badge

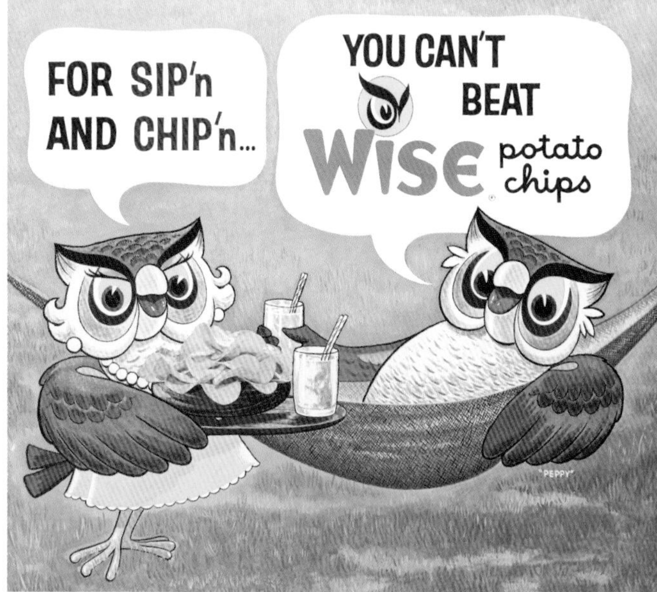

Peppy • c. 1955
Wise potato chips
Store sign

HARD BUMPS HURT ME

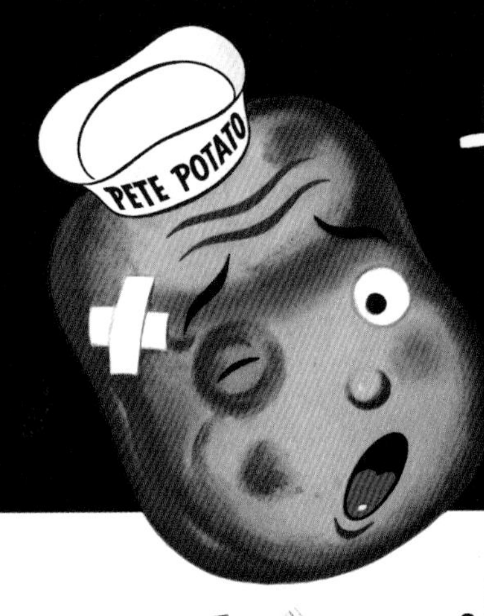

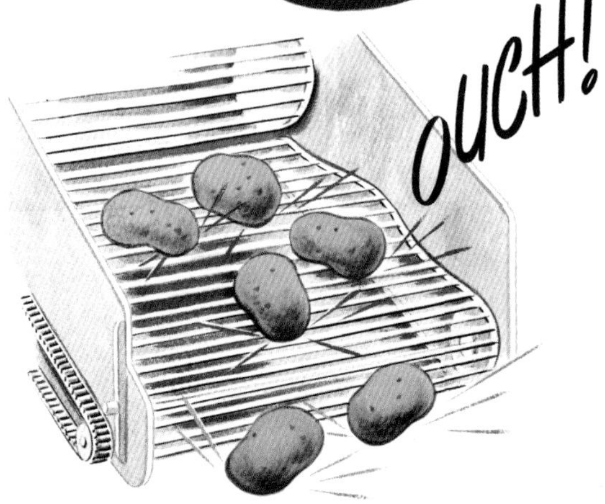

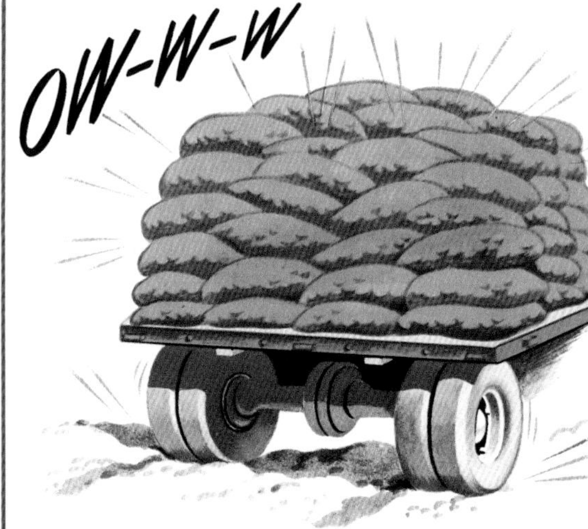

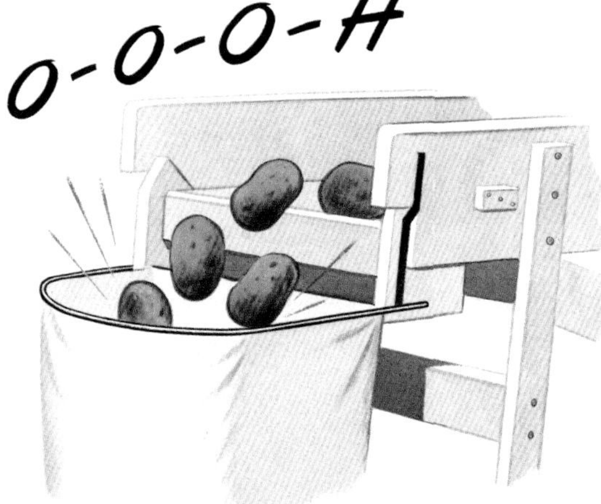

Handle Me Easy, Please

PETE POTATO

Pete Potato • c. 1961
National Potato Chip Institute
Promotional poster

DISTRIBUTED BY RESEARCH DEPARTMENT OF THE

NATIONAL POTATO CHIP INSTITUTE

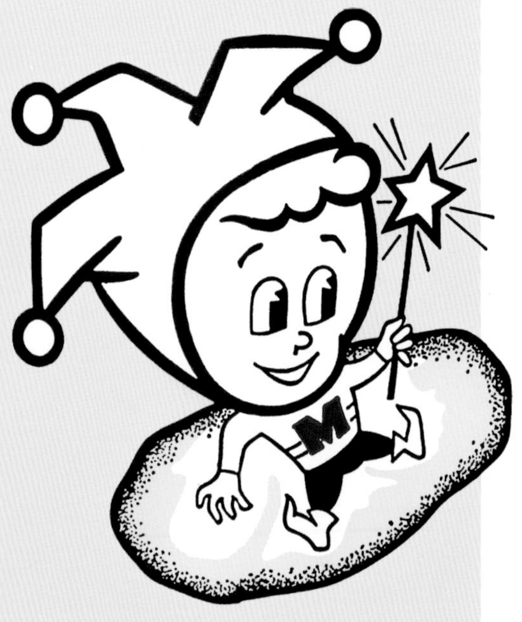

Moore's Boy • c. 1964
Moore's potato chips
Container detail

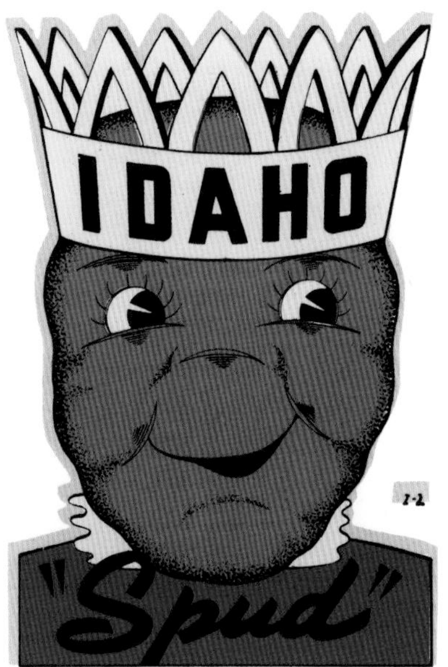

Spud • c. 1954
State of Idaho
Water decal

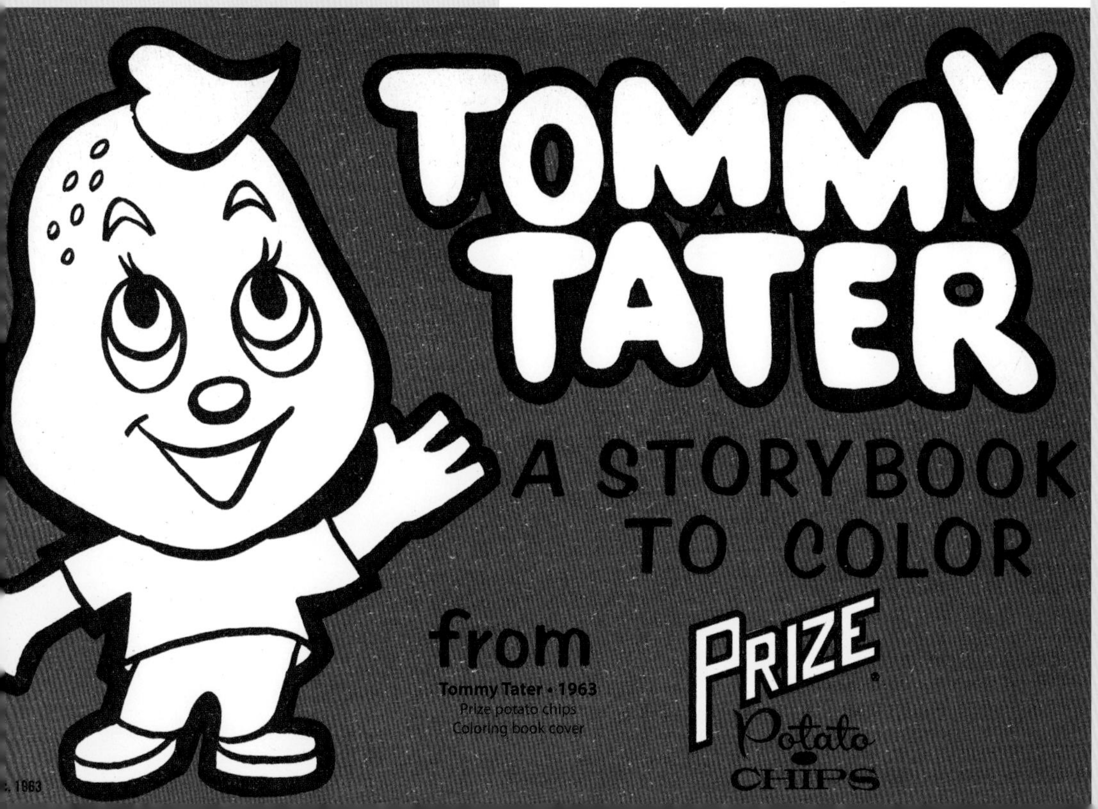

TOMMY
TATER
A STORYBOOK
TO COLOR
from
PRIZE
Potato
CHIPS

Tommy Tater • 1963
Prize potato chips
Coloring book cover

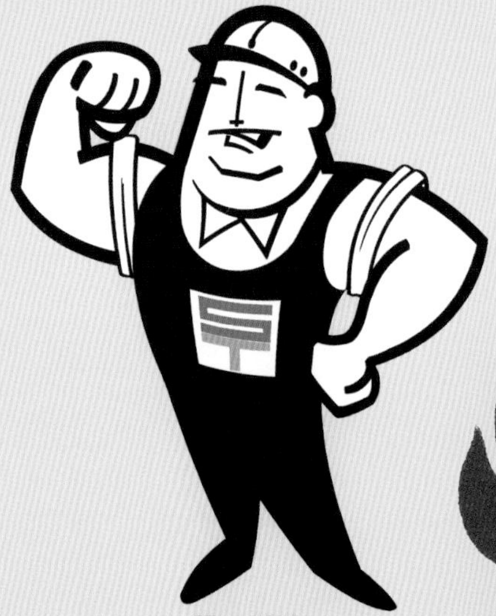

ST • c. 1965
Unknown
Company sign

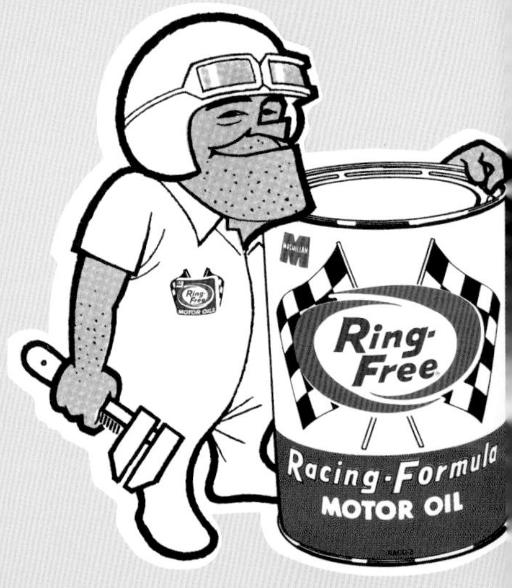

Ring-Free Mechanic • 1969
Ring-Free motor oil
Promotional sticker

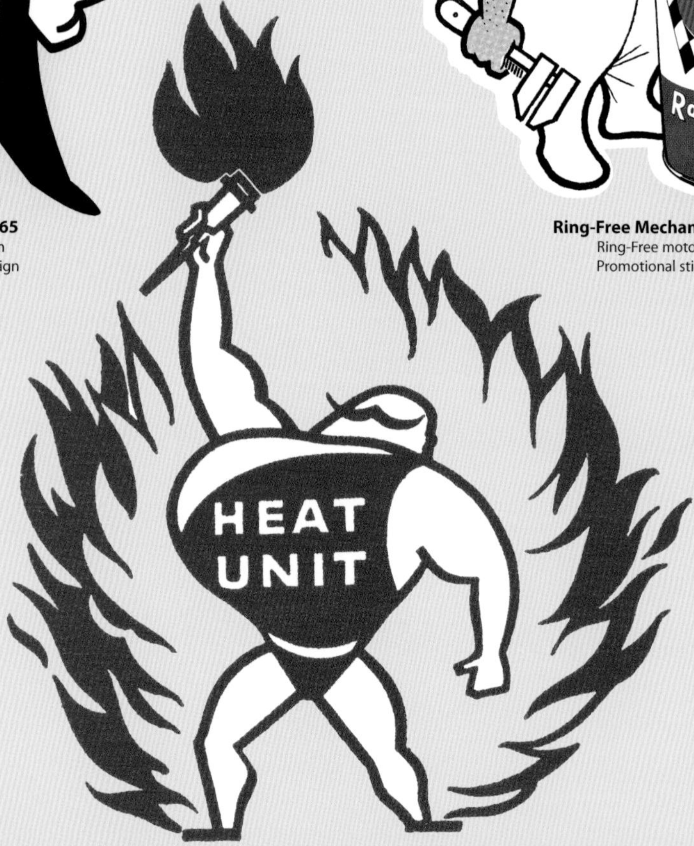

Heat Unit • c. 1948
Standard burner oils
Promotional brochure detail

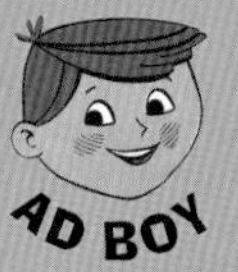

To be competitive in an increasingly crowded marketplace, products from gasoline to kitchen cleansers were often represented by "powerful" mascots. On the road, Esso claimed to put a Tiger in Your Tank and Sinclair offered the strength of Dino the Dinos While at home, Mr. Clean, always agleam in spotless white, flexed his muscular arms a making kitchen floors sparkle.

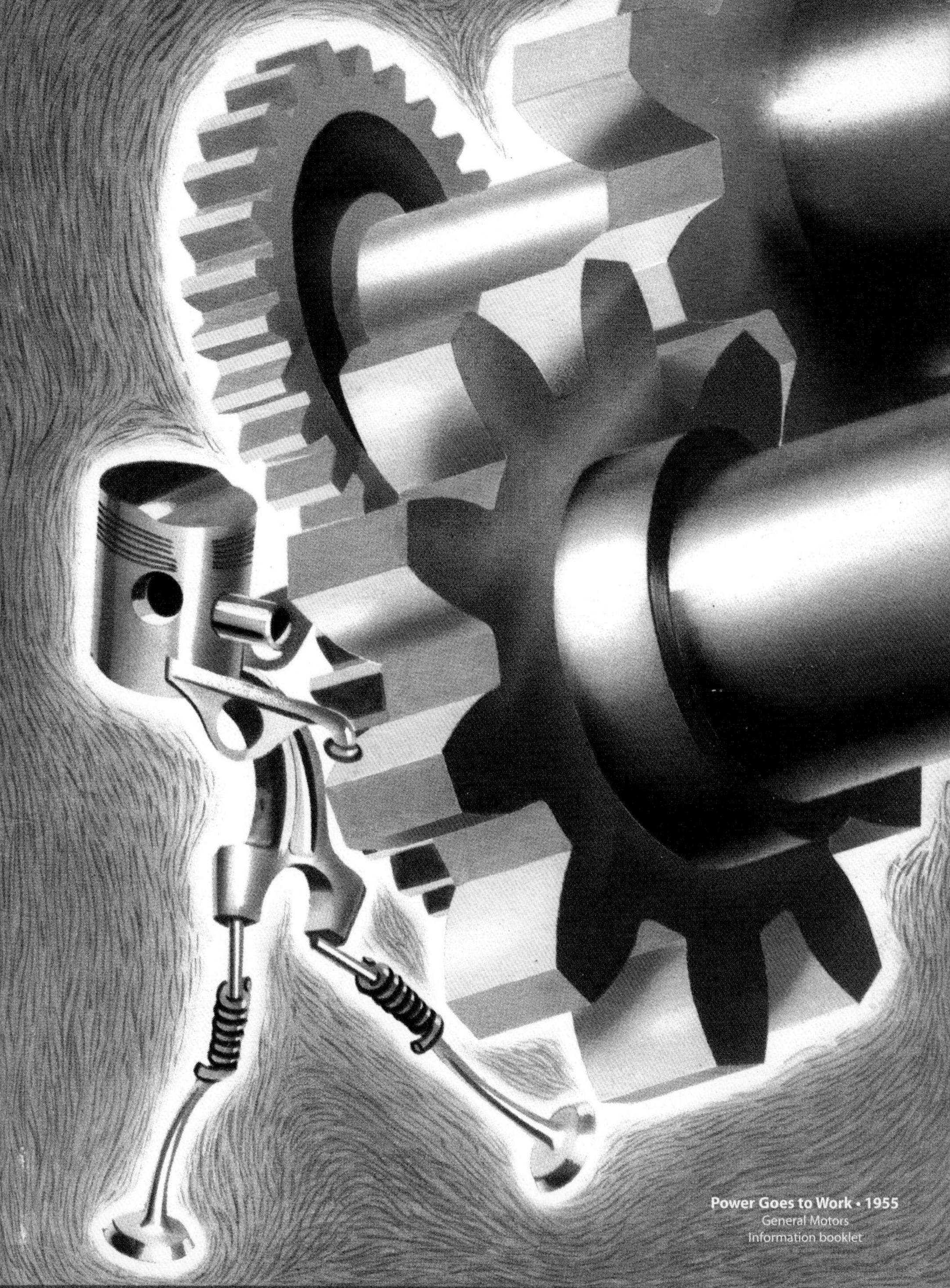

Power Goes to Work • 1955
General Motors
Information booklet

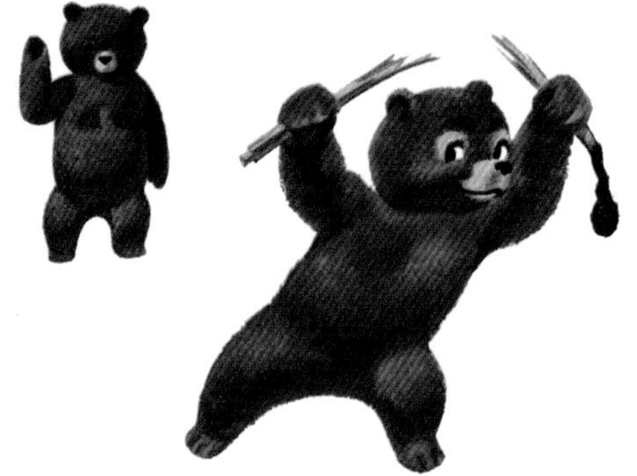

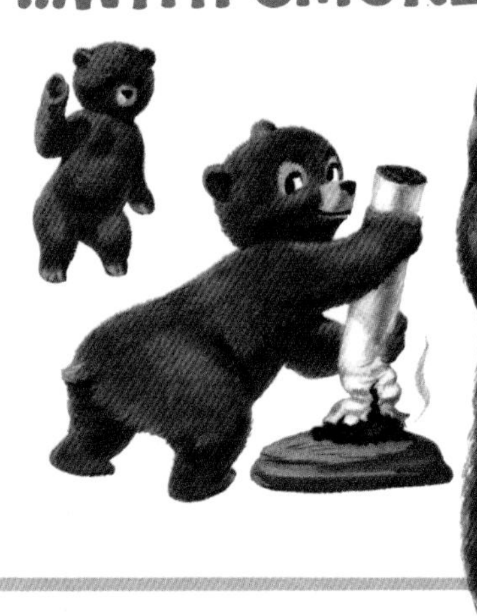

Smokey the Bear • 1953
U.S. Dept. of Agriculture, Forest Service
Public service poster

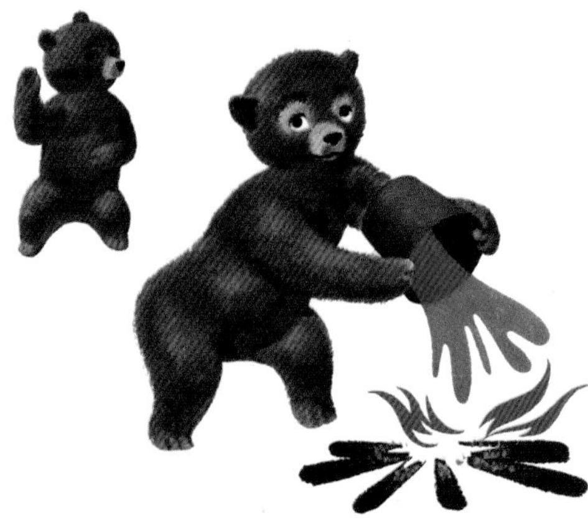

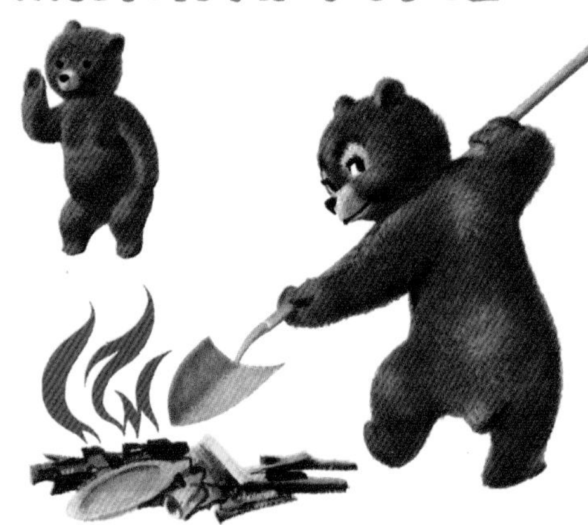

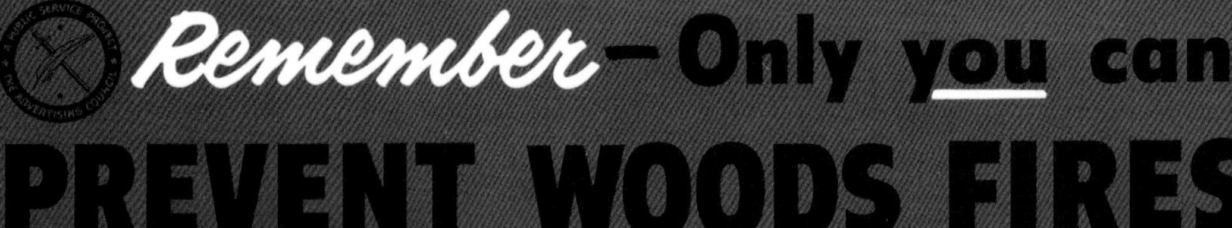

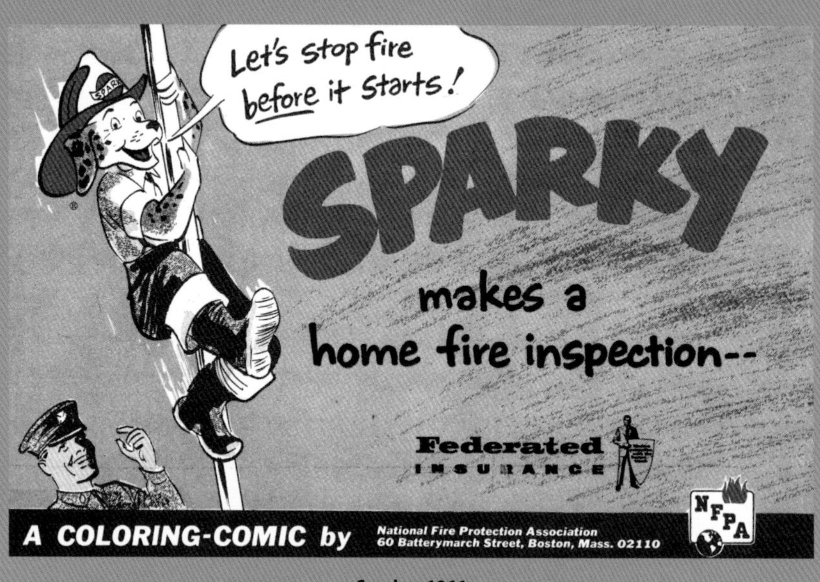

Sparky • 1966
National Fire Protection Association
Coloring book cover

Did you know that Smokey the Bear is not only the oldest spokesbear in America, he is also the star of the longest running public-service campaign in U.S. history? In 1965, at the height of his popularity with school children, Smokey was given his own Zip code—20252—to receive letters from the thousands of youngsters who looked up to the once-orphaned cub as a grown-up role model.

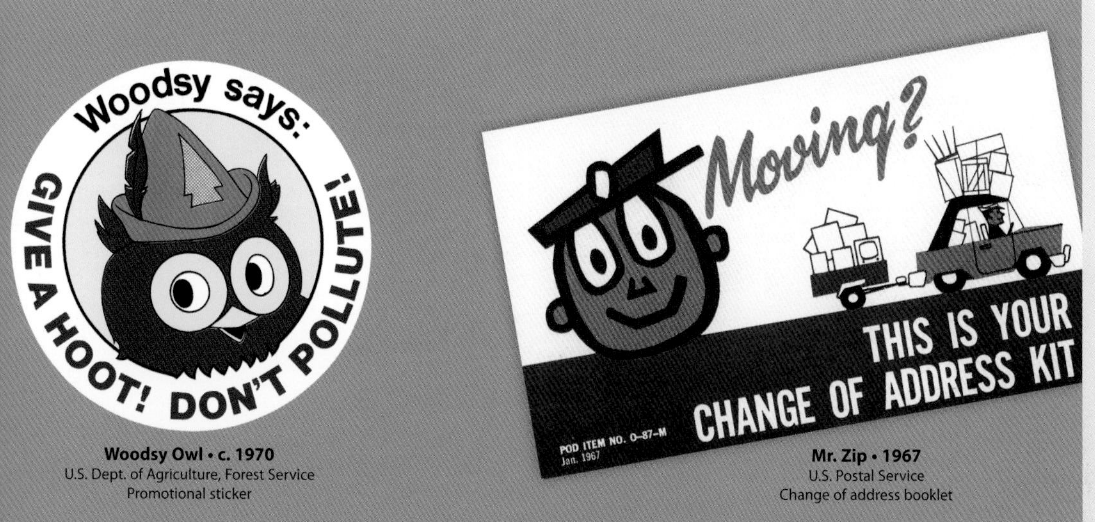

Woodsy Owl • c. 1970
U.S. Dept. of Agriculture, Forest Service
Promotional sticker

Mr. Zip • 1967
U.S. Postal Service
Change of address booklet

Howdy • c. 1968
Pennsylvania Forestry Association
Bag detail

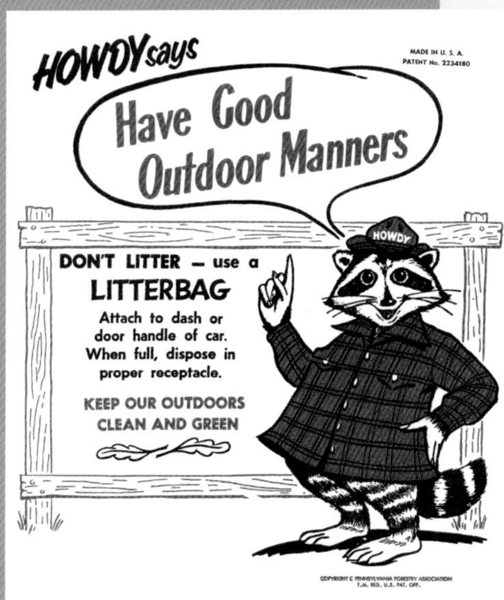

Torchy Timberloss • 1950
Wisconsin Conservation Department
Public service sign

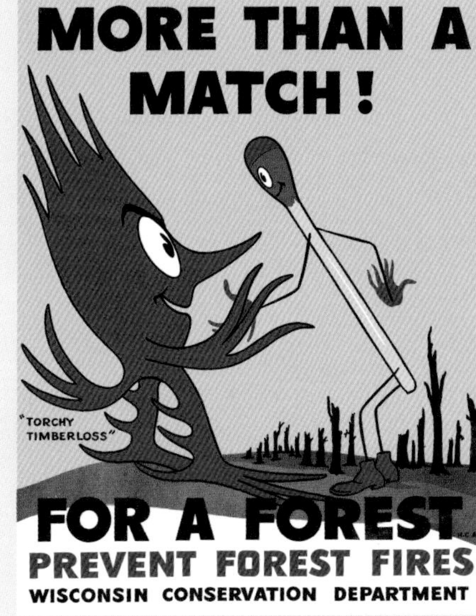

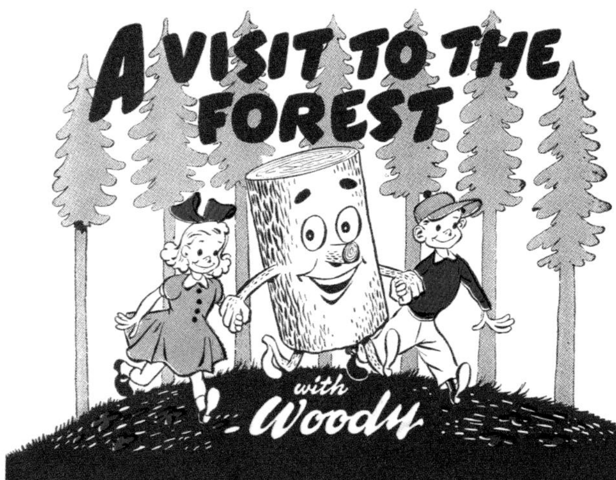

Woody • c. 1958
Maine Forest Service
Comic book cover

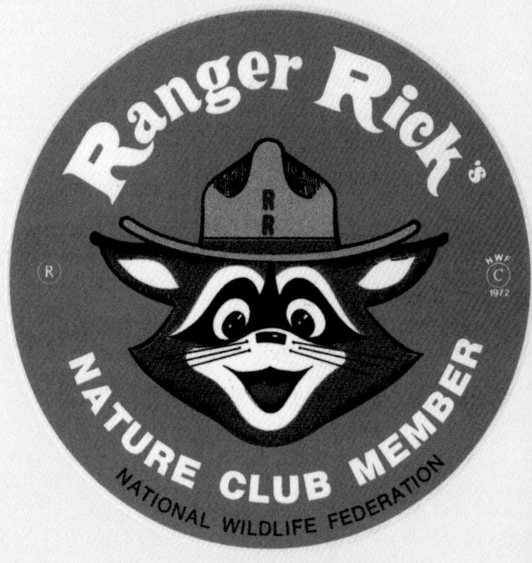

Ranger Rick • 1972
National Wildlife Federation
Water decal

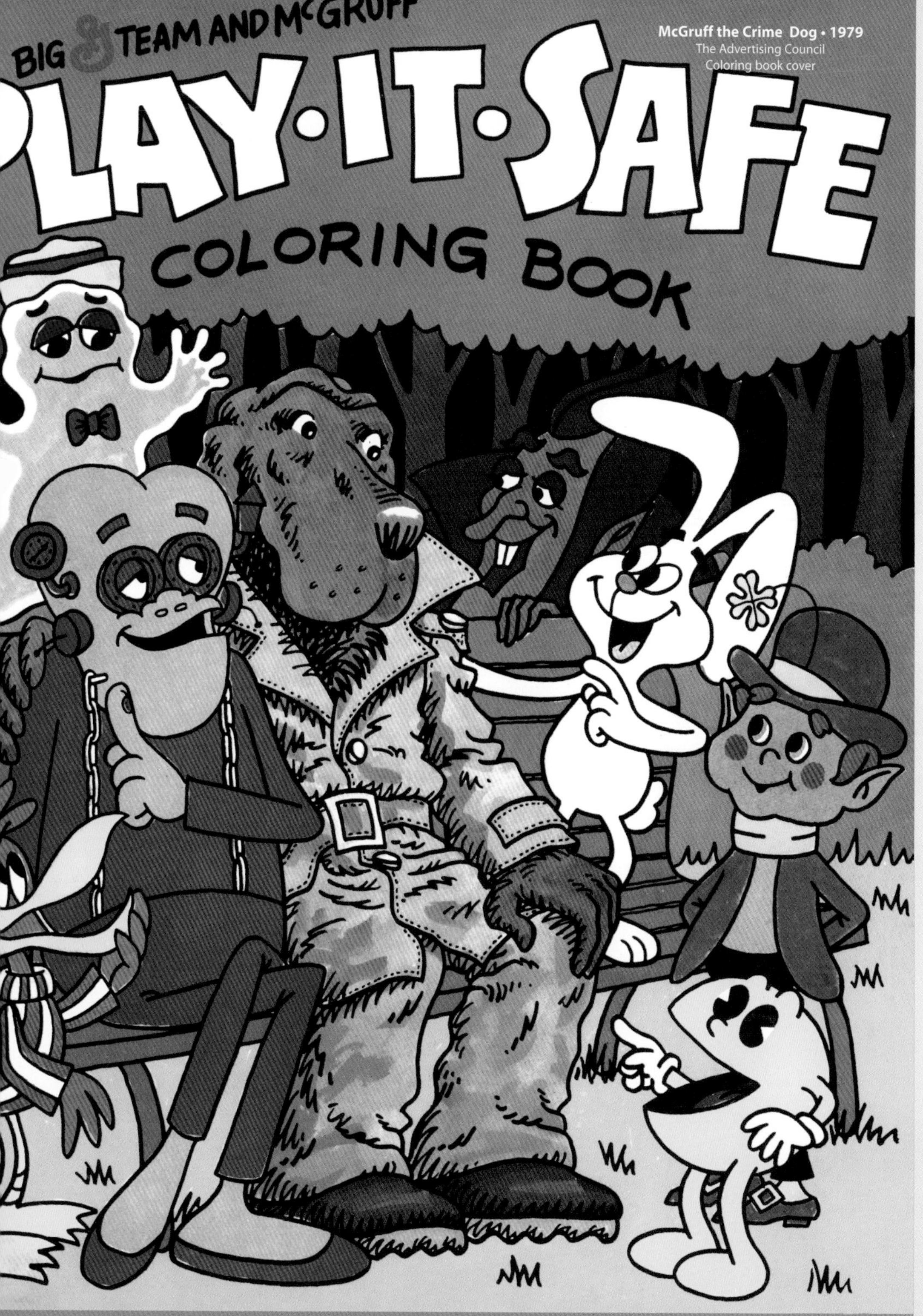

McGruff the Crime Dog • 1979
The Advertising Council
Coloring book cover

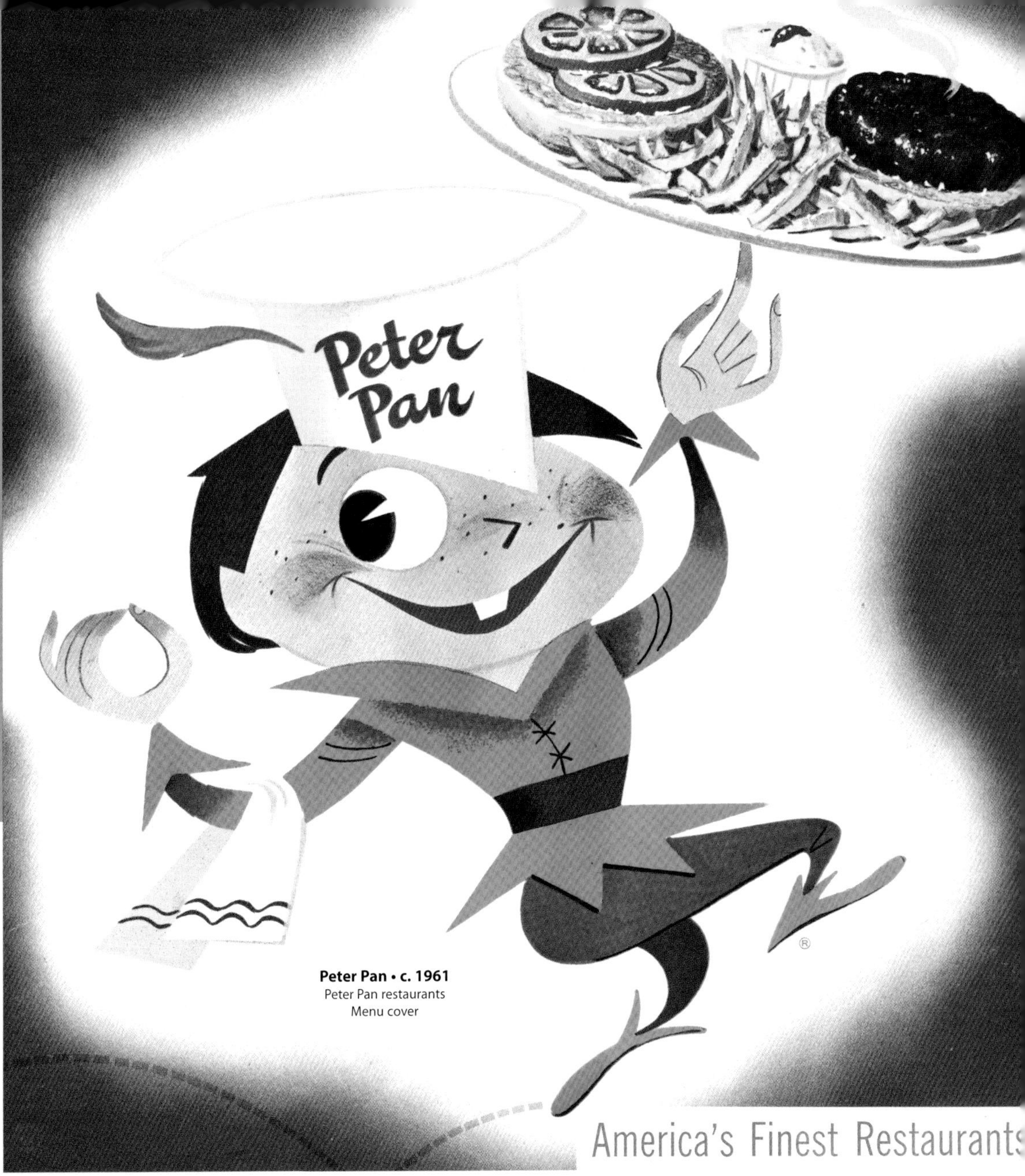

Peter Pan

Peter Pan • c. 1961
Peter Pan restaurants
Menu cover

America's Finest Restaurants

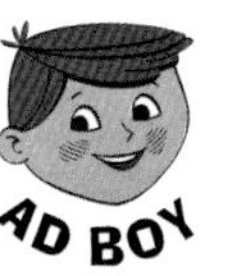

Fast-food franchise mascots, like Ronald McDonald and Colonel Sanders, have been w
us for decades. Some, like the Taco Bell Boy, enjoyed brief stardom at the chain's ince
tion, while others, like the Red Barn Hungries, were used for only a few years. Jack in t
Box's Jack and Burger King's King have had a resurgence in recent years, evolving fro
kiddie-centric mascots to TV hipsters and videogame stars.

Pizza Pete • c. 1973
Pizza Hut restaurants
Promotional sticker

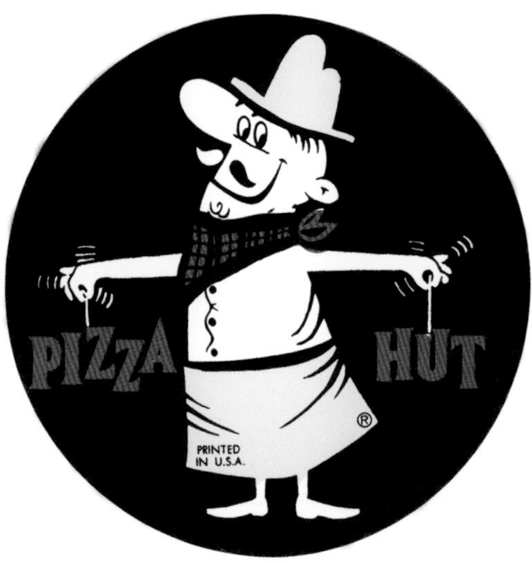

Sonic Man • c. 1969
Sonic restaurants
Paper cup detail

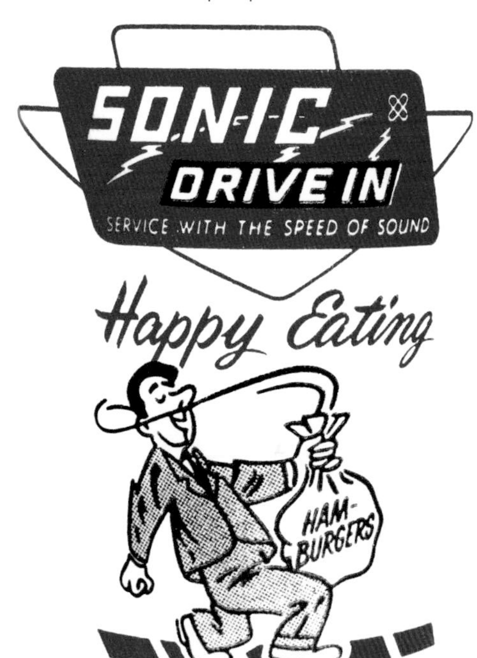

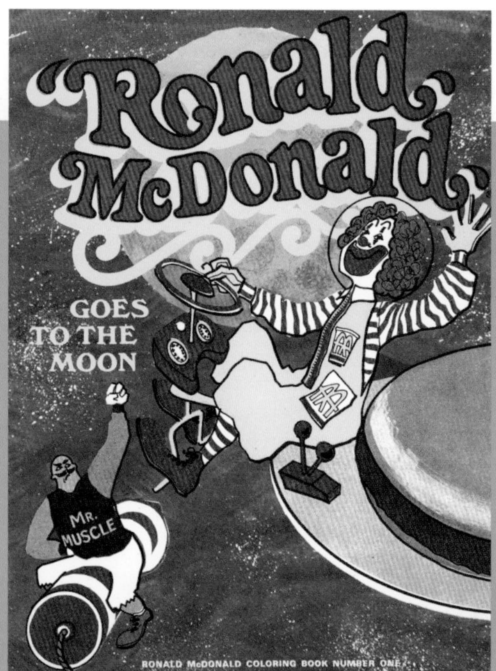

Ronald McDonald • 1967
McDonald's restaurants
Coloring book cover

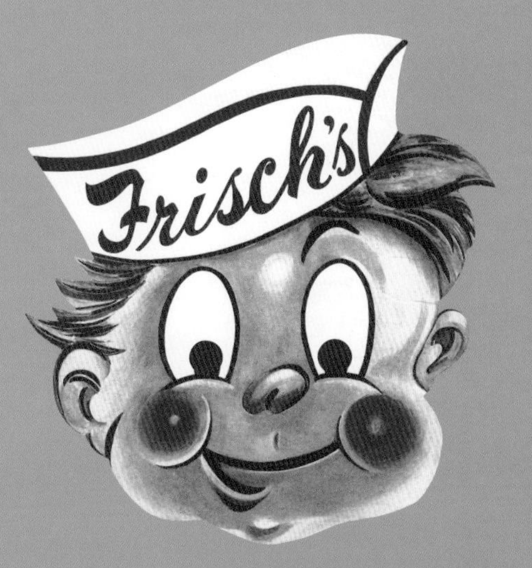

Big Boy • c. 1959
Frisch's Big Boy restaurants
Paper mask

Happy Star • c. 1974
Carl's Jr. restaurants
Hand puppet

Carl's Jr.®
HappyStar

Arby's®
ROAST
BEEF
Sandwich
IS DELICIOUS®

INSERT HAND HERE

Arby's Kid • c. 1974
Arby's restaurants
Hand puppet

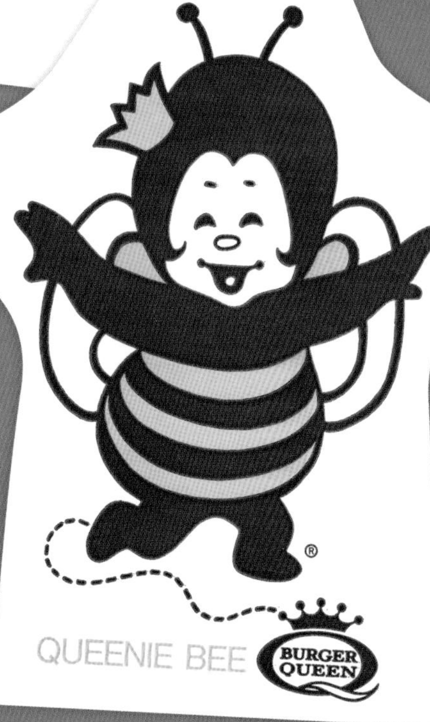

Queenie Bee • c. 1974
Burger Queen restaurants
Hand puppet

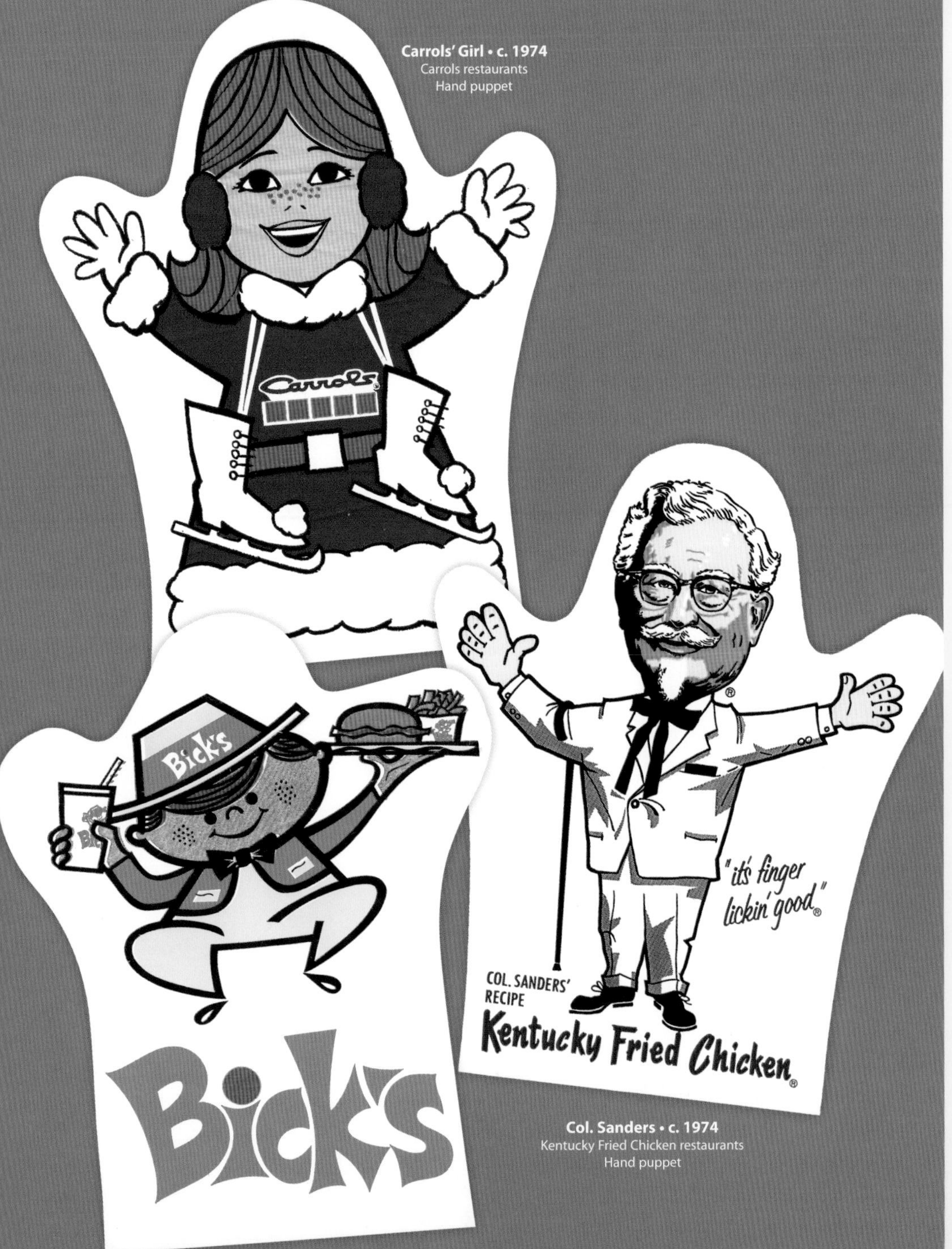

Carrols' Girl • c. 1974
Carrols restaurants
Hand puppet

Col. Sanders • c. 1974
Kentucky Fried Chicken restaurants
Hand puppet

Bick's Boy • c. 1974
Bick's restaurants
Hand puppet

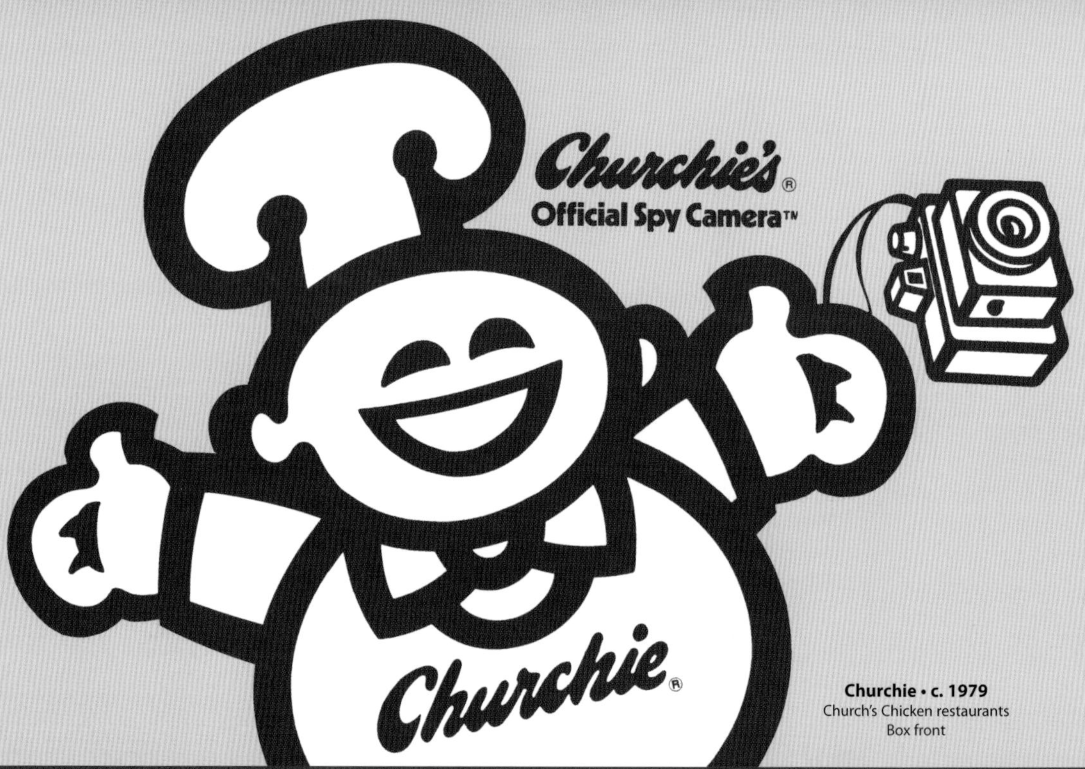

Churchie's®
Official Spy Camera™

Churchie®

Churchie • c. 1979
Church's Chicken restaurants
Box front

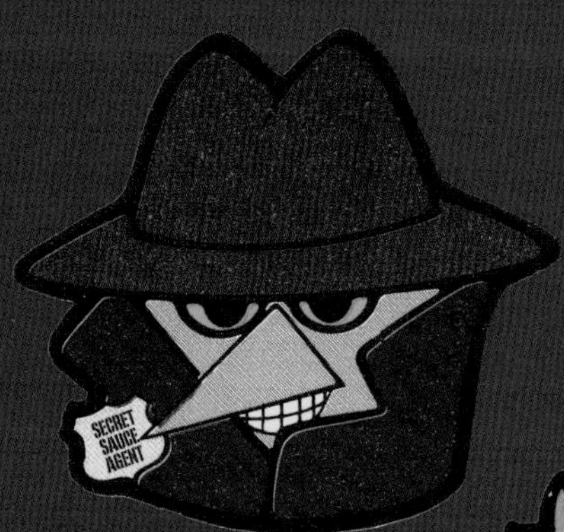

Secret Sauce Agent • 1972
Jack in the Box restaurants
Paper mask

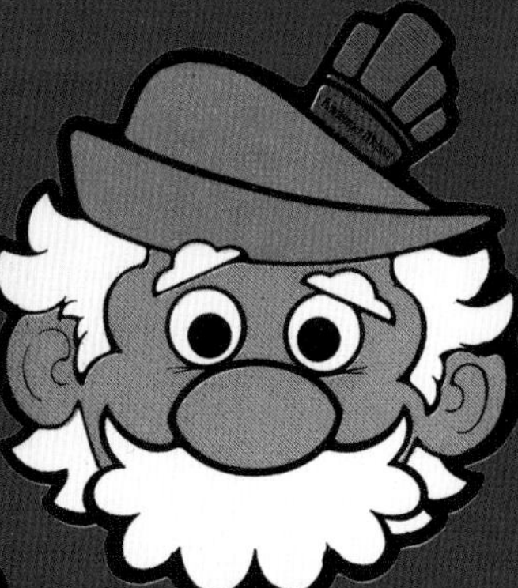

Hamburgermeister • 1972
Jack in the Box restaurants
Paper mask

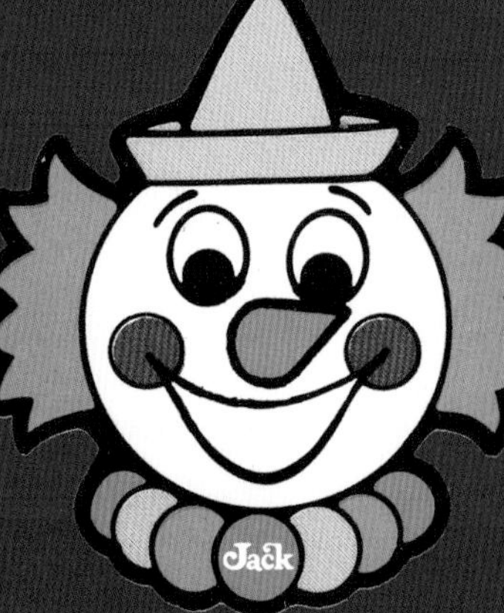

Jack • 1972
Jack in the Box restaurants
Paper mask

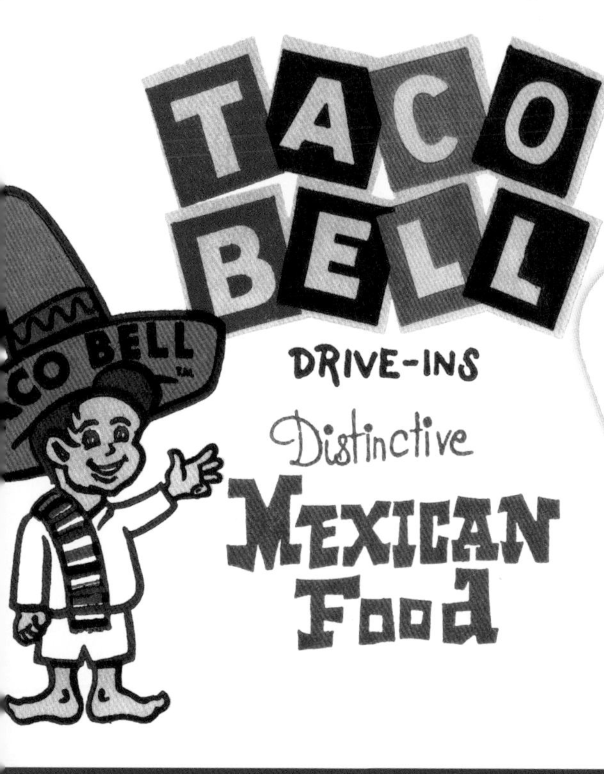

Taco Bell Kid • 1968
Taco Bell restaurants
Paper wrapper

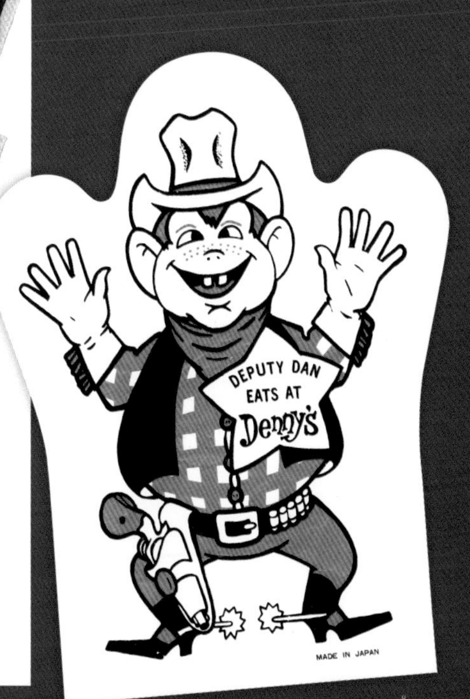

Deputy Dan • c. 1968
Denny's restaurants
Hand puppet

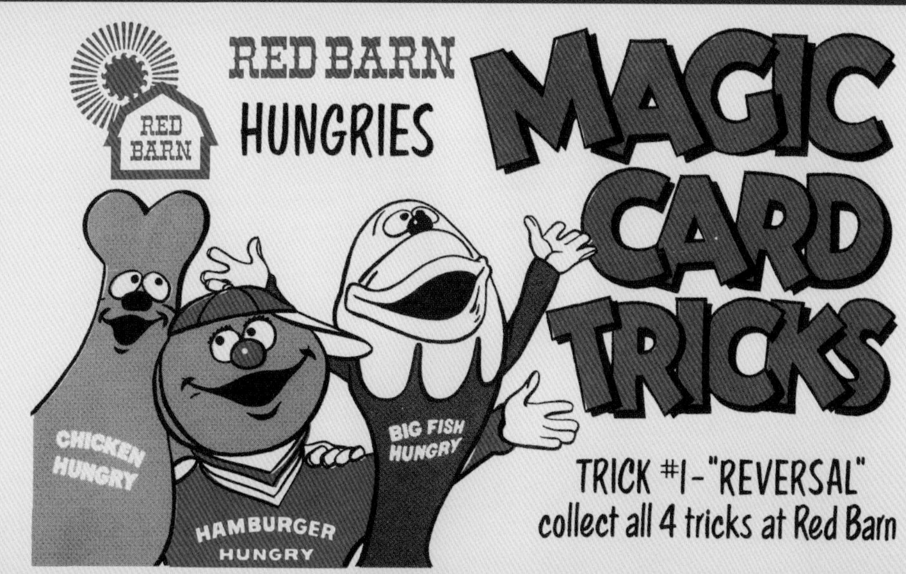

The Hungries • c. 1972
Red Barn restaurants
Paper envelope

Breakfast
KING

Breakfast King • 1958
Breakfast King restaurants
Menu cover

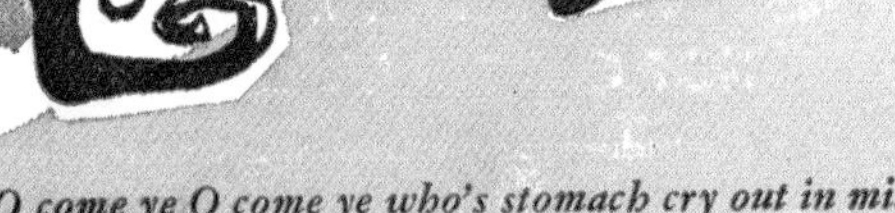

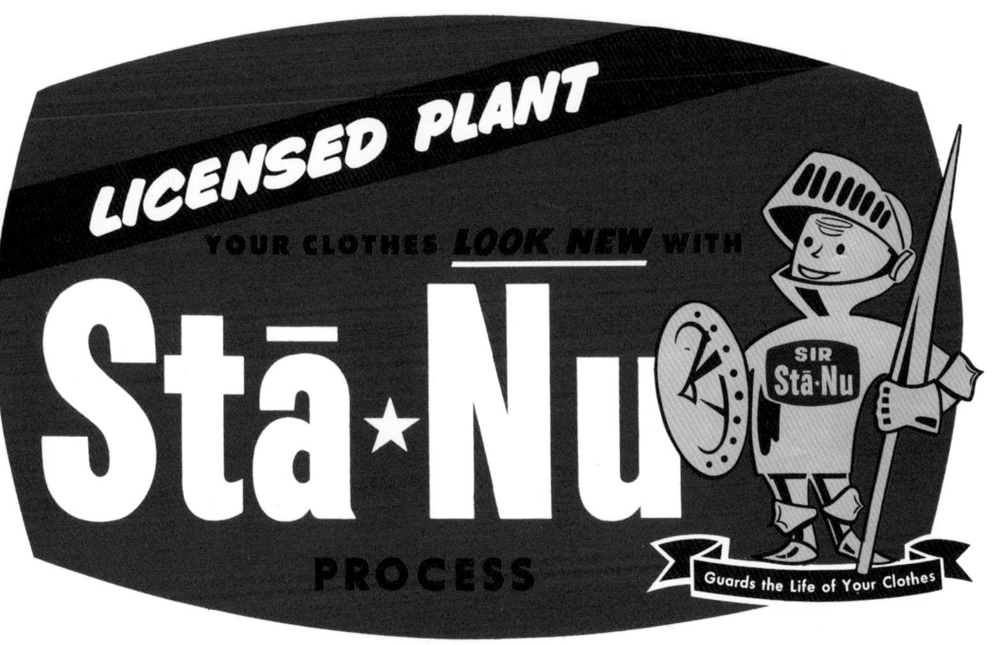

Sir Sta-Nu • 1960
Sta-Nu dry cleaning process
Water decal

During the 1940s and early 50s, many companies used royal ad characters in an effort to set their products apart from others within the same industry and solidify the superiority of their brands in the minds of consumers. By the late 1950s and 60s, kings and queens were used to represent the customer (and how he or she would be treated) rather than the product.

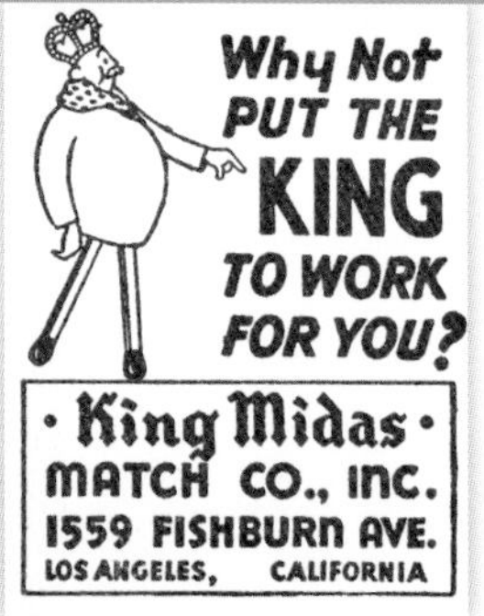

King Midas • c. 1948
King Midas matches
Matchbook cover

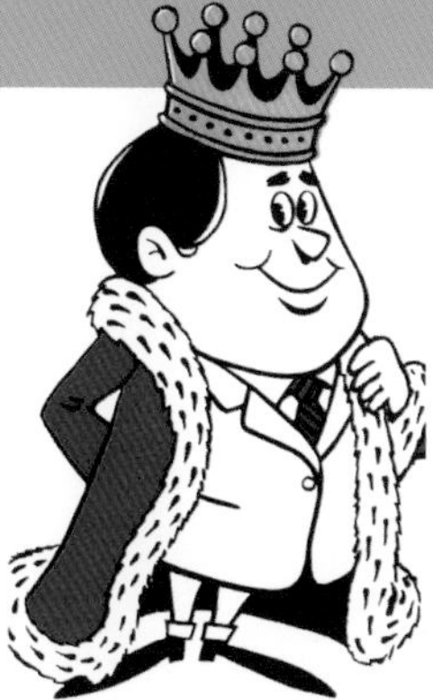

Our Customer Is King • c. 1982
Seaboard System railroad
Key chain fob detail

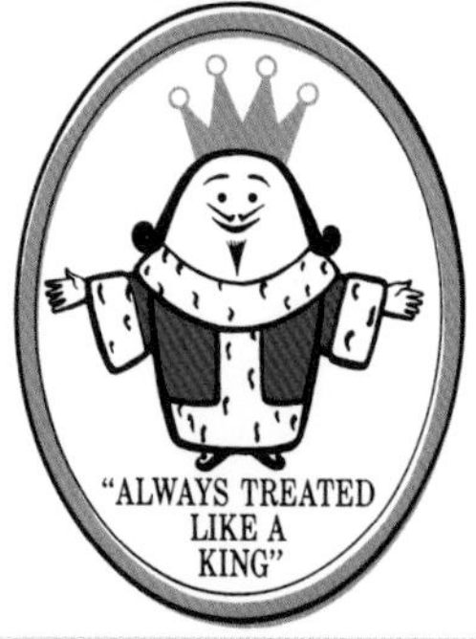

Royal Inn King • c. 1967
Royal Inn of America hotels
Matchbook cover

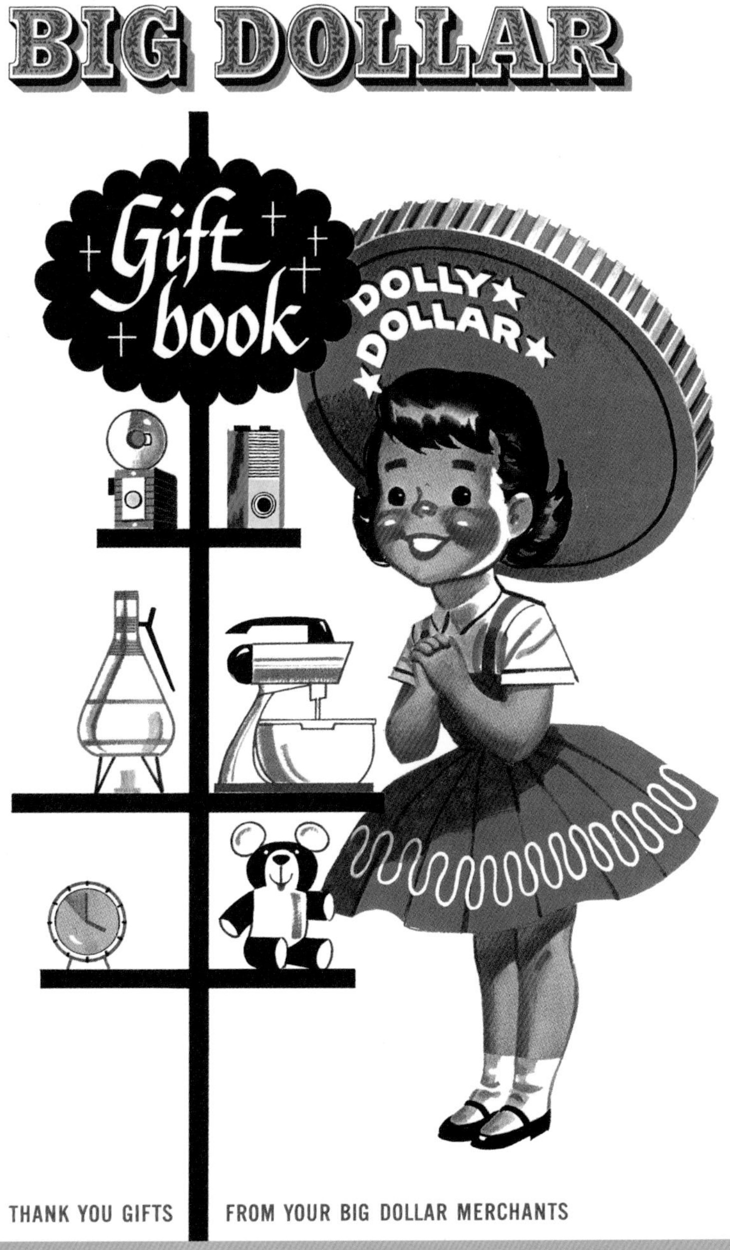

BIG DOLLAR

Gift book

DOLLY DOLLAR

THANK YOU GIFTS FROM YOUR BIG DOLLAR MERCHANTS

Dolly Dollar • c. 1957
Big Dollar savings stamps
Catalog cover

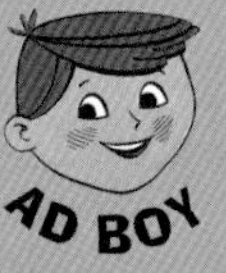

Two generations ago, amassing supermarket savings stamps was an all-American pa time. The concept was simple: the stamps were received with every purchase, and wh enough stamp books were filled, they could be used to acquire a variety of appliance or gifts. Three-quarters of all U. S. supermarkets offered savings stamps to attract and keep loyal shoppers, and many stores created ad characters to promote the concept.

Stampie • c. 1960
Family Discount savings stamps
Stamp saver book

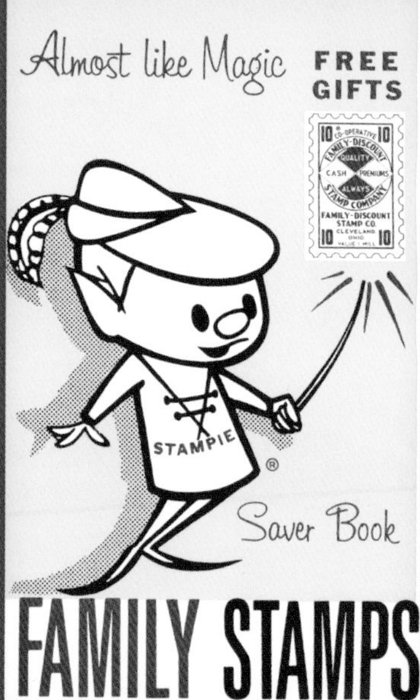

Colonial United Man • 1962
United savings stamps
Stamp saver book

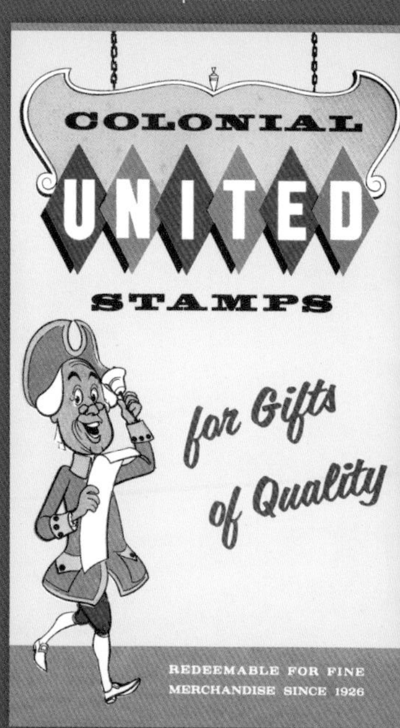

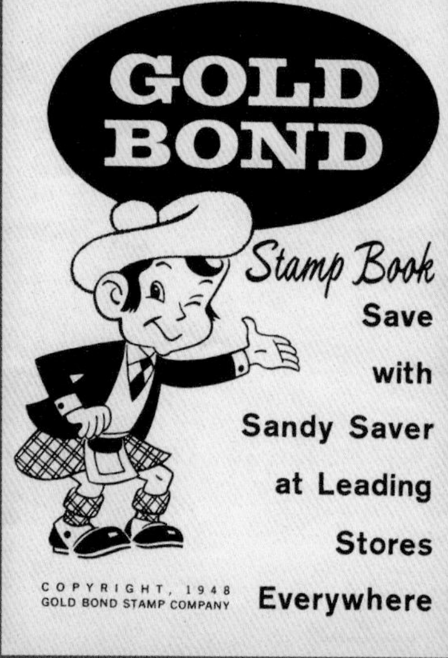

Sandy Saver • 1942
Gold Bond savings stamps
Stamp saver book

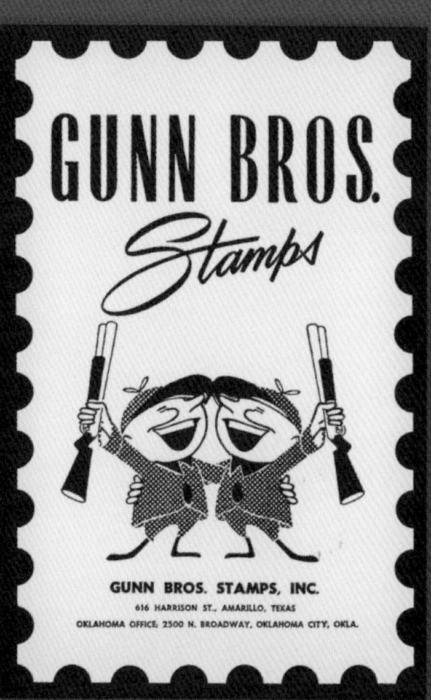

Gunn Bros. • 1949
Gunn Bros. savings stamps
Stamp book

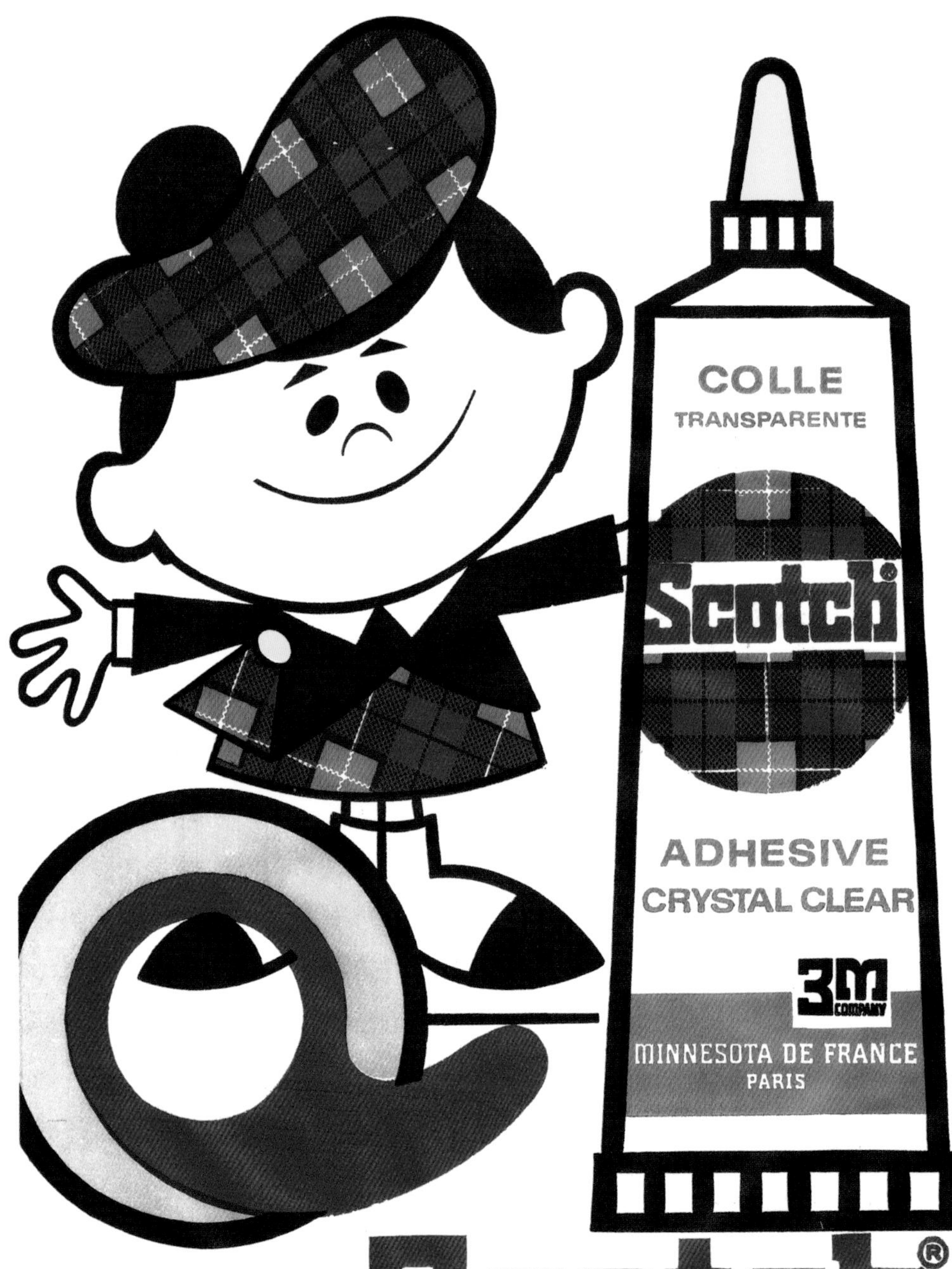

Scotch Boy • c. 1971
Scotch tape and adhesive
Bag detail

Sandy • c. 1965
Sandy's restaurants
Waxed paper cup

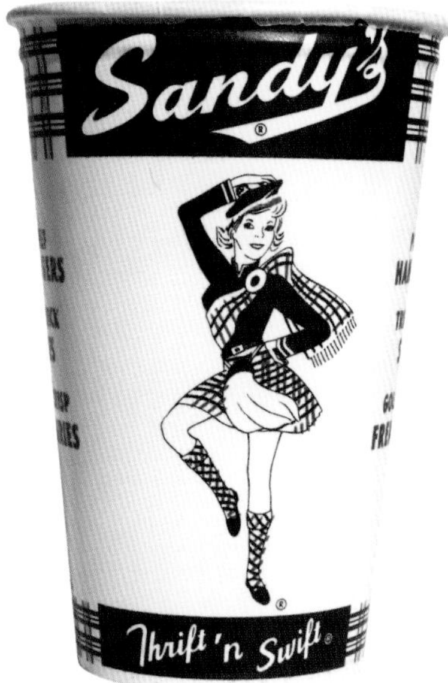

Plaid Girl • 1963
MacDonald Plaid Stamp savings stamps
Stamp saver book

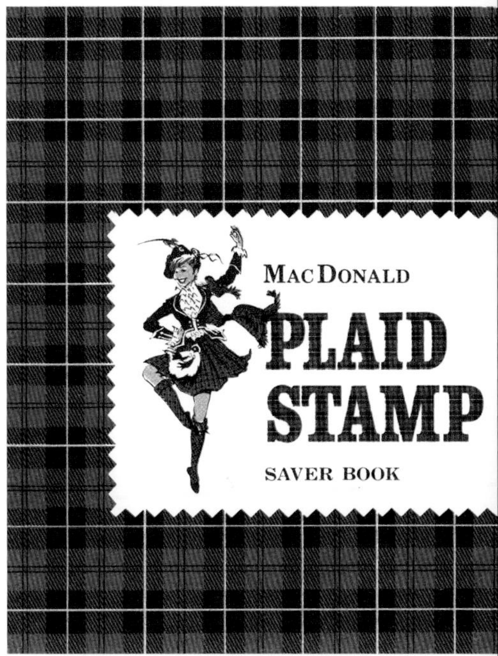

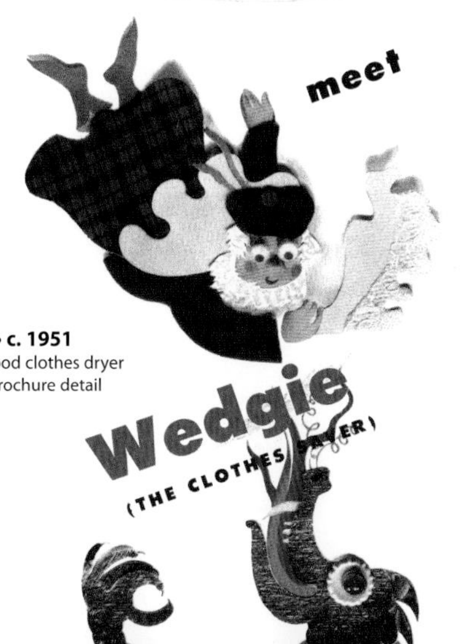

Wedgie • c. 1951
n Wedgewood clothes dryer
motional brochure detail

Shunk Man • 1957
Shunk blades
Playing card

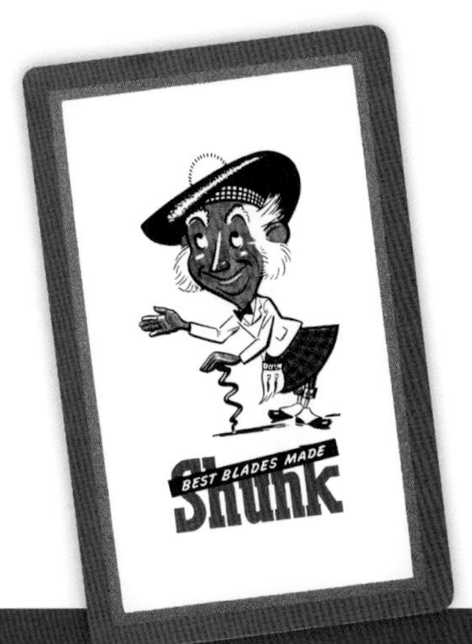

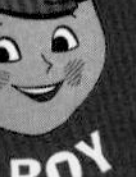

It might be considered politically incorrect these days, but in the mid-twentieth century Scottish plaid was a positive visual symbol of thriftiness that represented "a good buy for the money." Sprightly, tartan-clad characters reminded frugal shoppers of the Scottish saying, "Look after the pennies and the pounds will look after themselves."

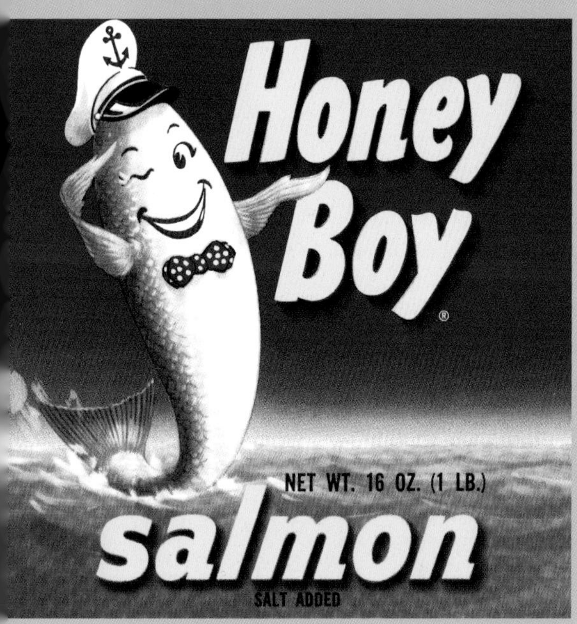

Honey Boy • c. 1975
Honey Boy salmon
Can label

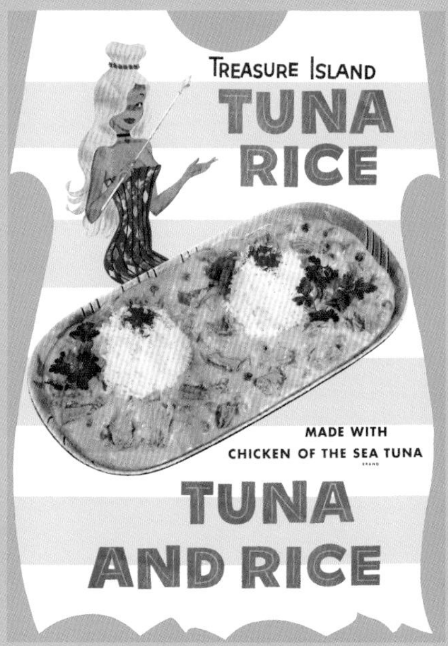

Chicken of the Sea Mermaid • 1951
Chicken of the Sea tuna
Store poster

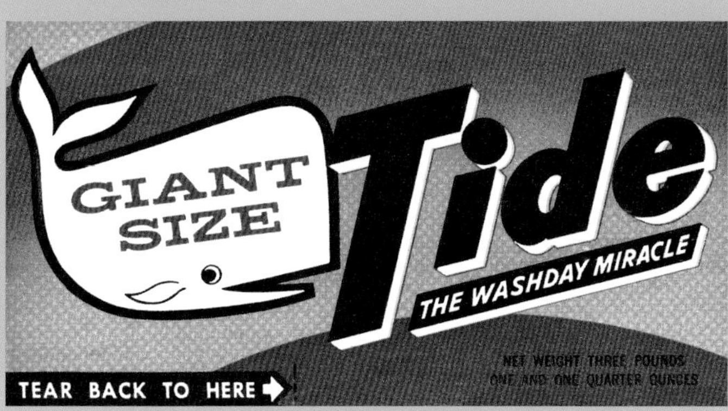

Giant Size Whale • c. 1949
Tide detergent
Box top

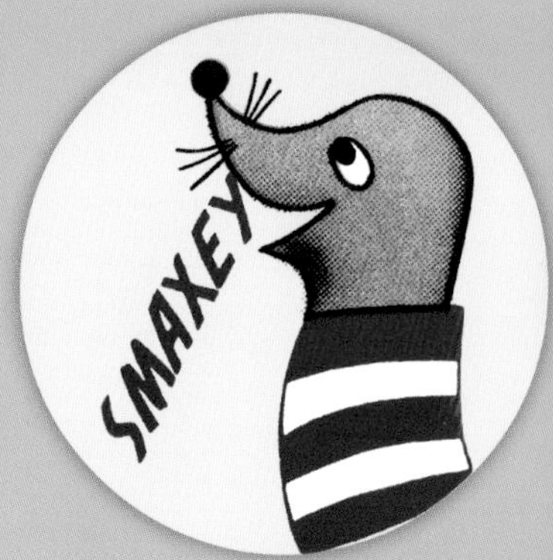

Smaxey the Seal • 1959
Sugar Smacks cereal
Pin-back button

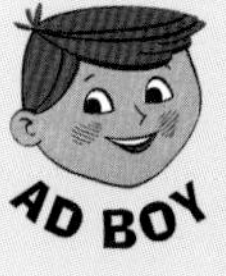

Sea creatures provided a variety of physical attributes that manufacturers could tie to product's promotion. Whales were added to packaging artwork to promote giant-size boxes. Octopus tentacles came in handy when tasting a delectable dessert or scrubbin autos at a car wash. Unduly happy and grinning fish commonly appeared on canned s food labels. Mermaids appeared too, with a considerably better fate.

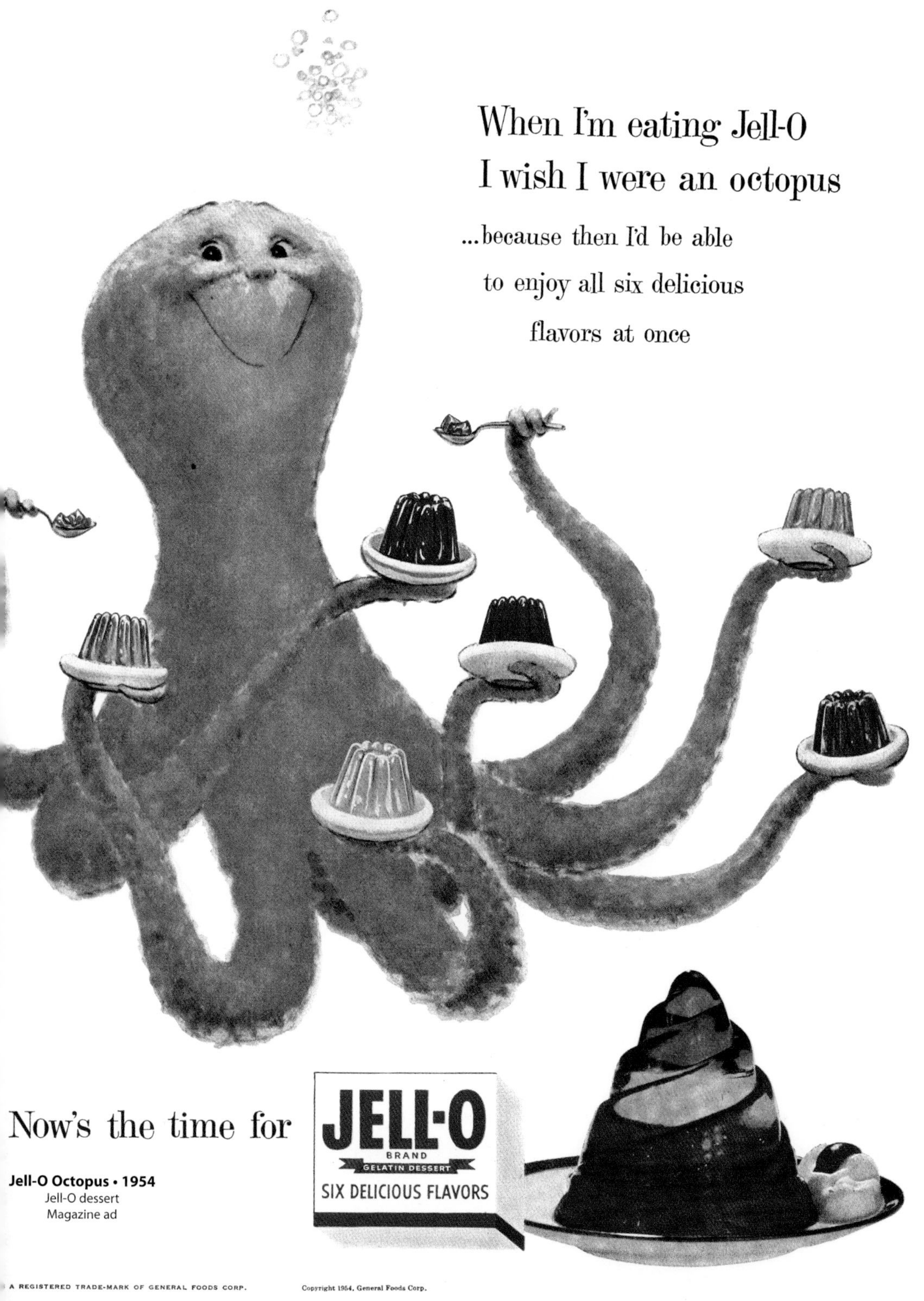

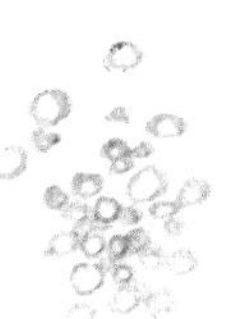

When I'm eating Jell-O
I wish I were an octopus

...because then I'd be able
to enjoy all six delicious
flavors at once

Now's the time for

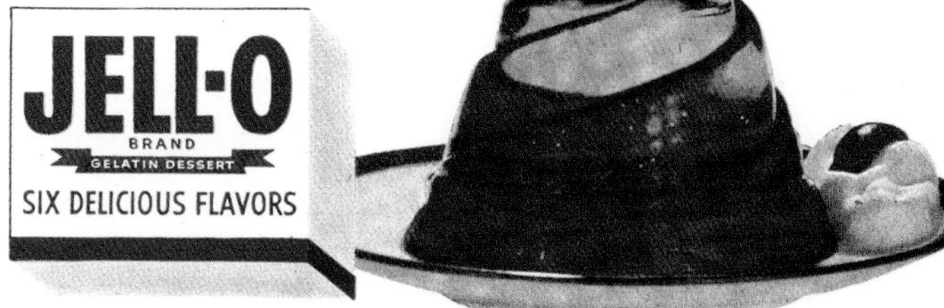

Jell-O Octopus • 1954
Jell-O dessert
Magazine ad

A REGISTERED TRADE-MARK OF GENERAL FOODS CORP.

Copyright 1954, General Foods Corp.

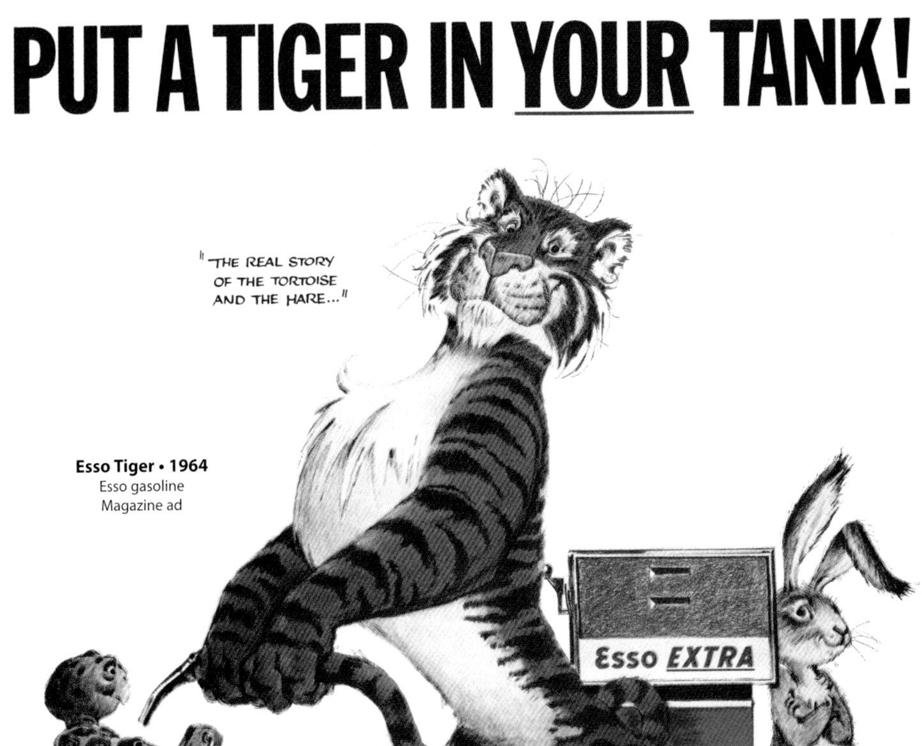

PUT A TIGER IN YOUR TANK!

"THE REAL STORY OF THE TORTOISE AND THE HARE..."

Esso Tiger • 1964
Esso gasoline
Magazine ad

Esso EXTRA

Watch for the Esso Report on NBC-TV. Check local listing for time and date.

NEW POWER-FORMULA ESSO EXTRA GASOLINE BOOSTS POWER THREE WAYS:

1 **Cleaning Power!** Dirt can clog even a new carburetor in a few months of normal operation—causing hard starting and rough idling. Your very first tankful of New Esso Extra will start to clear away these deposits—in new engines or old—to improve power and mileage.

2 **Firing Power!** Spark plug and cylinder deposits can cause misfiring, pre-ignition and hot spots. New Esso Extra neutralizes these harmful deposits—to help your engine fire smoothly, to help preserve the power of new cars and restore lost power to many older cars.

3 **Octane Power!** New Esso Extra has the high octane that most cars now need for full smooth performance without knocking.

You'll get *all* these extras with New Power-formula Esso Extra gasoline—it puts a tiger in your tank! *Happy Motoring!*

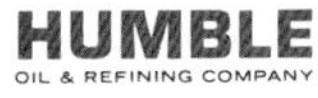

. . . AMERICA'S LEADING ENERGY COMPANY . . . MAKERS OF ESSO PRODUCTS

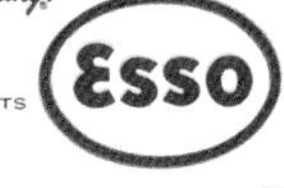

R5

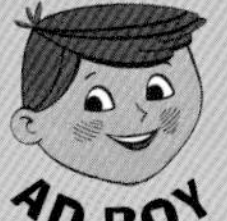

Memorable slogans and jingles are often part of an ad character's legacy. Mr. Whipple begged shoppers, "Please don't squeeze the Charmin." Chiffon's buttery margarine w "Good enough to fool Mother Nature." Actress Clara Peller screamed, "Where's the bee for Wendy's at a rival's unimpressive burgers, thereby launching a national catchphra that presidential candidate Walter Mondale used during his 1984 campaign.

Try It You'll Like It • 1971
Alka-Seltzer effervescent tablets
Pin-back button

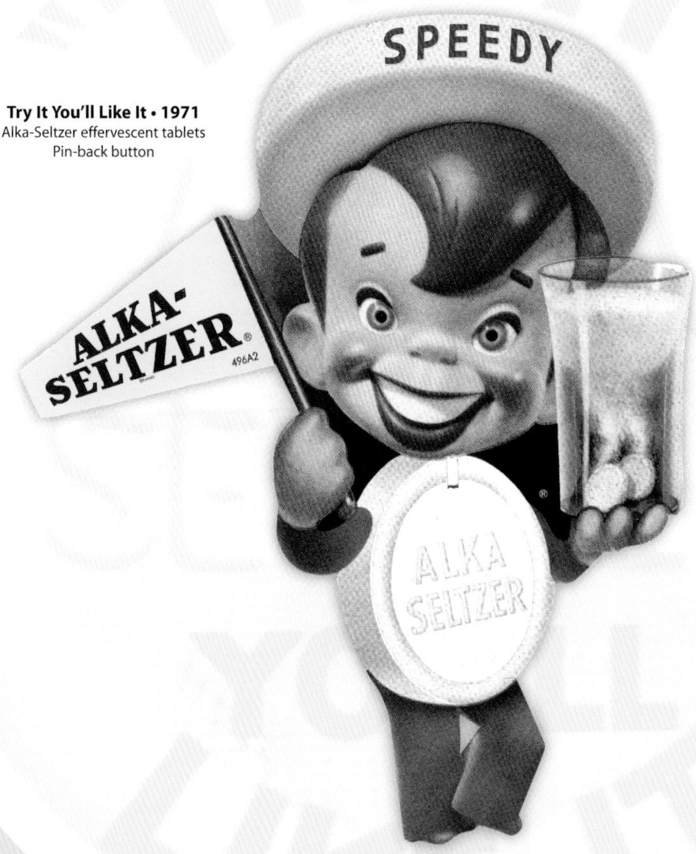

Speedy Alka-Seltzer • c. 1953
Alka-Seltzer effervescent tablets
Store display

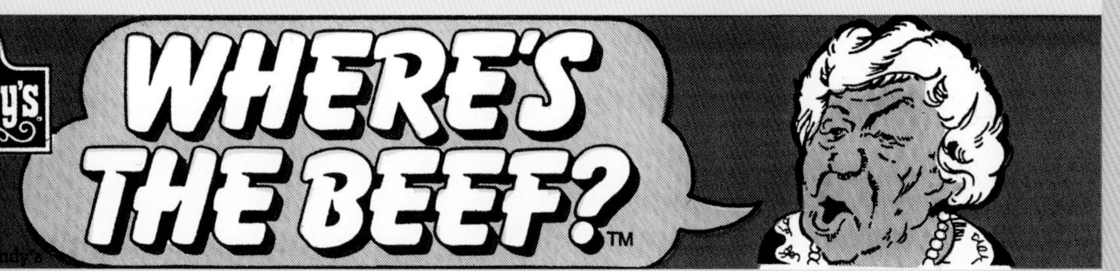

Where's the Beef? Lady • 1984
Wendy's restaurants
Promotional sticker

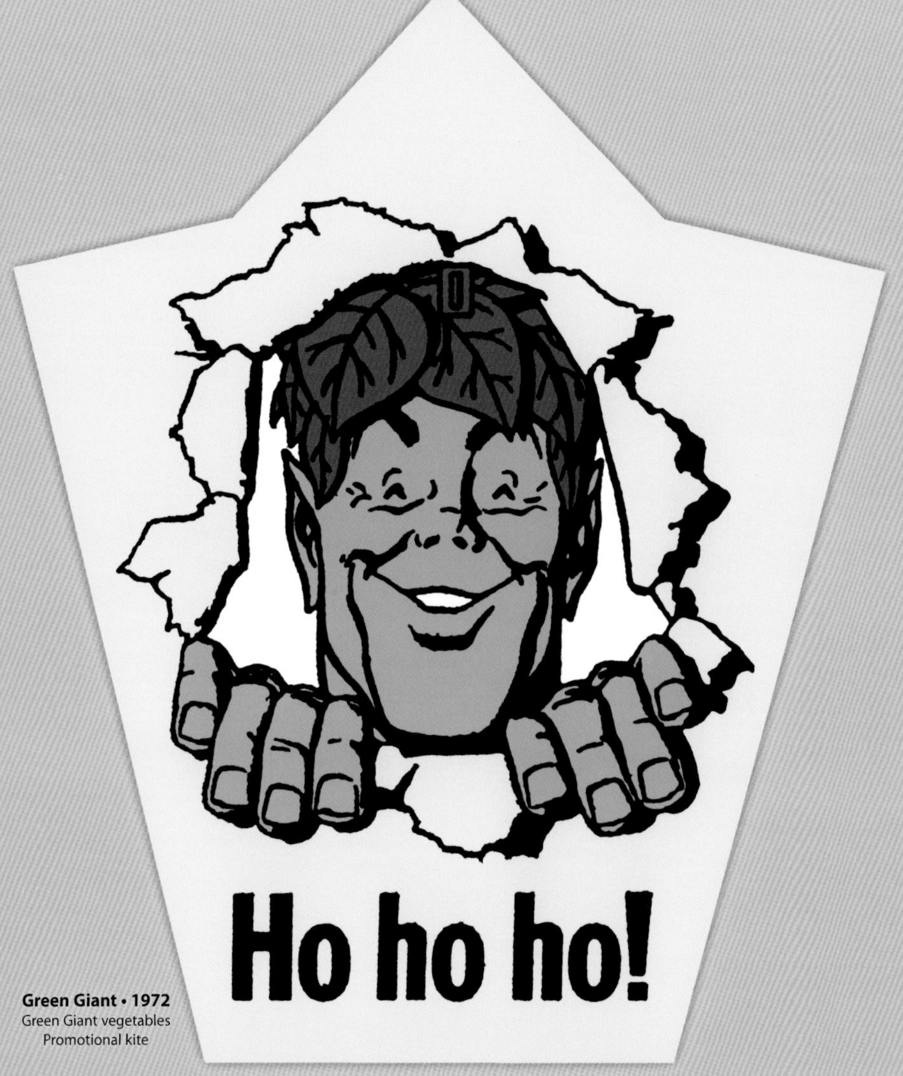

Green Giant • 1972
Green Giant vegetables
Promotional kite

Flick my BiC

BIC Boy • c. 1973
BIC lighters
Bumper sticker

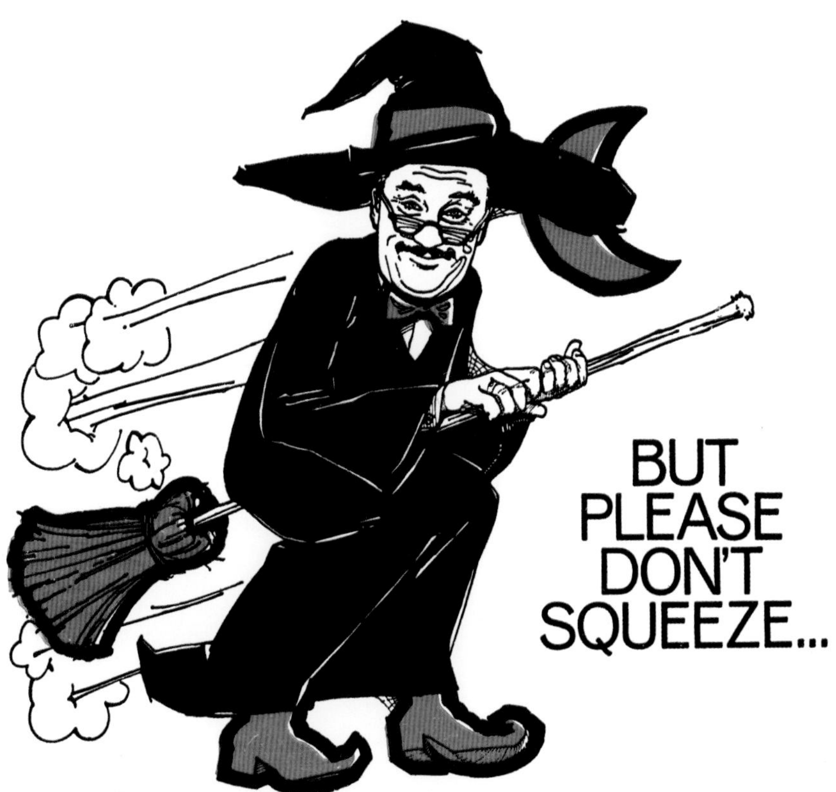

Mr. Whipple • c. 1977
Charmin toilet paper
Bag detail

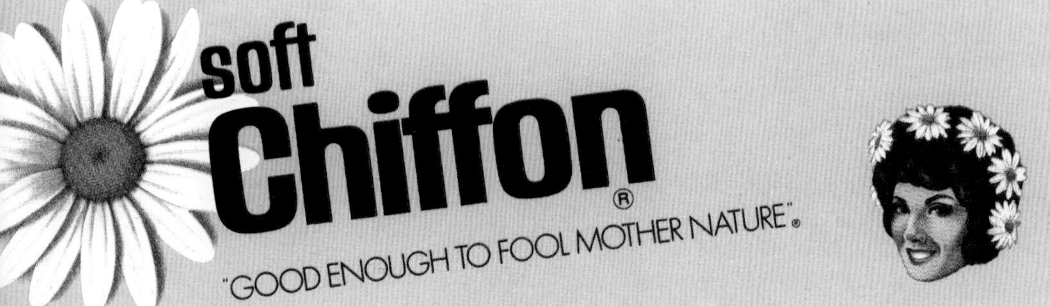

Mother Nature • 1976
Chiffon margarine
Package side panel

The Frito Kid • 1954
Fritos corn chips
Promotional booklet

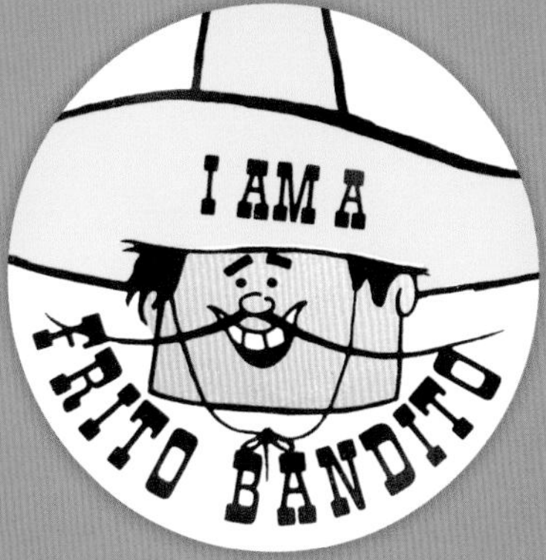

Frito Bandito • c. 1970
Fritos corn chips
Pin-back button

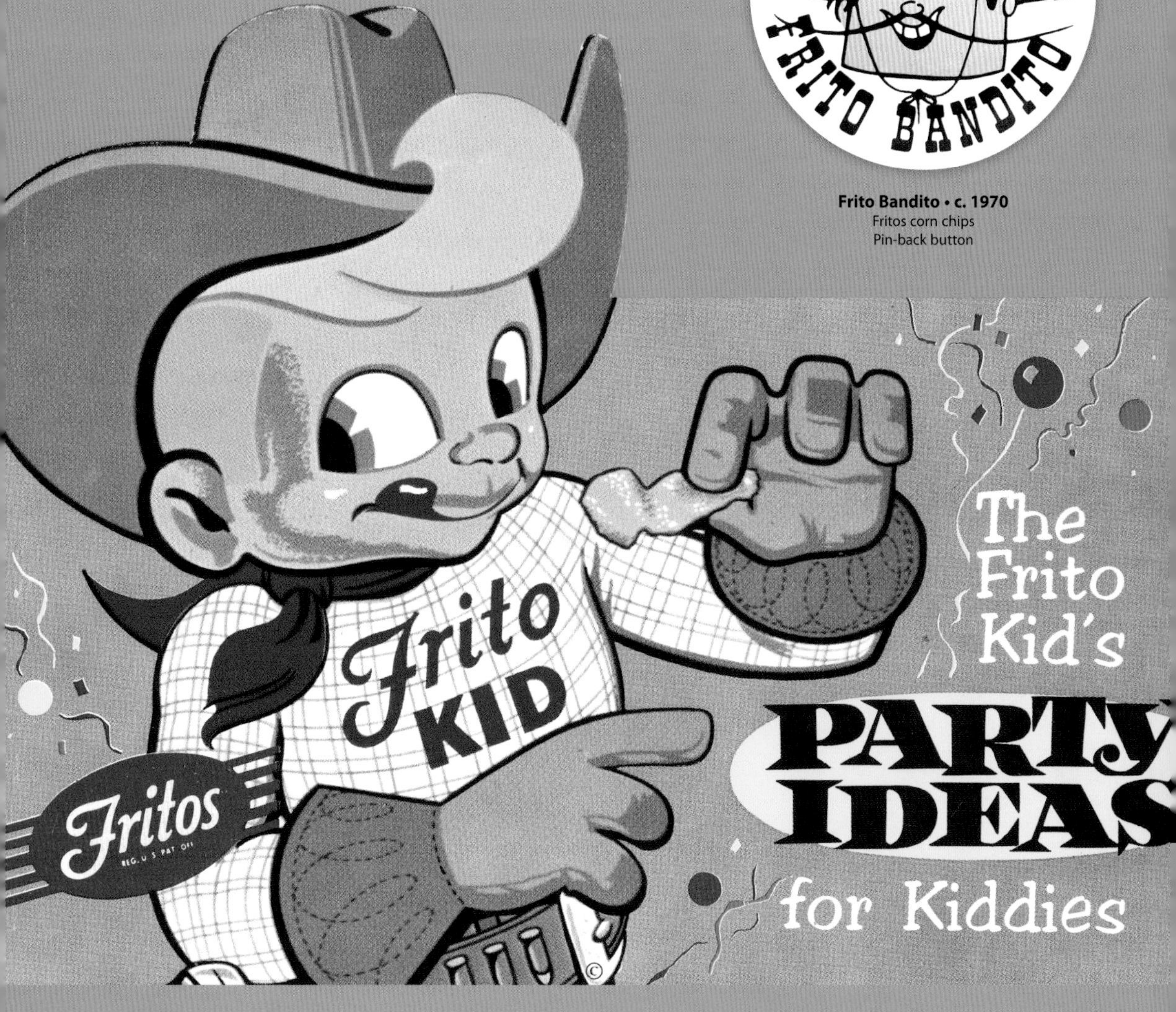

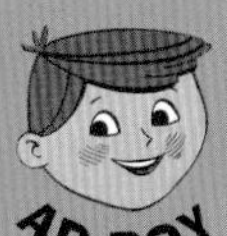

Is there a Frito Bandito in your house?

When Frito-Lay introduced the cartoon outlaw known as the Frito Bandito, this friend villain held up anyone snacking on his favorite corn chips. Although wildly popular, e in the Hispanic American community, the company eventually terminated the ad cam paign in response to critics' charges that it embodied an offensive ethnic stereotype.

WANTED
FOR THEFT
OF FRITOS® CORN CHIPS

THE FRITO BANDITO

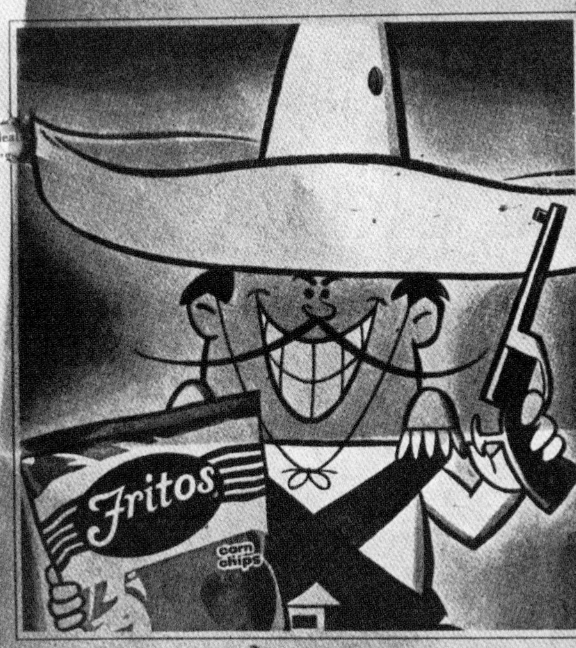

CAUTION:

He loves cronchy Fritos corn chips so much he'll stop at nothing to get yours. What's more, he's cunning, clever—and sneaky!

CITIZENS! PROTECT YOURSELVES!

NEVER BUY ONE BAG OF FRITOS CORN CHIPS ALWAYS BUY 2, AND HIDE 1 FOR YOU.

THERE MAY BE A FRITO BANDITO IN YOUR HOUSE.

Frito Bandito • 1968
Fritos corn chips
Magazine ad.

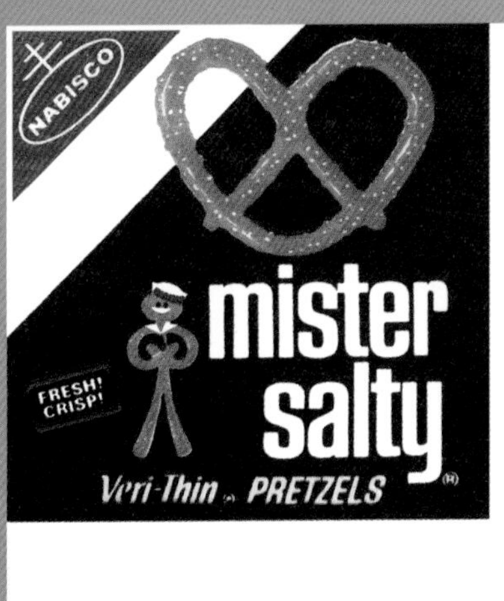

Mister Salty • c. 1984
Mister Salty pretzels
Paper napkin

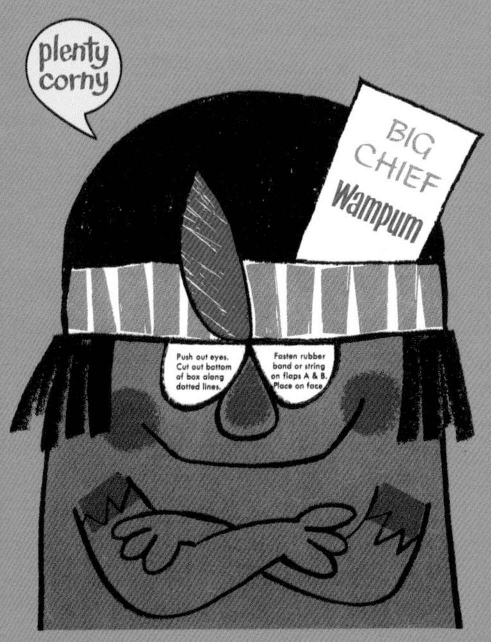

Big Chief Wampum • c. 1973
Wampum corn chips
Box back

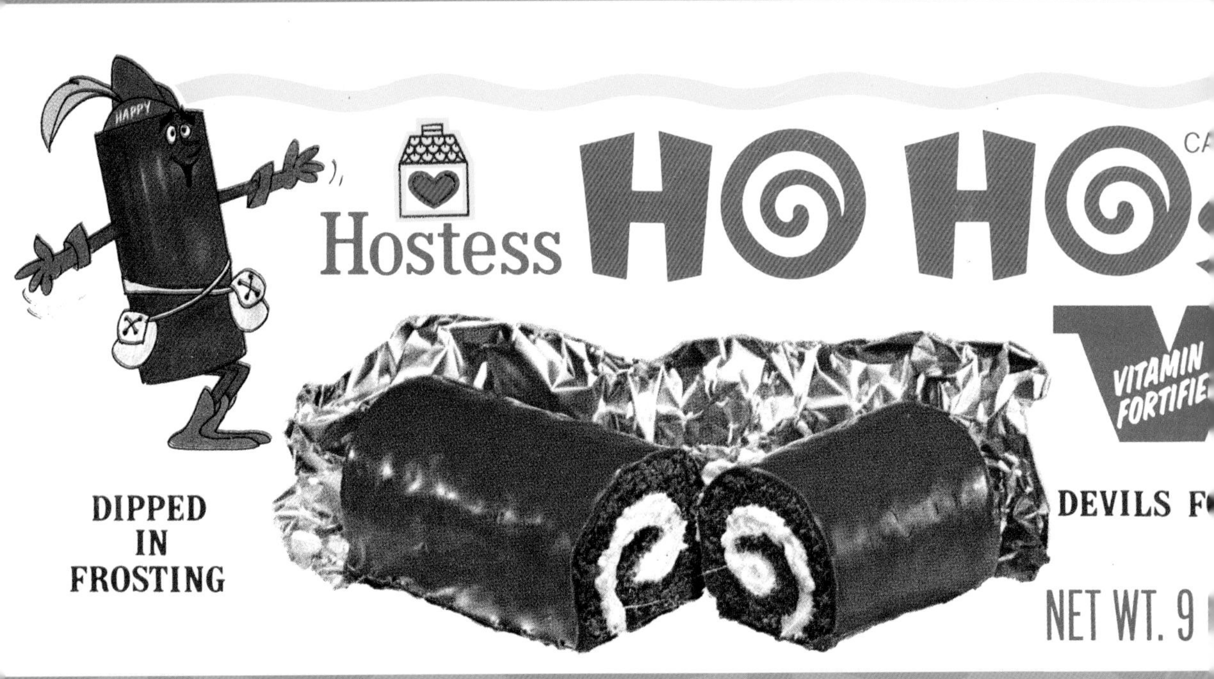

Happy Ho Ho • 1970
Hostess Ho Hos cake
Box cover

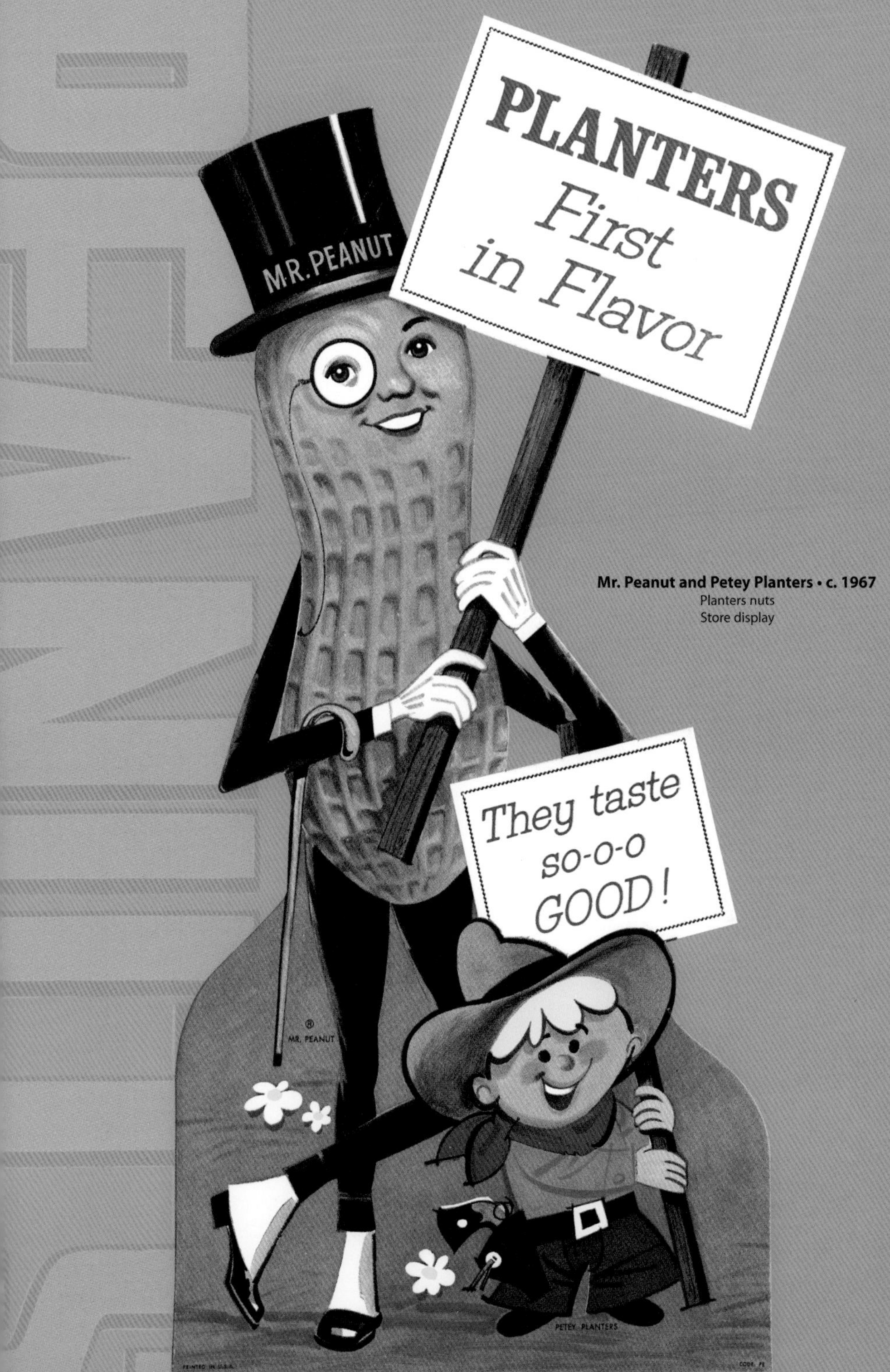

Mr. Peanut and Petey Planters • c. 1967
Planters nuts
Store display

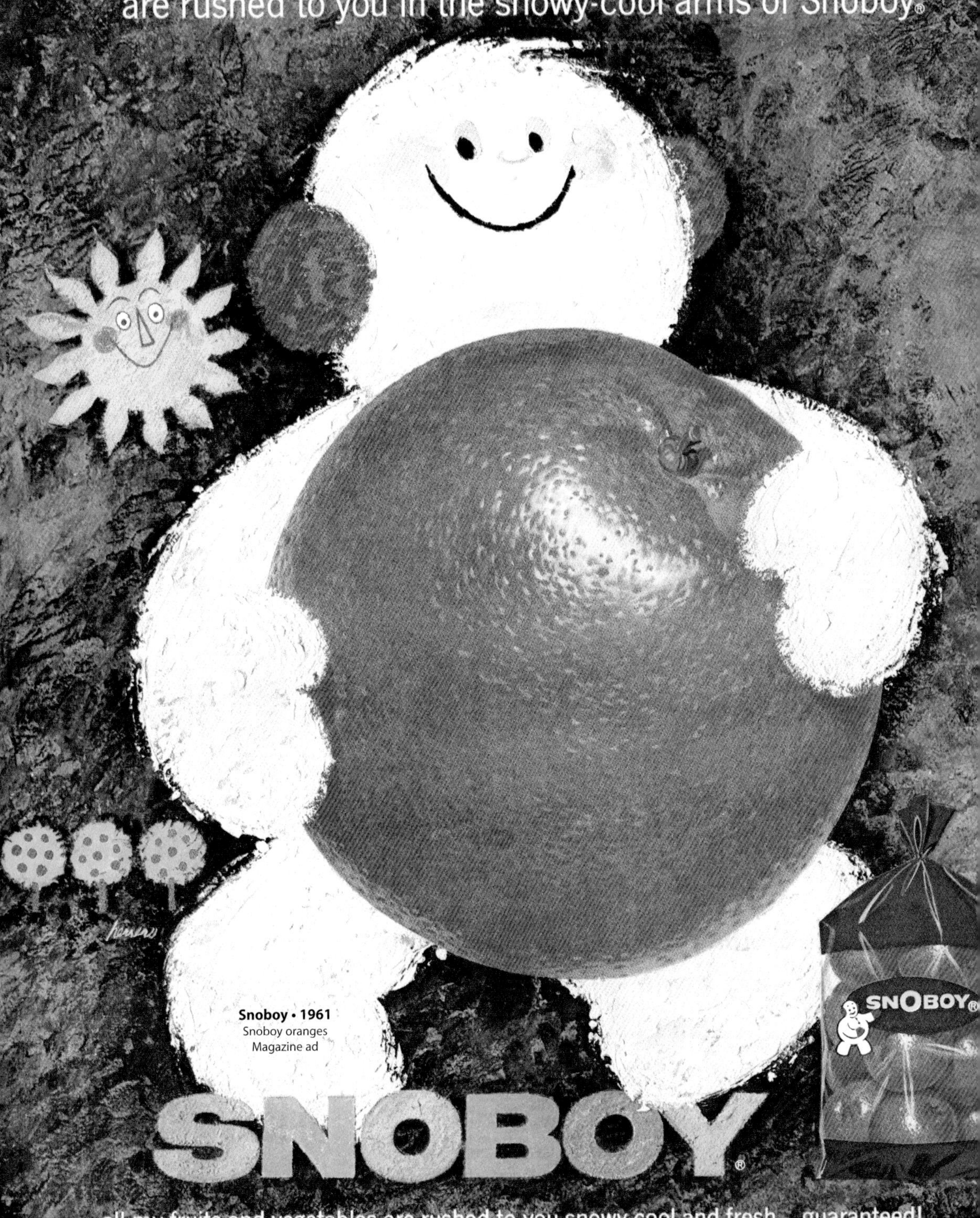

Snoboy • 1961
Snoboy oranges
Magazine ad

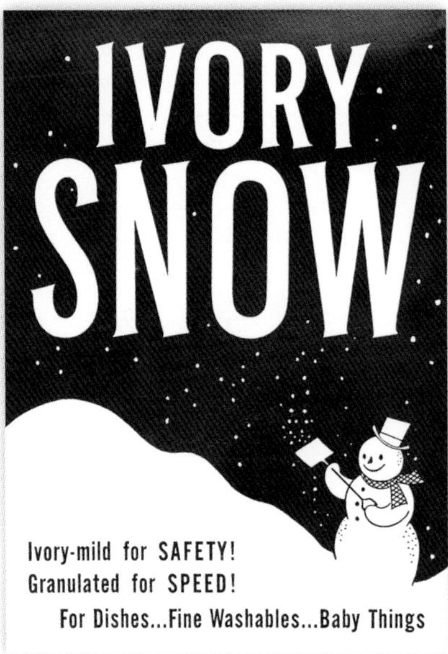

Ivory Snowman • 1951
Ivory Snow detergent
Box front

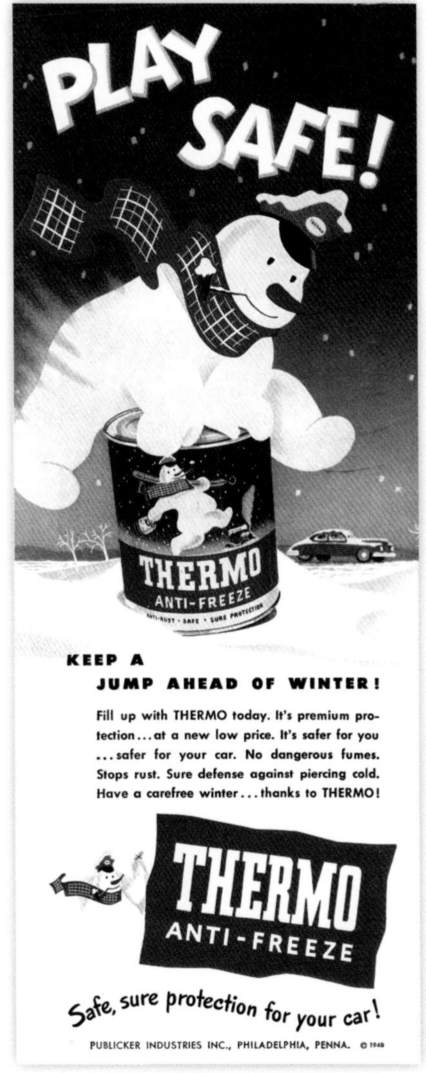

Thermo • 1948
Thermo anti-freeze
Magazine ad

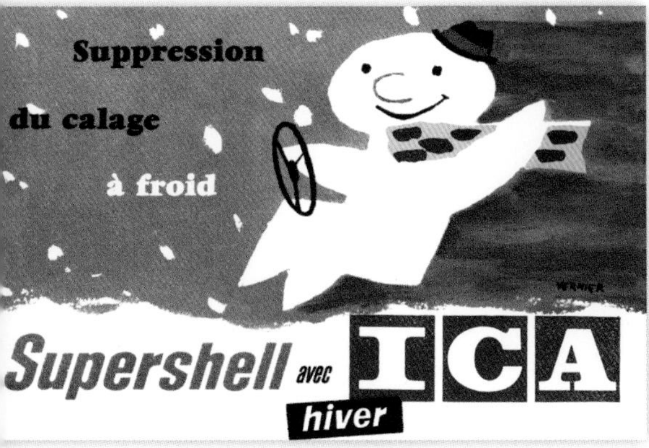

Supershell Snowman • c. 1955
Shell gasoline
Promotional postcard

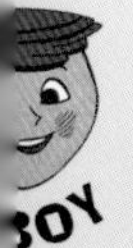

The snowman was a popular advertising character in the mid-twentieth century and was related either to products that had something to do with keeping things cold or, ironically, to products that prevented freezing. The Snoboy, on the other hand, symbolized freshness as in "fresh as snow," while Ivory Snow's snowman embodied the actual appearance of the product's pure white flakes.

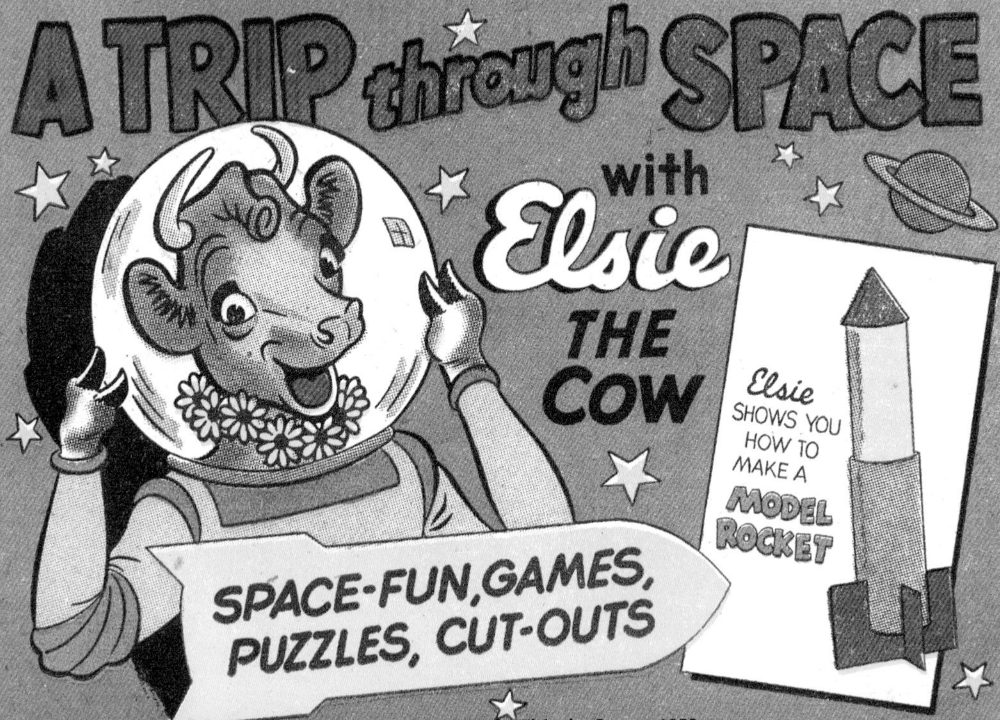

A TRIP through SPACE
with Elsie THE COW
Elsie SHOWS YOU HOW TO MAKE A MODEL ROCKET
SPACE-FUN, GAMES, PUZZLES, CUT-OUTS

Elsie the Cow • c. 1958
Borden dairy products.
Comic book cover

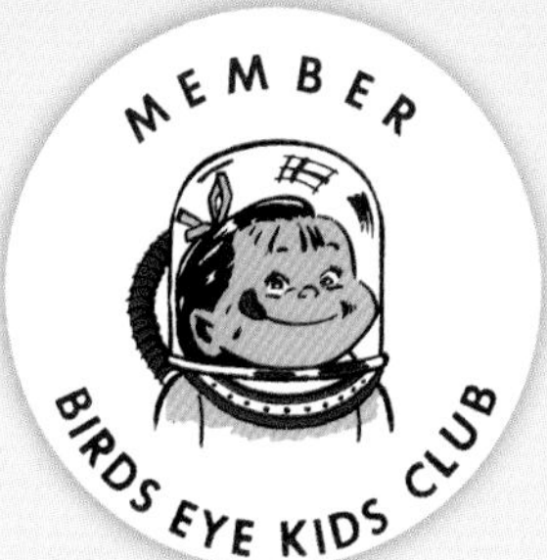

Birds Eye Kid • 1953
Birds Eye frozen foods
Tab button

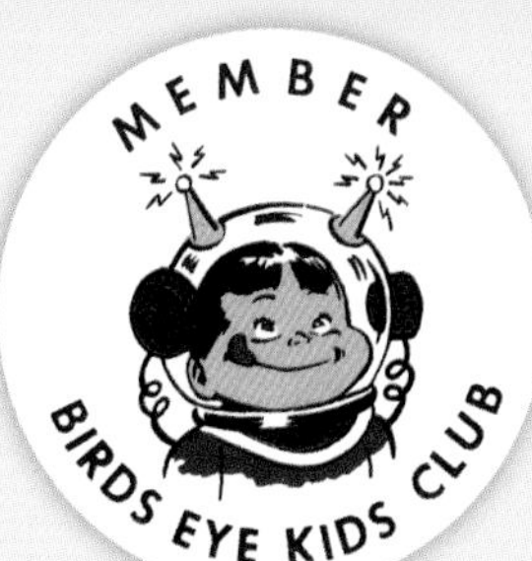

Birds Eye Kid • 1953
Birds Eye frozen foods
Tab button

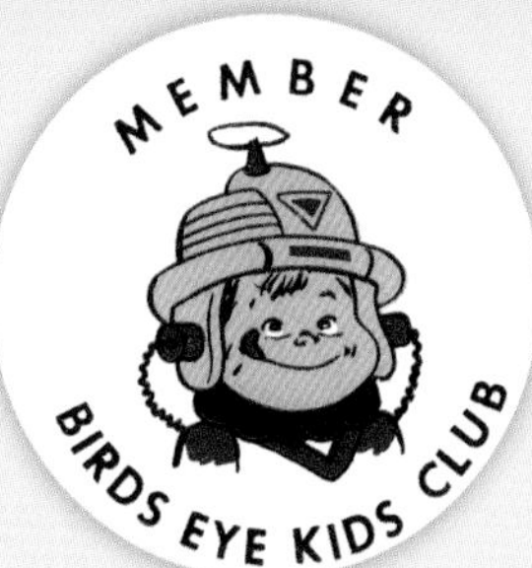

Birds Eye Kid • 1953
Birds Eye frozen foods
Tab button

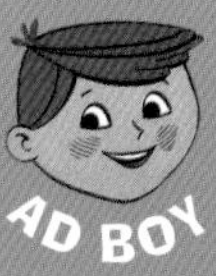

Thanks to enormous enthusiasm for America's space program and the perennial popularity of science fiction comics, books, and movies, the 1950s and 1960s saw the likes of Elsie the Cow, Speedy Alka-Seltzer, and many other previously earthbound ac characters don glass-bubble helmets and blast off into the gravity-free atmosphere o outer space.

Captain Ray-O-Vac • c. 1952
Ray-O-Vac batteries and flashlights
Store sign

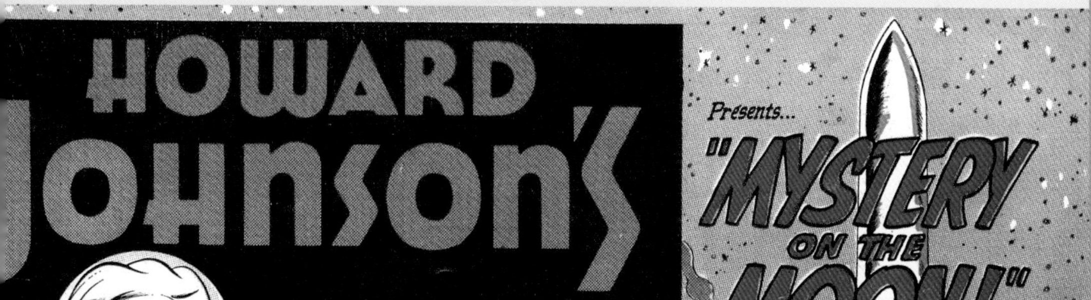

Simon and the Pieman • c. 1966
Howard Johnson's restaurants
Menu cover

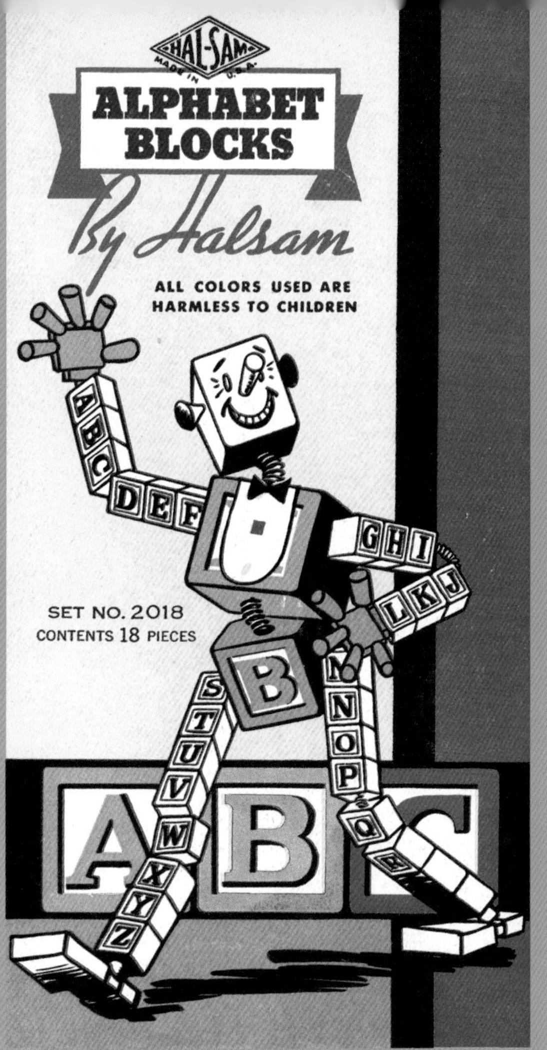

Alphabet Blocks Man • c. 1948
Alphabet Blocks toy
Box cover

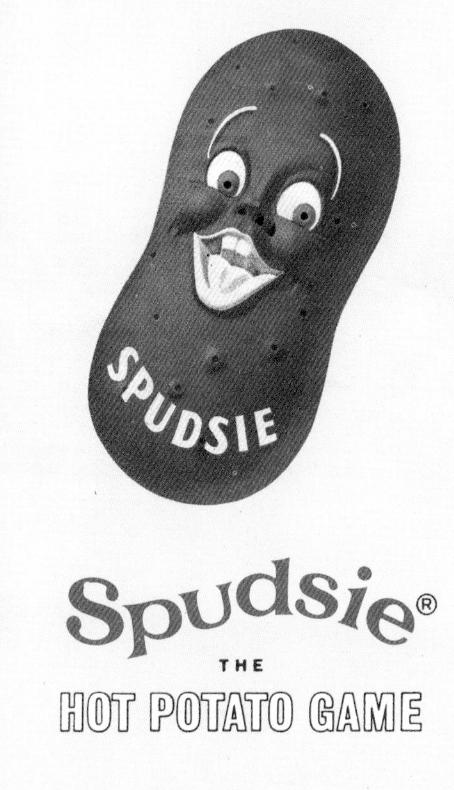

Spudsie • c. 1961
Spudsie hot potato game
Promotional pamphlet

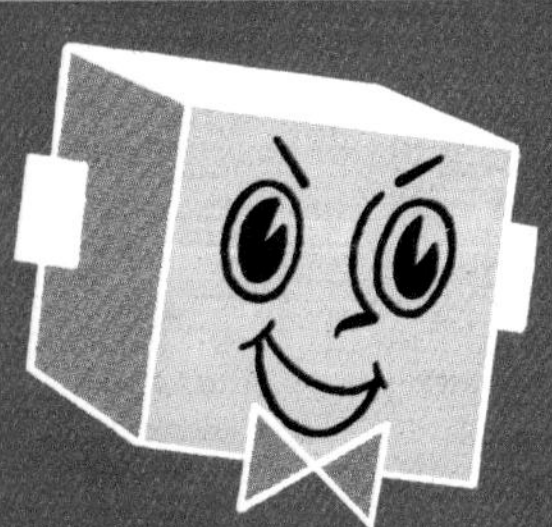

Blockhead • c. 1956
Blockhead game
Box side panel

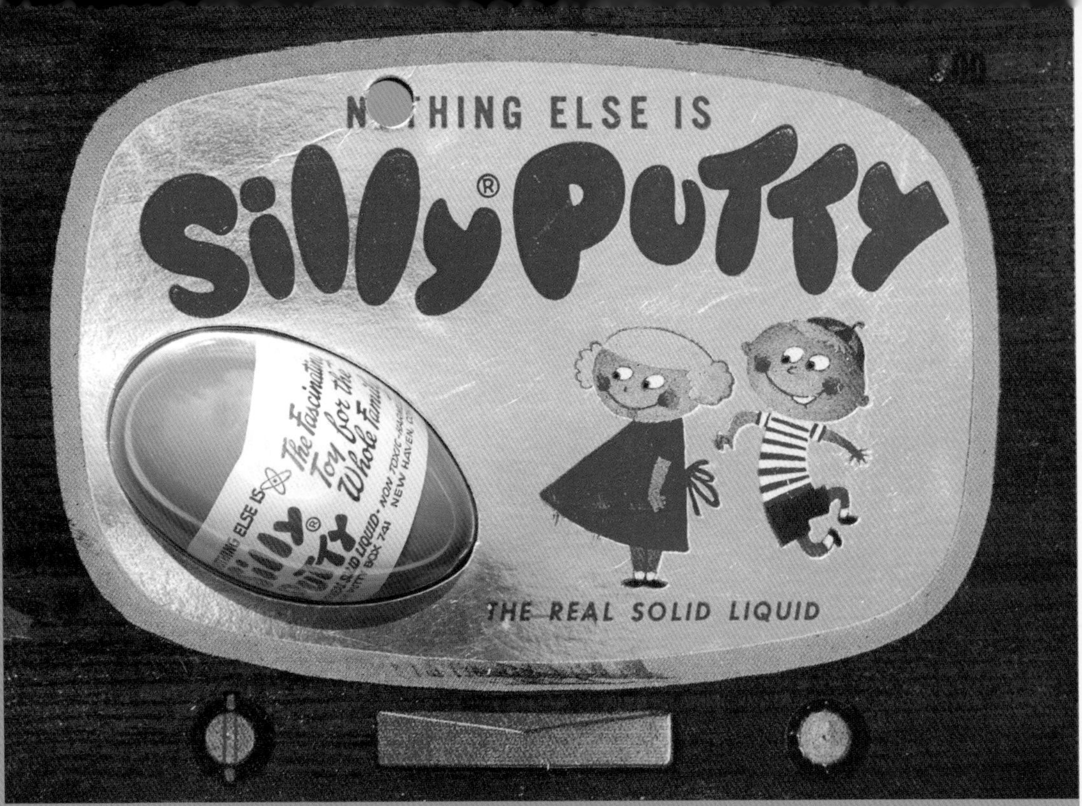

Silly Putty Kids • c. 1958
Silly Putty toy
Package front

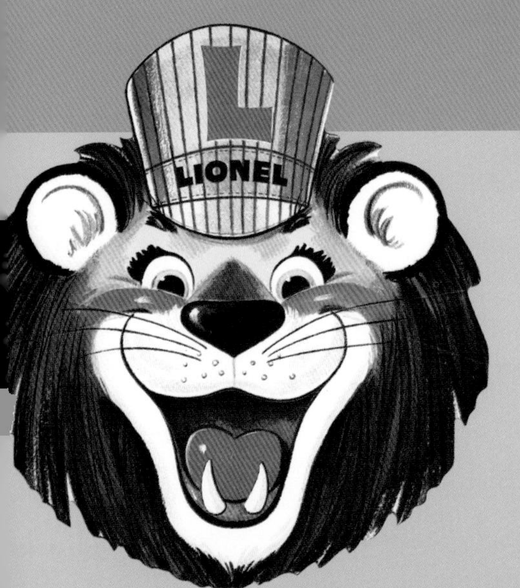

Lenny the Lion • 1957
Lionel toy trains
Paper mask

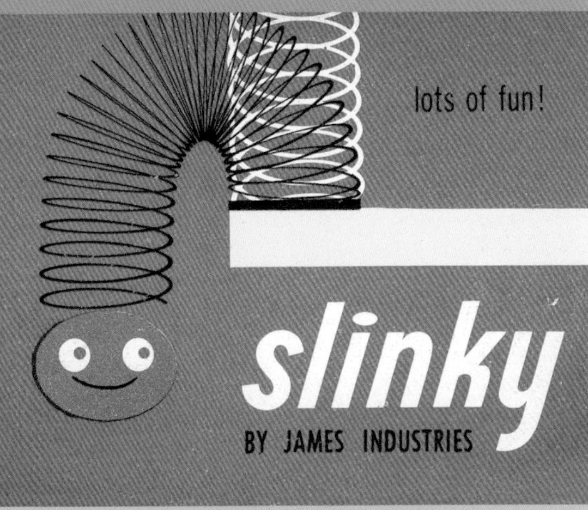

Slinky • c. 1954
Slinky spring toy
Box side panel

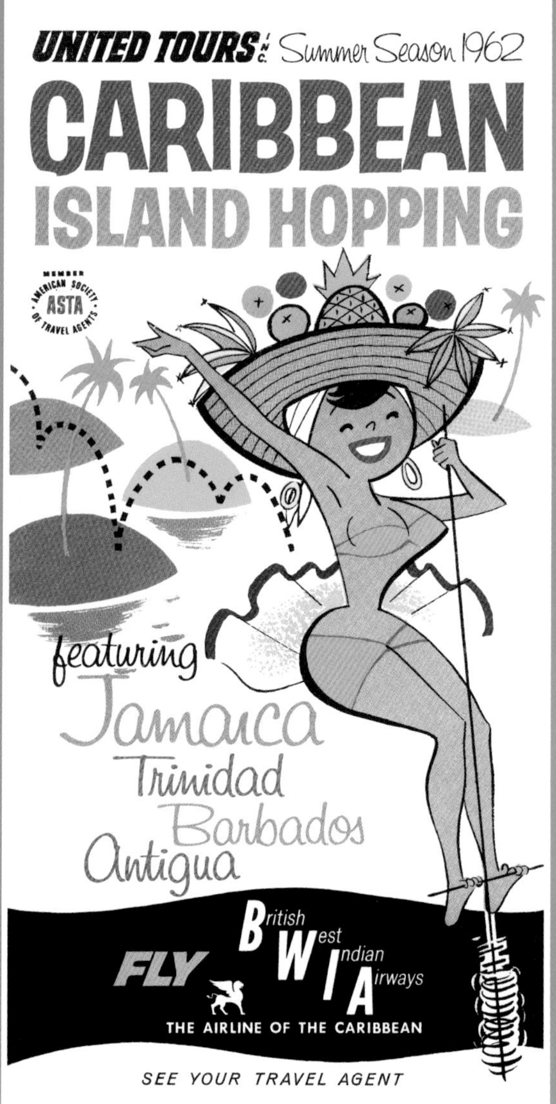

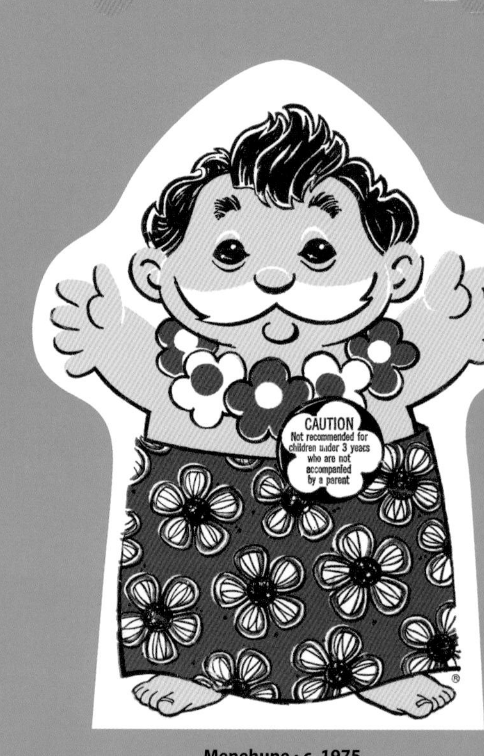

Menehune • c. 1975
United airlines
Hand puppet

Vicki • 1962
BWIA airlines
Travel brochure

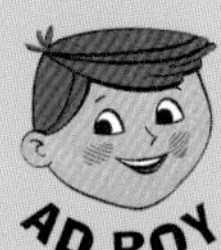

Who's that girl in the bikini?

Vicki, the bikini-clad babe from British West Indian Airways, was named after the Vick Viscount turboprop airliners that made up the BWIA Caribbean fleet. Although severa years before overt sex appeal would hit its stride in advertising, a brochure with Vicki gracing the cover might get a second look from the husband in the grey flannel suit.

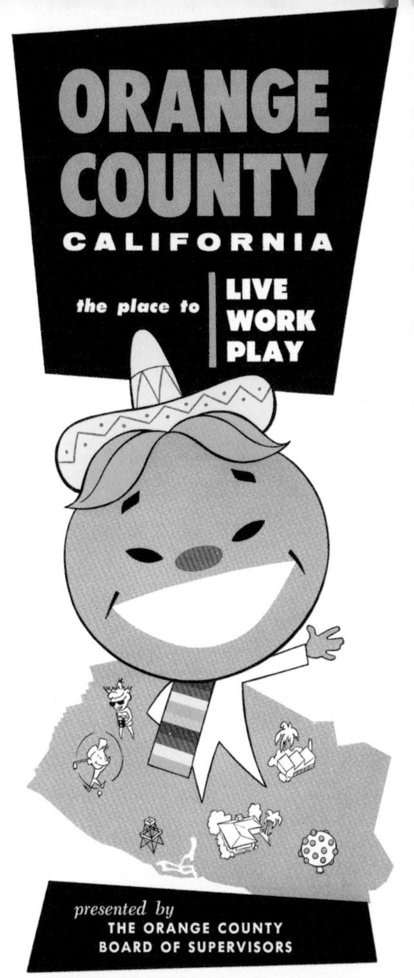

Orange County Orange • 1963
The Orange County Board of Supervisors
Travel brochure

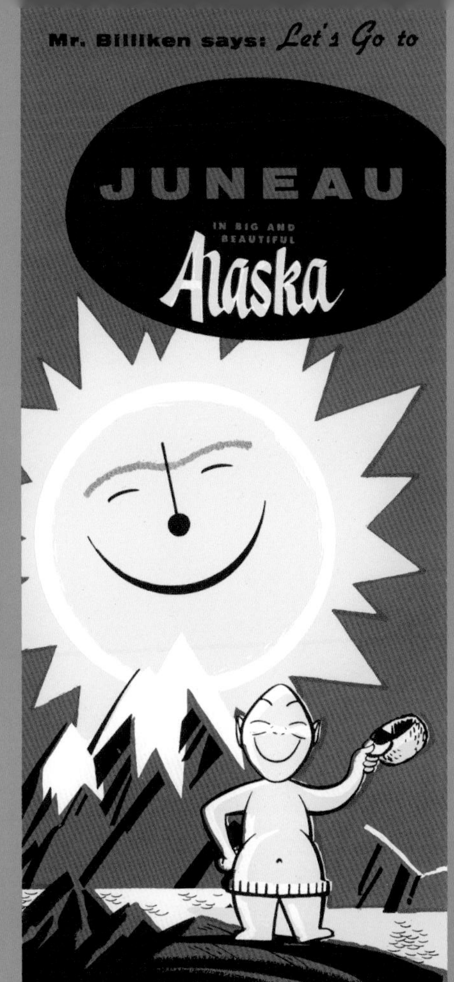

Mr. Biliken • c. 1960
Alaska Visitors Assocation
Travel brochure

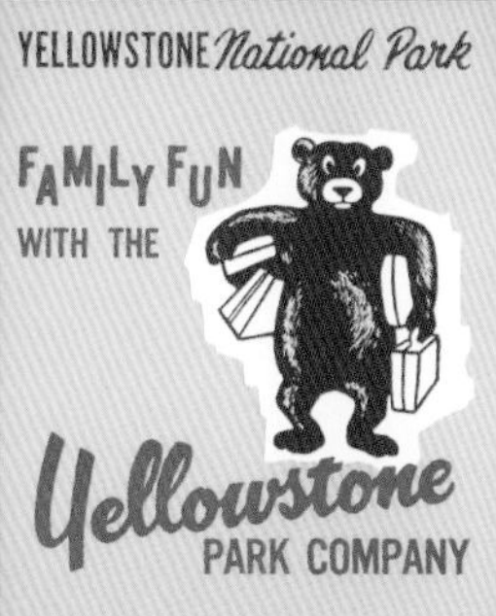

Yellowstone Bear • c. 1965
Yellowstone Park Company
Matchbook cover

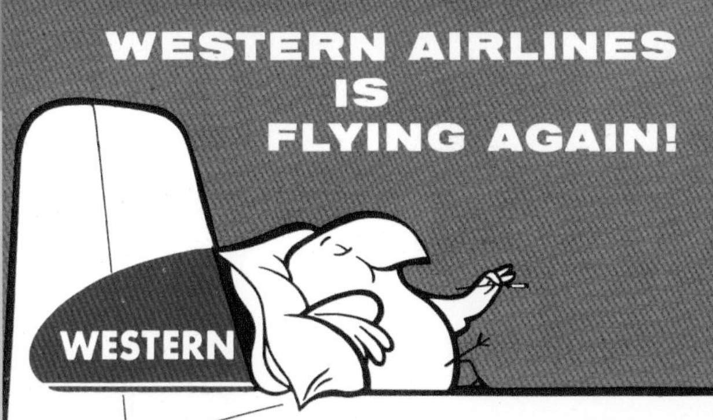

Wally Bird • c. 1955
Western airlines
Information pamphlet

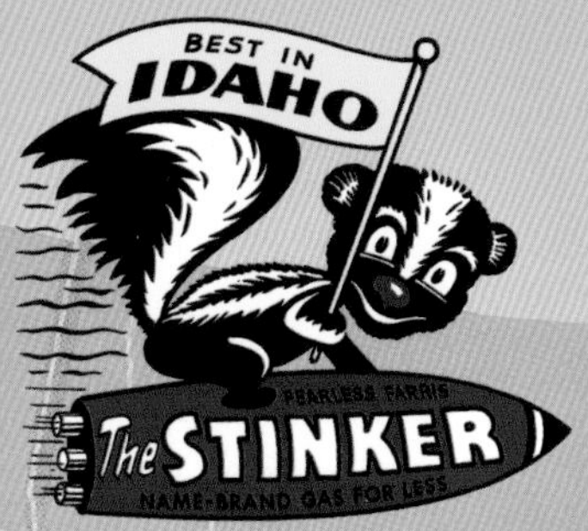

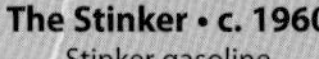

The Stinker • c. 1960
Stinker gasoline
Water decal

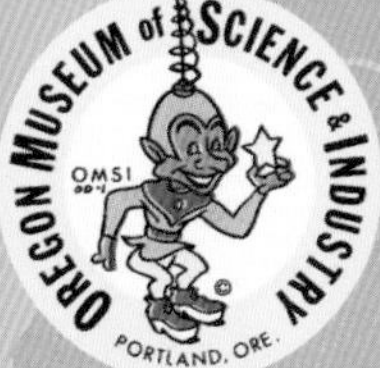

OMSI • c. 1963
Portland, Oregon
Water decal

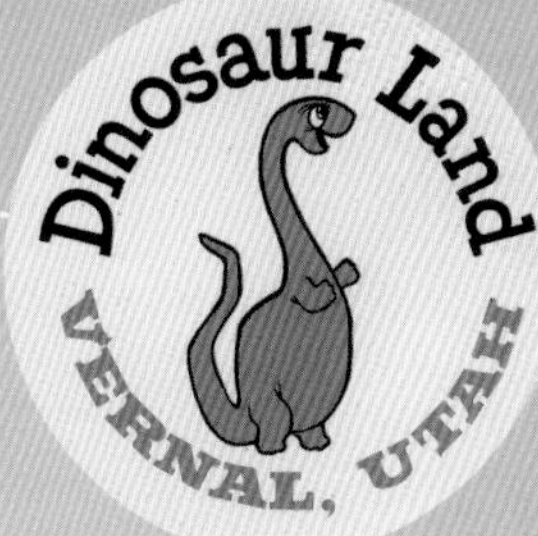

Dinah • 1970
Vernal, Utah
Water decal

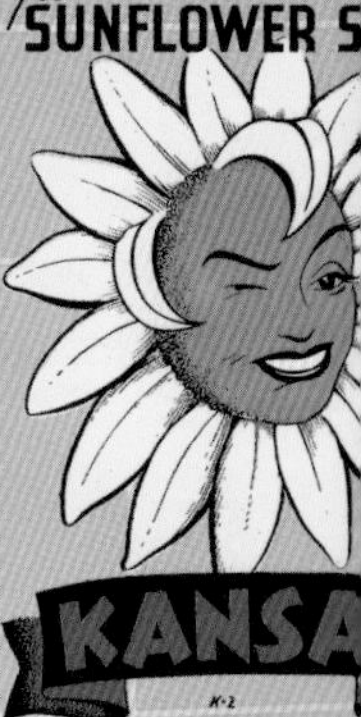

The Sunflower State •
State of Kansas
Water decal

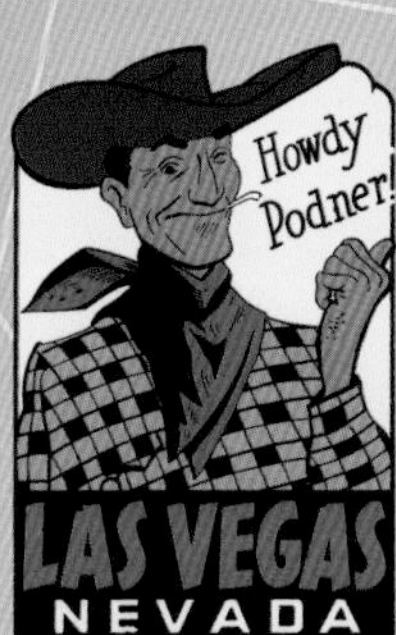

Vegas Vic • c. 1955
Las Vegas, Nevada
Water decal

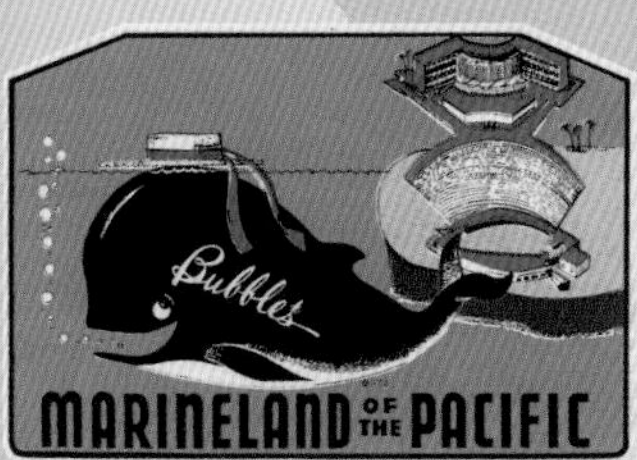

Bubbles • c. 1960
Palos Verdes, California
Water decal

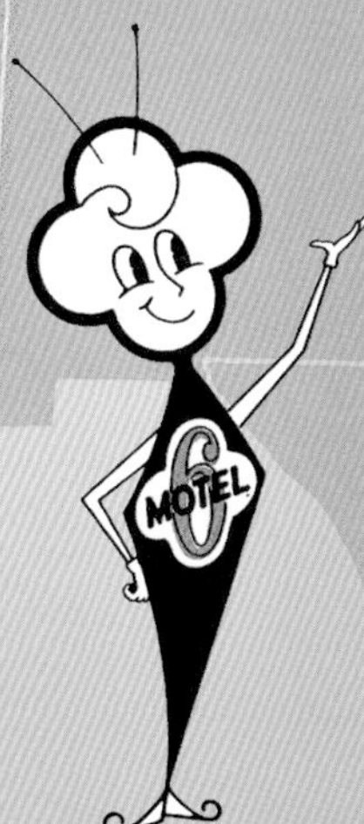

Miss Motel 6 • 1970
Motel 6 motels
Travel brochure detail

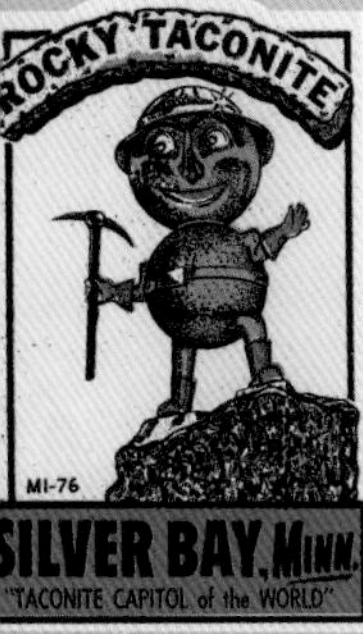

Rocky Taconite • c. 1964
Silver Bay, Minnesota
Water decal

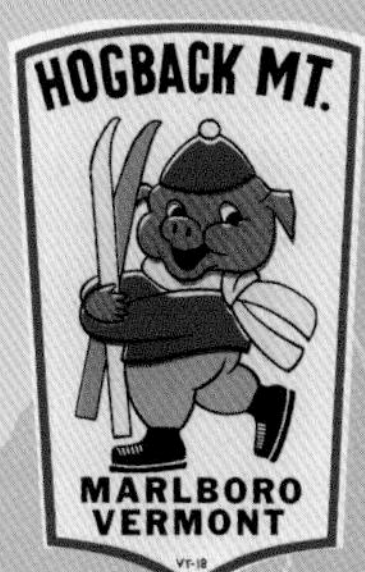

Hogback Mountain Hog • c. 1955
Marlboro, Vermont
Water decal

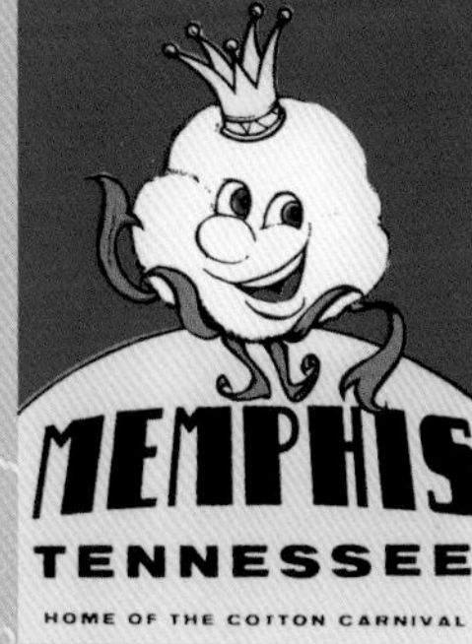

King Cotton • c. 1955
Memphis, Tennessee
Water decal

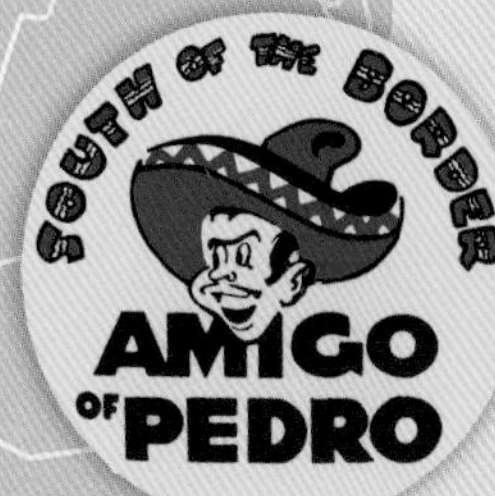

Pedro • c. 1955
Dillon, South Carolina
Pin-back button

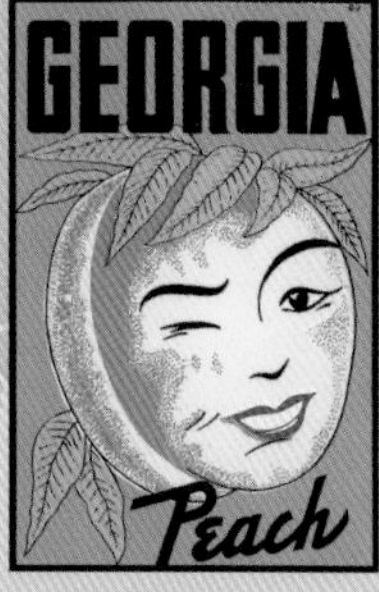

Georgia Peach • c. 1955
State of Georgia
Water decal

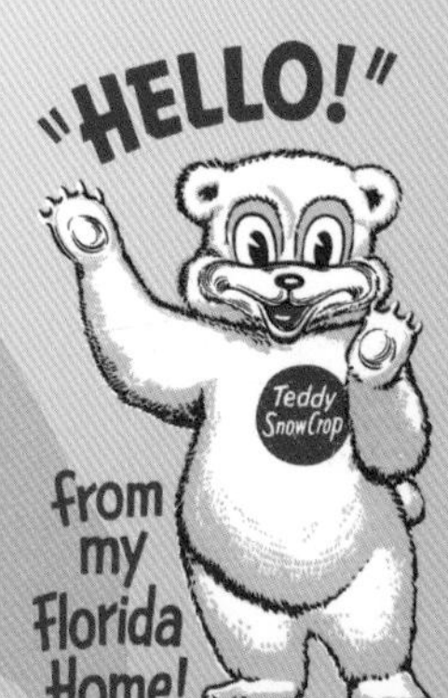

Teddy Snow Crop • 1959
Snow Crop orange juice
Water decal

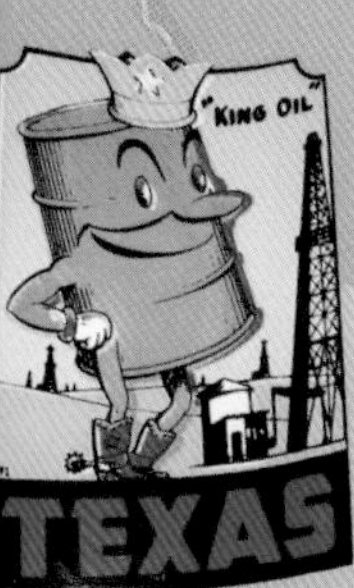

King Oil • c. 1955
State of Texas
Water decal

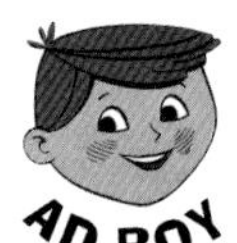

Should he stay or go?

In 1984, Big Boy Restaurants in the midst of adding salad bars and an expanded, more health-conscious menu wondered if the image of their rotund, checkered-pants-wearing Big Boy said "light, healthy and green." A public referendum was launched to see if should stay or go? When the votes were counted the Big Boy had won by a landslide.

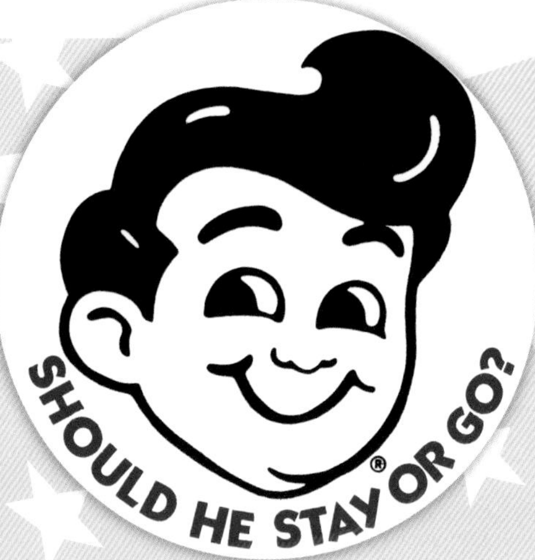

Big Boy • 1984
Big Boy restaurants
Pin-back button

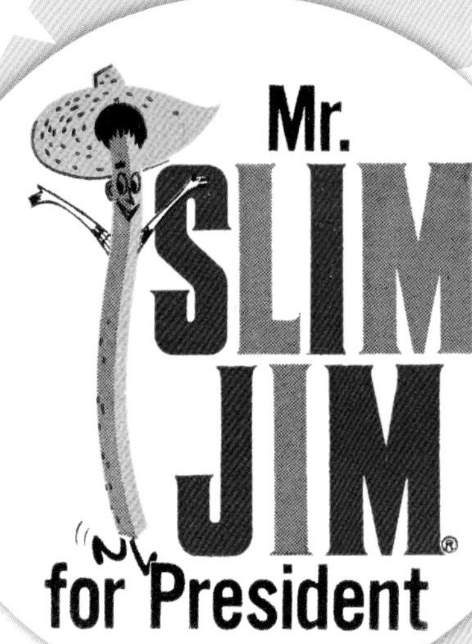

Mr. Slim Jim • c. 1972
Slim Jim beef jerky
Pin-back button

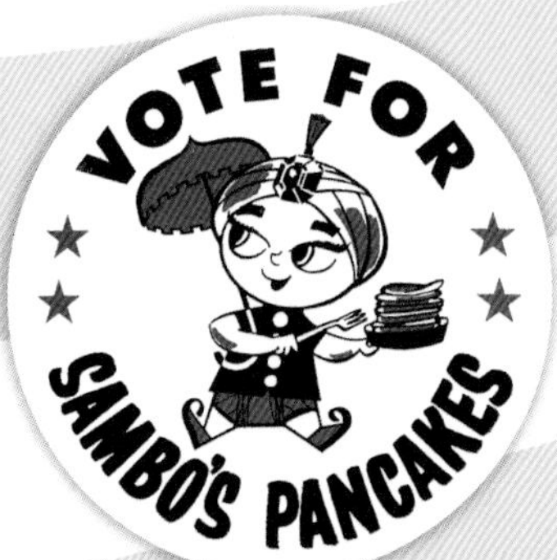

Sambo • c. 1970
Sambo's restaurants
Pin-back button

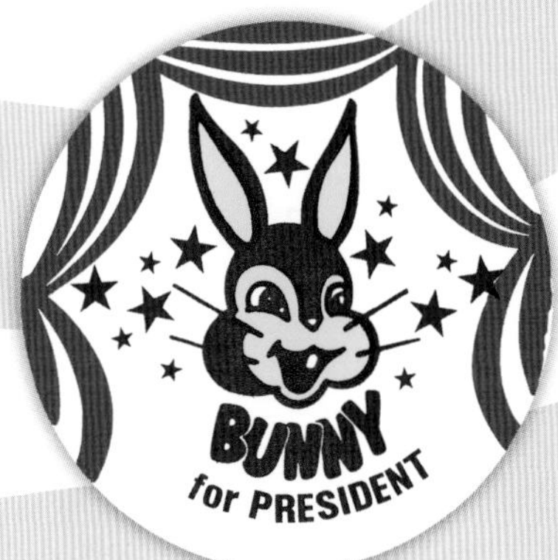

Bunny • c. 1972
Bunny bread
Pin-back button

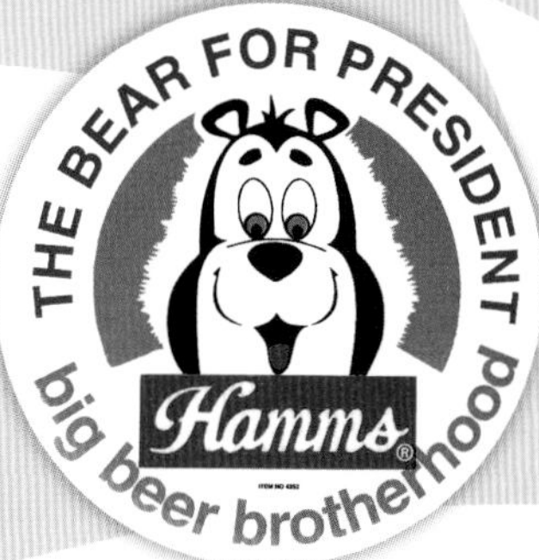

Hamm's Bear • 1972
Hamm's beer
Pin-back button

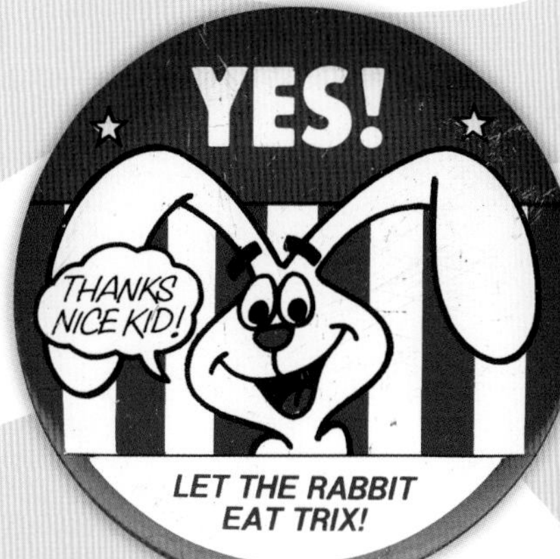

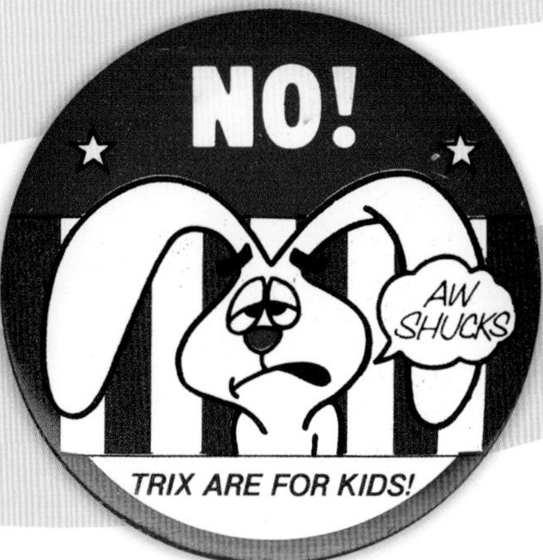

Trix Rabbit • 1976
Trix cereal
Clip-on buttons

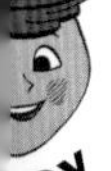

Yes! or No!?

During the U.S. presidential elections of 1976, General Mills launched a campaign that invited kids to vote for whether or not the Rabbit should finally be allowed to taste his beloved Trix. They voted by mailing in cereal box tops. Support was overwhelming and the Rabbit not only got to taste the Trix, he went berserk with ecstasy while doing so.

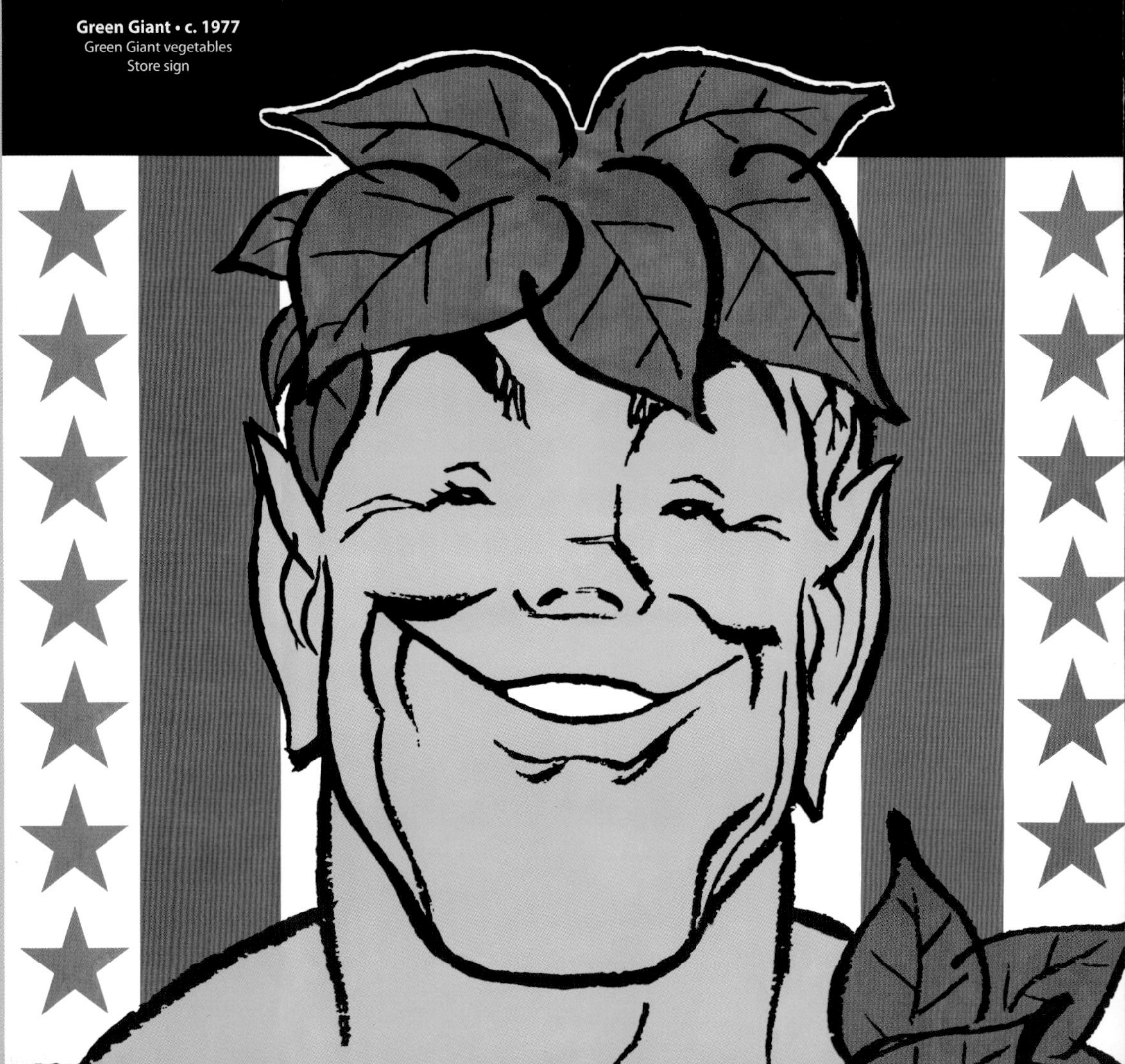

Green Giant • c. 1977
Green Giant vegetables
Store sign

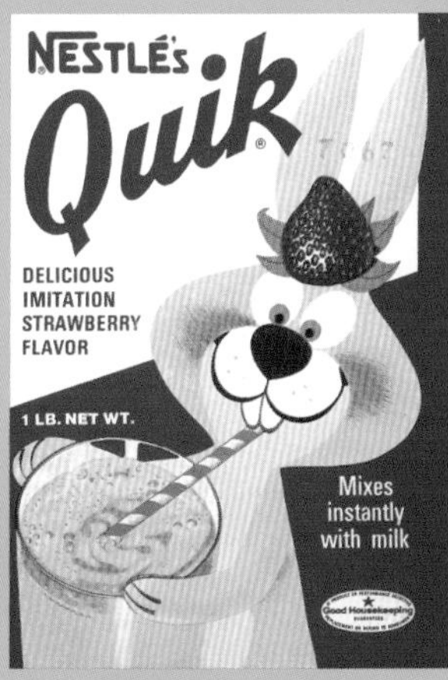

Quik Bunny • c. 1963
Quik strawberry drink mix
Container front

We would like to recognize and thank Phil Wood, founder and president of Ten Speed Press, for his remarkable accomplishments over the past 38 years in publishing. We are honored by his enthusiastic support of this project.

The authors are in gratitude to our multi-talented editor, Veronica (Fuzzy) Randall for her inspirational direction and creative contributions to the design and text of this book.

Thanks also to Randy Jones from Tikiranch as well as Dan Goodsell, and Jason Liebig for their wonderful websites that sparked our creativity. The authors would also like to express our appreciation to Takako Kikkawa, Sarah Donnelly, Dennis Weiss, Christine Freeman, Michelle Richards, and Eric Rollins for their interest and helpful feedback.

Masud Husain would like to extend personal thanks to his beloved wife, Jane Husain, for her support and inspiration in the making of *Ad Boy*.

Finally, we wish to thank all the corporate sponsors, illustrators, and graphic designers of advertising characters whose work appears in this book, and who have provided us with this glimpse of America's popular culture past.

Any omission of caption credit is inadvertent and will be corrected in future printings if notification is sent to the publisher. All the advertising artifacts in this book including pin-back buttons, hand puppets, paper ephemera, store signs, promotional displays, packages, and premiums are from the collections of the authors.

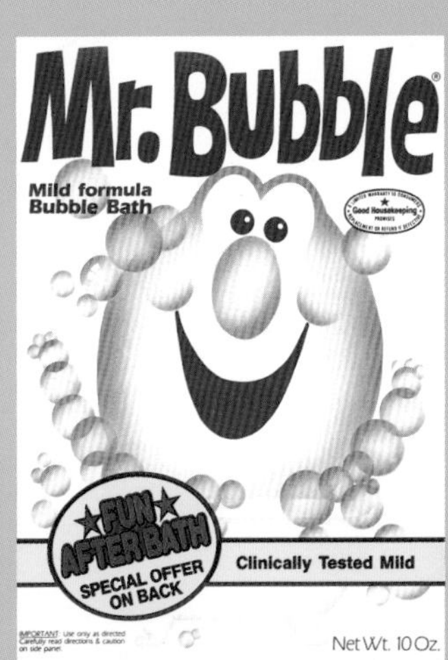

Mr. Bubble • 1990
Mr. Bubble bubble bath
Box front

 Published in the United States by Ten Speed Press, an imprint of the Crown Publishing Group, a division of Random House, Inc., New York.
www.crownpublishing.com
www.tenspeed.com

Ten Speed Press and the Ten Speed Press colophon are registered trademarks of Random House, Inc.

Library of Congress Cataloging-in-Publication Data

Dotz, Warren.
Ad boy : vintage advertising with character / Warren Dotz, Masud Husain.
p. cm.
1. Advertising characters—United States. I. Husain, Masud, 1962- II. Title.
HF6146.A27D67 2009
659.10973—dc22
2008030243

ISBN 978-1-58008-984-5 (alk. paper)

Printed in China

Book concept by Warren Dotz and Masud Husain
Cover and interior design by Masud Husain

11 10 9 8 7 6 5 4 3 2

First Edition

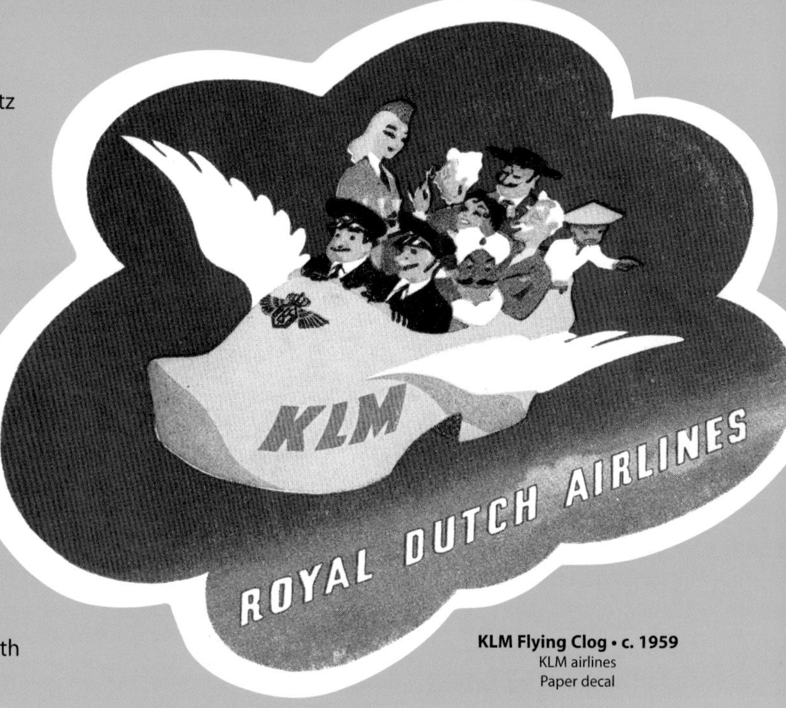

KLM Flying Clog • c. 1959
KLM airlines
Paper decal

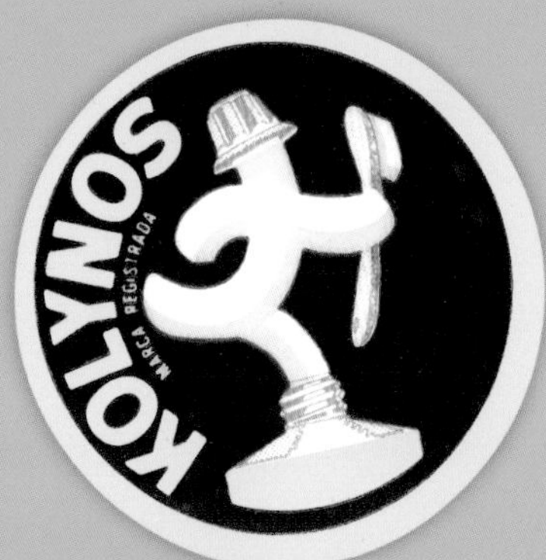

Kolynos • c. 1951
Kolynos toothpaste
Pin-back button